Slavery and the Death Penalty

It has long been acknowledged that the death penalty in the United States of America has been shaped by the country's history of slavery and racial violence, but this book considers the lesser-explored relationship between the two practices' respective abolitionist movements. The book explains how the historical and conceptual links between slavery and capital punishment have both helped and hindered efforts to end capital punishment. The comparative study also sheds light on the nature of such efforts, and offers lessons for how death penalty abolitionism should proceed in future. Using the history of slavery and abolition, it is argued that anti-death penalty efforts should be premised on the ideologies of the radical slavery abolitionists.

Dr Bharat Malkani researches and teaches in the field of capital punishment, and human rights and criminal justice more broadly. He is a member of the International Academic Network for the Abolition of Capital Punishment, and prior to joining academia he helped co-ordinate efforts to abolish the death penalty for persons under the age of 18 in America.

Slavery and the Death Penalty

A Study in Abolition

Bharat Malkani

Routledge
Taylor & Francis Group
LONDON AND NEW YORK

First published 2018 by Routledge
2 Park Square, Milton Park, Abingdon, Oxon OX14 4RN
605 Third Avenue, New York, NY 10017

First issued in paperback 2021

Routledge is an imprint of the Taylor & Francis Group, an informa business

Publisher's Note
The publisher has gone to great lengths to ensure the quality of this reprint but points out that some imperfections in the original copies may be apparent.

British Library Cataloguing in Publication Data
A catalogue record for this book is available from the British Library

Library of Congress Cataloging in Publication Data
Names: Malkani, Bharat, author.
Title: Slavery and the death penalty : a study in abolition / Bharat Malkani.
Description: New York, NY : Routledge, 2018. | Series: Law, justice and power | Includes index.
Identifiers: LCCN 2017060124 | ISBN 9781472452740 (hardback)
Subjects: LCSH: Capital punishment--United States. | Slavery--United States. | Antislavery movements--United States.
Classification: LCC KF9227.C2 M34 2018 | DDC 364.660973--dc23
LC record available at https://lccn.loc.gov/2017060124

ISBN 13: 978-0-367-89903-5 (pbk)
ISBN 13: 978-1-4724-5274-0 (hbk)

Typeset in Galliard
by Taylor & Francis Books

For Zoe and Lucas and to all those who, in whatever capacity, are bending the arc of the moral universe towards justice.

Contents

Acknowledgements viii

Introduction 1

1 The death penalty in the era of slavery 22

2 Capital punishment and the legacy of slavery, 1865–1976 32

3 The legacy of slavery in capital punishment since 1976 55

4 Abolitionism defined 79

5 Radical abolitionist constitutionalism 107

6 The experiential abolitionist 137

7 Abolitionism and "alternatives" 162

8 Non-complicity and abolitionism: from fugitive slaves to lethal injections 186

9 A peculiar abolition 220

Index 227

Acknowledgements

This project would not have come to fruition without the extraordinary help of many people. I owe particular thanks to Professor Austin Sarat who encouraged me to pursue the idea behind this book. Professors Manisha Sinha, Paul Finkelman, Julia O'Connell Davidson, and Zoe Trodd all took time to answer queries about slavery and abolition from a person whom they had never met. David Menschel, Abraham Bonowitz, Robert Dunham, and Mona Lynch also responded kindly to questions, and have helped me articulate my understanding of the nature of contemporary efforts to outlaw capital punishment. I was fortunate to be invited to the annual gathering of Witness to Innocence in Philadelphia in 2014, and I am exceptionally grateful to all those people who welcomed me and spoke with me about their role as abolitionists: Ray Krone, Sabrina Butler-Smith, Joe D'Ambrosio, Clarence Brandley, Harold Wilson, Juan Melendez, Shareef Cousin, Father Neil Kookoothe, Kathleen Lucas, Marshall Dayan, Scott Bass, and Steve Honeyman.

I am also grateful to the organizers and participants who provided me with invaluable feedback at the following conferences, where I presented various aspects of my research: the Law and Society Annual Meeting in Minneapolis in 2014, where the seeds for this book were sown; the Academic Meeting at the World Congress Against the Death Penalty in Oslo in 2016; the British Association of American Studies conference in Canterbury in 2017; and the Historians Against Slavery conference in Liverpool in 2017.

Much of my research and writing took place while I was a lecturer at Birmingham Law School, and in subtle but important ways, several colleagues helped ensure that I had the space to concentrate on this project. Robert Cryer, Stephen Smith, Rosa Freedman, Adrian Hunt, and Gavin Byrne deserve special mention. My then-Head of School, Professor Robert Lee, granted me an extended period of research leave, and I owe much thanks to him. I am also grateful for the financial assistance that covered travel and living costs for various research trips.

A number of people read drafts of chapters and helped me immeasurably with getting the manuscript into shape. Professors Roger Hood, John Bessler, Fiona de Londras, Erika Rackley, Dirk van zyl Smit, Kevin Barry, and Michael Radelet all provided valuable feedback, as did Andrew Novak, David Connor and the anonymous reviewer. Two former students of mine should also be singled out for their first-rate research assistance: thank you, Grace Checkland and Rachael Toon.

Finally, but perhaps most of all, thanks to my incredible wife and best friend, Zoe, for putting up with the lost evenings and weekends, and to our son Lucas. The subject matters of this book – enslavement and execution – may be bleak, but you've consistently brightened my days and nights.

Introduction

I. "...worse than slavery"

In June 1881, Sojourner Truth – a former slave and tireless campaigner for social justice – travelled from her home in Battle Creek, Michigan, to the state capitol in Lansing for what would be her final campaigning appearance. Legislators were considering a proposal to reinstate capital punishment in Michigan, which in 1846 had become the first English-speaking government in the world to abolish it. Truth's legislative testimony was unforgiving: "I have come here tonight to see about a thing that fairly shocked me. It shocked me worse than slavery. I've heard that you are going to have hanging again in this state.... Where is the man or woman who can sanction such a thing as that? We are the makers of murderers if we do it."[1] The Wykoff Hanging Bill was defeated, and Michigan has never since reinstated the death penalty.[2]

While there might have been an element of exaggeration in Truth's claim that the Bill "shocked [her] worse than slavery", many former slaves in that era were contemptuous of state-sanctioned executions because capital punishment had been a vital component in the machinery of slavery, and it had continued to play a central role in the subjugation of racial minorities that followed emancipation in 1865. Even today, it is widely recognized that capital punishment in the United States of America continues to be imbued with the legacy of slavery. The imposition of death sentences discriminates along racial lines and is disproportionately imposed on the poor, just as slavery was marked by divisions over race and class. Executions have occurred mainly, albeit not exclusively, in former slave states – the same places that witnessed the highest frequencies of lynchings. And capital punishment, like slavery, is predicated on the notion that some people do not belong to the political and moral human community.[3]

Although considerable attention has been paid to the historical and conceptual links between slavery, racial violence, and capital punishment in the US, relatively little attention has been paid to the relationship between today's anti-death penalty movement and the movement that worked to end slavery, and there is scant literature comparing the two movements' respective discourses of abolition. A rare exception is Bruce Ledewitz's "Abolition Then and Now", but this is a short, three-page article that appeared in print nearly 30 years ago.[4] The lack of a more thorough comparative study is regrettable because, as explained over the following chapters, the voluminous literature on the history of slavery and abolition provides useful analytical tools and a normative framework for understanding and evaluating the much less studied, yet more pressing subject, of contemporary efforts to outlaw capital punishment.

In undertaking such a comparative study, I make three central claims. The first is a methodological one: a comparative study is not just helpful, but also appropriate and necessary because today's anti-death penalty efforts are conceptually and historically linked to antebellum abolitionist efforts. My second claim is analytical: the literature on slavery and abolition helps us identify and understand the often-overlooked radicalism in contemporary abolitionist efforts. My third claim is a normative one: the history of emancipation and its aftermath suggests that death penalty abolitionism should be more explicitly radical in its outlook. Put more succinctly, I argue that today's efforts to end the death penalty in the US are the continuation of the project set in place by the slavery abolitionists, and such efforts should draw on the radicalism of those abolitionists. This involves expressly rooting anti-death penalty efforts in the idea of dignity.

This introductory chapter sets out the status of capital punishment and anti-death penalty efforts today, explaining the orthodox view that pragmatic and conservative anti-death penalty discourses are propelling America towards nationwide abolition. Such discourses set aside moral qualms with state-sanctioned executions, and focus attention instead on practical problems with the punishment. Rather than emphasize the incompatibility of the death penalty with the inherent dignity of the person facing execution, pragmatic and conservative discourses focus on issues such as the risk of executing an innocent person, and the exorbitant costs of capital punishment. In other words, they appeal to the existing moral values of those who support harsh retributivism.

Conservative and pragmatic anti-death penalty discourses, we will see, have been championed by some abolitionists for their perceived efficacy.[5] However, it is by no means clear that nationwide abolition is imminent, and such discourses have been criticized for perpetuating and entrenching wider problems with the criminal justice system, such as the use of life in prison without the possibility of parole.[6] It is with this in mind that I explain the benefits of using the history of slavery and abolition to understand and evaluate contemporary anti-death penalty efforts. This history suggests that anti-death penalty efforts are more radical than conservative or pragmatic, and such efforts should continue to be imbued with the idea of dignity that underpinned the radicalism of the slavery abolitionists.

II. The contemporary status of the death penalty

It is tempting to believe that the death penalty in America is in a state of terminal decline. A statistical comparison of capital punishment today compared to the late 1990s reveals the extent to which the use of, and support for, the death penalty has reduced since the turn of the century. In 1999, there were 98 state-sanctioned executions – the highest annual number since the United States Supreme Court ruled in 1976 that the death penalty is not per se unconstitutional.[7] Since 1999, the annual rate of executions has declined sharply, with just[8] 20 people executed in 2016. Thirty-one new death sentences were handed down in 2016, considerably fewer than the post-1976 high of 315 that were imposed in 1996. Throughout the 1990s, opinion polls suggested that 75–80% of the population supported capital punishment. The latest Gallup poll puts that number at just 55%.[9] And whereas 40 out of the 52 jurisdictions in the USA retained capital punishment on their statute books at the end of the 1990s, that number has declined to 33 at the time of writing.[10] These numbers led the *New York Times* to run an editorial on October 24, 2016, titled "The Death Penalty, Nearing its End".[11] Almost a year to the day earlier, the now late Justice Antonin Scalia – who had been a fervent supporter of capital punishment – said that "it would not surprise" him if the US Supreme Court soon outlawed executions, given the increasing number of anti-death penalty opinions emanating from the Bench.[12] Academic researchers have also confidently predicted the imminent demise of executions, with Brandon Garrett asserting in 2017 that "[t]he death penalty in the United States is at the end of its rope. We can abolish it not in a matter of generations, but in a matter of years."[13]

Despite this apparent trend towards abolition, it is also arguable that state-sanctioned executions are entrenched in the law, politics, and local cultures of many jurisdictions across America, and that abolition will not occur soon. On November 8, 2016, just two weeks after the *New York Times* editorial, the death penalty was on the ballot in Nebraska, California, and Oklahoma. In all three states, pro-death penalty measures succeeded. In Nebraska, the electorate voted to restore the punishment after state legislators had repealed it the year before.[14] In Oklahoma, voters approved an amendment to the state constitution to prevent state courts from outlawing capital punishment.[15] And in California, the electorate voted to speed up the appeals process so that those facing execution have fewer opportunities to challenge their sentences.[16] On the same day, pro-death penalty Donald Trump prevailed in the presidential elections, dashing any hopes that the seat left vacant on the Supreme Court by the death of Justice Scalia would be filled by a judge sympathetic to the abolitionists' cause. These election results led Andrew Cohen to assert in *The Marshall Project* the next day that "The Death Penalty is Alive and Well."[17] The ensuing months have done little to contradict Cohen. On April 10, 2017, Neil Gorsuch was sworn into office on the Supreme Court, and he has given every indication that he will uphold the constitutionality of capital punishment.[18] Later that same month, the Governor of Arkansas announced what was described as a "killing spree" by death penalty opponents, as state authorities attempted to carry out eight executions over the course of just 11 days.[19] In fact, Gorsuch's first vote was in a death penalty case emanating from this announcement. On April 20, 2017, he voted to deny a stay of execution for Ledell Lee, who had requested a chance to pursue claims relating to innocence, intellectual disability, and ineffective assistance of counsel.[20] Lee was executed later that evening. In July, Ohio followed Arkansas's lead, revealing plans to execute 27 people over a four-year period.[21] It is perhaps more accurate, then, to describe the death penalty in the US as being in a state of flux. There are myriad reasons why opponents of capital punishment have struggled to bring about nationwide abolition in an era in which every other Western liberal democracy has outlawed the practice,[22] and this is the context in which it is worth examining the strategies, tactics, and discourses of the anti-death penalty movement.

III. Understanding abolitionism

People oppose capital punishment for a range of reasons. These include the perceived incompatibility of the punishment with religious beliefs, or with more secular notions of human rights. Yet others might support the death penalty in the abstract, but believe that it does not and cannot ever operate fairly in practice. Whatever one's premise, it is the jurisprudence of the US Supreme Court that guides abolitionist strategies and tactics, particularly the cases of *Furman v. Georgia* (1972) and *Gregg v. Georgia* (1976).[23] The Court in these cases stated that as long as capital punishment serves the penological purposes of retribution and deterrence, it will be constitutional under the Eighth and Fourteenth Amendments to the Constitution, which prohibit "cruel and unusual punishments" and require due process and equal treatment under the law, respectively. To meet these penological aims, the Court said, the punishment must not be imposed arbitrarily, and must be restricted to those who commit the most heinous crimes and who are considered to be the most morally depraved of offenders. In *Gregg*, the Court also stated that the significant support for capital punishment among the general public at that time was indicative of its compatibility with "evolving standards of decency", and thus constitutional.[24] Later cases have clarified that "evolving standards of decency" are to be primarily determined with reference to public opinion as expressed through the sentencing decisions of juries, and in state legislation.[25]

In light of these decisions and the Court's subsequent death penalty jurisprudence, the anti-death penalty movement has pursued three concurrent tasks in an effort to convince a majority of the Supreme Court that the punishment is contrary to the Eighth and Fourteenth Amendments. The first has been to reduce the use of, and popular democratic support for, state-sanctioned executions, to illustrate that they are not compatible with contemporary standards of decency. The second has been to gather evidence that the punishment is arbitrarily and discriminatorily applied, and is both disproportionate under the Eighth Amendment and a violation of the Fourteenth Amendment's Equal Protection Clause. The third task is to show that the death penalty has no utilitarian justification as a deterrent to murder, and is therefore "nothing more than the purposeless and needless imposition of pain and suffering".[26]

The second and third tasks can be achieved by the work of social scientists and researchers who document the use, or misuse, of capital punishment, revealing its systemic bias against racial minorities and the indigent, its unequal use both within and across jurisdictions, and the lack of effect on homicide rates.[27] These studies are also used to achieve the first aim: to reduce the use of and popular support for executions, by showing that it is ineffective and unfairly applied. To further achieve this goal, abolitionists have undertaken three further activities. First, in courtrooms, lawyers seek to prevent death sentences from being handed down; they attempt to overturn existing death sentences; and they try to delay or prevent executions. Not all lawyers are necessarily abolitionists, and professional ethical considerations might compel a lawyer to allow their client to be executed if he or she is competent and wishes to waive their right to appeal.[28] Nonetheless, there is an inevitable abolitionist consequence to keeping convicted persons alive: the fewer people who are sentenced to death, and the fewer people who are executed, the stronger the grounds are for arguing that the death penalty has become "unusual".[29] Litigators have become adept at diverting people away from death sentences, and since the turn of the century lawyers have also persuaded the US Supreme Court to impose categorical bans on the execution of offenders who lack the capacity to be morally blameworthy, or whose crimes have not resulted in death.[30] The recent decision in *Hurst v. Florida*, outlawing death sentences imposed by judges rather than juries, also has the potential of reversing hundreds of such sentences.[31]

A second activity undertaken by anti-death penalty activists has been to focus on the political and public arena, where grassroots campaigners seek to change the minds of those who support or are apathetic about capital punishment. The inconsistent, biased, and ineffective use of the death penalty that has been documented by researchers plays a role in this, as do other arguments such as the risk of error, the high costs of capital punishment, and the incompatibility of state-sanctioned killing with religious precepts.[32] The hope is that state legislators will either respond to the public mood, or provide leadership on the issue and repeal relevant state statutes. The fewer states that permit capital punishment, the more evidence there will be that the American public considers such a punishment to be contrary to prevailing standards of decency.

In addition to legal and political efforts, abolitionists have adopted a third, more practical means of preventing executions from occurring. A striking example is the recent collaboration between anti-death penalty campaigners, pharmaceutical companies, and foreign governments to prevent US authorities from acquiring the drugs needed for lethal injections. The resulting shortage of drugs has rendered executions practically impossible to carry out, leading some commentators to surmise that this tactic might hold the key to permanent abolition.[33]

To understand why these various strands of abolitionism can be characterized as "conservative" and "pragmatic," it is helpful to consider Herbert Haines's critique of anti-death penalty efforts between the years 1972 and 1994.[34] Haines outlined the movement's then-largely unsuccessful attempts to stem the tide of death sentences and executions, and concluded that the movement

> need[s] to adopt a more pragmatic strategy, one that places less emphasis on moralistic appeals and more emphasis on tangible costs and on policy alternatives that resonate with widespread cultural sentiments... [O]nly some form of life-without-parole (LWOP) is likely to be seen by the largest segment of the American public as capable of making executions unnecessary.[35]

Haines also suggested that the movement needed to diversify, noting that the anti-death penalty movement consisted of "mostly… middle-class white people with professional backgrounds and liberal politics".[36] The movement, Haines surmised, therefore struggled to convert others to their cause.

A revised edition of Haines's book was published in 1999, and since around that time, there has been a discernible trend within the anti-death penalty community towards pragmatic discourses. For example, in November 1998, Northwestern University in Chicago, Illinois, hosted the first National Conference on Wrongful Convictions and the Death Penalty. The conference drew attention to the extent to which innocent people were being sentenced to death, and the risk of executing an innocent person has since played a considerable role in anti-death penalty efforts.[37] Since the financial crash of 2008, abolitionists have also increasingly drawn attention to the high costs of capital punishment compared to other criminal sanctions. Campaigners and activists have also been more willing to highlight the availability of life sentences in prison without the possibility of parole as an alternative punishment, in the hope of securing support from those who have concerns about state-sanctioned executions, but who still want to see convicted people suffer harsh punishments and be permanently excluded from society. Although these sorts of arguments had been raised prior to 2000, they have steadily become more central to abolitionist discourse since the turn of the century.[38]

These sorts of arguments are "pragmatic" in that they appeal to the existing moral views of those who support, or are apathetic about, capital punishment. Almost everybody agrees that it is wrong to execute a person who is not factually guilty of a crime. Those who support capital punishment in the abstract might be willing to forego such a penalty if doing so saves money, and if they are assured that people found guilty of heinous crimes will nonetheless suffer and be kept away from the rest of society. These sorts of arguments are "conservative" in that such discourses do not necessarily address broader concerns with the criminal justice system, such as the reliance on harsh retributivism, mass incarceration, police brutality, and so on.[39] The concern with *executing* an innocent person, for example, is unique to capital punishment. Similarly, the practical interference with the supply of lethal injection drugs that has proven so effective in stopping executions is "conservative" in that it is narrowly focused on the phenomenon of executions and, at first glance, says nothing about the measures that a society should adopt to prevent criminality, or how communities should respond to those found guilty of committing the most horrific offenses.

This apparent shift in abolitionist discourse, which has been characterized as rationalistic, conservative, and pragmatic, as opposed to emotional, progressive, and moralistic,[40] has been praised by some commentators for its apparent efficacy. Daniel LaChance expresses this view: "Arguing that the death penalty is an affront to human dignity just doesn't work. But portraying it as another failed government program just might."[41] However, it is not axiomatic that pragmatic and conservative approaches will secure nationwide abolition. While it is true that public support for state-sanctioned executions is declining, the 2017 Gallup poll referred to above shows that just 41% of Americans expressly oppose capital punishment.[42]

And even though state legislatures have been abolishing the death penalty at a remarkable rate, it is still a legally sanctioned punishment in the majority of states and by the military and federal government. Perhaps more strikingly, as noted above, abolitionist efforts in a number of states have not only been defeated recently, but actively pro-death penalty efforts – efforts to entrench capital punishment, and to curtail opportunities to appeal death sentences – have met with some success. And in response to the shortage of drugs needed for executions, states have utilized alternative chemicals, have procured drugs from unlicensed sources, have enacted measures to prevent such interference, and have introduced other methods of execution such as electrocution and gassing, in order to press ahead with executions.[43]

Even if these pro-death penalty successes are construed as blips on an otherwise straight line towards the end of executions, we should still be concerned about the potential collateral effect of a conservative and pragmatic-based abolition. Angela Davis, who advocates the abolition of prisons, complains that

> even the anti-death penalty campaign tends to rely on the assumption that life imprisonment is the most rational alternative to capital punishment. As important as it may be to abolish the death penalty, we should be conscious of the way the contemporary campaign against capital punishment has a propensity to recapitulate the very historical patterns that led to the emergence of the prison as the dominant form of punishment.[44]

Marie Gottschalk agrees, noting how the "disputes over capital punishment [in the 1960s and 1970s] helped solidify a zero-sum view of victims and offenders in capital and noncapital cases that bolstered the consolidation of the conservative victims' rights movement".[45] This, she writes, "facilitated the expansion of the carceral state,"[46] referring to the phenomenon of mass incarceration in the United States today. Thus, although situating anti-death penalty narratives within conservative discourses has reaped some rewards in the sense that there are fewer death penalty prosecutions, sentences imposed, and sentences carried out, this approach runs the risk of perpetuating the very values that (at least some) abolitionists are seeking to eradicate.[47] Michael McCann and David T. Johnson also state that "if abolition is separated from reform of the larger penal complex, the advance will be limited and perhaps even Pyrrhic". In their words, "[a]nother troubling possibility is that successful abolition could make other punishments harsher. Abolition was one precursor of America's massive prison expansion after the US Supreme Court effectively eliminated the death penalty in 1972."[48] In this book, I build upon these views by using historical lessons – namely, those from the abolition of slavery – to argue that contemporary anti-death penalty efforts are actually more radical than conservative or pragmatic, and should continue to be so.

IV. The comparative historical method

It is not immediately obvious that the history of slavery and abolition is an appropriate or helpful lens through which to understand and evaluate contemporary anti-death penalty efforts, but there are two reasons for doing so. The first lies in the benefits of a comparative-historical approach generally; the second lies in the specific relationship between slavery, capital punishment, and their respective abolition movements.

A. The benefits of a comparative historical approach

A comparative historical study is useful for the four purposes given by Jürgen Kocka when outlining why examples from history can and should be used to study modern phenomena, subject to certain methodological considerations. First, "[h]euristically, the comparative approach allows one to identify questions and problems that one might miss, neglect, or just not invent".[49] The experiences of slavery abolitionism help us identify actual and potential issues in contemporary anti-death penalty discourses that might otherwise be overlooked. Second, historical comparisons can help with definitional issues – we can better understand aspects of death penalty abolitionism by comparing and contrasting such aspects with those of slavery abolitionism. Third, the historical comparative approach helps us identify and answer certain causal questions about why contemporary anti-death penalty activities are the way they are. Finally, the comparative approach helps ensure that the researcher is not led by their own prejudices or personal history in relation to a particular subject matter. A researcher like myself who is personally opposed to the death penalty on moral grounds can find it difficult to assess contemporary abolitionism objectively, but the historical lens helps check any such prejudices.

B. The use of slavery and abolition specifically

While there are methodological benefits to the comparative historical approach, we must be clear why the history of the slavery and abolition specifically is useful and appropriate for examining modern anti-death penalty efforts. It might be argued that this exercise is ill-conceived because there is no conceptual link between antebellum slavery and the modern death penalty, or their respective abolitionist movements, and that such a comparison only serves propaganda purposes. Reformers of all kinds have drawn on the history of anti-slavery efforts primarily for propaganda purposes, because the term "abolitionist" is synonymous with "fighting the good fight".[50] For example, some people who favor the right of a woman to choose whether or not to continue with a pregnancy have likened state-control over reproductive choices as akin to slavery.[51] In direct contrast, the pro-life lobby has argued that abortion is comparable to slavery. Their argument is that the legality of abortion, as set out by the US Supreme Court in *Roe v. Wade*,[52] depends on the denial of personhood to the fetus in the same way that the Court denied legal and moral personhood to black people in the pro-slavery decision of *Dred Scott v. Sandford*.[53] The intention behind such a claim is transparent: *Dred Scott* has been described as the Court's "most dreadful" decision,[54] and if *Roe* is comparable in its jurisprudential approach, then it too must be a "dreadful" decision.[55]

Animal rights activists have also claimed that non-human animals are treated in the same way that slaves were treated. Writing in 1894, Henry Salt argued that "[t]he present condition of the more highly organized domestic animals is in many ways very analogous to that of the negro slaves... you will find in their case precisely the same exclusion from the common pale of humanity... [and] the same deliberate stubborn denial of their social 'rights.'"[56] More recently, on July 26, 2017, Anthony Scaramucci (who was Director of Communications at the White House) compared President Trump's efforts to repeal the Affordable Care Act to President Lincoln's efforts to outlaw slavery.[57] This followed Ben Carson's characterization of government control over healthcare to government control over the enslavement of black people.[58]

James Brewer Stewart – a notable historian of slavery and anti-slavery efforts – has questioned whether such "analogies involving abolitionism" can "be even conceivable, let alone defensible, since they do not in any way involve the pervasive historical problem of racial oppression".[59] In contrast, it is less controversial to suggest that contemporary efforts to stop human trafficking should draw on the work of the antebellum anti-slavery movement, given that modern slavery is conceptually linked to antebellum slavery.[60]

We need to be sure, then, that the comparative approach adopted in this book is methodologically rigorous and defensible. Let us consider why some readers might consider the contention that today's death penalty is rooted in the history of slavery is hyperbolic at best, or offensive at worst. It might seem hyperbolic to those who consider slavery and the death penalty to be separated by time, purpose, and scope. Such arguments would run along the following lines: Slavery ended in 1865; the modern death penalty is rooted in the US Supreme Court decisions of the 1970s. Slavery was centered on racial discrimination, unwaged labor and the economy; the death penalty is instead primarily about crime and punishment. Although death penalty systems across the US are affected by racial discrimination, many white people are sentenced to death and people are not sentenced to death solely because they are black, whereas people were enslaved solely because of the color of their skin. In terms of scope, it might be noted that in 1860, the population of the United States stood at nearly 31.5 million, of which 3.9 million were slaves.[61] In contrast, in a current population of nearly 325 million people, there are approximately 3,000 people awaiting execution.[62] We certainly cannot say that the issue of the death penalty today renders America "a house divided", notwithstanding divisions among Americans about the propriety of capital punishment.[63] Whereas the slavery abolitionists were calling for the destruction of hundreds of thousands of dollars' worth of property, and for the creation of millions of new citizens,[64] death penalty abolitionists are not seeking such dramatic changes to the American legal, political, and social order.

The comparison might also appear to be offensive because it conjures up images of death row inmates being compared to slaves, and death penalty supporters being cast as the moral equivalent of those who supported slavery. When state legislators in Connecticut were considering a bill in 2012 that would eventually lead to the end of the death penalty in that state, Bishop Peter Rosazza said:

"Connecticut was the last State in New England to abolish slavery. Hopefully we shall not have the shameful distinction as regards the death penalty."[65] Senator John Kissel balked at this testimony: "[T]o analogize folks that support [the death penalty] to people that supported slavery, that's so offensive. To analogize this to individuals that just act out of rage or vindictiveness, that's just not right... I take umbrage at the whole slavery thing because, once upon a time, one of my relatives was a surgeon in the union side of the Civil War. Come on, man, ... to make that analogy, I think, is a stretch."[66] When the Connecticut Supreme Court decided three years later in *State v. Santiago* that the legislative repeal applied retroactively to those already on death row, the majority referred to the legacy of slavery and the pervasiveness of racism in the administration of capital punishment.[67] This drew a sharp rebuke from the dissenters: "[T]he majority suggests that Southerners are *racists,* and so are those who support the death penalty. Painting Southerners and supporters of the death penalty with the broad brush of racism could appear to some to be racist itself and reinforces stereotypes that have no foundation in fact or law."[68]

Senator Kissel and the *Santiago* dissenters, it can be assumed, consider the analogy objectionable because, in contrast to slaves, those facing execution have been found guilty of committing horrific crimes. Many people were born into slavery and had no choice or control over their condition, whereas death row inmates are there because of an apparent personal choice to commit a crime. Similarly, everyone sentenced to death has an opportunity to plead for their lives at the sentencing stage of their trials, and to appeal their sentences and ask for mercy up to the point of execution. Slaves were rarely able to use the legal system to escape bondage, although there were a few notable exceptions to this.[69]

For these reasons, scholars have occasionally faced criticism for drawing comparisons between the struggle to end executions, and the struggle to end slavery.[70] To ensure that the comparative study in this book is justifiable and objective, the first three chapters explain the historical and conceptual links between slavery, capital punishment, and their respective abolitionist movements. The chapters are split across three eras: the relationship between capital punishment, slavery, and abolitionism in the antebellum era; the legacy of slavery in the death penalty between the years 1865 and 1976, when the US Supreme Court handed down its decision in *Gregg v. Georgia*; and the legacy of slavery and anti-slavery efforts on the death penalty and anti-death penalty efforts since *Gregg*. In all three chapters, we will see that anti-slavery and anti-racist campaigners often worked side-by-side with anti-death penalty campaigners, given their shared concerns, but that on occasion the different sets of campaigners have inadvertently hindered each other's progress. The success of the slavery abolitionists in bringing about the Thirteenth Amendment,[71] for example, quelled anti-death penalty sentiments in the mid-nineteenth century. The backlash to the success of the Civil Rights movement in the mid-twentieth century, we will see, contributed to the restoration of capital punishment in 1976, just four years after the Supreme Court had abolished it. And in the contemporary era, we will see that it was the failure of race-based litigation efforts – particularly the Supreme Court's rejection of such a claim in *McCleskey v.*

Kemp in 1987 – that compelled anti-death penalty activists to shift their focus from the courts, and to the political arena.[72] This is a point worth emphasizing: when the Court refused to overturn death sentences notwithstanding statistical evidence of racial bias, the focus of abolitionism changed in two particular ways. Many in the anti-death penalty community concluded that the case against capital punishment had to be taken to the public, and that the case would have to be framed in narrow terms that focused on the phenomenon of executions, rather than on issues such as racial bias which affect the criminal justice system more broadly. It is here, then, that we see the influence of race and the legacy of slavery on death penalty abolitionism: the rise of conservative and pragmatic anti-death penalty discourses can be traced, at least in part, to the failure of race-based abolitionist efforts.

V. Radical abolitionism

By the end of Chapter Three, it should be clear that the fate of death penalty abolitionism has been intertwined with America's legacy of slavery and racial injustice. I should be clear that capital punishment has not been *solely* formed by this history – discrete events such as particularly atrocious crimes; the personalities of the anti-death penalty movement's leaders; a lack of resources; and a whole range of other factors such as the decentralized nature of criminal justice in the American federal system have coalesced to inform the retention and use of capital punishment in the US.[73] But the history of slavery, and efforts to abolish slavery, have had an important and long-lasting impact on the American death penalty and on abolitionist strategies, tactics, and discourses. This statement, though, needs unpacking, since the movement that worked to end slavery was a divided one. Although the diverse ideologies, aims, and strategies and tactics of the anti-slavery movement are considered in depth in Chapter Four, it is necessary to outline the key differences here.

The first anti-slavery societies, such as the Pennsylvania Abolition Society, were conservative in nature. They rejected emotional appeals about the moral wrong of slavery, and focused instead on using the legal system to end involuntary bondage. Indeed, many of these initial societies prohibited blacks from taking up membership, betraying their own racism.[74] The principle of "gradualism" also underpinned conservative, or moderate, anti-slavery activism. Partly because of a concern with the social upheaval that would be caused by emancipation, and partly because of a belief that black people would struggle to cope with living a life of freedom, conservative reformers advocated the gradual abolition of slavery. They proposed laws, for example, that would only grant freedom to persons who were born into bondage after a particular date. Even then, these people would have to reach a certain age before achieving freedom. Those already in bondage at the time the law was passed, though, would remain enslaved.

Aileen Kraditor describes such conservative anti-slavery activists as "reformers rather than radicals in that they considered Northern society fundamentally good and believed that abolition of slavery would eliminate a deviation from its essential goodness and thereby strengthen and preserve its basically moral arrangements."[75] Put another way, they saw slavery as a standalone illness that could be treated in isolation to other social, political, and institutional injustices. This is not to say that all of them were unconcerned with other issues such as women's rights, but rather that they thought it unwise to fight several fronts simultaneously. Indeed, because of their narrow focus, some historians refrain from attaching the label "abolitionist" to such individuals, describing them as merely "anti-slavery" instead.[76]

Kraditor contrasts conservative anti-slavery activists with "radical abolitionists", who, in her words, "believed that American society, North as well as South, was fundamentally immoral, with slavery only the worst of its many sins, and who looked forward to a thoroughgoing change in its institutional structure and ideology."[77] That is, they viewed slavery as a symptom of a deeper sickness that pervaded America, and in their fight against involuntary human bondage they proposed a radical re-imagining of the American constitutional and social order. Radicals, such as William Lloyd Garrison and Wendell Phillips, differed from their more conservative or moderate counterparts in that they were uncompromisingly moralistic, and they insisted on the immediate rather than the gradual emancipation of all slaves. In this sense, they were critical of even Northern states that had initiated gradual emancipation laws. Not only did the principle of gradualism serve to keep black people in bondage, it also entrenched the principle of racial degradation that underpinned slavery. Radical abolitionists were also distinctive in advocating for a positive as well as a negative conception of abolition. While some opponents of slavery objected to human bondage but accepted the notion of white supremacy, radical abolitionists insisted both that black people should not be enslaved in a negative sense, and that black people should enjoy equal rights and opportunities in all other aspects of social and political life in a positive sense. Again, this led radicals to condemn communities which had ended slavery, but which subjected free black persons to mistreatment, and which were complicit in slavery. We will see, therefore, that radical abolitionists differed from their conservative allies by contending that slavery could not be divorced from other social ills such as the subjugation of women, the abuse of alcohol, the mistreatment of free blacks, and particularly for our purposes, the degrading treatment of those accused and convicted of criminal offenses.[78] Radical abolitionists recognized the similarities between the wrong of slavery and the wrong of the death penalty: both were symptomatic of the view that some people's lives are worth less than others.

Like today's anti-death penalty movement, then, opponents of slavery – consisting of moderates and radicals – undertook a range of activities. Some used the legal system to free the enslaved and to stifle the machinery of slavery; others focused on political activity. Yet others rejected the legal and political systems, complaining that they were the very problems. Perhaps the most notable of these abolitionists was William Lloyd Garrison, who advocated "moral suasion" as a primary abolitionist tactic. This involved appealing to the hearts and minds of the general public. And just as today's abolitionists have practically interfered with executions, so the antebellum abolitionists interfered with the machinery of slavery by helping slaves escape to freedom regardless of legal and political processes, and by refusing to be complicit in the recapturing of fugitive slaves. It is with this in mind, then, that I suggest that today's anti-death movement is more radical than it is conservative or pragmatic. To explain why, in Chapter Four I use the idea of dignity to encapsulate the spirit of radical abolitionism. Although the idea of dignity is a jurisprudentially and philosophically fraught one,[79] and although a number of commentators have rejected its usefulness in abolitionist efforts,[80] it is nonetheless a helpful organizing principle for the central tenet of radical abolitionism: the idea that the lives of all human beings – regardless of the color of their skin or their moral conduct – are equally important. Radical slavery abolitionists went further than emphasizing that slavery contravened the dignity of the condemned person, though. They also argued that slavery contravened the dignity of slaveholders and of communities that actively supported or passively acquiesced in such a practice. They also asserted that involuntary bondage threatened the dignity or integrity of the national constitutional order that permitted and provided legal support for slavery. As we will see, anti-death penalty discourses – even those that initially appear to be conservative and pragmatic – actually draw on this tripartite account of dignity: the dignity of the person, of the community, and of the legal system. Put another way, a radical approach to death penalty abolitionism places pragmatic and conservative discourses within a broader dignitarian framework, one that highlights that death sentences and executions are a symptom of a wider illness that continues to pervade criminal justice systems across America. These problems include issues such as mass incarceration, the use of solitary confinement, and sentences of life without the possibility of parole. Police brutality – particularly the phenomenon of black persons being killed with apparent impunity by police officers – also has the same root as capital punishment and slavery: a belief that some lives are worth less than others.

It is one thing to say that today's abolitionism is more radical than currently appreciated, but it is another thing to argue that it should be. The experience of emancipation and its aftermath are instructive for this normative question. We know from experience that the emancipation of slaves in 1865 was not accompanied by any significant change in moral sentiment, and that the lingering resentment among, in particular, Southern white communities resulted in the values that underpinned slavery rearing their heads again and again in the post-emancipation years. In *Black Reconstruction in America*, published in 1935, W.E.B. Du Bois explained how the freedom of slaves in 1865 had proven to be a pyrrhic victory: "The slave went free; stood for a brief moment in the sun; then moved back again toward slavery."[81] Du Bois was lamenting the shortcomings of the Reconstruction period, and it is hardly controversial to point to the Jim Crow era of lynchings and segregation to highlight how African Americans were not granted equal political rights or social opportunities, and were subjected to appalling treatment, notwithstanding their physical freedom from bondage.[82] The legacy of slavery continues to be felt to this day, as racial prejudices and injustices pervade all features of American life. This is particularly true of the over-representation of black people in the criminal justice system, the comparative neglect of black crime victims, and the administration of racially-constituted systems of capital punishment.[83] There are several reasons why racial inequality and degradation have persisted post-emancipation, but one reason is that conservative anti-slavery discourses in the antebellum era enabled the entrenchment and proliferation of the view that black-skinned people are not as important as white-skinned people. For example, one strategy of the conservative anti-slavery activists was colonization – the idea that slaves should be freed and then sent away from America because blacks and whites could never live alongside each other peacefully. Nicholas Guyatt explains how "colonization enabled 'moderate' opponents of slavery to denounce human bondage without accepting black citizenship, to believe that they were upholding their principles while denying non-whites a place in the expanding republic."[84] These views did not address the dignity of black people, and entrenched the idea of "separate but equal" in political, legal, and cultural conversations. In other words, it was the rhetoric of seemingly "enlightened Americans [that] invented racial segregation",[85] and which explains "why racial justice in the United States has remained such an elusive goal."[86]

If we accept Guyatt's thesis of how moderate, or conservative, anti-slavery activists contributed to the entrenchment of racial divisions and injustices today, then we can see why, as Angela Davis and others have argued, conservative anti-death penalty discourses might similarly perpetuate the very values that drive support for the degrading treatment of those found guilty of criminal offenses. Of course, we can never know if racial injustices would be less systemic and fewer and farther between today if radical abolitionist discourses had dominated discussions about emancipation. Indeed, in *Stamped from the Beginning*, Ibram X. Kendi suggests that even radical abolitionists such as William Lloyd Garrison contributed to the proliferation of racist ideas,[87] but we can surmise that a radical death penalty abolitionism will at least offer hope for systemic reforms that are needed in the criminal justice system.

Chapters Five through to Eight put this understanding of radical abolitionism into the context of contemporary anti-death penalty efforts. Chapter Five addresses abolitionist efforts in the courtroom. Using William Wiecek's definition of "radical anti-slavery constitutionalism", with its emphasis on natural law-inspired claims to equality and liberty, I suggest that Justice Kennedy's post-2005 death penalty jurisprudence, with its emphasis on dignity, offers a framework for a radical anti-death penalty constitutionalism which will open the doors for further reforms in the criminal justice system. Chapter Six focuses on abolitionism in the political and public sphere. A central tenet of radical slavery abolitionism was the inclusion of blacks and others with experience of slavery within abolitionist ranks, and it was the voice of experience that propelled the abolitionists towards a radical position. With this in mind, we will see that it is the voices of those with experience of capital punishment that are pushing death penalty abolitionism towards a more radical position.

Chapter Seven addresses the debate over the extent to which, if at all, abolitionists should advocate the use of life in prison without the possibility of parole in death's stead. For some, accepting LWOP is a necessary compromise in the fight against executions, whereas others abhor the idea of advocating or acquiescing in the sentencing of people to die behind bars. The contours of this disagreement mirror those of antebellum activists' disagreements over colonization. For some, colonization was a necessary means to securing abolition; for others, it ensconced the idea of white supremacy. Using David Walker's criticism of colonization, we will see the importance of establishing anti-death penalty discourses that do not entrench other degrading punishments.

Chapter Eight explores more practical types of abolitionism, including recent efforts to stem the supply of drugs needed for executions. While this has been incredibly effective in halting executions, it has provoked a backlash from the pro-death penalty lobby as authorities have pushed ahead with executions anyway. This chain of events finds a parallel in the history of fugitive slaves. Free states refused to co-operate with the machinery of slavery – particularly with respect to the non-return of fugitive slaves – and this was met with a backlash in the shape of adverse decisions from the US Supreme Court, and the adoption of pro-slavery measures by Congress. Slavery abolitionists, though, used these events to their advantage by alerting Northerners and those apathetic about slavery to the dangers that the pro-slavery lobby posed to their own self-interests and values. This history is used to illustrate how today's abolitionists can further their cause by drawing attention to the ways in which the pro-death penalty backlash threatens the rights and interests of those who do not normally consider themselves to be affected by capital punishment. The book concludes with an overview of how the abolition of the death penalty must be premised on America's peculiar history of slavery, and the ways in which this abolition can provide a framework for addressing other criminal and social injustices.

VI. An exploratory study

The parallels between antebellum and contemporary abolitionism are legion, and it has not been possible to provide an exhaustive comparative study. The parallels between the slavery abolitionists' uses of the nascent printing press with modern uses of social media, for example, is an interesting point of comparison that is not pursued here since it does not shed light on the radicalism of the movement, save to say that both sets of abolitionists have been innovative in making sure that their messages are delivered far and wide notwithstanding scarce resources. The comparative role of religious discourses is also not explored in any great depth, despite its centrality to much of slavery abolitionism. Religion might motivate people to oppose slavery or the death penalty, and it might drive people to the radical position, but it does not in and of itself tell us much about the nature or normativity of radical abolitionism. There is no place, in my view, for the violence of John Brown or Nat Turner in today's efforts to end state-sanctioned executions, and nor should today's abolitionists countenance disunion as William Lloyd Garrison did.

Constitutional, political, and social realities of the twenty-first century differ in many important ways from those of the nineteenth century: the Bill of Rights has since been incorporated against the states thus changing the relationship between the federal government and the states; new technologies have changed the way we interact and communicate; and America's relationship with the rest of the world has evolved, thus affecting the impact of international pressure in abolitionism. These factors also caution against a direct comparison between abolitionist efforts past and present. However, my point is not that discrete "actions" of the slavery abolitionists can and should be "copied" by today's abolitionists, but rather that the utopian rhetoric and visions of the radical slavery abolitionists can and should guide today's anti-death penalty movement. Robin D.G. Kelley has explained in his book on black radical social movements that we should not necessarily judge social movements on whether they succeed in realizing their aims, but rather we should judge them "on the merits or power of the visions themselves".[88] This is central to my argument: contemporary anti-death penalty efforts must be radical in their visions, in order to inspire much needed changes to the tendency to view some people's lives as less valuable than others.

Notes

1 Remarks published in an article in *Battle Creek Nightly Moon*, June 8, 1881 (reprinted in Larry G. Murphy, *Sojourner Truth: A Biography* (Greenwood Biographies 2011) 151). Also see Sojourner Truth, *Narrative of Sojourner Truth* (first published 1850, Vintage Books 1993); Margaret Washington, *Sojourner Truth's America* (University of Illinois Press 2009).

2 Eugene G. Wagner, 'Historical Reflections on Michigan's Abolition of the Death Penalty' (1996) 13 T.M. Cooley L. Rev 755.

3 Some of the central texts on the relationship between slavery and the death penalty include: Stuart Banner, 'Traces of Slavery: Race and the Death Penalty in Historical Perspective' in Charles J. Ogletree Jr and Austin Sarat (eds), *From Lynch Mobs to the Killing State: Race and the Death Penalty in America* (NYU Press 2006); Carol S. Steiker and Jordan M. Steiker, 'The American Death Penalty and the (In)visibility of Race' (2015) 82 University of Chicago Law Review 243; Jeffrey L. Kirchmeier, *Imprisoned by the Past: Warren McCleskey and the American Death Penalty* (OUP 2015), especially Chapters 4 and 5; Bryan Stevenson, *Just Mercy: A Story of Justice and Redemption* (Random House 2015). Although focused on the death penalty after slavery, there is some treatment of capital punishment's relationship with slavery in William J. Bowers, *Legal Homicide: Death as Punishment in America, 1864–1982* (Northeastern University Press 1974).

4 Bruce Ledewitz, 'Abolition Then and Now' *Southern Voices* (Spring 1989) 44.

5 See, for example, Daniel LaChance, 'What Will Doom the Death Penalty?' *The New York Times* (8 September 2014) http://www.nytimes.com/2014/09/09/opinion/what-will-finally-doom-the-death-penalty.html; Jolie McLaughlin, 'The Price of Justice: Interest-Convergence, Cost, and the Anti-Death Penalty Movement' (2014) 108 Northwestern University Law Review 675; Lawrence C. Marshall, 'The Innocence Revolution and the Death Penalty' (2004) 1 Ohio State Journal of Criminal Law 573.

6 Angela Y Davis, *Are Prisons Obsolete?* (Seven Stories Press 2003) 106; Marie Gottschalk, *The Prison and the Gallows: The Politics of Mass Incarceration in America* (Cambridge University Press 2006) Chapter 9.

7 Gregg v. Georgia, 428 U.S. 153 (1976). The numbers of executions and death sentences are taken from the website of the Death Penalty Information Center, which is a non-profit organization that provides information about capital punishment in the US. See https://deathpenaltyinfo.org/documents/FactSheet.pdf.

8 I use the word "just" with trepidation, for many people will consider even one execution to be an execution too many.

9 Gallup Polling, *Death Penalty* http://www.gallup.com/poll/1606/death-penalty.aspx (Polling carried out between 5–11 October 2017).

10 At the end of 1999, just 12 of the 52 jurisdictions in the United States of America (comprising 50 states, the military, and the federal government) outlawed capital punishment: Alaska (1957), Hawaii (1957), Iowa (1965), Maine (1887), Massachusetts (1984), Michigan (1846) Minnesota (1911) North Dakota (1973), Rhode Island (1984), Vermont (1964), West Virginia (1965), and Wisconsin (1853). Since 1999, a further seven jurisdictions have outlawed the punishment: Connecticut (2012); Delaware (2016); Illinois (2011); Maryland (2013); New Jersey (2007); New Mexico (2009); New York (2007). In 2015, legislators in Nebraska voted to repeal the death penalty, but it was reinstated by a popular ballot measure in 2016.

11 'Editorial: The Death Penalty, Nearing its End,' *The New York Times* (24 October 2016) http://www.nytimes.com/2016/10/24/opinion/the-death-penalty-nearing-its-end.html.

12 Associated Press, 'Supreme Court Justice says he wouldn't be surprised to see death penalty struck down' *New York Daily News* (21 October 2015) http://www.nydailynews.com/news/national/justice-wouldn-surprised-death-penalty-fell-article-1.2405429.

13 Brandon Garrett, *End of its Rope: How Killing the Death Penalty Can Revive Criminal Justice* (Harvard University Press 2017) 1. Also see Carol S Steiker and Jordan M Steiker, *Courting Death: The Supreme Court and Capital Punishment* (Belknap Press 2016) (arguing that the Court is in the process of regulating the death penalty out of existence).

14 Paul Hammel, 'Nebraskans vote overwhelmingly to restore death penalty, nullify historic 2015 vote by State Legislature' *Omaha World-Herald* (9 November 2016) http://www.omaha.com/news/politics/nebraskans-vote-overwhelmingly-to-restore-death-penalty-nullify-historic-vote/article_38823d54-a5df-11e6-9a5e-d7a71d75611a.html

15 Josh Sanburn, 'Oklahoma Votes to Add Death Penalty to its Constitution' *Time Magazine* (8 November 2016) http://time.com/4563488/oklahoma-death-penalty-referendum/.

16 Jazmine Ulloa and Julie Westfall, 'California voters approve an effort to speed up the death penalty with Prop. 66' *Los Angeles Times* (22 November 2016). http://www.latimes.com/politics/essential/la-pol-ca-essential-politics-updates-proposition-66-death-penalty-passes-1479869920-htmlstory.html

17 Andrew Cohen, 'The Death Penalty is Alive and Well' *The Marshall Project* (9 November 2016) https://www.themarshallproject.org/2016/11/09/the-death-penalty-is-alive-and-well#.vWFwrlIjk.

18 For an outline of Justice Gorsuch's approach to constitutional interpretation, including his views on the death penalty, see Eric Citron, 'Potential Nominee Profile: Neil Gorsuch' *SCOTUSblog* (13 January 2017) http://www.scotusblog.com/2017/01/potential-nominee-profile-neil-gorsuch/.

19 Editorial, 'Arkansas's State-sponsored Killing Spree' *The Washington Post* (10 April 2017); Meghan McCracken and Jennifer Moreno, 'Arkansas's Cruel and Unusual Killing Spree' *The New York Times* (20 March 2017).

20 Greg Stohr, 'Gorsuch's First Big Supreme Court Vote Allows Arkansas Execution' *Bloomberg Politics* (21 April 2017).

21 Mike Brickner, 'Tomorrow Ohio Plans to Restart Executions with Drugs Known to Torture' *American Civil Liberties Union* (25 July 2017) (noting that it 'will also mark the beginning of 27 planned executions' and that 'Gov. John Kasich can stop this execution spree…') https://www.aclu.org/blog/speak-freely/tomorrow-ohio-plans-restart-executions-drugs-known-torture.

22 Studies on America's retention of the death penalty in an era of global abolition include: David Garland, *Peculiar Institution: America's Death Penalty in an Age of Abolition* (Harvard University Press 2012); Franklin E. Zimring, *The Contradictions of American Capital Punishment* (OUP 2003).

23 Furman v. Georgia, 408 U.S. 238 (1972); Gregg v. Georgia, 428 U.S. 153 (1976).

24 The phrase "evolving standards of decency" was first used in Trop v. Dulles, 356 U.S. 86, 101 (1958) and has been used a guiding principle in Eighth Amendment analysis ever since.

25 The Court's approach to Eighth Amendment analysis is explained in Chapter Five.

26 Enmund v. Florida 458 U.S. 782, 798 (1982).

27 The literature on racial bias, unequal application, and deterrence is vast, and the following is a mere selection of works. On racial bias, see Glenn L. Pierce, Michael L. Radelet, and Susan Sharp, 'Race and Death Sentencing for Oklahoma Homicides Committed Between 1990 and 2012' (2017) 107 Journal of Criminal Law & Criminology 733; Frank R. Baumgartner, Amanda J. Grigg and Alisa Mastro '#BlackLivesDon'tMatter: race-of-victim effects in US executions, 1976–2013 (2015) 3 Politics, Groups, and Identities 209. On the unequal geographical distribution of death sentences and executions, see Robert J Smith, 'The Geography of the Death Penalty and its Ramifications' (2012) 92 Boston University Law Review 227. On deterrence, see National Research Council, *Deterrence and the Death Penalty* (The National Academies Press 2012) (arguing that the voluminous studies on the effect of capital punishment on homicide rates are inconclusive, and that there is no evidence that capital punishment does or does not deter homicides). For a more general statistical study of the death penalty that takes into account gender bias, and class, see Frank Baumgartner, Marty Davidson, Kaneesha Johnson, Arvind Krishnamurthy, and Colin Wilson, *Deadly Justice: A Statistical Portrait of the Death Penalty* (OUP 2017).

28 C. Lee Harrington, 'A Community Divided: Defense Attorneys and the Ethics of Death Row Volunteering' (2000) 25 Law and Social Inquiry 849.

29 Paul J. Kaplan, 'Forgetting the Future: Cause Lawyering and the Work of California Capital Trial Defenders' (2010) 14 Theoretical Criminology 211.

30 On the improvements in death penalty defence lawyering, see Garrett, *End of its Rope* (n.13) Chapter 6. The Court outlawed the death penalty for young offenders in Roper v. Simmons, 543 U.S. 551 (2005) and for the intellectually disabled in Atkins v. Virginia 536 U.S. 304 (2002). (reaffirmed in Hall v. Florida, 134 S. Ct. 1986 (2014) and Moore v. Texas, 137 S. Ct. 1039 (2017)).

31 Hurst v. Florida, 136 S. Ct. 616 (2016). See Michael L Radelet and G. Ben Cohen, 'The Predictable Disarray: Ignoring the Jury in Florida Death Penalty Cases' (Unpublished paper, 18 January 2017) (arguing that 201 death row prisoners in Florida may be eligible for resentencing hearings following the decision of the US Supreme Court, which ruled it unconstitutional to deny defendants the right to have their sentences in capital cases determined by a jury, and that unanimous verdicts were required for a death sentence to be imposed.) However, the Florida Supreme Court has decided a string of cases post-*Hurst* that have precluded relief to prisoners sentenced to death by non-unanimous juries. See Hitchcock v. Florida, No. SC17–445 (Fla. Aug. 10, 2017).

32 On religious arguments against capital punishment, see Shane Claiborne, *Executing Grace: How the Death Penalty Killed Jesus and Why It's Killing Us* (HarperCollins 2016).

33 See, for example, Lincoln Caplan, 'The End of the Open Market for Lethal Injection Drugs' *The New Yorker* (21 May 2016) http://www.newyorker.com/news/news-desk/the-end-of-the-open-market-for-lethal-injection-drug Clare Algar, 'Can Big Pharma end the death penalty in the US?' *The New Statesman* (22 October 2013) http://www.newstatesman.com/law/2013/10/could-big-pharma-end-death-penalty.

34 Herbert Haines, *Against Capital Punishment: The Anti-Death Penalty Movement in America, 1972–1994* (OUP 1999).

35 ibid 206.

36 ibid 103.

37 The role of innocence in abolitionist efforts is considered in depth in Chapter Six, but also see Daniel Medwed, *Wrongful Convictions and the DNA Revolution: 25 years of Freeing the Innocent* (Cambridge University Press 2017).

38 For the avoidance of confusion, I do not mean to suggest that there is a specific date or year in which pragmatic abolitionism came to the fore, but rather that such styles picked up prominence around the period of the late 1990s and early 2000s.

39 The literature on the problems with the criminal justice is vast, and following is a mere selection of texts. On mass incarceration, see John Pfaff, *Locked In: The True Causes of Mass Incarceration – and How to Achieve Real Reform* (Basic Books 2017) On racism within the criminal justice system, see Michelle Alexander, *The New Jim Crow: Mass Incarceration in the Age of Colorblindness* (The New Press 2012) (Pfaff and Alexander disagree with each other on the causes of mass incarceration). On life without parole, see Charles J. Ogletree Jr and Austin Sarat (eds) *Life Without Parole: America's New Death Penalty?* (NYU Press 2014).

40 Colleen Eren has written: "the leading [anti-death penalty organizations'] framing of the issue since 2000 has shifted away from 'moralistic,' allegedly 'emotional/non-rational,' traditionally progressive arguments to 'rational,' 'consensus-seeking,' crime-prevention frames and arguments that parallel those found in rightist, conservative movements, in the… belief that doing so is the best way to win abolition." Colleen Eren, 'The Right Anti-Death Penalty Movement? Framing Abolitionism for the Twenty-first Century' (2015) 15 New Politics 95, 95.

41 LaChance (n 5).

42 'Death Penalty', *Gallup* (n 9).

43 This is discussed in greater detail in Chapter Eight.

44 Davis (n 6) 106.

45 Gottschalk (n 6) 198.

46 ibid 201.

47 For similar criticisms of abolitionist efforts that neglect broader concerns with criminal justice, see Kerry Ann Akers and Peter Hodgkinson, 'A Critique of Litigation and Abolition Strategies: A Glass Half Empty' in Peter Hodgkinson (ed) *Capital Punishment: New Perspectives* (Ashgate 2013).

48 Michael McCann and David T. Johnson, 'Rocked but Still Rolling: The Enduring Institution of Capital Punishment in Historical and Comparative Perspective' in Charles Ogletree Jr and Austin Sarat (eds), *The Road to Abolition? The Future of Capital Punishment in the United States* (NYU Press 2009) 168.

49 Jürgen Kocka, 'Comparison and Beyond' (2003) 42 History and Theory 39, 40.

50 Jon Grinspan, 'Was Abolitionism a Failure?' *The New York Times* (30 January 2015) https://opinionator.blogs.nytimes.com/author/jon-grinspan/.

51 Robin Abcarian, 'Forcing Women to have Children is Akin to Slavery, says a devoutly Christian Abortion Doctor' *Los Angeles Times* (21 May 2017) http://www.latimes.com/local/abcarian/la-me-abcarian-abortion-doctor-201705121-story.html.

52 Roe v. Wade, 410 U.S. 113 (1973).

53 Dred Scott v. Sandford, 60 U.S. 393 (1857).

54 Paul Finkelman, '*Scott v. Sandford*: The Court's Most Dreadful Case and How it Changed History' (2007) 82 *Chicago-Kent Law Review* 3.

55 On the connections between contemporary abortion politics and the legacy of slavery, see Justin Buckley Dyer, *Slavery, Abortion, and the Politics of Constitutional Meaning* (Cambridge University Press 2013).

56 Henry Salt, *Animals' Rights: Considered in Relation to Social Progress* (Macmillan & Co. 1894) 21. More recently, Corey Lee Wrenn has set out "tactical" lessons that animal rights activists might draw from the abolitionists. See Corey Lee Wrenn, 'Abolition Then and Now: Tactical Comparisons Between the Human Rights Movement and the Modern Nonhuman Animal Rights Movement in the United States' (2014) 27 Journal of Agricultural and Environmental Ethics 177.

57 Julia Gregory, 'Trump Battle over Obamacare Reminds Scaramucci of Lincoln's Fight to Abolish Slavery', *The Guardian*, (27 July 2017) https://www.theguardian.com/us-news/2017/jul/27/trump-battle-obamacare-reminds-scaramucci-lincolns-fight-abolish-slavery.

58 Abby D. Phillip, 'Ben Carson: Obamacare is "Slavery"', *ABC News*, (11 October 2013) http://abcnews.go.com/blogs/politics/2013/10/ben-carson-obamacare-is-slavery/.
59 James Brewer Stewart, 'What Does it Mean to Study the Abolitionists?' (2005) 5 Pennsylvania Legacies 36, 37.
60 Joel Quirk, *The Anti-Slavery Project: From the Slave Trade to Human Trafficking* (Pennsylvania University Press, 2011). Also see Historians Against Slavery, which is "a community of scholar-activists who contribute research and historical context to today's antislavery movements in order to inspire and inform activism and to develop collaborations that empower such efforts." http://www.historiansagainstslavery.org/main/about-us/
61 These figures are from the 1860 Census, which is available online from the United States Census Bureau. See '1860 Census: Population of the United States' https://census.gov/library/publications/1864/dec/1860a.html. The Introduction to the Census contains an overview of the number of free persons and slaves.
62 The United States Census Bureau keeps a tab on the current population of the US. See https://www.census.gov/. The Criminal Justice Project of the National Association for the Advancement of Colored People, Legal Defense and Educational Fund keeps tab on the death row population. See http://www.naacpldf.org/death-row-usa.
63 Abraham Lincoln famously declared that "A house divided against itself cannot stand", referring to the divisions within the United States over the issue of slavery. See 'A House Divided: Speech Delivered at Springfield, Illinois, at the Close of the Republican State Convention, 16 June 1858, reprinted in Roy P. Basler, *Abraham Lincoln: His Speeches and Writings* (2nd edn, Da Capo Press 2001) 372.
64 Gerald Sorin, *Abolitionism: A New Perspective* (Praeger Publishers 1972) 58.
65 Hrg. on Raised Bill No. 280, An Act Revising the Penalty for Capital Felonies, Before the Connecticut General Assembly Joint Committee on Judiciary, March 14, 2012 (statement of Bishop Peter Rosazza), https://www.cga.ct.gov/2012/juddata/chr/2012JUD00314-R001100-CHR.htm.
66 Hrg. on Raised Bill No. 280, An Act Revising the Penalty for Capital Felonies, Before the Connecticut General Assembly Joint Committee on Judiciary, March 14, 2012 (statement of Sen. John Kissel), https://www.cga.ct.gov/2012/juddata/chr/2012JUD00314-R001100-CHR.htm.
67 State v. Santiago, 122 A.3d 1, 66–68 (Conn. 2015).
68 ibid at 394–95 (Espinosa, J., dissenting).
69 On the use of "freedom suits" by slaves to secure their freedom, see Anne Twitty, *Before* Dred Scott*: Slavery and Legal Culture in the American Confluence, 1787–1857* (Cambridge University Press 2016).
70 See, for example, Willam S. McFeely, *Proximity to Death* (W.W. Norton & Co. 2000). McFeely compares contemporary death penalty lawyers to the Underground Railroad, which was the moniker given to the elaborate system for helping slaves escape from bondage (102, 105). McFeely also writes that "the anti-death penalty effort is not far apart from the nineteenth century's anti-slavery movement" (22). Stuart Banner criticizes McFeely, though, for failing to justify this comparison, and for not being objective in his account of defense lawyers. Stuart Banner, *Too Close for Insight (Review of Proximity to Death)* (2000) 28 Reviews in American History 460.
71 Section 1 of the Thirteenth Amendment reads: "Neither slavery nor involuntary servitude, except as a punishment for crime whereof the party shall have been duly convicted, shall exist within the United States, or any place subject to their jurisdiction."
72 McCleskey v. Kemp, 481 U.S. 279 (1987).
73 See, for example, Garland (n 22); Zimring (n 22).
74 Richard S. Newman, *The Transformation of American Abolitionism: Fighting Slavery in the Early Republic* (University of North Carolina Press, 2002).
75 Aileen S. Kraditor, *Means and Ends in American Abolitionism: Garrison and His Critics on Strategy and Tactics, 1834–1850* (Pantheon Books 1969) 8.

76 Stanley Harrold, *American Abolitionists* (Routledge 2001) 4–5.
77 Kraditor (n 75) 8.
78 Indeed, such were the differences among opponents of slavery that the movement suffered a schism in 1840, when several members left the American Anti-Slavery Society because of their differences of opinion over the proper scope and strategies of abolitionism. See Ronald G. Waters, *The Antislavery Appeal: American Abolitionism after 1830* (John Hopkins University Press 1976).
79 See Christopher McCrudden, 'In Pursuit of Human Dignity: An Introduction to Current Debates' in Christopher McCrudden (ed) *Understanding Human Dignity* (OUP 2013).
80 LaChance (n 5).
81 W.E.B. Du Bois, *Black Reconstruction in America 1860–1880* (first published 1935, The Free Press 1998) 30.
82 On the Reconstruction era, see Eric Foner, *Reconstruction: America's Unfinished Revolution, 1863–1877* (Harper & Row 1988).
83 See generally, Stevenson (n 3).
84 Nicholas Guyatt, *Bind Us Apart: How Enlightened Americans Invented Racial Segregation* (Basic Books 2016) 11.
85 Ibid.
86 ibid 13.
87 Ibram X. Kendi, *Stamped From the Beginning: The Definitive History of Racist Ideas in America* (The Bodley Head 2017).
88 Robin D. G. Kelley, *Freedom Dreams: The Black Radical Imagination* (Beacon Press 2002) ix.

1 The death penalty in the era of slavery

I. Introduction

On October 7, 1858, Frederick Douglass – who had escaped from slavery 20 years earlier and was by now a particularly famous slavery abolitionist – chaired an anti-capital punishment rally at the City Hall in Rochester, New York. The meeting had been called to protest the impending execution of Ira Stout, who had been convicted of murder and sentenced to death by hanging. Douglass set forth what have now become traditional arguments against the death penalty:

> the gallows blunt all the better feelings of human nature, and stimulates all the bad.... [L]ife is the great primary and most previous and comprehensive of all human rights – that whether it be coupled with virtue, honor, or happiness, or with sin, disgrace and misery, the continued possession of it is rightfully a matter of volition; that it [ought not to be] deliberately or voluntarily destroyed, either by individuals separately or combined in what is called Government.[1]

The *Rochester Daily Union and Advertiser* reported on the meeting, titling Douglass's address: "Capital Punishment is a Mockery of Justice."[2] The report also recounted the racial slurs that were aimed at Douglass by some members of the crowd that had gathered to listen. Although Douglass did not explicitly dwell on the fact that slaves and free black people were disproportionately subjected to capital punishment, his concerns were driven by the same values that underpinned his objection to slavery and racism: all human life is important and has value.

Since black people were considered to be of less value than whites, they had long been particularly prone to execution. This is not to say that the death penalty was solely a cog in the machinery of slavery, but rather that the machinery of slavery had an indelible impact on the workings of capital punishment. Even though neither slavery nor the death penalty were uniform, monolithic practices in colonial America, (slavery in the Northern colonies was very different from slavery in the South, just as different colonies employed capital punishment in a range of ways), the practice of slavery affected the imposition and execution of death sentences. In colonies with large numbers of slaves, for example, authorities expedited the process of trying and punishing slaves accused of capital crimes. In 1692, Virginia began using local justices of the peace in capital cases involving slaves, rather than juries or trained judges. Other colonies adopted similar measures, and as such, slaves were executed at a greater rate than whites. At least a hundred slaves were executed in North Carolina in just 25 years between 1748 and 1772, far more than the number of whites who were executed over the course of the colony's entire history, which spanned over a century from 1629 to 1789.[3]

The multifarious ways in which the two institutions interrelated and complemented one another perhaps made it inevitable that those opposed to human bondage would speak out against capital punishment. In the late 1700s, Quakers simultaneously called for the abolition of slavery and the abolition of capital punishment.[4] Louis P. Masur has suggested that William Lloyd Garrison and Wendell Phillips – two of the leading slavery abolitionists in the mid-nineteenth century – understood that "[b]oth slavery and capital punishment… represented systems of brutality".[5] However, as this chapter seeks to demonstrate, attacking both institutions was no easy feat, because an attack on one had the effect of strengthening the other.

II. Attacking capital punishment in the era of slavery

In 1764, a book titled *On Crimes and Punishments*, written by the Italian philosopher Cesare Beccaria, was translated into English.[6] Beccaria provided a searing critique of capital punishment, stating that it served no useful purpose and was unnecessary. Punishments, he argued, should be focused on preventing the criminal from doing further harm to society, and on deterring others from committing a similar offense. For Beccaria, the certainty of being punished was a greater deterrent than the severity of punishment, but in any event he considered the "momentary spectacle" of an execution to be less powerful than the sight of a person in "perpetual slavery". That is, lengthy terms of imprisonment would be a greater deterrent than a death sentence: "Much more potent than the idea of death, which men always regard as vague and distant, is the efficacious because often repeated reflection that I too shall be reduced to so dreary and so pitiable a state if I commit similar crimes."[7] Capital punishment was also not useful because it had a brutalizing effect on the wider community, "because of the example of savagery it gives to men."[8]

Beccaria's tract caught the attention of those who would go on to lead America to independence and write the US Constitution.[9] Many of the Framers, inspired by Beccaria's ruminations, had considerable doubts about capital punishment, though they were reluctant to espouse complete abolition. In 1778, Thomas Jefferson sought to limit the death penalty in Virginia to the crimes of murder and treason, but when his Bill for Proportioning Crimes and Punishments in Cases Heretofore Capital was finally introduced to the legislature in 1785, it was defeated by one vote.[10] When the Bill of Rights was ratified in 1791, the wording of the Fifth Amendment confirmed that, notwithstanding any reservations that the

Framers had, capital punishment was legal if certain processes were followed: "No person shall be… deprived of life… without due process of law."

Not all of the revolutionaries were tentative about abolition, though. Benjamin Rush – one of the signers of the Declaration of Independence – published "Considerations on the Injustice and Impolicy of Punishing Murder by Death" in 1792, in which he developed Beccaria's arguments and added that capital punishment was not compatible with republican ideology. Republics, in Rush's view, were to be defined in opposition to monarchies, and since monarchies relied on capital punishment as a show of sovereign power, it followed that republics must reject such a punishment. Every execution, he argued, resembled monarchical rule.[11] Rush also lamented the effects of capital punishment on the virtue of the people, noting that public hangings in particular debased the communities that took part in them.[12] Additionally, for Rush, executions were not compatible with religious impulses. Theology led him to encourage efforts to reform the criminal, rather than destroy them.[13] With his colleague, William Bradford, Rush managed to galvanize an anti-death penalty movement of sorts.[14] By 1850, societies devoted to the abolition, or at least the regulation, of capital punishment had been formed in Tennessee, Ohio, Alabama, Louisiana, Indiana, Iowa, New York, Pennsylvania, and Massachusetts.[15] Writers and poets railed against capital punishment too, with John Greenleaf Whittier and Walt Whitman among those who published solemn pieces highlighting the humanity of the condemned.[16]

It is little surprise, but important to acknowledge, that many of those who spoke out against the death penalty in this era were also active in anti-slavery efforts, such as Rush and Benjamin Franklin. This is not to say that all opponents of one were opponents of the other, though. Reverend George B. Cheever was firmly against slavery, but published two tracts in defense of capital punishment. In contrast, the Ohioan politician Clement L. Vallandigham was prominently outspoken against the death penalty, but showed support to the South over the issue of slavery.[17]

Those who opposed both practices generally cited religious and ethical grounds for their position, and many took their cue from the founding principles of the United States. Robert Rantoul Jr, who was elected to the Massachusetts House of Representatives in 1834, explained in a report to the state legislature in 1836 that capital punishment was just as repugnant to the spirit of the Constitution of Massachusetts as slavery was: "our Constitution does not forbid capital punishment; for neither does it, by that name, forbid slavery… yet [both] are confessedly contrary to the spirit of the Constitution." He went on to note that the incompatibility of slavery with the constitutional principles of freedom and equality had been recognized by the Massachusetts Supreme Court, and argued that the gallows "must soon follow in their train."[18]

Although many activists opposed the death penalty because they understood it to be a component in the system of bondage, in several respects these activists inadvertently contributed to the use of capital punishment as a tool of slavery and racial subjugation. This had the effect of consolidating and normalizing the racial prejudices that underpinned slavery. Likewise, anti-slavery efforts in this era had the effect of entrenching the death penalty. To explain this, we can consider two ways in which the reforms that the anti-death penalty movement achieved did not extend to slave populations, thus normalizing the disparate treatment of people based on the color of their skin, and institutionalizing the death penalty for black people. We can then consider how the fight for racial justice in turn halted the progress of death penalty abolitionism.

A. Restricting capital punishment; entrenching racial injustice

Slaves and free blacks had long been subjected to the death penalty at a greater rate than free whites. In 1740, for example, slaves and free blacks could be executed in South Carolina for destroying grain, for enticing other slaves to escape captivity, or for maiming or bruising a white person.[19] Inadvertently, anti-death penalty activists entrenched these racially disparate laws by successfully campaigning to limit the death penalty's use. In 1794, for example, Pennsylvania took the then radical step of dividing homicides into two categories so that death sentences would only be handed down in the most serious cases. This model was replicated in other states, and Americans soon claimed that the restriction of the death penalty to only the most serious crimes was a mark of progress for the fledging nation. In fact, Americans took great pride in the fact that they were not as barbaric as their former colonial rulers – the English – who at that time imposed capital punishment for a long list of criminal offenses.[20] These reforms, though, did not extend to slave populations. When the Mississippi state legislature revised its criminal code in 1835 and restricted the use of the death penalty to the crime of murder, it did so only in cases involving white defendants. Slaves could still be executed for any one of 38 separate offenses. By 1856, there were 66 crimes for which a slave could be executed in Virginia, yet just one crime for which a white person could be executed in that state.[21] A similar state of affairs occurred in Tennessee. By 1858, slaves and free blacks faced a mandatory death penalty for 11 offenses, and a discretionary death penalty for two further offenses. White people, meanwhile, faced execution for murder and accessory to murder in the first degree only.[22]

There were several rationales for these formal, legal, and transparent disparities, and these explanations set the scene for understanding the lasting influence of slavery on today's death penalty. For many, it was believed that black offenders were somehow more deserving of death. A black slave raping a white woman was considered to be a more heinous offense than a white man raping a black slave, and thus in many states the death penalty could be imposed for the former offense but not for the latter. The death penalty was also made more readily available against the slave population because death, it was thought, was the only punishment that would sufficiently deter slaves from committing offenses. After all, the threat of imprisonment would hardly act as a deterrent on those who already lived in captivity.[23] If anything, "imprisonment would have been a reward, giving the slave time to rest."[24]

The threat of death was also designed to deter the slave population from rising up in rebellion against their masters. Slave revolts were considered to be as treacherous as treason, in the sense that the slave was expected to show the same loyalty to his or her slave-owner as a citizen was expected to show to the state. The official name for slave revolts was "petit treason," which reflected the perceived gravity of such offences. In fact, one of the first American-made capital punishment statutes was passed in New York in 1712 in response to a slave revolt, and was only applicable to blacks,[25] illustrating clearly the historical connections between slavery and the death penalty. The revolution in Haiti at the end of the eighteenth century, in which slaves overthrew their French colonial rulers, also stoked the fears of American slave-owners. When the slave Nat Turner led a revolt in August 1831 that culminated in the deaths of 61 white people, state authorities in Virginia felt compelled to use the harshest penalty available against Turner and his comrades, and these executions played a pivotal role in the fate of slavery.[26]

Religion was also a factor in the racially disparate capital statutes. Slaves, it was believed, had "less faith than whites in the system of eternal rewards and penalties provided by the Christian concepts of heaven and hell, so they were understood to need more conspicuous penalties in this life."[27] Slaves, according to one authority, had "no civic virtue or character to restore, no freedom to abridge",[28] thus warranting capital punishment for a long list of offenses. A further reason for making the death penalty more readily available against slaves than whites was because slaveholders needed the assistance of state authorities when it came to disciplining the growing slave population.[29]

Despite the greater scope for imposing death sentences on slaves, there is some disagreement over whether or not slaves were actually executed at such a high rate. Lawrence Friedman writes that the "gallows was by no means sparingly used" against slaves, and that "[c]apital punishment was an important pillar of the southern social-control system."[30] However, as a number of other scholars have noted, slaves were considered to be property – often very valuable property – and thus slave-owners would object to the potential execution of a slave. In order to ensure that slave-owners did not protect slaves from facing capital charges, almost all southern states agreed to compensate the owner for any slave that was executed. In Louisiana, the public treasury would pay up to a maximum of $750 per slave executed. In South Carolina, slave-owners would usually be paid $122.45 per slave sentenced to death.[31] However, it made little financial sense for a slave-owner to lose a worker, and for the state to spend its money on compensation. Therefore, rather than execute slaves who had been found guilty of committing death-eligible crimes, slaves were often sold instead. This ensured that they were punished as they were separated from their family, that the slave-owner was not at a financial disadvantage, and that the state did not incur any monetary losses.[32]

In any event, these racially disparate death penalty statutes had an effect that has lasted to the present day. The statutes were part of the "Slave Codes", which was the body of law that regulated the behavior of slaves and governed the relationship between slaves and free persons. These codes were inevitably disadvantageous to black people, premised as they were on the belief that black people were degenerate and had to be kept under the control of whites. The codes also served to institutionalize and normalize antipathy on the parts of whites towards blacks. Writing about South Carolina's 1740 slave code, A. Leon Higginbotham notes that this law "must be understood not only for what it did to blacks and slaves – assuring their submissiveness, guaranteeing their ignorance, and sanctioning great brutality; but it also imposed an obligation on white inhabitants to set aside any natural human compassion and granted extraordinary inducements to those who would revel in brutality against blacks."[33]

Beyond the slave population, free blacks were similarly exposed to capital punishment in circumstances that whites were not. In 1816, Georgia passed a law that mandated death for a slave or a "freeman of colour" found guilty of the rape or attempted rape of a white woman, while simultaneously reducing the punishment for white men convicted of rape. Whereas a white male would face a minimum term of seven years, they would now face just two years imprisonment. Moreover, if the victim was a slave or a free black woman, the white male could escape with a mere fine.[34]

These racially disparate death penalty statutes normalized and institutionalized the dehumanizing treatment of black bodies. Indeed, North Carolina – like many other states – expressly construed the black body as "property" rather than human. An 1837 statute made "slave-stealing", "concealing a slave with intent to free him", "inciting slaves to insurrection", and "circulating seditious literature among slaves" capital offenses, reflecting the view that slaves were the property of their owners and as such should not be interfered with by others.[35] The myriad ways in which these laws concretized the perception of blacks as inferior to whites is a phenomenon that exists to this day and which forms the bedrock of much scholarly work in critical race theory.[36]

B. "Humanizing" death; institutionalizing racial subjugation

The second way in which anti-death penalty efforts contributed to the normalization and institutionalization of racial subjugation can be found in activists' attempts to ensure that executions were as humane as possible. Benjamin Rush had argued that executions corrupted the public, and that public executions tended to draw drunken and unruly crowds that caused disturbances and incited criminality.[37] Armed with these sorts of arguments, reformers managed to outlaw public hangings in numerous states, such as Pennsylvania and New York in 1834 and 1835 respectively. In another ten years, all the states in New England and in the Mid-Atlantic region had replaced public with private executions.[38]

It was hoped that the elimination of public executions would usher in the death penalty's abolition, as people came to realize that society was a better place without such spectacles. However, many anti-death penalty campaigners opposed the end of public hangings, presciently arguing that driving the practice away from the public gaze would only hinder their efforts to mobilize public opinion against the death penalty.[39] We can never know whether their concerns were well founded, although there is a growing view today that the "medicalization" of death through lethal injection as the prevailing modern method of execution serves to stifle abolitionist sentiments and thus keeps the death penalty alive.[40] Either way, critics of so-called humane and non-barbaric executions could only focus on the executions of white people, since the shift towards private and allegedly humane executions did not apply to slaves and free blacks. The proffered rationale was straightforward: it was believed that slaves and blacks were prone to violence and criminality, and thus public, gruesome executions were needed as a deterrent measure. Whereas free whites would be hanged for the crime of murder, slaves found guilty of rebellion were sometimes burned alive. To further increase the deterrent effect of capital punishment on slaves, executed slaves were occasionally dismembered and put on public display. The corpse of the executed would be placed in a gibbet, which was essentially an iron cage that would be suspended above the ground to enable public viewing. Put another way, whereas white bodies were merely executed, black bodies were also publicly humiliated and degraded. Once again, this reflected the view that the black body had no dignity that required respect. They were, instead, construed as objects whose primary function was to serve the purpose of deterrence.

Execution ceremonies were also designed to reflect and reinforce racial hierarchies and the perceived distinctions between blacks and whites, particularly slaves and free whites.[41] In the moments before being executed, slaves were often coerced into using their final words to remind their brethren to respect white superiority. A slave named Arthur reportedly said the following words before his execution: "I would solemnly warn those of my own Color, as they regard their own Souls, to avoid Desertion from their Masters."[42] These rituals further degraded black people in the eyes of society, reinforcing the perception that black people were not as dignified or as worthy of respect as whites.

III. A vicious circle

Racially disparate death penalty statutes and methods of executions have, in the long-term, had a twofold effect on the problem of racial injustice. First, they normalized and institutionalized capital punishment for black offenders; and second, they entrenched racial prejudices in a more general sense. As Stephen John Hartnett has written, "one of the functions of the death penalty… was *to create race*: to segregate the myriad social positions of the New World into hard and fast categories of white and black, free and enslaved."[43]

By creating racially-divided death penalty systems across America, anti-death penalty campaigners not only contributed to racial injustices. They also, contrary to their central aim, put up an insurmountable barrier in the path towards abolition of capital punishment. So long as death sentences and executions were considered necessary for slaves and free blacks, such a punishment could never be completely outlawed. In other words, anti-death penalty efforts had a circular effect. They created racially disparate laws and practices, which normalized and institutionalized racial subjugation that, as we will see in the next chapter, further entrenched the death penalty.

IV. Conclusions

David Brion Davis has explained how the partial successes of the anti-death penalty movement in the antebellum era – notably the end of public executions and the restriction of death-eligible crimes – "produced a mood of self-satisfaction" among anti-death penalty activists, "which is always a bulwark against reform."[44] The campaigns against the death penalty in this era did bring about three unequivocal victories: Michigan abolished capital punishment outright in 1846, Rhode Island followed in 1852, and Wisconsin in 1853. These successes were not built upon, though. By the mid-point of the nineteenth century, slavery was perceived to be the greater evil and the campaign against capital punishment ended up being stifled by the surging anti-slavery movement. In Davis's words, it became "difficult… to evoke sympathy for a few murderers when the attention of sympathetic people was focused increasingly on a different and more numerous group of oppressed aliens."[45] Stuart Banner has also pointed out that "[t]he movement to abolish the death penalty tailed off in the late 1850s, as sectional controversy and slavery crowded out other issues, and then the movement virtually ceased during the Civil War."[46] The brutality of the war rendered discussions about the death penalty at best inappropriate, and Wisconsin legislator Marvin Bovee delayed the publication of his anti-death penalty book until after the cessation of the Civil War, on the grounds that campaigning to save the lives of criminals would be insensitive at a time when so many gallant soldiers were losing their lives on the battlefield.[47]

The end of the Civil War and the abolition of slavery in 1865 did not see a revival of the anti-death penalty movement though. Although Bovee published his treatise against the death penalty in 1869, the war had rendered the American public less sensitive to killings, thus dissipating anti-death penalty sentiments: "After the Civil War, men's finer sensibilities, which had once been revolted by the execution of a fellow being, seemed hardened and blunted."[48] The war also shattered the economy, and raised tensions between Northern and Southern states that overshadowed issues such as capital punishment. Perhaps more devastatingly for those opposed to capital punishment, though, was the text of the Thirteenth Amendment to the Constitution, which was adopted on December 18, 1865. Although this Amendment is usually considered to have abolished slavery, it did not. The Amendment expressly permits slavery as a punishment for crimes: "Neither slavery nor involuntary servitude, *except as a punishment for crime* whereof the party shall have been duly convicted, shall exist within the United States, or any place subject to their jurisdiction."[49] In the years following emancipation, proponents of white supremacy took advantage of this text and turned to the criminal justice system as a replacement for plantation-based slavery. Such people were in no mood to entertain the idea that capital punishment should be abolished. Thus, in the post-emancipation era, the death penalty continued to be marred by the legacy of slavery.

Notes

1 Frederick Douglass, 'Capital Punishment is a Mockery of Justice' in John Blassingame (ed.), *The Frederick Douglass Papers* (Vol. 3, Yale University Press 1985) 242–248. See also Paul Christian Jones, *Against the Gallows: Antebellum American Writers and the Movement to Abolish Capital Punishment* (University of Iowa Press 2011).

2 Blassingame (n 1).
3 Stuart Banner, *The Death Penalty: An American History* (Harvard University Press 2002) 9.
4 On the Quakers' efforts to abolish the death penalty in antebellum America, see David Brion Davis, *From Homicide to Slavery: Studies in American Culture* (OUP 1986) 22. On the role of the Quakers in the anti-slavery movement, see Ryan P Jordan, *Slavery And The Meetinghouse: The Quakers And The Abolitionist Dilemma 1820–1865* (Indiana University Press 2007).
5 Louis P Masur, *Rites of Execution: Capital Punishment and the Transformation of American Culture, 1776–1865* (OUP 1991) 157.
6 Cesare Beccaria, *On Crimes and Punishments and Other Writings* (ed Richard Bellamy) (Cambridge University Press 2003).
7 ibid 67.
8 ibid 70.
9 For a thorough account of the pervasive and wide-ranging influence that Beccaria's tract had on the Founders, see John D. Bessler, *The Birth of American Law: An Italian Philosopher and the American Revolution* (Carolina Academic Press 2014).
10 Banner (n 3) 95–96.
11 Davis, *From Homicide To Slavery* (n 4) 21; Masur (n 5) 64.
12 Masur (n 5) 50; 64–65.
13 ibid 66–70.
14 On the movement to abolish the death penalty in the post-colonial era, see David Brion Davis, 'The Movement to Abolish Capital Punishment, 1787–1861' (1957) 63 The American Historical Review 23; Masur (n 5) Chapters 6 and 7; Philip English Mackey, *Hanging in the Balance: The Anti-Capital Punishment Movement in New York State, 1776–1861* (Garland Publishing 1982); Philip English Mackey, '"The Result May be Glorious": The Anti-Gallows Movement in Rhode Island, 1838–1852' (1974) 33 Rhode Island History 19; Louis Filler, 'Movements to Abolish the Death Penalty in the United States' (1952) 284 The Annals of the American Academy of Political and Social Sciences 124.
15 Davis, 'The Movement to Abolish Capital Punishment' (n 14) 42.
16 Philip English Mackey, *Voices Against Death: American Opposition to Capital Punishment, 1787–1975* (Burt Franklin & Co. 1976) 70 and 102 respectively.
17 Filler (n 14) 128.
18 Robert Rantoul Jr., 'Has Society the Right to Take Away Life' (1836) in Mackey, *Voices Against Death* (n 16) at 46–47. Rantoul Jr did not explicitly refer to the Massachusetts Supreme Court, but he was most likely referring to the decisions of that Court in Walker v. Jennison, which was widely considered to have effectively, if not formally, abolished slavery in that state. See John D. Cushing, 'The Cushing Court and the Abolition of Slavery in Massachusetts: More Notes on the "Quock Walker Case"' (1961) 5 American Journal of Legal History 118.
19 Banner (n 3) 8–9.
20 ibid 99.
21 George M. Stroud, *A Sketch of the Laws Relating to Slavery in the Several States of the United States of America* (2nd edn, H. Longstreth 1856) 75–87 (cited in Stuart Banner, 'Traces of Slavery: Race and the Death Penalty in Historical Perspective' in Charles J. Ogletree, Jr. and Austin Sarat (eds), *From Lynch Mobs to the Killing States: Race and the Death Penalty in America* (NYU Press 2006) 99.
22 Margaret Vandiver, 'Abolitionist Efforts in Tennessee from Statehood to 1959' in Amy L. Seward and Margaret Vandiver (eds) *Tennessee's New Abolitionists: The Fight to End the Death Penalty in the Volunteer State* (University of Tennessee Press 2010) 28.
23 Banner (n 3) 9; Banner, 'Traces of Slavery' (n 21) 98.
24 Brief of *Amici Curiae* National Association for the Advancement of Colored People et al., Aikens v. California, 1971 WL 134376, at *9 (U.S. Aug. 31, 1971). Also see Banner, *The Death Penalty* (n 3) 142.

25 Banner (n 3) 8. Previous death penalties had been imported from Britain during colonial rule.
26 Jeffrey L Kirchmeier, *Imprisoned By The Past: Warren McCleskey And The American Death Penalty* (OUP 2015) 53–54.
27 Banner, 'Traces of Slavery' (n 21) 98.
28 Edward Ayers, *Vengeance and Justice: Crime and Punishment in the 19th Century American South* (OUP 1984) 61 (quoted in David Oshinsky, *Worse than Slavery: Parchman Farm and the Ordeal of Jim Crow* (Free Press 1997) 6).
29 Carol S. Steiker and Jordan M. Steiker, 'The American Death Penalty and the (In)visibility of Race' (2015) 82 University of Chicago Law Review 243, 245.
30 Lawrence M. Friedman, *Crime and Punishment in American History* (Basic Books 1993) 88.
31 Laws La. 1854, Act No. 215, p.149; Acts and Resolutions of the General Assembley [sic] of the State of South Carolina, 1830, p.17 (cited in Friedman, ibid 88).
32 James Q Whitman, *Harsh Justice: Criminal Punishment and the Widening Divide Between America and Europe* (OUP 2003) 169 ("Masters, too, sometimes asked that they slaves be pardoned, so that they not suffer the property loss occasioned by an execution.") *citing* Douglas Greenberg, *Crime and Law Enforcement in the Colony of New York, 1691–1776* (Cornell University Press 1976) 129. Also see Paul Finkelman, *Prosecutions in Defense of the Cornerstone*, 17(3) Reviews in American History 397–403 (1989) (reviewing Philip J Schwarz, *Twice Condemned: Slaves and the Criminal Laws of Virginia, 1705–1865* (Louisiana State University Press 1988).
33 A. Leon Higginbotham Jr, *In the Matter of Color: Race and the American Legal Process, The Colonial Period* (OUP 1978) 199.
34 William J. Bowers, *Legal Homicide: Death as Punishment in America, 1864–1982* (Northeastern University Press 1984) 140 (citing *Brief of Amici Curiae* NAACP Legal Defense and Educational Fund Inc., Jackson v. Georgia No. 69–5031Appendix B).
35 Bowers (n 34) 139.
36 For an outline of the central tenets of critical race theory, see Richard Delgado and Jean Stefancic, *Critical Race Theory: An Introduction* (2nd edn, NYU Press 2012).
37 Banner (n 3) 103–104.
38 Masur (n 5) 94. Also see John D. Bessler, *Death in the Dark: Midnight Executions in America* (Northeastern University Press 1997).
39 Mackey, *Voices Against Death* (n 16) xx.
40 Deborah W. Denno, 'For Execution Methods Challenges, the Road to Abolition is Paved with Paradox' in Charles J. Ogletree Jr and Austin Sarat (eds) *The Road to Abolition? The Future of Capital Punishment in the United States* (NYU Press 2009) 204 ("Some death penalty opponents believe… that enhancing the humaneness of an execution method may make executions far more acceptable scientifically and politically than ever before.")
41 Banner, 'Traces of Slavery' (n 21) 101–107; Steiker and Steiker (n 29) 246.
42 *The Life and Dying Speech of Arthur, A Negro Man* (Boston: s.n., 1768) quoted in Banner, 'Traces of Slavery'(n 21) 102.
43 Stephen John Hartnett, *Executing Democracy (vol. 1): Capital Punishment & the Making of America, 1683–1807* 20 (Michigan State University Press 2010) 20 (quoted in Carol S Steiker and Jordan M Steiker, *Courting Death: The Supreme Court And Capital Punishment* (Belknap Press 2016) 20.
44 Davis, 'The Movement to Abolish Capital Punishment' (n 14) 28.
45 Davis, *From Homicide To Slavery* (n 4) 40.
46 Banner (n 3) 134.
47 Marvin Bovee, *Christ and the Gallows, or, Reasons for the Abolition of Capital Punishment* (first published 1869, Gale, Making of Modern Law 2010) Also see Bessler (n 38) 45–46.
48 Davis, *From Homicide To Slavery* (n 4) 40.
49 Emphasis added.

2 Capital punishment and the legacy of slavery, 1865–1976

I. Introduction

The end of the Civil War did not lead to a resurrection of anti-death penalty sentiments, and the apathy of those previously committed to stopping executions contributed to the resurgence of capital punishment in the post-emancipation era. The death penalty not only survived, but flourished in this era precisely because of the way in which the abolition of chattel slavery had been forced upon Southern states, and because of the ways in which Northern and Southern societies, and the federal government, reacted to the emergence of millions of new citizens, all seeking jobs, homes, and participation in social and political life. Despite the valiant attempts of black activists and others to ensure that emancipation would usher in an era of racial equality, the period of Reconstruction came to end in 1877 and was followed by laws and social practices that entrenched racial discrimination and which subjected the newly-emancipated to grossly unfair treatment in all areas of public life, including education, employment, and housing opportunities.[1] Communities that clung to the moral and economic values that had underpinned chattel slavery went to great lengths to ensure that newly emancipated black people remained subjugated. Groups such as the Ku Klux Klan emerged in order to terrorize black neighborhoods and communities; and electoral processes were routinely interfered with so that black people could not exercise their recently granted right to vote.[2]

This is not to say that Reconstruction was an abject failure. W.E.B. Du Bois rightly noted that many freed black persons rose to the challenge of freedom, and the Fourteenth and Fifteenth Amendments have, over time, been used to defeat some racist laws and policies.[3] However, it is in the context of the shortcomings of Reconstruction that we must understand the criminalization of black people, and the increasing racialization of capital punishment. In his Pulitzer-prize winning book *Slavery by Another Name*, Douglas Blackmon describes how the subjugation and degradation of African Americans in that era and beyond was particularly notable in the criminal justice system. Freed blacks were routinely arrested and convicted of criminal offenses on spurious grounds so that they could then be leased out for unpaid work, usually to corporations, thus rendering them "slaves in all but name."[4] Put another way, the criminal justice system was used as a replacement for the plantation, leading to the creation of what Blackmon calls "neoslavery" – the use of the criminal justice system to re-enslave black Americans.[5] As the apex of all legally sanctioned punishments, capital punishment came to symbolize the legacy of slavery in the post-emancipation era. As such, opponents of racial injustices tended to advocate for the abolition of the death penalty. Once again, though, those concerned with tackling racial injustices inadvertently stifled anti-death penalty efforts; and those concerned with limiting or ending the death penalty unintentionally hindered progress towards racial equality.

II. The "condemnation of blackness"[6]

There were several factors that led to the criminalization of black people in particular, but also of lower working-class whites. One such factor was an underlying belief that black people could not cope with freedom. Slavery had been justified, in part, on the grounds that black people were degenerate, prone to violence and sexual impulses, and in need of a civilizing force. Senator James Calhoun put forward the thesis of slavery as a "positive good" in a speech in 1837, in which he proclaimed: "Never before has the black race of Central Africa, from the dawn of history to the present day, attained a condition so civilized and so improved, not only physically, but morally and intellectually."[7] It was believed that without discipline and control, blacks would give in to their primitive violent and sexual urges. Upon emancipation, then, there was a very real concern – among proponents and opponents of racial subordination alike – that black people were too unskilled and poor to cope with freedom. In this sense, the imprisonment of blacks was sometimes justified as a "positive good" since it allowed blacks to be controlled, disciplined, and civilized.[8]

There was also a perception that, in their desperation to forge a living, free black people would turn to criminality as a means of survival. W.E.B. Du Bois noted in 1899 that "[i]t is impossible for such a social revolution to take place without giving rise to a class of men, who, in the new stress of life, under new responsibilities, would lack the will and power to make a way, and would consequently sink into vagrancy, poverty and crime."[9] Even though the waves of lawlessness that washed over Southern communities in the decades following emancipation were often perpetrated by whites against other whites, a narrative emerged that the growing crime rate was a result of a degenerate or desperate black population.[10] These sociological beliefs were compounded by practical considerations. Transgressions of the law by slaves had usually (but not always) been dealt with informally by their owners, especially when the crime in question was relatively minor. Things that used to be classed as an offense against a slaveholder, and thus within the slaveholder's purview, were now classed as an offense against the state.[11] That is, prior to emancipation, crimes by black people had not always attracted the attention of the criminal justice system. Now, they did.

White populations did not only turn to the criminal justice system for allegedly benevolent reasons, or because of the propaganda that attributed high crime rates to blacks. The Civil War had shattered the economy, yet there was no longer any free labor for work in the plantations. This gave rise to the convict leasing system.[12] People who were imprisoned were leased out to work, marking a return to the days of slavery when black people undertook hard labor without pay. Although Blackmon brought popular attention to this phenomenon in 2008, Thorsten Sellin had noted in 1976 that "[t]he revived convict lease system would for decades place the stamp of slavery on the penal systems of the South,... offering a good illustration of the debasing effects of the 'peculiar institution' on the evolution of penal systems for men."[13] Du Bois published an essay in 1901 that was titled "The Spawn of Slavery: The Convict Lease System of the South."[14] Put starkly, the post-emancipation criminal justice system was designed in such a way that it enabled the legal re-enslavement of black people.

Given prevailing racial prejudices, it was unsurprising that white communities pushed on the door that had been opened by the text of the Thirteenth Amendment, which permitted slavery as a punishment for criminal offenses. Laws referred to as the "Black Codes" were swiftly enacted, which sought to criminalize certain activities when carried out by free black people, but not by whites.[15] Although the Black Codes were overturned by the federal Civil Rights Act of 1866, which stated that everyone "shall be subject to like punishment, pains, and penalties," it is nonetheless clear that the text of the Thirteenth Amendment encouraged proponents of racial subjugation to use the criminal justice system as a means of preserving white supremacy, since it tied the discourse of slavery, and by extension the idea of white supremacy, to discourses of crime and punishment.

It is important to be clear though that the alignment of punishment with slavery did not solely mean that punishment was now imbued with racism. Slavery was also underpinned by the belief that some humans could be degraded to the status of "chattel personal", and could be denied full legal and moral personhood. Such values, then, came to infuse approaches to punishment.[16] This is a theme more fully explained in Chapter Four, but for now we can see the makings of a criminal justice system that can be described as a *racialized system of degradation*. It was racialized in the sense that racial prejudices clearly affected the operation of criminal justice processes, and it was a system of degradation in that it was premised on the belief that certain groups of people do not deserve the moral and legal status of full personhood. This extended to the use of capital punishment, and it affected the progress of death penalty abolitionism.

III. The relationship between "neoslavery" and capital punishment

It was noted in the previous chapter that although the death penalty was more readily available for use against slaves throughout the revolutionary and antebellum periods, slaves were often spared for financial reasons. Although the post-emancipation convict lease system and the criminal justice system in general have been described as "slavery by another name," it should not be inferred that black people were still viewed as financial assets in the post-emancipation era. After emancipation, black people could not be used as collateral for borrowing money or as payment of debts. They could not be sold for profit, or contribute to the economic advancement of their owners in any other way. Therefore, notwithstanding their value as laborers, black people in the convict leasing system, or in neoslavery, were less insulated from physical harm or even death than they had been in the days of chattel slavery.[17] It follows that black people were at greater risk of the death penalty – and extrajudicial killings, known as lynchings – in the post-emancipation years, than they were during slavery.

In this sense, the abolition of slavery actually contributed to an increase in the use of the death penalty against black people in the late 1800s and throughout much of the 20th Century. Despite capital statutes being framed in racially neutral language in light of the Civil Rights Act of 1866 and the Fourteenth Amendment of 1868,[18] it was almost inevitable that death sentences would be disproportionately imposed on black defendants. Prosecutors would exercise their discretion and seek death sentences against black defendants at a higher rate, and the phenomenon of all-white juries systematically sentencing African Americans to death after patently unfair trials soon emerged.[19] While overt racist attitudes certainly played their part in many cases, in many other instances subtler racial biases afflicted the use of capital punishment.

There are innumerable cases that could be used to illustrate the phenomenon of black people being sent to their death by all-white juries. One such case is that of George Stinney, who was executed in South Carolina on June 16, 1944, for the murder of two white girls. The only evidence against him was the testimony of three police officers, who claimed that Stinney had confessed to them. Stinney denied this, and there was no written confession either. However, his lawyer did not challenge these testimonies in court, and did not call any witnesses to testify on his client's behalf. The trial lasted just two and a half hours, and the all-white jury took ten minutes to decide that he should die. George Stinney was not just black – he was also just 14 years old at the time of his execution. In 2014, 70 years after his execution, a South Carolina court vacated his conviction on the grounds that he did not receive a fair trial.[20] While he would end up being the youngest person to be executed in the 20th Century, the other circumstances of his case were far from unique. Between 1870 and 1950, 771 people of identified race were executed for rape. 701 of these people were black. Thirty-one out of the 35 people who were executed for robberies during that period were black, and for burglary the numbers were 18 black people out of a total of 21 executed.[21]

It is not just the statistics that illustrate how the criminal justice system and capital punishment came to be used as a means of racial control. The development of Louisiana's death row also anecdotally illustrates capital punishment's historical association with slavery. The Confederate Major Samuel James came to be in charge of the Louisiana Corrections system in1869, and eleven years later he purchased a plantation that was to become the Louisiana State Penitentiary. The plantation was called "Angola," named after the place in Africa where former slaves who worked on the plantation had come from. James began to house inmates in the Old Slave Quarters there, and Angola, with all its connotations of slavery, is where death row inmates in Louisiana sit today.[22]

It is little surprise to find, then, that those who took action against racial injustices in the period from 1865 tended to also take issue with the racially discriminatory death penalty. That is, the connections between racial prejudices and the death penalty led numerous individuals and groups to simultaneously fight for equality and abolition, just as they did in the era of slavery. Once again, though, the fight for racial justice occasionally contributed to the use of the death penalty, and in some cases the fight against the death penalty widened racial divisions. This is perhaps most clearly illustrated by the campaigns against lynchings.

IV. The inadvertent effects of anti-lynching campaigns

Lynchings had occurred during slavery, but took on a different meaning in the Reconstruction and Jim Crow eras. Lynchings primarily served to terrorize the free black population, and involved the violent killing of racial minorities for an assortment of reasons.[23] Sometimes, people were lynched because they were suspected of transgressing the law, but the community did not want to wait for the suspect to be tried in the criminal justice system. Sometimes, no law had been allegedly broken, but a person was lynched for failing to observe social norms that had been created and implemented by whites. The lynching of Emmett Till in 1955, who like George Stinney was just 14 years of age, is perhaps the pre-eminent example of this. Till was lynched for allegedly whistling and speaking inappropriately to a white woman named Carolyn Bryant. His murder is generally believed to have been a catalyst for the emerging Civil Rights movement, as communities across America expressed outrage when confronted with pictures of his disfigured and mutilated body. Despite the wealth of evidence that implicated Bryant's husband and his half-brother in Till's murder, the two men were acquitted of all charges. Moreover, in 2007, Carolyn Bryant admitted to fabricating the "case" against Till.[24] On other occasions, black people were lynched for speaking out against their subordination, and for demanding equal treatment. In many cases, black people were lynched because of an exaggerated fear of inter-racial sex. The mere suspicion that a black man was sexually interested in a white female could result in that man being lynched, regardless of whether or not there was any basis to that suspicion, and regardless of whether the interest was reciprocated by the white person in question.

The Equal Justice Initiative – a legal charity founded in 1989 that represents minorities and the indigent caught up in the criminal justice system – has documented over 4,000 lynchings of African Americans between 1877 and 1950 across 20 states.[25] Although lynchings were predominantly public spectacles and took place outside the criminal justice system, they nonetheless had a quasi-judicial nature to them. Law enforcement personnel would sometimes be involved in the apprehension of, more often than not, black men accused of raping white women, and the crowd would take on the role of the jury, condemning the person to death. Lynchings were also characterized by the absence of any prosecution against those who participated in them, thus giving them an air of legal acceptability. Therefore, while lynchings were not strictly the product of judicial procedures, they bore close resemblance to criminal trials and, in particular, they mimicked legal executions.

When the fight for racial justice centered on taking action against lynchings, the result was the entrenchment of the death penalty. As people began to oppose lynchings, proponents of racial subjugation sought other avenues for disciplining and controlling the black population, and since lynchings were criticized on the grounds that they were illegal, then legal killings were the logical replacement. In the words of James W. Clark: "perhaps the most important reason that lynching declined is that it was replaced by a more palatable form of violence",[26] namely, capital punishment. Clarke documents the correlation between the decline of lynchings from the 1890s until 1959, and the rise of state-sanctioned executions over the same period. In Kentucky, for example, 76 percent of all lynchings of black people took place before 1900, yet 65 per cent of executions occurred after 1900, when the rate and numbers of lynchings declined.[27] In 1915, court-ordered executions outnumbered lynchings in the former slave states for the first time as more use was made of the official criminal justice system. Even though African Americans made up just 22 percent of the South's population between 1910 and 1950, 75 percent of those executed during that period in the South were black.[28]

Lynchings not only led to the increased use of state-sanctioned executions; they also reversed anti-death penalty developments. In their study of the abolition and reinstatement of the death penalty across ten states in the Progressive era and early 20th Century, John Galliher, Gregory Ray, and Brent Cook note that states with small populations of non-whites tended to pass abolition bills, with only two of the ten states that repealed the death penalty in this era having minority populations of over 5 percent. Moreover, of these ten states, eight reinstated capital punishment between 1901 and 1939. Although a number of reasons coalesced to foster reinstatement in each of these states, the authors contend that "[l]ynchings emerged as the most important common triggering event in reinstatement of the death penalty."[29] Carol Steiker and Jordan Steiker agree: "the practice of lynching helped to insulate the institution of capital punishment from lasting abolition."[30] The experiences of Colorado provide a vivid illustration of the relationship between race, lynching, and the abolition and re-instatement of the death penalty in this period. Colorado became the first state to outlaw the death penalty in the Progressive Era, Governor Alva Adams signing abolition into law in 1897 with very little opposition.[31] However, it was reinstated just four years later after some highly publicized lynchings. The aim of reinstatement, though, was not to punish the lynch mobs. Rather, reinstatement reflected a belief that black people should be punished by death for certain crimes. J.E. Cutler, an Assistant Professor of Political Economy at the University of Michigan in the early 1900s, argued that the abolition of capital punishment in Colorado was misguided because the death penalty was the only suitable punishment for black people, on account of their intellectual and moral inferiority. According to Cutler, black people committed atrocious crimes because of their biological impulses, and it was not appropriate to expect the superior white population to impose a punishment less than death. In the face of these crimes, and in the absence of the death penalty, it was only natural that the white population should take the law into their hands. Thus, for Cutler, it was the abolition of the death penalty that was to blame for the lynchings, and not a racist mentality on the part of those carrying out the lynchings.[32] Newspaper reports and testimonies from the time support this view. On May 24, 1900, the *Rocky Mountain Daily News* reported the lynching of a person described as a "mulatto", and proclaimed: "The people of Colorado and the next legislature might as well face the fact that in the absence of capital punishment, under the law it is inflicted through the angry mob violence whenever an especially atrocious crime is committed … To prevent the recurrence of such horrors the death penalty should be restored in this state."[33] When, just a few months later, a 16-year-old African American named Preston Porter was accused of murdering a 13-year-old white girl, he was burned at the stake. A former lieutenant governor expressed a view that was shared by many: "Capital punishment has been abolished in Colorado and the only resource left to an outraged citizenship is that which overtook Porter this afternoon at Limon. Lynch law may be objectionable to some sentimentalists, but there was little of sentiment or pity in Porter when he outraged and murdered Louise Frost."[34]

When an abolition bill was being considered by state legislators in Tennessee in 1915, a politician spoke out against the proposal: "if this bill should become law it would be almost impossible to suppress mobs in their efforts to punish colored criminals."[35] Several opponents of the Bill did not even pretend to be concerned with punishing mob violence, with one citizen writing to the Governor: "negroes fear nothing but death, and this law would increase the crimes of homicide among that race."[36] A local business leader agreed: "We have a large negro population in our state, many of them are ignorant and brutal. I honestly think that there are thousands of them that would commit murder for ten dollars if they thought they would not be hung or electrocuted."[37] The Bill passed, but notably it did not impose outright abolition. Capital punishment remained for the crime of rape, and for murder committed by persons already serving a term of life imprisonment. Efforts to reinstate capital punishment began immediately, and in 1919 the punishment was once again available for murder.[38] In Iowa, a similar pattern emerged. The legislature passed an abolition bill in 1872, but capital punishment was restored just six years later after citizens complained that the absence of the death penalty was to blame for the rise in lynchings.[39] We can see, then, how the legacies of slavery and racial violence worked to sustain capital punishment in the post-emancipation and post-Reconstruction eras.

Two further factors played a part in the continuing entrenchment of the death penalty, particularly against black people, up until 1972 when the US Supreme Court temporarily outlawed capital punishment. The first factor was death penalty processes, including the expansion of discretionary death penalty schemes and the exclusion of black people from juries. The second factor behind the institutionalization of capital punishment as a racialized system of degradation was the strategies and tactics of the emerging anti-death penalty movement. These are considered in turn.

V. The impact of death penalty processes

Just as attempts to fight racial prejudices in the shape of lynchings led to a rise in the use of the death penalty and a stifling of abolitionist efforts, so attempts to minimize the harsher effects of the death penalty led to the disproportionate imposition of capital punishment on black defendants, thus perpetuating and institutionalizing racial inequalities which, in a cyclical process, have concretized the use of capital punishment. In the early 20th Century, several states replaced mandatory death penalty schemes with discretionary procedures ostensibly in order to ensure that mercy could be shown in appropriate cases, and that only the worst of the worst would be sentenced to death. Three states – Alabama, Louisiana and Tennessee – had introduced such schemes prior to the Civil War, but between 1900 and 1941, 18 more states introduced discretionary schemes.[40] While this might initially seem like progress for opponents of the death penalty, such schemes allowed juries to hand down death sentences on the basis of race, rather than on the basis of guilt or deservingness. Stuart Banner takes the view that the schemes were not primarily intended to ensure that only the deserving were executed, stating instead that "[t]he purpose of these early discretion statutes was almost certainly to allow jurors to take race into account in setting the penalty. In the years immediately following the Civil War, most of the southern states adopted the same strategy with respect to some crimes."[41]

The replacement of mandatory schemes with discretionary schemes must be understood in light of the phenomenon of all-white juries, discussed above.[42] In *Strauder v. West Virginia*, decided in 1880, the US Supreme Court outlawed statutes that forbade black persons from sitting on juries, ruling that such laws violated the Equal Protection Clause of the Fourteenth Amendment. In the Court's words, such a law "lessened the security of the right of the colored race, and was a step toward reducing them to a condition of servility."[43] However, the Court did not conclude that the racial make-up of juries must reflect the race of the defendant or victim, and limited its holding to the categorical exclusion of black people from juries. Thus, authorities found it relatively easy to ensure that juries would continue to be racially skewed. Prosecutors developed a practice of using their peremptory challenges – challenges that are used to strike potential jurors from the pool without offering any reason for doing so – to prevent African Americans from sitting on juries. In *Swain v. Alabama*, decided in 1965, the US Supreme Court betrayed the impotency of the *Strauder* rule by holding that Robert Swain – a black man sentenced to death for the rape of a white girl – had failed to show that the prosecutor in his case had acted with purposeful and intentional discrimination when striking blacks from the jury. Thus, even though the prosecutor had struck out all potential black jurors from the jury pool by using his peremptory challenges, Swain's death sentence was upheld.[44]

Other tactics included the enactment of criteria that could be used to surreptitiously exclude blacks from juries. In Alabama, for example, a statute passed in 1923 set out the requisite qualifications for jurors, giving the state jury commission broad discretion to determine who was "esteemed in the community for their integrity, good character and sound judgment" and thus eligible for jury service.[45] In practice, black people were routinely excluded from juries on these grounds. In a challenge to the practice in Alabama in 1935, the US Supreme Court acknowledged that there were many blacks who satisfied the criteria for jury service but who had been systematically removed from jury pools.[46] Despite the admonition of the Court, though, the practice of constructing all-white juries to try black people accused of harming white people would continue.

The racial composition of juries served two purposes: to increase the likelihood of convictions against black defendants, and to decrease the likelihood of white defendants being convicted for crimes against blacks. With respect to the former, Edward Ayers notes how blacks in Tennessee complained about "the continued, persistent and unlawful manner in which they are tried, condemned, hanged, and enslaved, by individuals who have been taught from cradle to the jury box, that the negro is naturally inferior to them."[47] With respect to the latter, James Forman Jr notes that between 1865 and 1866, 500 white people in Texas were tried for the murder of black people. In all 500 cases, all-white juries acquitted the defendant.[48] While the criminal convictions of black people were certainly a problem in the years after the Civil War, a major problem was the lack of protection for black victims of crimes. In Ayers's words again, the problem with Southern justice in the post-emancipation years was "not so much that the negro fails to get justice before the Courts ... but too often it is that the native white man escapes it."[49]

VI. The death penalty and abolitionism in the Civil Rights era

The rapid rise in the use of the death penalty during the late 19th and early 20th Centuries posed considerable challenges for death penalty abolitionists. Most organized groups operated at the local and state level, and as noted above, although they succeeded in convincing 10 states to abolish the death penalty between 1897 and 1917, most of these successes were short-lived.[50] In 1925, the American League to Abolish Capital Punishment (ALACP) was formed with the aim of coordinating campaigns for state abolition by engaging in advocacy and public education. However, the ALACP's activities were stymied by the Great Depression and the Second World War, and it was not until the 1940s, 50s and 60s that death penalty abolitionism really picked up steam.

Unsurprisingly, the anti-death penalty movement of this era could not be divorced from the movements that worked for racial equality. In 1905, W.E.B. Du Bois expressly drew on the work of the slavery abolitionists when setting up the Niagara Movement in order to press for equal rights. Four years later, the Niagara Movement merged into the National Association for the Advancement of Colored People (NAACP), which was formed by, inter alia, the descendants of slavery abolitionists.[51] In 1911, a keynote speaker for the NAACP explained how the group was bound up with the legacy of slavery and the abolitionists: "In every charge we make against the forces of oppression we have a right to feel that [William Lloyd] Garrison and [Wendell] Phillips ... are riding at our side."[52]

Garrison and Phillips, as any reader of American history will know, were two of the most prominent slavery abolitionists. As editor of the NAACP's magazine, *The Crisis*, Du Bois frequently referred to the organization as the "New Abolition Movement."[53]

One of the major "forces of oppression" that the NAACP fought against was the unequal treatment of black people caught up in the criminal justice system, particularly those facing a sentence of death. Leaders of the emerging civil rights movement in the 1950s, including Martin Luther King Jr, identified the connection between the death penalty and civil rights, noting how capital punishment had been used to subjugate African Americans.[54] According to Jeffrey Kirchmeier, "[t]he civil rights movement of the 1960s influenced the death penalty debate as the general public became more aware of racial discrimination's effects on the death penalty."[55] However, although the civil rights movement gave momentum to the anti-death penalty movement, it also hampered the prospects for abolition.[56] To understand the contradictory effect of the civil rights movement on anti-death penalty activism, we need to explore how the NAACP came to lead general anti-death penalty efforts.

The NAACP initially provided assistance to black defendants in capital and non-capital cases, and a legal arm – the Legal Defense Fund (LDF) – was set up in 1940 in order to more formally use the legal system to challenge racial discrimination and protect African Americans facing criminal charges, including death sentences.[57] At first, these lawyers focused solely on cases involving aspects of race discrimination, given the remit and purpose of the LDF. Others also took up the cause, and a body of race-based capital punishment jurisprudence soon emerged which would shape the administration of the punishment more broadly. The Scottsboro Boys Case is illustrative of how litigation efforts shaped not just death penalty abolitionism, but also responses to abolitionism. In 1931, nine young black men were accused of raping two white women on a freight train in Alabama. The case stoked immense controversy, with local passions stirred by the accusation that black men had attacked white women in such a way. Before they could stand trial, crowds gathered outside the jail where they were held, with the express intention of lynching them. Concerned by the strength of local feelings, the trial judge insisted on bringing the case to trial speedily, giving the defense little time to prepare. All nine were tried and sentenced over the course of just two days, and eight of them were sentenced to death, despite scant evidence and contradictory statements from the women.[58]

In November 1932, the US Supreme Court ordered retrials on the grounds that the boys had received woeful legal representation, in violation of the Due Process Clause of the Fourteenth Amendment.[59] This was the first time that the Court declared a constitutional right to adequate legal counsel for those accused of criminal offenses, but the holding only applied to capital cases. This marked the beginning of the Supreme Court's "death is different" jurisprudence, whereby it adopts unique approaches to constitutional questions concerning the death penalty because of the uniqueness of the punishment itself. It would take another 30 years before the Supreme Court extended a similar right to counsel in non-capital cases.[60] Although the Scottsboro Boys case is famous for the holding of the Court, the facts were far from unique. As outlined above, many capital prosecutions in the South during this era were akin to "legal lynchings", in that black people were sentenced to death after trials in which due process was virtually illusory.[61] Moreover, we can see how the issue of race – which had led to the rushed trial – was central in prompting the Supreme Court to intervene in the way in which states implemented capital punishment, which, as we will see below, has ultimately shaped the anti-death penalty movement's contemporary litigation strategy.[62]

Notwithstanding the ruling in the Scottsboro Boys case, the Supreme Court did not regulate the death penalty with any degree of vigor. In 1947, the Court rejected a constitutional challenge from a prisoner who had experienced a failed electrocution, and who was facing a second time in the electric chair. In *Louisiana v Resweber,* Willie Francis complained that "to require him to undergo [the psychological strain of preparation for an electrocution] again subjects him to a lingering or cruel and unusual punishment", but the Court held that "[t]he fact that an unforeseeable accident prevented the prompt consummation of the sentence cannot, it seems to us, add an element of cruelty to a subsequent execution. There is no purpose to inflict unnecessary pain, nor any unnecessary pain involved in the proposed execution."[63]

While lawyers filed challenges to specific aspects of the administration of capital punishment, such as trial processes and methods of execution, there was little appetite to challenge the constitutionality of death sentences per se. The LDF had many other pressing civil rights issues to deal with such as voting and employment rights, and it would not have made sense to devote precious resources to a relatively marginal issue such as capital punishment. Indeed, the anti-death penalty activist Norman Redlich recounts how, "in the early 1960s there was considerable debate whether the death penalty was a civil liberties issue... Many civil rights groups argued that it was not a racial issue."[64] It took Martin Luther King Jr's leadership, though, to convince racial justice groups that the fight for equality entailed the condemnation of capital punishment. In November 1957, King explained the criminological and religious grounds for his opposition to the death penalty, stating that "[c]apital punishment is against the best judgment of modern criminology and, above all, against the highest expression of love in the nature of God."[65] Five months later, he delivered a speech on the steps of the state capitol in Montgomery, Alabama, in protest at the electrocution of Jeremiah Reeves. Reeves – an African American – was 16-years-old when he was accused of raping a white woman. King was explicit about the racial dimension of the death penalty:

> ...the issue before us now is not the innocence or guilt of Jeremiah Reeves. Even if he were guilty, it is the severity and inequality of the penalty that constitutes the injustice. Full grown white men committing comparable crimes against Negro girls are rare ever punished, and are never given the death penalty or even a life sentence. It was the severity of Jeremiah Reeves penalty that aroused the Negro community, not the question of his guilt or innocence.[66]

As lawyers at the LDF continued to help black defendants, they soon came to recognize that racism could not be weeded out from the systems of capital punishment. Michael Meltsner – one of the lead LDF attorneys of that time – has recounted how he and his colleagues "came to believe that it was impossible to separate racism from the death penalty; that the only remedy for discrimination was to ensure that the opportunity to execute blacks simply did not arise."[67] Not only did the lawyers recognize that racism was inherent to the system of capital punishment, they also felt morally unable to stand aside when white people faced the death penalty. Another LDF attorney – Anthony Amsterdam – explained how, once they knew which legal arguments saved the lives of black people, they could not refuse their assistance to non-blacks: "We could no more let men die that we had the power to save, than we could have passed by a dying accident victim sprawled bloody and writhing on the road without stopping to render aid as we could."[68] Meltsner makes the same point: "once the lawyers knew the legal theories that could win stays of execution, they felt morally obliged to use them" for all death row inmates, regardless of race.[69]

The LDF therefore extended its remit to include fighting for the abolition of the death penalty regardless of race, and assumed leadership of anti-death penalty efforts.[70] It is somewhat ironic, then, that the architects of the Jim Crow laws were partly responsible for the birth of a systematic and sustained campaign against the death penalty in all circumstances, and it is noteworthy that the anti-death penalty movement was historically and conceptually linked to the civil rights movement, which had grown out of the anti-slavery movement.

Even though the LDF resolved to oppose the death penalty in all circumstances, attorneys still saw race as the key issue. This troubled some abolitionists. Emanuel Redfield, who was counsel to the New York Civil Liberties Union, believed that the racism argument weakened abolitionism, for it either invited efforts at reform rather than abolition, or logically inferred that all punishments that were affected by racism should be abolished.[71] From its inception in 1920, until 1963, the American Civil Liberties Union (ACLU) took no position on capital punishment because it simply did not see the death penalty as a civil rights issue. The ACLU only formally adopted an abolitionist position when Norman Dorsen, a law professor at New York University, presented a memorandum that portrayed capital punishment as antithetical to "the spirit of civil liberties" and which "dehumanizes a society which employs it."[72] Nonetheless, the LDF by this point was firmly established as the leading abolitionist organization, and its lawyers still believed that the issue of race was central to challenging the constitutionality of the death penalty as a whole.

Race-based litigation efforts picked up speed over the 1960s, brought some triumphs for the anti-death penalty movement in 1972, but ultimately contributed to the entrenchment of capital punishment in 1976. The chain of events began in 1963, when US Supreme Court Justice Arthur Goldberg asked his law clerk, Alan Dershowitz, to examine whether or not there existed grounds for challenging the constitutionality of state-sanctioned executions. Up until then, the Court had never entertained the idea that the punishment might be unconstitutional, since the death penalty had been endorsed by the Framers in the Fifth Amendment to the Constitution, and reaffirmed by the drafters of the Fourteenth Amendment in 1868.

A. The Goldberg dissent

Dershowitz identified two grounds for questioning the constitutionality of capital punishment. First, he highlighted the problematic use of the death penalty in non-homicide cases, setting the scene for future challenges based on the alleged disproportionality of capital punishment. Second, he expressed concern with the racially discriminatory way in which death sentences were handed down.[73] In light of this, Goldberg drafted a memorandum for the Court, but only two other justices were willing to entertain the idea of granting a review in the death penalty cases that were being presented to the Court. Goldberg therefore published his views in a dissent to a denial of certiorari in the case of *Rudolph v Alabama*, in which two black men had been sentenced to death for the rape of white women.[74]

An initial draft of Goldberg's memo included a reference to racial disparities. Setting out the constitutional case against the death penalty for rape, Goldberg wrote that abolition "would also eliminate the well-recognized disparity in the imposition of the death penalty for sexual crimes committed by whites and non-whites. See, e.g., National Prison Statistics, April 1952, which indicates that between 1937 and 1951, 233 Negroes and 26 whites were executed for rape in the United States."[75] However, Chief Justice Earl Warren successfully persuaded Goldberg to remove all references to race and racial discrimination from his dissent.[76] For the reasons outlined below, this sequence of events was the precursor to the Court's habitual avoidance of the question of systemic racial discrimination in the administration of capital punishment, and this in turn has had a detrimental effect on discussions about race, the death penalty, and abolition. The Supreme Court's silence has given the appearance that systemic racism is either not present in the death penalty today, or that even if it is present, it is legally acceptable.

To explain this, we must be clear about how Goldberg's dissent in *Rudolph* was received by the LDF and others. The dissent, joined by Justices Brennan and Douglas, alerted the LDF to the fact that a growing section of the Supreme Court was concerned with the death penalty, thus triggering a concerted effort to devise a litigation strategy. Thus began a distinct era of death penalty abolitionism, one which foregrounded legal efforts and a focus on racial discrimination. Herbert Haines has noted that the litigation strategy of this era often came at the expense of public and political-facing efforts to advance abolition:

> During the legalistic era of the 1960s and 1970s, the [anti-death penalty movement] often behaved as though the attitudes of the American people did not matter very much. What mattered was the Constitution and its interpretation by federal judges. If the judges could be convinced that capital punishment violated the Eighth and Fourteenth Amendments, executions would be consigned to the history books.[77]

In his account of challenging the death penalty at that time, attorney Michael Meltsner explains why he and his colleagues at the Legal Defense Fund resolved to pursue abolition in the courts: "Political action to abolish the death penalty was not in fashion. Only a few maverick moralists..., professional organizations..., lawyers..., and a rare public official... considered the continued existence of the death penalty in the 1960's an issue worthy of public commitment."[78]

On the issue of race discrimination, even though the dissent said nothing about race, it did address the issue of the death penalty for rape that was undeniably affected by racism. Therefore, the LDF began a project of documenting the racially discriminatory use of the death penalty in rape cases, in the hope that it could persuade a majority of the Court that the death penalty, at least for rape, was unconstitutionally discriminatory. Marvin Wolfgang – a criminologist at the University of Pennsylvania – studied rape convictions in 11 states during the period 1945–1965, and found that black men were 11 times more likely than white men to be sentenced to death.[79] An opportunity to present these statistics to the Court arose in the case of *Maxwell v Bishop* in 1968, but when the Court granted certiorari, it only agreed to hear claims relating to (a) the fact that jurors and prosecutors enjoyed wide discretion in death penalty cases, and (b) the suggestion that unitary trial processes were unfair.[80] Even though the Court declined to review Maxwell's claim of racial discrimination, Maxwell's lawyers and various amici laid bare in their submissions the pernicious influence of racial prejudices. An amicus curiae brief on behalf of various Jewish organizations described the death penalty for rape as a "badge of slavery".[81]

Ultimately, the Supreme Court granted Maxwell relief on the grounds set out in *Witherspoon v Illinois*.[82] In *Witherspoon*, decided in 1968 while *Maxwell* was pending, the Court outlawed Illinois's overbroad approach to barring potential jurors who expressed any level of conscientious reservations about the death penalty from sitting on capital trials. The LDF urged the *Maxwell* Court to reconsider its refusal to consider the issue of race, but the Court declined and once again handed down a decision in a case that was racially charged without even mentioning the issue of racial discrimination.[83] The pleadings in *Witherspoon* had also contained ample reference to the phenomenon of black people being excluded from capital cases because they objected to the death penalty, thus leading to all-white juries deciding the fates of black defendants.[84] However, as in Goldberg's dissent in *Rudolph*, and as in *Maxwell*, the Court side-stepped the issue of race in its opinion.

It can be seen that although the anti-death penalty movement achieved several judicial victories during the 1960s, lawyers repeatedly failed to engage the Court in discussions about race. The reasons for this are complex, but important for understanding how slavery continues to leave its mark on today's death penalty. During the 1950s and 1960s, the Court was engaged in variety of other issues that involved aspects of racial discrimination, and the Court's decisions invariably attracted criticisms from proponents of racial segregation. In the *Brown v Board of Education* cases,[85] for example, the Court struggled to enforce the desegregation of schools, and many of the Court's decisions that favored blacks were met with a considerable backlash. Opponents of the Court either abhorred the notion of racial equality, or abhorred interference by the federal court in state affairs. Often, they abhorred both. Supporters of segregation challenged "judicial overreaching and disregard of federalism," and advanced "moral arguments about the breakdown of social values and discipline that would result from too much change."[86] The political and social backlashes were extraordinary, and as Carol Steiker and Jordan Steiker have noted, "[i]n light of the Court's ongoing role in the school-desegregation battle, it is no wonder that Chief Justice Warren, the architect of the Court's unanimous opinion in *Brown*, hesitated to add capital punishment to the simmering pot of racial issues. Black murders and rapists presented a much less sympathetic face for civil rights enforcement than schoolchildren."[87] Put another way, the Court was concerned that any decisions that highlighted the racial aspects of capital punishment would be met with fierce condemnation. The Court therefore avoided addressing the race issue in death penalty cases because it wanted to avoid fanning racial fires, and because it anticipated that decisions focused on race would not enjoy the same degree of perceived legitimacy as decisions focused on more procedural aspects of criminal justice.

Steiker and Steiker identify a second reason for the Court's silence on the race issue. During the 1960s and 1970s, crime rates were rising, and there was particular fear about the militancy of some black radicals: "Rising crime rates and fear of black crime not only increased the likelihood of political backlash to a race-based judicial curtailment of capital punishment, but they also may have engendered ambivalence among some of the justices about the underlying racial discrimination claim."[88] A perceived breakdown in social order was attributed to the activism of the civil rights movement, which had begun to use arrest and imprisonment as a tactic in their reform efforts. As explained above, black people had long been subjugated through the criminal justice process, and they thought that if they actively sought arrest, then this would nullify the stigmatizing and degrading aspects of imprisonment. Partly as a response, Southern states set about the enactment of "tough on crime" policies, which included increasing support for the death penalty.[89] Once again, then, the actions and successes of those concerned with racial justice had a negative impact on the progress of anti-death penalty activism.

Whatever their reasons, some Justices on the Supreme Court were concerned with capital punishment but wanted race-neutral grounds for curtailing or abolishing the death penalty. This situation shaped the outcome of *Furman v Georgia* in 1972,[90] in which the Court temporarily outlawed capital punishment. The Court did so, though, on grounds that would eventually entrench racial discrimination and the legacy of slavery within the death penalty when it was restored in 1976, in the case *Gregg v. Georgia.*[91]

VII. The predominance and absence of race in *Furman* and *Gregg*

In *Furman*, LDF lawyers argued that the lack of legal guidelines in death penalty systems across the US led to racial disparities in the application of the death penalty. They argued that the discretion given to prosecutors resulted in death sentences generally being sought against racial minorities and other marginal groups. Similarly, the lack of direction to juries resulted in death sentences being handed down disproportionately against blacks and other minorities, in circumstances in which whites would escape death sentences. The death penalty, lawyers argued, only remained because it was applied in an arbitrary and discriminatory manner. One of the petitioner's briefs set out this argument in stark terms: "A legislator may not scruple to put a law on the books (still less, to maintain an old law on the books) whose general, even-handed, non-arbitrary application the public would abhor – precisely because both he and the public know that it will not be enforced generally, even-handedly, non-arbitrarily."[92] That is, petitioners suggested that the death penalty is only maintained *because* (white people know that) it is applied discriminatorily and arbitrarily.

Petitioners' briefs and the various briefs of amici curiae that were submitted in the conjoined cases detailed the history and legacy of racism in the death penalty in incredible detail.[93] The brief submitted by the NAACP in particular explained why capital punishment could not be separated from America's history: "Slavery was exclusively a Southern phenomenon, and the general data with respect to all crimes, and particularly the crime of rape, indicates that the South has been the prime contributor to the disproportionate application of the death penalty to blacks."[94] However, the five Justices who decided in Furman's favor and struck down all capital statutes generally refrained from addressing racial discrimination at all. Justices Brennan and White avoided all mention of race, and Justice Marshall addressed racial discrimination in just one paragraph in his 60-page opinion. Justice Douglas gave considered attention to the race-based arguments, noting that death sentences were "disproportionately imposed and carried out on the poor, the Negro, and the members of un-popular groups."[95] However, as with Justice Stewart, he concluded that racial discrimination had not been proven in this particular case. In all, none of the Justices were willing to engage with the LDF's suggestion that states retained the death penalty *because* of its racially discriminatory application, as a tool of racial control. In fact, Justice Marshall hypothesized that Americans would reject the death penalty if they were aware of how the penalty was applied discriminatorily, thus contradicting the thesis of the LDF.[96]

Given the extensive attention to racial discrimination in the pleadings before the Court, the Justices must have been aware of the race dimension, and must have made conscious decisions to side-step the issue. As Evan Mandery states in his in-depth exploration of *Furman* and *Gregg*, "whatever the justices may have intended, everyone understood *Furman* as having been about race."[97] Just as Chief Justice Warren implored Justice Goldberg to remove the issue of race from his dissent in *Rudolph* nearly ten years earlier, so the Justices in *Furman* tactfully avoided basing their judgments on concerns with racial injustices. They instead addressed the arbitrary application of the death penalty both within and across jurisdictions, stemming from the lack of any guidelines to decision-makers in capital cases.

The *Furman* Court had reasons for avoiding the race issue. One reason for the Court's reluctance to strike down the death penalty on race-related grounds is that to do so would have been to admit that racial injustices could not be rectified. This would have run counter to the Court's insistence in other civil rights cases that racial inequalities could be tackled. In the words of Carol Steiker and Jordan Steiker: "[t]o have invalidated the death penalty on the ground of racial disparities in its administration would have betrayed [the] hope that such disparities could be remedied by the right procedural interventions or interim corrective measures."[98] Just as Emanuel Redfield had cautioned a few years earlier, the issue of race did not *require* abolition as such. Rather, it warranted reform: "A race-based abolition of the death penalty would have constituted an acknowledgement that the effects of institutionalized racism could not be erased by constitutional intervention – the very last message that the Supreme Court wanted to send in the era of constitutionally mandated school desegregation and criminal procedure reform."[99]

The Supreme Court was also still reeling from the political and social backlash to its civil rights cases of the 1960s. Proponents of racial segregation and inequality succeeded in practically scaring the Court into receding from public debates about race. The Court shared Chief Justice Warren's concern that a race-based opinion would be rejected by the public, weakening the legitimacy of the decision. Moreover, Warren had cause to believe that a race-based opinion was unnecessary, since in the five years leading up to the US Supreme Court's decision, there had not been a single execution in the entire country. Luis Monge had been gassed in Colorado on June 2, 1967, after waiving his appeals and volunteering to be executed, but those who fought their sentences benefitted from the unofficial moratorium that came to be as the courts grappled with the raft of litigation that the LDF and others had filed. Given the decline in actual executions and in popular support for capital punishment, Warren likely shared abolitionists' confidence that the Court's decision in *Furman* sent capital punishment the way of slavery – consigned to the country's history books. Both the Court and death penalty abolitionists were to be proven wrong.

The backlash to *Furman* was fierce and swift, in part because people genuinely supported capital punishment, but also in part because the decision brought to the fore the simmering resentment that many states felt for the federal court's more liberal decisions of the past decade or so. For many, the decision was the latest in a long line of illegitimate interferences with states' rights – a concept which derived from discussions about slavery during the Constitutional Conventions nearly 200 hundred years previously. Between 1972 and 1976, 35 states re-crafted their death penalty statutes in light of the Court's fractured reasoning in *Furman*. Since the Court had criticized the arbitrary nature in which death sentences were sought, handed down, and ultimately carried out, the various states enacted schemes that purported to guide and constrain decision-making at all stages of the capital process. The sheer scale of legislative activity led the Court to surmise four years later, in *Gregg v. Georgia*, that "a large proportion of American society continues to regard [capital punishment] as an appropriate and necessary criminal sanction".[100] In upholding the constitutionality of most of the new schemes, the Court explained that the Eighth Amendment "requires…that we look to objective indicia that reflect the public attitude toward a given sanction".[101] Although emphasis was placed on public opinion as expressed through state legislation and the decisions of juries,[102] the Court also held that "the infliction of death as a punishment for murder is not without justification and thus is not unconstitutionally severe".[103] The retributive purposes of capital punishment were explained: "the decision that capital punishment may be the appropriate sanction in extreme cases is an expression of the community's belief that certain crimes are themselves so grievous an affront to humanity that the only adequate response may be the penalty of death".[104]

Troy Leon Gregg, like most of the other defendants in the five conjoined cases, was white. As David Oshinsky has explained, the selection of white defendants to challenge these statutes had the effect of "taking race, for the moment, off the table".[105] It has since become clear that the *Furman* and *Gregg* Courts' failure to address the issue of race has been partly responsible for the continued racial discrimination in today's death penalty. In this sense, the Court's neglect of race – in part because of the backlash to the success of the civil rights movement – has ended up contributing to racial divisions in the sense articulated by A. Leon Higginbotham, as outlined in the previous chapter. That is, racial disparities in today's death penalty serve to institutionalize and normalize racial discrimination not just in the criminal justice system, but also in other areas of American life.[106]

VIII. Conclusions

Between 1865 and 1976, the death penalty was linked to the defunct system of slavery in two ways: the racial discrimination in the application of the death penalty, and the rise of the death penalty abolitionist movement from the ashes of the slavery abolitionist movement. And, just as the slavery abolitionists first helped but ultimately hindered the anti-death penalty movement of the 19th Century, so the civil rights movement first helped, but ultimately hampered, the efforts of the anti-death penalty movement in the 20th Century, even though they largely shared the same agenda. It might be said that the defeat of the Radical Republicans to have their vision of Reconstruction realized in the aftermath of emancipation contributed to the entrenchment of capital punishment, but it is worth noting that even the radicals' major success had the effect of institutionalizing capital punishment. The Fourteenth Amendment, which is often considered the hallmark of the abolitionists' achievements so far as advancing racial equality goes, contained language that constitutionalized the death penalty: "nor shall any State deprive any person of life, liberty, or property, without due process of law." Indeed, for all his efforts in condemning capital punishment, Frederick Douglass was unnervingly silent about the post-Civil War systems of convict leasing systems, a point raised by Angela Davis. Although Davis refrains from apportioning blame to Douglass for the construction of "ideological equations of blackness and criminality", she rightly draws attention to his silence on the matter, making it clear that the inability of the abolitionists to fully tackle such matters contributed to the propensity towards harsh punishments.[107] Later anti-racists, as Naomi Murakawa has argued, also contributed to mass incarceration by both advocating the use of prison to tackle racial violence, such as lynchings, while simultaneously neglecting to note that the prison was itself a systemic form of racial violence.[108]

The relationship between slavery, racial injustice, capital punishment, and their respective abolitionist movements, has therefore been profound, complex, and contradictory. Although the US Supreme Court invalidated the death penalty in the racially-charged case of *Furman*, the legacy of slavery was so deeply woven into the fabric of capital punishment that it contributed to its resurrection four years later in *Gregg*. And even though the *Gregg* Court purported to demand a death penalty that would be free from discrimination, research has consistently shown that today's post-*Gregg* death penalty continues to be infected with the same strains of racism and degradation, as outlined in the next chapter.

Notes

1 See, for example, Eric Foner, *Reconstruction Updated Edition: America's Unfinished Revolution, 1863–1877* (HarperPerennial 2014); W.E.B. Du Bois, *Black Reconstruction In America 1860–1880* (first published 1935, The Free Press 1998); George C. Rable, *But There Was No Peace: The Role Of Violence In The Politics Of Reconstruction* (University of Georgia Press 2007); Kenneth M. Stampp, *The Era of Reconstruction, 1865–1877* (Vintage 1967).

2 Wyn Craig Wade, *The Fiery Cross: The Ku Klux Klan In America* (OUP 1998); Douglas A Blackmon, *Slavery By Another Name: The Re-Enslavement Of Black Americans From The Civil War To World War II* (Anchor Books 2009) 42.

3 Perhaps the most famous example is the US Supreme Court's decision in Brown v. Board of Education of Topeka, 347 U.S. 483 (1954), in which the Court held that racially segregated schools contravened the Equal Protection Clause of the Fourteenth Amendment.

4 Blackmon (n 2) 2.

5 ibid 402.

6 Khalil Gibran Muhammad, *The Condemnation Of Blackness: Race, Crime, And The Making Of Modern Urban America* (Harvard University Press 2011).

7 John C. Calhoun, 'Slavery is a Positive Good' Speech to U.S. Senate, 6 February 1837, reprinted in Jolyon P. Girard, Darryl Mace, and Courtney Smith (eds) *American History Through its Greatest Speeches: A Documentary History of the United States* (ABC CLIO 2017) 44–45.

8 Thorsten Sellin, *Slavery and the Penal System* (Elsevier 1976) 145; David M Oshinsky, *'Worse Than Slavery': Parchman Farm And The Ordeal Of Jim Crow Justice* (The Free Press 1996) 18–19.

9 W.E.B. Du Bois, 'The Negro and Crime' *Independent* (18 May 1899) quoted in Oshinsky (n 8) 98–99.

10 Blackmon (n 2) 25, 69 (outlining the arrest records of several counties in Alabama, Florida, and Georgia)

11 Oshinsky (n 8) 32.

12 Blackmon (n 2) 53.

13 Sellin (n 8) 145. Also see Oshinsky (n 8) Chapter 3.

14 W.E.B. Du Bois, 'The Spawn of Slavery: The Convict Lease System of the South' *Missionary Review of the World* (October 1901).

15 Oshinsky (n 8) 20–21.

16 James Q Whitman, *Harsh Justice: Criminal Punishment and the Widening Divide Between America and Europe* (OUP 2003) 173–177.
17 Blackmon (n 2) 96.
18 Carol S. Steiker and Jordan M Steiker, 'The American Death Penalty and the (In) visibility of Race' (2015) 82 University of Chicago Law Review 243, 250.
19 J.R. Gillespie, 'The Constitution and the All-White Jury' (1950) 39 Kentucky Law Journal 65; James Forman Jr, 'Juries and Race in the Nineteenth Century' (2004) 113 Yale Law Journal 895.
20 See Lindsey Bever, 'It Took 10 Minutes to Convict 14-year-old George Stinney Jr. It Took 70 Years after his Execution to Exonerate Him' *Washington Post* (18 December 2014). (The headline is misleading, since the court did not exonerate Stinney.)
21 Stuart Banner, *The Death Penalty: An American History* (Harvard University Press 2002) 230.
22 For a history of the Louisiana State Penitentiary, see Mark T. Carleton, *Politics and Punishment: The History of the Louisiana State Penal System* (LSU Press 1984).
23 On the use of lynching to subjugate and terrorize black populations in the post-emancipation era, see W. Fitzhugh Brundage, *Lynching in the New South* (University of Illinois Press 1993); W. Fitzhugh Brundage (ed) *Under Sentence of Death: Lynching in the South* (University of North Carolina Press 1997); James Cutler, *Lynch-Law* (Patterson Smith 1969); Ida B. Wells-Barnett, *On Lynchings* (Introduction by Patricia Hill Collins; Prometheus Books 2002).
24 For a definitive account of the lynching of Emmett Till, see Timothy Tyson, *The Blood of Emmett Till* (Simon & Schuster 2017). For an overview of how Till's death catalysed the emerging civil rights movement, see Christopher Benson and Mamie Till-Mobley, *Death of Innocence: The Story of the Hate Crime That Changed America* (One World 2004) and Clenora Hudson-Weems, *Emmett Till: The Sacrificial Lamb of the Civil Rights Movement* (Revised edn, AuthorHouse 2006).
25 The website of the Equal Justice Initiative has a section titled 'Lynching in America' which contains up-to-date information about their on-going research. See https://lynchinginamerica.eji.org/. Also see 'Lynching in America: Confronting the Legacy of Racial Terror, (3rd edn) available at https://lynchinginamerica.eji.org/report/.
26 James W. Clarke, 'Without Fear or Shame: Lynching, Capital Punishment and the Subculture of Violence in the American South' (1998) 28 British Journal of Political Science 268, 284.
27 ibid 285.
28 Stephen B. Bright, 'Discrimination, Death and Denial: The Tolerance of Racial Discrimination in Infliction of the Death Penalty' (1995) 35 Santa Clara Law Review 433, 439.
29 John F. Galliher, Gregory Ray, and Brent Cook, 'Abolition and Reinstatement of Capital Punishment During the Progressive Era and Early 20th Century' (1992) 83 The Journal of Criminal Law & Criminology 538, 574. Economics is another factor that the authors attribute to the reinstatement of capital punishment.
30 Carol S. Steiker and Jordan M. Steiker, *Courting Death: The Supreme Court And Capital Punishment* (Belknap Press 2016) 23.
31 Galliher et al (n 29) 553.
32 J.E. Cutler, 'Capital Punishment and Lynching' (1907) 29 The Annals of the American Academy of Political and Social Science 182.
33 'Restore Capital Punishment,' *Rocky Mountain Daily News* (24 May 1900) 4 (cited in Galliher et al (n 29) 561).
34 'Citizens Express Themselves on the Burning of Porter,' *Rocky Mountain Daily News* (17 November 1900) 7 (cited in Galliher (n 29) 562).
35 Letter from B.F. Murrell to Gov. Thomas Rye (Mar. 27, 1915) (on file with the Tennessee State Historical Society) (cited in Galliher et al (n 29) 557).

36 Letter from D. J. Currie to Gov. Thomas Rye (Mar. 29, 1915) (on file with the Tennessee State Historical Society) (cited in Galliher et al (n 29) 557).
37 Letter from John P. Williams to Gov. Thomas Rye (Apr. 7, 1915) (on file with the Tennessee State Historical Society) cited in Galliher et al (n 29) 557).
38 Margaret Vandiver, 'Abolitionist Efforts in Tennessee from Statehood to 1959', in Amy L. Seward and Margaret Vandiver (eds), *Tennessee's New Abolitionists: The Fight to End the Death Penalty in the Volunteer State* (Tennessee University Press 2010) 30–32.
39 Jeffrey L. Kirchmeier, *Imprisoned By The Past: Warren McCleskey And The American Death Penalty* (OUP 2015) 57.
40 ibid 58.
41 Stuart Banner, 'Traces of Slavery: Race and the Death Penalty in Historical Perspective' in Charles J. Ogletree, Jr. and Austin Sarat (eds), *From Lynch Mobs to the Killing States: Race and the Death Penalty in America* (NYU Press 2006) 100.
42 See Forman Jr (n 19).
43 Strauder v West Virginia, 100 U.S. 303, 305 (1880).
44 Swain v. Alabama, 380 U.S. 202 (1965).
45 Alabama Code, 1923 §8603 (cited in Norris v. Alabama, 294 U.S. 587, 590 (1935)).
46 Norris (n 45) 587.
47 Edward L. Ayers, *Vengeance and Justice: Crime and Punishment in the Nineteenth-Century American South* (OUP 1984) 175 (internal quotation marks omitted).
48 Forman Jr (n 19) 916.
49 Ayers (n 47) 179.
50 Herbert H. Haines, *Against Capital Punishment: The Anti-Death Penalty Movement In America, 1972–1994* (OUP 1999) 10.
51 James McPherson, *The Abolitionist Legacy: From Reconstruction to the NAACP* (2nd edn Princeton University Press 1998). The grandson of William Lloyd Garrison – Oswald Garrison Villard – was one of the founding members of the NAACP.
52 ibid 390.
53 Ibid.
54 Martin Luther King Jr, 'Statement Delivered at the Prayer Pilgrimage Protesting the Electrocution of Jeremiah Reeves' Montgomery Ala, 6 April 1958 (reprinted in Clayborne Carson (ed) *The Papers of Martin Luther King, Jr: Vol IV Symbol of the Movement January 1957–December 1958* (University of California Press 2000) 396–397.
55 Kirchmeier (n 39) 72.
56 In the words of Michael McCann and David T. Johnson, "the legacy of civil rights activism during the cold war shaped the future of capital punishment in the United States in contradictory ways." (Michael McCann and David T. Johnson, 'Rocked but Still Rolling: The Enduring Institution of Capital Punishment in Historical and Comparative Perspective' in Charles J. Ogletree Jr and Austin Sarat, *The Road to Abolition? The Future of Capital Punishment in the United States* (NYU Press 2009) 149).
57 On the role of the LDF in death penalty litigation, see Michael Meltsner, *Cruel and Unusual: The Supreme Court and Capital Punishment* (Random House 1973); Eric L. Muller, 'The Legal Defense Fund's Capital Punishment Campaign: The Distorting Influence of Death' (1985) 4 Yale Law and Policy Review 158.
58 For an account of this case, see David Cates, *The Scottsboro Boys* (ABDO Publishing 2012). For the sake of clarity, the LDF did not initially play a leading part in this case.
59 Powell v Alabama, 287 U.S. 45, 71 (1932).
60 ibid. Also see Steiker and Steiker (n 30) 36. On the Court's "death is different" jurisprudence, see Chapter Five of this book.
61 See Rev. Jesse Jackson, *Legal Lynching: Racism, Injustice and the Death Penalty* (Marlowe & Co. 1996).

62 Steiker and Steiker (n 30) 37.
63 Louisiana ex rel. Francis v. Resweber, 329 US 459, 464 (1947).
64 Norman Redlich, 'Fighting the Death Penalty: A Thirty-Five Year Perspective' (1990) 54 Albany Law Review 617, 620.
65 Martin Luther King Jr., 'Advice for Living' *Ebony* (November 1957).
66 King Jr, 'Statement Delivered at the Prayer Pilgrimage' (n 54).
67 Meltsner (n 57) 36.
68 ibid 108 (quoting Anthony Amsterdam). Also see Banner (n 21) 252, n 43.
69 ibid.
70 For a criticism of the LDF's adoption of this mantel, and of the approach taken by the LDF, see Muller, 'The Legal Defense Fund's Capital Punishment Campaign' (n 57).
71 Evan J. Mandery, *A Wild Justice: The Death and Resurrection of Capital Punishment in America* (W.W. Norton & Company 2013) 36.
72 ibid.
73 ibid 15–25.
74 Rudolph v. Alabama, 375 US 889 (1963) (Goldberg J., dissenting from denial of certiorari).
75 Memorandum to the Conference from Mr Justice Goldberg re. Capital Punishment (r.e., Rudolph v. Alabama, Oct. Term 1963, Misc. 308) (unpublished papers of Justice Tom C Clark, University of Texas Law School Library, Austin, TX) 18 (cited in Dennis D. Doran, 'Two Different Worlds: Criminologists, Justice and Racial Discrimination in the Imposition of Criminal Punishment in Rape Cases' (1981) 72 Journal of Criminal Law and Criminology 1667, 1694.
76 Mandery (n 71) 25–28.
77 Haines (n 50) 83.
78 Meltsner (n 57) 54.
79 Kirchmeier (n 39) 141.
80 Maxwell v Bishop, 393 US 997, 997–98 (1968) (granting certiorari).
81 Brief Amici Curiae of the Synagogue Council of America and its Constituents and the American Jewish Congress, Maxwell v. Bishop, No. 622–13 (filed 15 September 1969) (available on Westlaw at 1969 WL 136886), 26–30 (quoted in Steiker and Steiker (n 30) 83).
82 Witherspoon v. Illinois, 391 US 510 (1968).
83 For a full account of *Maxwell v. Bishop*, see Mandery (n 71) 37–40.
84 Steiker and Steiker (n 30) 85.
85 Brown v. Board of Education of Topeka, 347 U.S. 483 (1954). See James T. Patterson, *Brown v. Board of Education: A Civil Rights Milestone and Its Troubled Legacy* (OUP 2002).
86 McCann and Johnson (n 56) 150.
87 Steiker and Steiker (n 18) 278.
88 Ibid.
89 McCann and Johnson (n 56) 150.
90 Furman v. Georgia, 408 U.S. 238 (1972).
91 Gregg v. Georgia, 428 U.S. 153 (1976).
92 Brief for Petitioner, *Aikens v California*, No 68–5027, *39–43, 50–53 (US filed Sept 10, 1971) (available on Westlaw at 1971 WL 134168) at 22.
93 For a thorough outline, see Steiker and Steiker (n18) 263–265.
94 Brief for NAACP et al. as Amici Curiae Supporting Petitioners, *Furman v. Georgia*, Nos. 68–5027, 69–5030, 69–5003, and 69–5031) (available on Westlaw at 1971 WL 134376) 5–6.
95 *Furman*, 408 U.S. at 249–50 (Douglass concurring) (internal citations omitted).
96 On the Marshall Hypothesis, see Gavin M. Lee, Robert M. Bohm, and Lynn M. Pazzani, 'Knowledge and Death Penalty Opinion: The Marshall Hypotheses Revisited' (2014) 39 American Journal of Criminal Justice 642 (calling into question Justice

Marshall's beliefs that information and knowledge about capital punishment would swing supporters towards the abolitionist camp).

97 Mandery (n 71) 276.

98 Steiker and Steiker, 'The (In)visibility of Race' (n 18) 285

99 ibid

100 Gregg (n 91) 179

101 ibid 173.

102 ibid 179–181 ("The most marked indication of society's endorsement of the death penalty for murder is the legislative response to Furman. The legislatures of at least 35 States have enacted new statutes that provide for the death penalty for at least some crimes that result in the death of another person." And "The jury also is a significant and reliable objective index of contemporary values because it is so directly involved.").

103 ibid 187.

104 ibid 184.

105 David M. Oshinsky, *Capital Punishment on Trial:* Furman v. Georgia *and the Death Penalty in Modern America* (University Press of Kansas 2010) 61.

106 A. Leon Higginbotham Jr, *In the Matter of Color: Race and the American Legal Process, The Colonial Period* (OUP 1978).

107 Angela Y. Davis, 'From the Prison of Slavery to the Slavery of Prison: Frederick Douglass and the Convict Lease System' in Joy James (ed), *The Angela Y. Davis Reader* (Blackwell 1998) 74, 92.

108 Naomi Murakawa, *The First Civil Right: How Liberals Built Prison America* (OUP 2014).

3 The legacy of slavery in capital punishment since 1976

I. Introduction

In *Gregg v. Georgia*, the US Supreme Court made it clear that although capital punishment is permitted by the text of the US Constitution, the imposition of death sentences must not be arbitrary and must not be marred by racial prejudices.[1] In the 40 years since *Gregg* was decided, though, research has consistently shown that such prejudices and imperfections continue to infect death penalty systems across America, from the decision to seek death in particular cases; to the process of plea bargaining; to the empaneling of juries; through to the decision to sentence a person to death. There is also evidence that race plays a role in decisions to grant clemency.[2] This is not to say that the map of slavery and the map of the modern death penalty are identical, though. California currently has the highest number of people on death row, yet it entered the Union as a free state; Pennsylvania, which was one of the first states to enact laws to end slavery, has the fifth most populous death row.[3] Nonetheless, actual executions tend to occur in those states that practiced slavery, and which saw lynchings carried out with some frequency.[4]

The centrality of race to capital punishment has therefore inevitably continued to influence the path of abolitionism, but again the impact of slavery and concerns with race have been mixed. Post-1976 research has mainly highlighted how the race of the victim has had a greater impact on the imposition of capital punishment than the race of the defendant.[5] That is, whereas it used to be the case that black people were sentenced to death at a disproportionate rate, since the 1970s it has been the killers of white people who are sentenced to death at a disproportionate rate. In other words, the lives of white people are considered to be more valuable than those of blacks. This puts anti-death penalty campaigners in a quandary, for a solution to this disparity would be to ensure that more people who are convicted of killing black people – and other minority populations such as Latinos and Native Americans, for that matter – are put to death. This would hardly further the anti-death penalty cause. Also, the focus on the race of victims, when coupled with the emerging paradigm of "victims' rights" discourses that came to prominence in the early 1980s, draws attention away from the degradation of the person facing death. Similarly, the failure in 1987 of a race-based challenge to the constitutionality of capital punishment – in the now notorious case of *McCleskey v.*

Kemp[6] – propelled the anti-death penalty movement towards an emphasis on political abolitionism, and the shift towards pragmatic and non-offender focused argumentation that such efforts entail. The prevailing view today, then, is that abolitionist efforts since the turn of the 21st Century have succeeded *because* they have marginalized the moral case against capital punishment.

This chapter sets out the initial successes of the anti-death penalty movement in the courts in the immediate years post-*Gregg*. It then considers the central role that discourses of victims' rights assumed in the early 1980s, and the continued resistance of the US Supreme Court to engage in discussions about the systemic racial bias that has afflicted the death penalty. It is with these issues in mind that we can then understand how and why abolitionism shifted from litigation-based efforts, to more political-based efforts that appear to neglect the plight of the person facing execution. The problems with these pragmatic and conservative anti-death penalty discourses are then outlined, to set the scene for the defense of radical abolitionism that follows this chapter.

II. Race, the death penalty, and abolitionism: 1976–1983

In the immediate aftermath of *Gregg* in 1976, the anti-death penalty community faced a dilemma. On the one hand, the litigation strategy had clearly failed, and concerns with racial discrimination were not gaining traction in the courts. Ten days after the ruling was announced, an ACLU memo declared that "The Supreme Court has now rejected the major constitutional arguments against the death penalty which have stopped executions in the United States during the past ten years. ... [The constitutional] attack has failed".[7] On the other hand, though, the Court had indicated that the administration of capital punishment was very much a matter for judicial oversight, and thus abolitionists were attuned to the possibility of persuading the Court that the best efforts of legislators to craft constitutionally-appropriate death penalty schemes would not be good enough to eliminate arbitrariness and discrimination.

Following *Gregg*, abolitionists were largely successful in drawing the Court's attention to the practical and procedural flaws in the new death penalty statutes. In *Lockett v. Ohio*, decided in 1978, the Court held that defendants could introduce whatever mitigating factors they wished to (as long as such factors related to the characteristics of the offender, or the circumstances of the crime) whereas prosecutors were, theoretically at least, limited to a list of statutorily enumerated aggravating factors.[8] Notwithstanding the argument that aggravating factors have been so broadly worded so as to include almost anything, the sentiment behind the Court's ruling was clearly weighted in favor of the defendant.[9] In *Presnell v. Georgia*, decided in the same year, the Court reversed a state court's decision to uphold a death sentence on the basis of an aggravating factor that the trial jury had not itself relied.[10]

In terms of racial discrimination, the most pertinent case in this era was *Coker v. Georgia*, decided in 1977.[11] As we saw in the previous chapter, it was in inter-racial rape cases that the legacy of slavery was most vivid: black men accused of raping white women were the class of people most likely to be sentenced to death. When the *Coker* Court outlawed the death penalty for rapes that did not result in death, this inevitably led to a decline in the numbers of black people being sentenced to death. Three years later, in 1980, the Massachusetts Supreme Judicial Court referred to the racially discriminatory use of capital punishment when holding that the death penalty violated the state constitution. In *District of Attorney v. Watson*, the Court stated that "[t]he conclusion is inescapable that the death penalty is reserved for those who kill whites, because the criminal justice system in these states simply does not put the same value on the life of a black person as it does on the life of a white." The Court also noted that the race of the defendant had a bearing on who was sent to death row, with "a disproportionate number of non-white offenders being sentenced to death."[12]

The Massachusetts state court's opinion applied only to that state, though, and it was notable that the *Coker* Court did not explicitly address the racially discriminatory use of capital punishment either generally, or for the crime of rape. Instead, the *Coker* Court focused on the dearth of political support for imposing death for such crimes, and on the justices' own perception of the disproportionality of capital punishment for crimes such as rape which did not result in death. That is, the Court did not officially denounce the impact of racial prejudices in the administration of death sentences, even though abolitionists continued to raise awareness of the extent to which such prejudices determined who died and who did not.[13] On the one hand, it might be argued that the Court did not need to consider the issue because both the perpetrator and the victim in this case were white. However, the year before Ehrlich Anthony Coker was sentenced to death, three black men were sentenced to death in Georgia for the crime of rape, and it is telling that the Court chose to review Coker's case rather than any of those three.[14] Randall Kennedy suggests that the Court purposely chose to review Coker's case so that they could effectuate protection for African Americans implicitly, rather than explicitly.[15] However, the Court should not be given credit for protecting black people, since the silence on the issue of race gave the impression that racial prejudices were not a problem. Steiker and Steiker describe it as "astonishing that concerns about race did not merit even a mention in the ultimate *Coker* opinions", noting that "*Coker* represents the height of the Court's avoidance of race".[16]

In terms of the anti-death penalty community, the ACLU Capital Punishment Project, the Legal Defense Fund, and other people and organizations opposed to executions convened a meeting a week after *Gregg* at which the National Coalition Against the Death Penalty was formed, which would later change its name to the National Coalition to Abolish the Death Penalty (NCADP).[17] A year later, the international non-governmental organization Amnesty International formally joined the fray. Amnesty had long opposed executions that were politically motivated, but the United States section of Amnesty initially felt reluctant to champion the cause of death row inmates on US soil. It had encountered no problems when expressing concerns about capital punishment in other countries when imposed on prisoners of conscience, because it "was easy to imagine prisoners of conscience…

as morally pure and heroic figures, abused by evil tyrants."[18] However, those sentenced to death for committing brutal acts of murder could not be cast as "morally pure and heroic". American abolitionists were well aware that attempts to evoke sympathy for them could be portrayed as a distasteful attempt to paint the death row inmate as a "victim", or even as a tragic hero.[19] If this was done without due regard to the horrific crime that the death row inmate had committed, it would clearly not serve to sway the minds of those who support capital punishment, and could instead be counter-productive. Nonetheless, as Herbert Haines notes, Amnesty's "entrance into the movement... introduced an entirely novel abolitionist frame: *the incompatibility of capital punishment with international human rights standards.*"[20] The Stockholm Declaration, which had been issued in 1977 at Amnesty's first major international meeting concerning capital punishment, listed racial discrimination as one of the primary faults with state-sanctioned executions. After noting that "[t]he death penalty is the ultimate cruel, inhuman and degrading punishment and violates the right to life", the Declaration went on to condemn the use of the death penalty as "an instrument of repression against opposition, racial, ethnic, religious and underprivileged groups".[21]

The American use of capital punishment during the first half of the 20th Century rarely drew criticisms from abroad because most other countries continued to impose such punishment themselves. By the 1980s, though, European countries in particular had generally outlawed state-sanctioned executions, and used the human rights frame to criticize other countries that continued to sentenced people to death. In this sense, by the 1990s the anti-death penalty movement was a transnational movement – much like how the antebellum movement to abolish slavery was transnational. However, while the international community was increasingly coming to see the death penalty as a violation of the human rights of the person facing death, the US was increasingly seeing capital punishment as a means of upholding the rights of the victim of the crime in question.[22] The discourse of victims' rights, we will see, has hindered the efficacy of race-based arguments against capital punishment.

III. Race, the death penalty, and abolitionism: 1983–1989

A. The centrality of "victims' rights" in debates about capital punishment

Paul Kaplan has written that, in the US, the death penalty is seen as "a public service conducted on behalf of victims."[23] Marie Gottschalk notes how the concept of victims' rights and community justice came to shape public and political discourses about crime and punishment during the 1960s and 1970s, stating that the anti-death penalty movement's failure to grapple with this emerging paradigm is a reason why the movement was unable to permanently end capital punishment at a time when it seemed ripe for outright abolition.[24] David Garland also suggests that the politics of crime control that emerged during the Nixon years is a prime reason for the survival of capital punishment,[25] and the Reagan-era of the 1980s fared no differently. In 1982, the Reagan Administration published a report entitled the President's Task Force on Victims of Crime, aimed in part at promoting the role of victims and their families in the criminal justice system.[26] In the same year, Congress passed the Victim and Witness Protection Act, which permitted the introduction of "victim impact evidence" in the sentencing process. The next year, albeit not in a death penalty case, then Chief Justice Burger wrote that "[i]n the administration of justice, courts may not ignore the concerns of victims."[27]

By 1987, 44 states and the federal government permitted victim impact evidence during the sentencing phase of capital trials.[28] That year, in *Booth v. Maryland*, the US Supreme Court narrowly outlawed such schemes. Writing for a bare majority, Justice Powell insisted that evidence relating to the impact of a homicide on the victim's family had no bearing either on the gravity of the crime, or the moral culpability of the offender.[29] This, however, proved to be only a temporary victory for abolitionists.

B. The marginalization of race: 1983–1987

The focus on the rights of victims and their families might seem to have little relevance to the question of race and the legacy of slavery. But there are at least two ways in which these topics are inter-related. First, we see that some victims are considered more valuable than others by virtue of their race, since killers of white people are far more likely to receive a death sentence than killers of black persons. Second, the centrality of victims' rights to debates about capital punishment shifted attention away from the rights of the person facing execution, and compelled abolitionists to take their fight into the political domain.

Abolitionists knew that the decision in *Gregg*, with its emphasis on guided discretion, would do little to eliminate the effect of racial prejudices and unconscious biases in the administration of capital punishment. After all, they had argued during the 1960s and 1970s that the death penalty survived precisely *because* the discretion afforded to decision-makers enabled them to apply capital punishment non-systematically and in racially biased ways.[30] Purported limits on such discretionary power, they feared, would be easily circumvented. A study published in 1984 by William Bowers, Glenn Pierce, and John McDevitt revealed racial disparities in the application of capital punishment. They studied capital convictions across four states in the period between 1972 and 1977, and found that in Florida, Georgia, Texas, and Ohio, "black killers and the killers of whites are substantially more likely than others to receive a death sentence".[31] A central reason for these disparities lies in the racial make-up of juries.

In 1880, the US Supreme Court outlawed state statutes that barred black people from sitting on juries, but the phenomenon of all-white juries trying black defendants has persisted.[32] This is problematic because research has repeatedly shown that the racial make-up of a jury has a bearing on findings of guilt and innocence, and on decisions to sentence a person to death.[33] A study by the Capital Jury Project published in 2001 revealed a "white male dominance effect" in capital cases involving black defendants and white victims. The presence of five or more white males on a jury, the Project found, substantially increased the likelihood of a death sentence being passed. Likewise, the presence of African Americans on the jury substantially reduced the chances of a death sentence.[34] Based on interviews with jurors, the researchers offered numerous reasons for this. In particular, it was found that the differences in jurors' approaches to mitigation evidence reflected the differences in jurors' life experiences. Thus, whereas white jurors saw a black defendant as incorrigible and lacking in emotion or remorse, black jurors in the same case saw the defendant as a victim of a disadvantaged upbringing, and demonstrative of remorse and sincerity.[35] These differences, the researchers surmise, stem from America's history of racial prejudices:

> Unconsciously perhaps, whites as jurors carry into the jury box and the jury room this cultural baggage of the dangerous black male predator and the need for punitiveness... Not surprisingly, the perspectives of blacks on crime and the criminal justice system diverge widely from those of whites. Blacks are more likely to believe that... capital punishment [is] tainted with racial bias.[36]

In an interview with one white juror, the interviewee stated that she believed that it would be beneficial to the mother of the defendant for the person to be executed, since a death sentence would not "burden her with this boy being behind prison [bars] and what he would go through."[37] The authors draw attention to both the juror's choice of words, and underlying justification for imposing a death sentence: "Note that this juror began referring to the defendant as 'boy' in her patronizing explanation of why his execution would probably be good for his mother."[38] Both the choice of words and underlying justification mirror are emblematic of the legacy of slavery. The term "boy" was often used in a patronizing, derogatory way to refer to male slaves, and slavery was similarly justified on occasion as a "positive good" for black people.

There are at least two explanations for the prevalence of all-white, or primarily-white, juries in cases involving black defendants. First, there can be a genuine difficulty in finding black jurors. African Americans, after all, make up only 12 percent of the population. Moreover, in *Witherspoon v. Illinois* (1968) and *Wainwright v. Witt* (1985), the Court reinforced what is known as the "death qualification" process for empaneling juries.[39] To sit on a capital case, a potential juror must show that their personal views about capital punishment will not "prevent or substantially impair" them from carrying out their duties impartially.[40] Public opinion polls have invariably demonstrated a distaste for capital punishment among African American communities, in large part because of their general distrust of the criminal justice system as a whole, given the ways in which they have historically been disadvantaged by the system.[41] Thus, we find that many potential black jurors are struck for cause, on the grounds that they will not be able to impartially consider whether a death sentence is appropriate on the evidence.

The second explanation lies in the surreptitious practices of prosecutors who go to great lengths to ensure that an all-white jury is empaneled. They do this because they know that they are more likely to secure a conviction and a death sentence if the jury cannot empathize or identify with the defendant. They are similarly more likely to secure a conviction and death sentence if the jury can empathize and identify with the victim. Thus, even if a potential black juror demonstrates an ability and willingness to consider death as per the *Witherspoon* test, prosecutors often seek to strike the person off the pool for another reason. And if they cannot demonstrate potential bias on the part of the prospective juror, the prosecutor can use their peremptory strikes to remove jurors from the pool without providing any reasons for doing so.

In the non-capital case of *Batson v. Kentucky*, decided in 1986, petitioner appealed his sentence on the grounds that the prosecuting attorney had used his peremptory strikes to remove all black people from the jury, in the knowledge that an all-white jury would be more likely to convict.[42] The Court in *Batson* offered a mixed judgment. On the one hand, it agreed that striking black jurors on account of their race violates the Equal Protection Clause of the Fourteenth Amendment. However, the Court provided a three-stage test for determining whether there has been such a violation, and this test has been notoriously difficult to satisfy. First, the defense must challenge the prosecutor's use of a peremptory challenge. Second, the prosecutor must then offer an explanation for why they struck that particular juror. Third, the trial court must determine whether the explanation offered is racially neutral.[43]

In his concurring opinion in *Batson*, Justice Marshall warned that the decision would not eliminate racial discrimination, noting that such a "goal can be accomplished only by eliminating peremptory challenges entirely."[44] Marshall's concerns were twofold. First, the rule meant that defendants could only realistically successfully challenge the discriminatory use of peremptory strikes if they "are so flagrant as to establish a prima facie case."[45] Second, even when a prima facie case can be established, the trial court still has the difficulty of assessing the prosecutor's true motives. As Marshall wrote,

> [a]ny prosecutor can easily assert facially neutral reasons for striking a juror... [and a] prosecutor's own conscious or unconscious racism may lead him easily to the conclusion that a prospective black juror is 'sullen,' or 'distant,' a characterization that would not have come to his mind if a white juror had acted identically. A judge's own conscious or unconscious racism may lead him to accept such an explanation as well supported.[46]

Although Justice Marshall did not explicitly refer to slavery, he nonetheless tied conscious and unconscious racism to America's past: "It is worth remembering that 114 years after the close of the War Between the States and nearly 100 years after *Strauder*, racial and other forms of discrimination still remain a fact of life, in the administration of justice as in our society as a whole."[47]

If *Batson* was a qualified victory for those working to eliminate racial discrimination, then *McCleskey v. Kemp*,[48] decided the next year, was an outright defeat for those concerned with racial justice, and for those opposed to the death penalty. Warren McCleskey – an African American man sentenced to death for killing a white police officer – claimed that his death sentence had been predicated on his race, and the race of the victim, rather than on the gravity of the crime or his moral culpability. The Legal Defense Fund introduced statistical evidence relating to racial disparities in the death penalty in Georgia, where McCleskey had been convicted. David Baldus, Charles Pulaski, and George Woodworth studied 2,484 homicide prosecutions in Georgia from 1973 to 1979, and found that prosecutors tended to seek death sentences with much more vigor when the homicide victim was white, than when the victim was black. Prosecutors sought the death penalty in 70 percent of cases involving black defendants and white victims; 32 percent of cases involving white defendants and white victims; 19 percent of cases involved white defendants and black victims; and 15 percent of cases involving black defendants and black victims.[49] They also found that actual death sentences handed down were significantly skewed along racial lines. The evidence suggested that the odds of a death sentence for those accused of killing a white person were 4.3 times higher than in cases where the victim was black.

Statistical studies had been carried out before, but had been rejected by the courts for their lack of methodological rigor. In 1968, the US Court of Appeals for the Eighth Circuit had rejected similar evidence from the criminologist Marvin Wolfgang in *Maxwell v. Bishop* because Wolfgang had not sufficiently accounted for different variables that might have explained why some cases resulted in death sentences when others did not.[50] Baldus and his colleagues, though, had accounted for 230 non-racial variables that could have accounted for these discrepancies. Their study, therefore, was contemporaneously regarded as one of the most robust statistical analyses of racial discrimination in capital punishment cases. Given the rigorous methodology behind the study, the Supreme Court was reluctant to reject the evidence outright. However, in a 5–4 decision, the majority ruled that individuals cannot rely on these general statistical studies to have their death sentences vacated. The Court declared that "at most, the Baldus study indicates a discrepancy that appears to correlate with race",[51] and accepted that "[a]pparent disparities in sentencing are an inevitable part of our criminal justice system."[52] Such discrepancies, though, are to be tolerated unless it could be shown that specific actors in a specific case acted with intent to discriminate against a specific person on the basis of race. In the Court's words: "to prevail under the Equal Protection Clause, McCleskey must prove that the decisionmakers in *his* case acted with discriminatory purpose."[53]

The Court appeared to be reluctant to accept McCleskey's claim because of the broader impact it would inevitably have: "McCleskey's claim, taken to its logical conclusion, throws into serious question the principles that underlie our entire criminal justice system… Thus, if we accepted McCleskey's claim that racial bias has impermissibly tainted the capital sentencing decision, we could soon be faced with similar claims as to other types of penalty."[54] In other words, the Court rejected the application of the statistical evidence so that it would not be faced with a barrage of similar claims. Dissenting, Justice Brennan refused to ignore the historical roots of racial discrimination: "we cannot pretend that in three decades [since the Civil Rights Act] we have completely escaped the grip of a historical legacy spanning centuries. Warren McCleskey's evidence confronts us with the subtle and persistent influence of the past… we remain imprisoned by the past as long as we deny its influence in the present."[55] Brennan also chastised his colleagues for their "unwillingness to regard petitioner's evidence as sufficient [because] recognition of McCleskey's claim would open the door to widespread challenges to all aspects of criminal sentencing." In Brennan's view "such a statement seems to suggest a fear of too much justice."[56] Presaging the central tenet of today's BlackLivesMatter movement, Brennan wrote that the decision in *McCleskey* "reflects a devaluation of the lives of black persons."[57]

Notwithstanding Brennan's dissent, it is plausible to argue that the Court in *McCleskey* was not avoiding the question of race simply because it wanted to avoid a controversial topic. In the cases of the 1960s and 1970s, the Court avoided the race question because its other race-based decisions were causing considerable controversy. However, there was nothing in 1987 to suggest that a decision in favor of racial minorities would stoke unrest. Instead, perhaps the *McCleskey* Court avoided the question because it considered it inappropriate to base constitutional reasoning on statistical analysis. Justice Powell authored the majority opinion in *McCleskey*, but admitted in a memorandum to one of his law clerks that his "understanding of statistical analysis – particularly what is called regression analysis – range[d] from limited to zero."[58] This is not to say that they avoided the question because they did not understand it. Rather, it might be that the Justices saw their role as one of evaluating evidence and points of law in individual cases. Using general statistical evidence to create policy, though, is outside the realm of the judiciary. Such a task, as Justice Powell explained in *McCleskey*, is better left to legislative bodies.[59]

One of the most significant effects of the decision in *McCleskey* – apart from, of course, hastening Warren McCleskey's death – was the legitimization of both capital punishment, and of racial discrimination. That is, once again, a race-focused attempt at abolition backfired. Baldus and Woodworth later wrote that the decision "significantly legitimated tolerance for race discrimination" in death penalty cases,[60] and Carol Steiker and Jordan Steiker have written that the case "contribute[d] substantially to the stabilization and perpetuation of capital punishment as a social practice."[61] Jerome McCristal Culp Jr, like other critical race scholars, has noted that this decision, and the reasoning offered by the Court, reminds black people that American law has long served to subjugate the value of black people.[62] For this reason, *McCleskey* has been compared to the pro-slavery decision *Dred Scott v. Sandford*,[63] since it entrenched and legitimized a legal system that perpetuates racial subjugation. Anthony Amsterdam, who led the abolitionist efforts of the 1960s and 1970s, described *McCleskey* as "the *Dred Scott* of our time",[64] and Michelle Alexander has written that "*McCleskey v. Kemp* and its progeny serve much the same function as *Dred Scott* and *Plessy*."[65] Powell, who authored the majority opinion, candidly announced after his retirement that if he could change one decision during his tenure on the Court, it would be his opinion in *McCleskey*. In an interview with his biographer, Powell said that he not only accepted that McCleskey should have had his life spared, but that capital punishment as a whole was unworkable.[66]

Justice Powell's hope that legislatures would take up the task of addressing systemic racism in the death penalty was misplaced because the Court's decision gave the impression that the death penalty was working, and thus hardly encouraged state legislatures or Congress to address the issue of racial discrimination.[67] Congress did consider passing a Racial Justice Act in 1988 that would have allowed defendants to use statistical evidence to invalidate their death sentences, but the attempt, and a later attempt, failed.[68] There are a number of reasons why members of Congress have opposed the idea of a Racial Justice Act. Randall Kennedy opines that, for some, "the death penalty retains an assuring symbolic association with the racial hierarchies of the past and becomes even more significant symbolically when challenged directly on the grounds of racial justice."[69] Less overtly, there are those who might well abhor racial discrimination, but who engage in a cost-benefit analysis of a Racial Justice Act. To these people, a Racial Justice Act would not advance racial equality to the same extent that it would slow down the capital process, and it is more important to them that death penalty systems are allowed to operate unhindered by concerns with racial justice.[70] Similarly, some opponents of the Racial Justice Act stated that the answer was not to set aside death sentences, but to impose more death sentences in cases involving black victims. When the House of Representatives Committee on the Judiciary issued a report that was generally favorable to the proposed Act, Henry Hyde dissented: "[T]he solution", he said, "would be to seek the death penalty in more cases in which black defendants murder black [people]".[71]

While the national government failed to introduce such legislation, two states succeeded. In 1998, Kentucky became the first state to pass a Racial Justice Act, but its effects have been unclear. On the one hand, the law imposes a high burden of proof for defendants to demonstrate, and still requires a link between the evidence and the individual case. Thus, there have been no successful claims based on Kentucky's Racial Justice Act. On the other hand, though, it has been argued that the mere presence of the law has encouraged prosecutors to check their explicit or unconscious bias when exercising their discretion to seek a death sentence in any given case, and during jury selection.[72] In 2009, North Carolina became the second state to pass a Racial Justice Act, and in 2012 Marcus Robinson became the first person to use the Act to have their death sentence overturned. This success was met with criticism, though. Prosecutors in particular complained that executions were being illegitimately held up as death row inmates abused the law. One year after Robinson was freed, the legislature repealed the Racial Justice Act.[73]

The decision in *McCleskey* was also a turning point in anti-death penalty strategies and tactics since, in Herbert Haines's words, it "signaled the futility of continuing to place hope for abolishing the death penalty on the constitutional strategy that had once been so successful."[74] Jeffrey Kirchmeier also states that, following the decision, the "decades-long litigation strategy to abolish the death penalty appeared to suffer a final defeat."[75] In 1988, the *New York Times* reported that the decision "ended what may well have been the last sweeping challenge to the death penalty in our time."[76] This is not to say that the anti-death penalty community ceased challenging the death penalty in the courts altogether. However, the decision dramatically changed the nature of these efforts. The constitutional case had been framed in terms of arbitrariness and discrimination, issues that are also applicable in non-capital criminal justice contexts. The majority's explicit concern with "fac[ing]… similar claims as to other types of penalty",[77] though, dissuaded abolitionists from continuing with a strategy that so clearly worried the Court. The Court's reasoning in *McCleskey*, then, compelled abolitionists to frame future constitutional challenges to the death penalty in terms that were unique to capital punishment – it encouraged, in other words, a conservative approach to abolition.[78]

The hopes of those abolitionists who clung to the belief that the Supreme Court would strike down capital punishment were diminished further in 1989 when the Court handed down judgments in two cases on the same day: *Stanford v. Kentucky*, and *Penry v. Lynaugh*.[79] In *Stanford*, the Court rejected an Eighth Amendment challenge to the executions of persons who committed their offenses while under the age of 18, and in *Penry* the Court rejected a similar challenge to the executions of persons suffering from what was then termed "mental retardation." These cases, considered below, forced abolitionists to take their case to the court of public opinion instead.

IV. Race, the death penalty, and abolitionism: 1989–1998

From *Gregg* up until 1989, the Court tended to adopt a two-pronged approach to Eighth Amendment analysis in death penalty cases. It would look at objective indicia of national opinion to gauge whether a particular punishment offended "evolving standards of decency", and it would invoke its own independent proportionality analysis. In *Stanford*, though, Justice Scalia signaled the outright primacy of national opinion over the Court's proportionality analysis. Writing for a plurality, Scalia asserted that "…we emphatically reject petitioner's suggestion that the issues in this case permit us to apply our 'own informed judgment.'"[80] Scalia instead placed objective indicia of a national consensus front and center of Eighth Amendment analysis: "…proportionality analysis itself can only be conducted on the basis of the standards set by our own society; the only alternative, once again, would be our personal preferences."[81] This approach was echoed in *Penry*, and it was clear to the anti-death penalty movement that if the death penalty was ever to be ruled unconstitutional in the courts, it would first have to be rejected by a majority of state legislatures, and that juries across America would need to stop imposing such sentences.

In a series of cases over the next few years, the Court continued to deregulate the death penalty, steadily withdrawing federal oversight over the various states' administration of capital punishment. In 1990, the Court upheld a Pennsylvania statute that mandated the death penalty where aggravating factors were found in the absence of any mitigating factors.[82] The next year, the Court reversed its earlier decision in *Booth v. Maryland*, and permitted schemes that allowed victims' families to testify at the sentencing stage of capital trials.[83] In 1993 the Court affirmed a death sentence even though the jury in the case had been unable to consider the relevant mitigating factor of the defendant's age.[84] In that same year, the Court declared that evidence of actual innocence did not necessarily amount to a constitutional right to have an execution halted.[85] And also in 1993, the Court upheld the validity of a state statute that permitted jurors to sentence a person to death on the grounds that the defendant had shown "an utter disregard for human life."[86] Every person who commits murder has shown "an utter disregard for human life", thus broadening the pool of people who are eligible for the death penalty.[87] In light of the Court's retreat, and the *Stanford* rule relating to the importance of public opinion, abolitionists retreated from the judiciary and took their grievances to the public.

Public-facing abolitionist efforts in the 1990s suffered from the fact that public support for capital punishment was high. Ever since the Court in *Furman* and *Gregg* validated the role of "popular sentiments and passions"[88] in debates about capital punishment, the pro-death penalty movement manipulated anti-death penalty discourses relating to the right to life, and framed capital punishment as, in part, a necessary tool to protect the right to life of actual and potential victims of crime.[89] Thus, public debates tended to revolve around "victims' rights" and the wishes of murder victims' families, resulting in the strengthening of public support for the ultimate punishment.

Popular support for the death penalty was so high in this period that politicians generally did not dare signal their opposition to it. During the presidential debates in 1988, the Democratic nominee Michael Dukakis was asked if he would support capital punishment if somebody raped and murdered his wife. When he answered by expressing his distaste for capital punishment, he was widely chastised for his apparent lack of emotion. Many observers considered his answer to be the pivotal moment in the election campaign, with his opponent George H. Bush going on to win.[90] Dukakis's answer could not be separated from the now infamous "Willie Horton" advertising campaign of the Republican party, in which voters were told that Dukakis was to blame for the escape of a black prisoner named Willie Horton, who went on to rape and murder a white woman. Michelle Alexander describes this as "Bush's most famous racial appeal", and notes that the "ad was stunningly effective; it destroyed Dukakis's chances of ever becoming president."[91] During the next election campaign in 1992, the Democratic nominee – Bill Clinton – made sure that he would not suffer the same fate as Dukakis. On January 24, 1992, Clinton broke form the campaign trail to witness, in his capacity as Governor of Arkansas, the execution of Ricky Ray Rector. Rector was black, and had suffered significant brain damage after an attempted suicide attempt. Clinton not only won the primary to run for President; he also won the election.[92]

In 1994, Congress passed the Violent Crime Control and Law Enforcement Act, which included the Federal Death Penalty Act. This expanded the number of death-eligible federal offenses to 60 crimes, including some non-lethal offenses. The Congressional Black Caucus fought for the inclusion of a Racial Justice Act, but their efforts failed.[93] The bombing of the Alfred P. Murrah Federal Building in Oklahoma City on April 19, 1995, which was the deadliest act of terrorism on US soil until the attacks of September 11, 2001, also entrenched support for capital punishment as a nation grieved for the lost lives of 168 people. When Timothy McVeigh was apprehended and charged for the bombing, there was little support for sparing him from the ultimate punishment.[94] The crime also inspired the adoption of the Antiterrorism and Effective Death Penalty Act in 1996, which curtailed the opportunities for death row inmates to file for habeas corpus review in federal courts.

Although McVeigh was white, it was still widely acknowledged that capital punishment was infected with the strain of racism that had bred since the days of slavery. In 1994, Justice Blackmun emphasized the "vestiges of racism"[95] when announcing that he would no longer "tinker with the machinery of death."[96] In a dissent from a denial of certiorari in *Callins v. Collins*, Blackmun explained that he found it impossible to reconcile the constitutional requirement that death sentences be consistent and non-arbitrary, with the constitutional requirement of individualized sentencing so as to ensure that only the most deserving suffer death. He explained that the "arbitrariness inherent in the sentencer's discretion to afford mercy is exacerbated by the problem of race",[97] and that there was "no indication that the problem of race in the administration of death will ever be addressed."[98]

In 1997, the American Bar Association added its voice to the chorus of concerns about racial prejudices when calling for a moratorium on all executions. The Death Penalty Moratorium Resolution urged the implementation of "policies and procedures … intended to (1) ensure that death penalty cases are administered fairly and impartially, in accordance with due process, and (2) minimize the risk that innocent people may be executed." To satisfy these demands, the Resolution enjoined jurisdictions to ensure competent defense counsel, to strengthen post-conviction appeals proceedings, and to eliminate capital punishment for the "mentally retarded" and persons under the age of 18 at the time of their crime. Notably, the Resolution also urged authorities to strive "to eliminate discrimination in capital sentencing on the basis of the race of either the victim or the defendant."[99] The Report that accompanied the Resolution documented the statistical evidence of racial discrimination, and condemned both the Supreme Court and Congress for failing to take action to deal with the problem.[100]

In the years following *Gregg*, executions had resumed at a slow pace as cases worked their way through the appeals systems, but 17 death penalty states resumed executions during the 1990s,[101] and there were 98 executions in 1999 – the highest number in a calendar year since the death penalty was restored in 1976. Not a single state repealed their death penalty statutes during the 1990s, with New York re-instating capital punishment in 1995. Popular support consistently registered between 75–80 percent,[102] and men and women were sentenced to death at a remarkable rate. In every year of the 1990s at least 250 new death sentences were handed down.[103]

V. The anti-death penalty movement until 1998

In 1999, a revised edition of Herbert Haines's *Against Capital Punishment: The Anti-Death Penalty Movement in America, 1972–1994* was published.[104] In this thoroughly researched and engaging account, Haines used social movement theory to explain and critique the anti-death penalty movement of that era. Given how entrenched the death penalty was at the time, his book struck a despondent tone for abolitionists. However, it provided valuable insights into the workings of the anti-death penalty movement, and offered suggestions for going forward.

Haines described adherents to the anti-death penalty cause as "mostly … middle-class white people with professional backgrounds and liberal politics",[105] and he criticized the predominance of "moralistic critique[s]" of capital punishment in abolitionist discourses.[106] He also highlighted the movement's inability to appeal to the values held by death penalty supporters: "There have been too few members, too little money, and too little broad appeal in the messages the movement has tried to deliver."[107] More recently, in 2014, Andy Hoover and Ken Cunningham reiterated some of Haines's critique: "Research indicates that arguing against the death penalty by making moral arguments against it… is fruitless."[108]

On the basis that emotional claims about the immorality of state-sanctioned executions are ineffective, Haines used social movement theory to argue that abolitionists should adopt a more pragmatic approach to framing the case against capital punishment. Drawing on the work of David Snow and his colleagues,[109] he suggested that death penalty abolitionists had pursued "frame transformation" in vain. "Frame transformation" involves trying to change the moral outlook and values of one's target audience, but such a task is very difficult, time-consuming, and is often of little practical use. After all, there is just as much chance of a death penalty supporter changing the moral outlook of an abolitionist. Instead, Haines asserted, abolitionists should adopt a framing technique that involves relating the goals of abolition to the "*existing* values of the public."[110] This would involve framing the case for abolition in such a way that resonates with the existing conservative values of harsh retributivism: "the restriction or elimination of capital punishment could be 'marketed' as not merely humanitarian reform, but an intelligent step toward a realistic crime control policy. This is a message with broader appeal, capable of being taken more seriously by people who are deaf to the primarily moral claims of traditional death penalty opponents."[111] Haines identified concerns with government spending as another feature of conservatism, and thus argued that the "cornerstone of a more effective assault on the death penalty would most likely be its crippling cost."[112] In all, Haines writes, the anti-death penalty movement "need[s] to adopt a more pragmatic strategy, one that places less emphasis on moralistic appeals and more emphasis on tangible costs and on policy alternatives that resonate with widespread cultural sentiments… [O]nly some form of life-without-parole (LWOP) is likely to be seen by the largest segment of the American public as capable of making executions unnecessary."[113]

VI. Death penalty abolitionism since 1998

Herbert Haines's book makes passing reference to the anti-death penalty movement's use of the "innocence" narrative that has come to dominate abolitionism since the turn of the century.[114] This is likely because the book was initially published *before* the 1998 National Conference on Wrongful Convictions and the Death Penalty, with a revised edition appearing shortly afterwards. Although Haines notes in an Afterword that the conference "received widespread press coverage in the United States and abroad",[115] he was writing before the effects of this conference took hold. Since then, abolitionists have tended to marginalize "moralistic critique[s]" and have focused instead on rational and pragmatic arguments against state-sanctioned executions. Although things did not change overnight, the National Conference on Wrongful Convictions was something of a watershed moment in the course of death penalty abolitionism. The conference, which took place at Northwestern University in Chicago, Illinois, on November 13–15, 1998, drew some 800 lawyers, academics, journalists, and other interested persons, and largely succeeded in challenging the assumption that instances of innocent people being sentenced to death were few and far between. The media reports that followed the conference confirmed that this message had been delivered: the scale of innocent people facing execution was now firmly in the spotlight.[116] I do not mean to suggest that this one conference propelled America on the path towards abolition, but it did draw attention to what Haines would describe as a "pragmatic" reason for outlawing executions: whatever one's moral disposition on capital punishment in the abstract, we can all agree that people should not be sentenced to death or executed for a crime that they have not committed. Six years after this conference, Lawrence Marshall, noting that the "[innocence] revolution… has just begun",[117] confidently asserted that "it is the issue of innocence that carries the real potential to transform American opinion on the use of capital punishment."[118] Noting this shift in abolitionist argumentation, Marshall described this "new group" of anti-death penalty activists as "pragmatic abolitionists".[119] While Marshall was possibly biased in his assessment of the strength of the discourse of innocence – he organized and ran the conference – he was not incorrect to describe these abolitionists as "pragmatic."

The "pragmatic abolitionists" have not only focused on innocence. They have also appealed to the economic interests of its target audience by raising awareness of the exorbitant costs of the death penalty.[120] This has been particularly relevant to the movement's target audiences since the economic crash of 2008. Writing in 2014, Jolie McLaughlin asserted that:

> Within the past decade, anti-death penalty advocates have placed less emphasis on the moral arguments against capital punishment, focusing more on the costs and inefficiencies of the practice. In turn, state legislatures have been receptive to the anti-death penalty movement's cost arguments, especially in light of the recent economic crisis. In other words, by giving state legislatures a self-interested reason to abolish capital punishment – saving their constituents millions of dollars (and increasing their chances of re-election) – anti-death penalty advocates have aligned state lawmakers' interests with their own. The result has been an apparent turning point for death penalty reform in America.[121]

The attention to innocence and costs is interconnected with the endorsement of life in prison without the possibility of parole as an alternative punishment. Haines's account of the anti-death penalty movement was published at a time when abolitionists were reticent about endorsing sentences of LWOP. In his words: "A few anti-death penalty activists and litigators have given their explicit support to LWOP," but "most of them resist coming out in favour of LWOP".[122] Since his book was published, it is increasingly common for anti-death penalty activists and practitioners to refrain from criticizing the use of LWOP as an alternative to executions, and we will see in Chapters Six and Seven that several in the anti-death penalty community have explicitly endorsed such sentences. In this sense, we can see how abolitionists have accepted conservative values of harsh retributivism, rather than emphasize that it is precisely such severe punishment without hope of redemption that is their objection to capital punishment in the first place.

In many respects, this pragmatic, conservative approach to abolition in the public and political arenas has been successful in converting more and more people to the anti-death penalty cause. The website of the National Coalition to Abolish the Death Penalty lists 59 state-wide affiliate organizations, in addition to 60 national and nine international affiliates. There are also 51 local branches of the American Civil Liberties Union that are affiliated with the NCADP.[123] While many of these groups are the orthodox human rights-based and religious groups that have long been part of the anti-death penalty camp, and which emphasize the moral case against executions, many are newer groups that bring a fresh and more pragmatic perspective to the abolitionist campaign. Witness to Innocence (WTI) was set up in 2003, and draws attention to the particular problem of wrongful convictions. Conservatives Concerned About the Death Penalty (CCATDP) was set up in 2013, and draws attention to the incompatibility of executions with conservative values of limited government and tight fiscal policy.[124] And in 2016, over 70 current and former law enforcement officials, prosecutors, and corrections officials founded Public Safety Officials on the Death Penalty (PSODP), which adds a unique perspective – that of law enforcement personnel – on the propriety of capital punishment. The multifarious ways in which these groups feed into conservative and pragmatic discourses are outlined in Chapter Six, since it is in the political and public spheres that these groups tend to operate, but for present purposes it is worth noting that while the anti-death penalty movement is thus broader and much more diverse than it was at the time Haines was writing, much anti-death penalty discourse is narrowly framed around problems that are unique to capital punishment.

The advance of conservative and pragmatic discourses has coincided with a decline in race-based argumentation. Conservatives Concerned About the Death Penalty lists five issues that, in their view, warrant abolition: innocence, cost, victims, public safety, and fairness.[125] While one might expect the issue of race discrimination to appear under the topic of "fairness", it does not.[126] Writing in 2006, Austin Sarat observed that "the rhetorical center of abolitionist argument has come to focus less on race and more on claims of actual innocence."[127]

Fatimah Loren Muhammad agrees: "the death penalty repeal movement has not always prioritized the call for racial justice".[128] Given the pervasiveness of race and the legacy of slavery on the use of the death penalty, Sarat urges abolitionists to "resist the temptation to further marginalize the discourse of race in their rhetoric and politics… because no critique of state killing in the United States is, or can be, adequate if it neglects or marginalizes race."[129] It is not just the marginalization of race that is problematic, though. The reluctance to object to life without parole has been criticized for perpetuating the belief that some people deserve to die behind bars, in the custody of the state.[130] The focus on innocence has been criticized for drawing attention away from the importance of ensuring that even the guilty are treated humanely. As Angela Davis and others have noted, these approaches to abolition fail to address the root of the problem, which is that the criminal justice system – with its historic links to slavery – institutionalizes and normalizes the belief that some lives are worth less than others.[131] It is these critiques that drive the rest of this study.

VII. Conclusion

Before explaining why abolitionism can and should be more radical, rather than pragmatic or conservative, it is worth clarifying that the anti-death penalty movement is not a monolithic group which pursues one strategy or abolitionist discourse to the exclusion of all others, and it is inaccurate to state that the groups mentioned above – WTI, CCATDP, and PSODP in particular – are representative of the movement as a whole. Equal Justice USA (EJUSA), for example, used to be a single-issue organization that focused on death penalty repeal, but has recently broadened its scope to "work[] to transform the justice system from one that harms to one that heals. Our work includes ending the death penalty, strengthening programs that help crime survivors address trauma and rebuild their lives, and promoting trauma-informed responses to violence that can save lives and help heal communities."[132] Writing in November 2017, Fatimah Loren Muhammad explains that EJUSA recognized that the tendency to sideline race-based concerns was inappropriate, and that therefore "over the past decade EJUSA has expanded its work beyond the death penalty and developed a broader vision focused on building a justice system that works for everyone impacted by violence."[133]

In addition to these groups, The Eighth Amendment Project, which was set up in 2014 by Henderson Hill, co-ordinates the national campaign against capital punishment by collating evidence relating to the decline in the use of the death penalty; highlighting the inherent flaws with the system in those few counties that do impose capital punishment; and by illustrating that those who are sentenced to death are usually not the "worst of the worst", but are the poor, the vulnerable, and the unlucky. The Project's "ultimate mission", though, is to identify and bring a case to the US Supreme Court in which the justices will be asked to consider the constitutionality of the death penalty per se.[134] In this sense, the litigation strategy still dominates. Carol Steiker and Jordan Steiker suggest that this Project, alongside long-standing centers such as the Equal Justice Initiative (EJI) in Montgomery,

Alabama and the Southern Center for Human Rights (SCHR) in Atlanta, Georgia, "are in some meaningful sense the descendants of the LDF",[135] illustrating the enduring legacy of the slavery abolitionists in today's anti-death penalty efforts. The EJI does not just focus on capital punishment – it addresses all aspects of the criminal justice system that impact racial minorities and the poor. And the SCHR has long drawn connections between the South's resistance to emancipation and abolition, with the race-based problems that afflict criminal justice systems across Southern states.[136]

Perhaps the clearest link between anti-slavery and anti-racist efforts on the one hand, and anti-death penalty efforts on the other, can be found in the Policy Platform of the BlackLivesMatter movement, which was founded in 2012 in response to widely publicized incidents of black people being shot by police officers. The Policy Platform, which was adopted in 2016, lists abolition of capital punishment as one of the movement's core aims because the "death penalty devalues Black lives" and has "targeted Blacks and other people of color and poor people throughout… history."[137]

Over the following chapters we will see yet a clearer link between the slavery abolitionists and death penalty abolitionists. In short, we will see that the contemporary anti-death penalty movement should be understood as embodying the vision and rhetoric of the radical slavery abolitionists. These men and women understood that slavery and racial prejudices were part of a broader problem: the failure to treat each and every person with respect for their dignity. When we recognize that, notwithstanding appearances to the contrary, today's abolitionists likewise frame the case against the death penalty within such terms, we see that today's anti-death penalty discourses still draw on the legacy of the slavery abolitionists. Perhaps more importantly, recognizing these historical and conceptual links leads to the conclusion that anti-death penalty efforts should be more radical going forward.

Notes

1 Gregg v. Georgia, 428 U.S. 153 (1976).

2 For examples, see Frank R. Baumgartner, Amanda J. Grigg and Alisa Mastro '#BlackLivesDon'tMatter: race-of-victim effects in US executions, 1976–2013 (2015) 3 Politics, Groups, and Identities 209; Nick Petersen, 'Examining the Sources of Racial Bias in Potentially Capital Cases: A Case Study of Police and Prosecutorial Discretion' (2017) 7 Race and Justice 7; US Dept. of Justice, *The Federal Death Penalty System, A Statistical Survey*, (12 September 2000) 34–35 http://www.usdoj.gov/dag/pubdoc/dpsurvey.html; John Kraemer, 'An Empirical Examination of the Factors Associated with the Commutation of State Death Row Prisoners' Sentences Between 1986 and 2005' (2008) 45 American Criminal Law Review 1389, 1410.

3 The Death Penalty Information Center keeps up-to-date figures of death row populations across America. See 'Death Row Prisoners by State' at https://deathpenaltyinfo.org/death-row-inmates-state-and-size-death-row-year?scid=9&did=188.

4 Franklin E. Zimring, *The Contradictions of American Capital Punishment* (OUP 2003) 66; Carol S Steiker and Jordan M Steiker, *Courting Death: The Supreme Court and Capital Punishment* (Belknap Press 2016) 17 ("One of the strongest predictors

of a state's propensity to conduct executions today is its history of lynch mob activity more than a century ago. Given this connection, it is no surprise that the current map of active death penalty states is predominantly a map of the former Confederacy.").

5 One of the most recent studies is Baumgartner et al (n 2).

6 McCleskey v. Kemp, 481 U.S. 279 (1987).

7 'Background paper on the Supreme Court's death penalty decisions.' Unpublished document, American Civil Liberties Union Archives, Princeton University (cited in Herbert Haines, *Against Capital Punishment: The Anti-Death Penalty Movement in America, 1972–1994* (OUP 1999) 55).

8 Lockett v. Ohio, 438 U.S. 586 (1978).

9 For criticisms of "vague, open-ended terms in [the] list[s] of aggravating factors", see Steiker and Steiker, *Courting Death* (n 4) 159. They give the example of Georgia's statute, which provides as an aggravating factor that the offense "was outrageously or wantonly vile, horrible or inhuman in that it involved torture, depravity of mind, or an aggravated battery to the victim." As they note, most murders are "horrible", and phrases such as "depravity of mind" invite "subjective, idiosyncratic judgments."

10 Presnell v. Georgia, 439 U.S. 14 (1978).

11 Coker v. Georgia, 433 U.S. 584 (1977).

12 District Attorney for Suffolk Dist. v. Watson, 411 N.E.2d 1274, 1285–86 (Mass. 1980). But see Dennis D. Dorin, 'A Case Study of the Misuse of Social Science in Capital Punishment Cases: The Massachusetts Supreme Judicial Court's Findings of Racial Discrimination in *Watson* (1980)' in Kenneth C. Haas and James A. Inciardi (eds) *Challenging Capital Punishment: Legal and Social Sciences Approaches* (Sage 1988) (criticizing the decision on the grounds that there was scant empirical evidence that racial discrimination had had an impact on the death penalty in Massachusetts.) In 1982, voters approved by referendum an amendment to the state constitution that would prevent the judiciary from construing any part of the Constitution as "prohibiting the imposition of the punishment of death" (Article 116). Despite attempts to introduce capital punishment, though, Massachusetts remains an abolitionist state.

13 Coker's attorney raised the issue at oral argument, noting Georgia's authorities' "notorious and unsavory reputation for racial discrimination." Briefs of Amici Curiae also raised the point. See Randall Kennedy, *Race, Crime, and the Law* (Vintage Books 1998) 324.

14 See Eberheart v. Georgia, 206 S.E.sd 12 (1974); and Hooks v. Georgia, 210 S.E.2d 668 (1974). Cited in Kennedy, *Race* (n 13) 325.

15 ibid 325.

16 Steiker and Steiker, *Courting Death* (n 4) 97.

17 Haines, *Against Capital Punishment* (n 7) 61. For the history of the NCADP, see Eugene G. Wanger, 'National Coalition to Abolish the Death Penalty: A 30th Anniversary History' (NCADP 2006) available at http://b.3cdn.net/ncadp/715d47acf83838ca54_rlm6y8vx3.pdf.

18 Haines (n 7) 66.

19 ibid 127–128.

20 ibid 64 (emphasis in original).

21 Amnesty International, 'Declaration of Stockholm Conference on the Abolition of the Death Penalty', ACT 50/001/1977 (11 December 1977) available at https://www.amnesty.org/en/documents/act50/001/1977/en/

22 See generally, Zimring (n 4).

23 Paul J. Kaplan, 'American Exceptionalism and Racialized Inequality in American Capital Punishment' (2006) 31 Law & Social Inquiry 149, 150.

24 Marie Gottschalk, *The Prison and the Gallows: The Politics of Mass Incarceration in America* (Cambridge University Press 2006) 228–230.

25 David Garland, *Peculiar Institution: America's Death Penalty in an Age of Abolition* (OUP 2010) 22.

26 Joel F. Donahoe 'The Changing Role of Victim Impact Evidence in Capital Cases' (1999) 2 Western Criminology Review [online publication] available at http://www.westerncriminology.org/documents/WCR/v02n1/donahoe/donahoe.html.
27 Morris v Slappy 461 U.S. 1, 14 (1983).
28 See Donahoe (n 26).
29 Booth v Maryland 482 US 496 (1987).
30 Brief for Petitioner, *Aikens v California*, No 68–5027, *39–43, 50–53 (US filed Sept 10, 1971) (available on Westlaw at 1971 WL 134168) at 22.
31 William J. Bowers, *Legal Homicide: Death as Punishment in America, 1864–1982* (Northeastern University Press 1984) 226.
32 Strauder v. West Virginia, 100 U.S. 303 (1880).
33 Kenneth Williams, *Most Deserving of Death? An Analysis of the Supreme Court's Death Penalty Jurisprudence* (Ashgate 2012) 52 (arguing that "the presence of African Americans on a capital jury can literally mean the difference between life and death for the defendant.")
34 William J. Bowers, Benjamin D. Steiner, and Marla Sandys, 'Death Sentencing in Black and White: An Empirical Analysis of the Role of Jurors' Race and Jury Racial Composition' (2001) 3 University of Pennsylvania Journal of Constitutional Law 171, 192.
35 ibid 179–189; 248–249.
36 ibid 180.
37 ibid 249.
38 ibid.
39 Witherspoon v. Illinois, 391 U.S. 510 (1968); Wainwright v. Witt, 470 U.S. 412 (1985).
40 Wainwright, 470 U.S., 424 (1985) (quoting Adams v. Texas, 448 U.S. 38, 45 (1980).
41 Williams (n 33) 51. Remarkably, though, Sandra Jones has found that despite their likelihood to oppose capital punishment, black people are generally not active in the anti-death penalty movement. See Sandra J Jones, *Coalition Building in the Anti-Death Penalty Movement: Privileged Morality, Race Realities* (Lexington 2010).
42 Batson v. Kentucky, 476 U.S. 79 (1986).
43 For criticisms of the *Batson* ruling, and illustrations of its limited effect in practice, see Bowers et al, 'Death Sentencing in Black and White' (n 34); Steiker and Steiker, *Courting Death* (n 4) 106–107.
44 Batson, 476 U.S., 103 (1986) (Marshall J. dissenting).
45 ibid 105.
46 ibid 106.
47 ibid 106–07.
48 McCleskey (n 6). For a detailed exposition of this case, and its implications more broadly, see Jeffrey L Kirchmeier, *Imprisoned by the Past: Warren McCleskey and the American Death Penalty* (OUP 2015). Also see Randall Kennedy, '*McCleskey v. Kemp*: Race, Capital Punishment, and the Supreme Court' (1988) 101 Harvard Law Review 1388.
49 The authors updated their study and published it in 1990. See David C. Baldus, George G. Woodworth, and Charles A. Pulaski, Jr. *Equal Justice and the Death Penalty: A Legal and Empirical Analysis* (Northeastern University Press 1990).
50 Kirchmeier (n 48) 141. See Marvin E. Wolfgang, and Marc Riedel, 'Rape, Racial Discrimination, and the Death Penalty' in Hugo Adam Bedau and Chester M. Pierce (eds.), *Capital Punishment in the United States* (AMS Press 1976) 99–121.
51 McCleskey (n 6) 312.
52 ibid 313.
53 ibid 292.
54 ibid 314–315.

55 ibid 344 (Brennan J. dissenting).
56 ibid 339 (Brennan J. dissenting).
57 ibid 336 (Brennan J. dissenting).
58 Justice Lewis Powell, Memorandum to Law Clerk *27 (16 September 1986), archived at http://perma.cc/2F2T-DBQZ (cited in Steiker and Steiker, *Courting Death* (n 4) 102).
59 Steiker and Steiker, *Courting Death* (n 4) 102–103.
60 David C. Baldus and George Woodworth, 'Race Discrimination and the Legitimacy of Capital Punishment: Reflections on the Interaction of Fact and Perception' (2004) 53 DePaul Law Review 1411, 1438.
61 Carol S. Steiker and Jordan M. Steiker, 'Sober Second Thoughts: Reflections on Two Decades of Constitutional Regulation of Capital Punishment' (1995)109 Harvard Law Review 355, 438.
62 Jerome McCristal Culp Jr, 'Autobiography and Legal Scholarship and Teaching: Finding the Me in the Legal Academy' in Richard Delgado and Jean Stefancic (eds) *Critical Race Theory: The Cutting Edge* (2nd edn Temple University Press 2000) 487, 490 (using *McCleskey* to explain why it is imperative for legal academia to include the lived experiences of black persons, so that those who go on to serve on the US Supreme Court or Congress and so on have been imbued with an understanding of the lives of black people).
63 Dred Scott v. Sandford, 60 U.S. 393 (1857).
64 Quoted in Adam Liptak, 'A New Look at Death Sentences and Race' *The New York Times* (29 April 2008) http://www.nytimes.com/2008/04/29/us/29bar.html.
65 Michelle Alexander, *The New Jim Crow: Mass Incarceration in the Age of Colorblindness* (The New Press 2012) 77 (referring to Plessy v. Ferguson, 163 U.S. 537 (1896), in which the Court upheld the constitutionality of laws that mandated racial segregation. It was this case that gave rise to the doctrine of "separate but equal").
66 John C. Jeffries Jr., *Justice Lewis F. Powell Jr: A Biography* (Charles Scribner's Sons 1994) 451. Also see David Von Drehle, 'Retired Justice Changes Stand on Death Penalty' *Washington Post* (10 June 1994).
67 Scott Sunby, The Loss of Constitutional Faith: *McCleskey v Kemp* and the Dark Side of Procedure' (2012) 10 Ohio State Journal of Criminal Law 5.
68 Racial Justice Act (1989–1990; 101st Congress H.R. 4618) *and* Racial Justice Act (1993–1994; 103rd Congress H.R. 4017).
69 Kennedy (n 13) 347.
70 Ibid.
71 Dissenting Views on Racial Justice Act, Report 103–458, House Committee on the Judiciary, 103rd Congress, 2d Sess., 24 March 1994, at 13. Also see Daniel E. Lungren and Mark L. Krotoski, 'The Racial Justice Act of 1994 – Undermining Enforcement of the Death Penalty without Promoting Racial Justice' (1995) 20 University of Dayton Law Review 655 (the authors of this article were, respectively, the Attorney General of California and the Special Assistance Attorney General of California.)
72 Kirchmeier (n 48) 275–276.
73 Barbara O'Brien and Catherine M. Grosso, 'Confronting Race: How a Confluence of Social Movements Convinced North Carolina to Go Where the McCleskey Court Wouldn't' (2011) Michigan State Law Review 463; Kirchmeier, *Imprisoned by the Past* (n 48) 276–277; Kim Severson, 'North Carolina Repeals Law Allowing Racial Bias Claim in Death Penalty Challenges' *The New York Times* (5 June 2013) http://www.nytimes.com/2013/06/06/us/racial-justice-act-repealed-in-north-carolina.html.
74 Haines (n 7) 76.
75 Kirchmeier (n 48) 215.
76 David G. Stout, 'The Lawyers of Death Row' *New York Times Magazine* (14 February 1988) http://www.nytimes.com/1988/02/14/magazine/the-lawyers-of-death-row.html.

77 McCleskey (n 6) 315.

78 Carol S. Steiker and Jordan M. Steiker, 'Opening a Window or Building a Wall? The Effect of Eighth Amendment Death Penalty Law and Advocacy on Criminal Justice More Broadly' (2008) 11 Journal of Constitutional Law 155, 168 (stating that as a result of *McCleskey*, anti-death penalty litigators were compelled to "fram[e] constitutional challenges to the death penalty in uniquely capital terms.")

79 Stanford v. Kentucky, 492 U.S. 361 (1989); Penry v. Lynaugh, 492 U.S. 302 (1989).

80 Stanford (n 79) 378.

81 ibid 380.

82 Blystone v. Pennsylvania, 494 U.S. 310 (1990).

83 Payne v. Tennessee, 501 U.S. 808 (1991).

84 Johnson v. Texas, 509 U.S. 350 (1993).

85 Herrera v. Collins, 506 U.S. 390 (1993).

86 Arave v. Creech, 507 U.S. 463 (1993).

87 Jeffrey Kirchmeier, 'Casting a Wider Net: Another Decade of Legislative Expansion of the Death Penalty in the United States' (2006) 34 Pepperdine Law Review 1, 9.

88 Gottschalk (n 24) 216–218; Randall McGowen, 'Through the Wrong End of the Telescope: History, the Death Penalty, and the American Experience', in David Garland, Randall McGowen, and Michael Meranze (eds), *America's Death Penalty: Between Past and Present* (NYU Press) 122.

89 Gottschalk (n 24) 218–227.

90 Jack W. Germond and Jules Witcover, *Whose Broad Stripes and Bright Stars? The Trivial Pursuit of the Presidency 1988* (Warner Books 1989) (The first chapter of this book is titled "A Killer Question" emphasizing the central role that this part of the campaign played in the outcome of the election. Also see Roger Simon, 'Questions that Kill Candidate's Careers' *Politico* (20 April 2007) http://www.politico.com/story/2007/04/questions-that-kill-candidates-careers-003617 (noting that Dukakis's poll numbers dropped from 49 percent on the day before the debate, to 42 percent the day after.)

91 Alexander (n 65) 54.

92 Peter Applebome, 'The 1992 Campaign: Death Penalty; Arkansas Execution Raises Questions on Governor's Politics' *The New York Times* (25 January 1992) http://www.nytimes.com/1992/01/25/us/1992-campaign-death-penalty-arkansas-execution-raises-questions-governor-s.html Marshall Frady, 'Death in Arkansas' *The New Yorker* (22 February 1993).

93 Kirchmeier, *Imprisoned by the Past* (n 48) 217.

94 For a discussion of the impact of the Oklahoma bombings on discussions about capital punishment, see Austin Sarat, *When the State Kills: Capital Punishment and the American Condition* (Princeton University Press 2001) 3–19.

95 Callins v. Collins, 510 U.S. 1141, 1148 (1994) (Blackmun J., dissenting from denial of writ of certiorari).

96 ibid 1145.

97 ibid 1153.

98 ibid 1156.

99 ABA House of Delegates, Resolution 107 (adopted 3 February 1997).

100 Leslie Harris, ABA Section on Individual Rights and Responsibilities, *Report to the House of Delegates* (1997).

101 Arkansas (1990); Illinois (1990), Oklahoma (1990); Arizona (1992); California (1992); Delaware (1992); Wyoming (1992); Washington (1993); Idaho (1994); Maryland (1994); Nebraska (1994); Montana (1995); Pennsylvania (1995); Oregon (1996); Colorado (1997); Kentucky (1997); Ohio (1999). This data is taken from Death Penalty Information Center, Executions in the United States https://deathpenaltyinfo.org/executions-united-states.

102 Gallup, 'Death Penalty' http://www.gallup.com/poll/1606/death-penalty.aspx
103 Death Penalty Information Center, 'Death Sentences by Year Since 1976' .https://deathpenaltyinfo.org/death-sentences-year-1977-present.
104 Haines (n 7).
105 ibid 103.
106 ibid 163.
107 ibid 5.
108 Andy Hoover and Ken Cunningham, 'Framing, Persuading, Messaging, and Messengers: How the Death Penalty Abolition Movement Succeeded in New Jersey' (2014) 38(4) Humanity and Society 443, 458.
109 David Snow, E. Burke Rochford Jr, Steven K. Worden, and Robert D. Benford, 'Frame Alignment Process, Micromobilization, and Movement Participation' (1986) 51 American Sociological Review 464 (cited in Haines, 19).
110 Haines (n 7) 19 (emphasis in original).
111 ibid 169.
112 ibid.
113 ibid 206.
114 ibid 87–92 (noting that the issue of innocence has been stressed by anti-death penalty campaigners, but that the "relatively few instances" of innocent people being convicted and actually executed means that such episodes are taken as "indications of how *well* the nation's procedural safeguards worked").
115 ibid 199.
116 Rob Warden, 'How and Why Illinois Abolished the Death Penalty' (2012) 30 Minnesota Journal of Law & Inequality 245.
117 Lawrence C. Marshall, 'The Innocence Revolution and the Death Penalty' (2004) 1 Ohio State Journal of Criminal Law 573, 574.
118 ibid 577.
119 ibid 576.
120 There are many studies about the costs of capital punishment. This is a mere selection: Nicole C. Brambila and Liam Migdail-Smith, 'Executing Justice: A Look at the Cost of Pennsylvania's Death Penalty' *Reading Eagle* (19 June 2016) (finding that Pennsylvania has spent $272 million on each execution since 1978); Peter A. Collins, Robert C. Boruchowitz, Matthew J. Hickman, and Mark A. Larrañaga, 'An Analysis of the Economic Costs of Seeking the Death Penalty in Washington State' (Seattle University, 1 January 2015) (finding that the state spends on average $1 million more on a death penalty case than for cases in which death has not been sought); 'An Analysis of the Economic Costs of Capital Punishment in Oklahoma' Appendix 1B of the Report of the Oklahoma Death Penalty Review Commission (March 2017) https://www.courthousenews.com/wp-content/uploads/2017/04/OklaDeathPenalty.pdf See generally 'Costs of the Death Penalty' Death Penalty Information Center https://deathpenaltyinfo.org/costs-death-penalty#financialfacts.
121 Jolie McLaughlin, 'The Price of Justice: Interest-Convergence, Cost, and the Anti-Death Penalty Movement' (2014) 108 Northwestern University Law Review 675, 675.
122 Haines (n 7) 137 ("A few anti-death penalty activists and litigators have given their explicit support to LWOP," and "most of them [anti-death penalty activists] resist coming out in favour of LWOP".
123 This is correct as of December 2017. See 'Affiliates by State' NCADP, http://www.ncadp.org/affiliates/all.
124 See http://conservativesconcerned.org/ . CCADP is part of Equal Justice Initiative USA, which is an affiliate of the NCADP.
125 Conservatives Concerned About the Death Penalty, 'Why We're Concerned' http://conservativesconcerned.org/why-were-concerned/fairness/.
126 Conservatives Concerned About the Death Penalty, 'Fair and Equal Under the Law?' http://conservativesconcerned.org/why-were-concerned/fairness/.

127 Austin Sarat, 'The Rhetoric of Race in the 'New Abolitionism'' in Charles J. Ogletree Jr and Austin Sarat (eds), *From Lynch Mobs to the Killing State: Race and the Death Penalty in America* (NYU Press 2006) 263.
128 Fatimah Loren Muhammad, 'Justice from Within: The Death Penalty and a New Vision for Criminal Justice through a Racial Justice Lens' *Nonprofit Quarterly* (28 November 2017) https://nonprofitquarterly.org/2017/11/28/justice-within-death-penalty-new-vision-criminal-justice-racial-justice-lens/.
129 Sarat (n 127) 277.
130 This is explained and discussed in Chapter Seven.
131 Angela Y Davis, *Are Prisons Obsolete?* (Seven Stories Press 2003)
132 See 'About Us', on the website of Equal Justice USA at https://ejusa.org/about-us/
133 Muhammad (n 128)
134 The website of the Eighth Amendment Project contains scant information about the Project itself. See http://www.8thamendment.org/#ABOUT. The Head of the Project – Henderson Hill – and the litigation director – Robert Smith – revealed more about the Project in an interview with the online newspaper, BuzzFeed. See Chris Geidner, 'The Most Ambitious Effort Yet To Abolish The Death Penalty Is Already Happening' *BuzzFeed* (9 November 2015)
135 Steiker and Steiker, *Courting Death* (n 4) 210
136 See Mary Sidney K. Harbert, *Justice Taking Root: A 40 Year History of the Southern Center for Human Rights 1976–2016* (Southern Center for Human Rights 2016) https://www.schr.org/files/post/files/Justice-Taking-Root-40-Year-History-of-SCHR.pdf
137 See The Movement for Black Lives https://policy.m4bl.org/end-war-on-black-people/. The Movement lists 10 demands in its quest to "End the War on Black People", and the abolition of capital punishment is the second in the list.

4 Abolitionism defined

I. Introduction

A recurrent theme since the days of legal slavery is that anti-slavery and anti-racist efforts have shaped anti-death penalty efforts. We need to unpack this, though, since abolitionism is not a monolithic phenomenon. The men and women who opposed slavery, like those who oppose capital punishment today, had diverse aims and ideologies, which led to differences in their preferred strategies and tactics. A central contention of mine is that anti-death penalty efforts are an iteration of *radical* slavery abolitionism, and it follows that a detailed explanation of "radical abolitionism" is required. After setting out the usual distinctions that are drawn between the radical abolitionists and others, we will see the centrality of the idea of dignity to radical abolitionism. This provides us with the framework for understanding and evaluating anti-death penalty efforts in the rest of the book.

II. Distinguishing between "slavery abolitionism" and "anti-slavery activism"

Ira Berlin – one of America's most prominent historians – has said: "History is not about the past; it is about arguments that we have about the past."[1] Academic understandings, as well as popular attitudes, towards the slavery abolitionists are not uniform, and have been the subject of much disagreement. Some of these disagreements have been premised on political agendas. When white communities in the post-emancipation era sought to entrench domination over non-whites, for example, slavery abolitionists were cast as fanatics who caused a needless Civil War.[2] The civil rights activists of the 1950s and 1960s, on the other hand, painted a more favorable picture of the abolitionists, as they claimed to be continuing the work of those who fought for racial justice in the antebellum era.[3]

Scholars without a political agenda have also disagreed over the historical record. Manisha Sinha, for example, has recently argued that historians have tended to overlook the centrality of black abolitionists to the movement.[4] And while many people today admire the abolitionists, some scholars have cast doubt on whether they should be praised as such. Andrew Delbanco and Thomas Fleming, for example, have argued that the radical abolitionists were too uncompromising in their rhetoric and actions, and should have adopted a more centrist approach to ending bondage.[5]

With these disagreements in mind, a useful starting point is to look at the diverse aims, ideologies, and strategies of those who opposed slavery. The term "anti-slavery" has been used to describe the ideologies and the tactics and strategies of a certain group of people who opposed slavery, but maintained a belief in keeping society segregated on grounds of race. They espoused genteel, non-emotional types of argumentation, and supported the idea of gradual emancipation. "Anti-slavery" activists tended to limit their focus to slavery, eschewing other social injustices such as the subjugation of women. It was not that they did not care about such issues, but rather that they thought it prudent to concentrate their efforts on one issue. And in some instances, they endorsed notions of white supremacy and suggested that freed black people should not be permitted to live alongside whites in America. It was in these senses that they were moderate, or conservative, rather than radical in their outlook or actions.

The Pennsylvania Abolition Society (PAS), established in 1775, was emblematic of the "anti-slavery" point of view. Richard Newman writes that

> the PAS condemned "overzealous" abolitionist activity, including emotionalism, enthusiasm, or anything that smacked of fervent behavior. Fever-pitched tactics, many of the group's legal counselors and official representatives warned, threatened the reasoned, sure-handed approach of PAS elites. The Pennsylvania society regarded its members as diligent reformers and respectable men who pursued specific legal and political objectives with vigor but never fervency.[6]

Moreover, "the group cherished elite activists, particularly lawyers. In short, the PAS believed that abolitionism would succeed only by utilizing the governmental and legal institutions of men (certain men), not the universe of God, to end slavery."[7] In other words, they generally rejected appeals to a "higher law" against which slavery could be judged. The PAS concentrated on legal argumentation instead of issuing polemics against the immorality of slavery: "We hope to subserve the cause in courts of adjudicature",[8] read a 1789 declaration. Although members also urged legislators to bring about an end to slavery, they resolutely avoided moralistic critiques of slavery, and refrained from questioning the virtues of the wider legal and political system.

The principle of "gradualism" was central to PAS and other conservative anti-slavery activists. They proposed legislation such as that adopted in Pennsylvania, which only provided for the freedom of those born after March 1, 1780. In other words, slavery would gradually be abolished as existing slaves passed away, and no new black people would replace them.[9] There were several reasons for endorsing the gradual emancipation of slaves, revealing some of the different motivations and ideologies of those opposed to bondage. Some truly believed that all slaves deserved to be freed with immediate effect, but felt that a phased abolition was preferable so that the social and political order could manage the upheaval that emancipation would bring. Others truly believed that black people were not ready for freedom, either because they were biologically and morally inferior, or because decades of bondage had rendered them unprepared for the duties and responsibilities of citizenship. A gradual approach to emancipation was therefore required so that black people could be educated about how to live a life of freedom.[10]

The same beliefs that underpinned gradualism also underpinned the suggestion of colonization. Founded in 1816, the American Colonization Society proposed that black people be freed from bondage but sent to colonies outside America. There were pragmatic and principled rationales for this suggestion. Some believed that white communities would not agree to emancipation if that meant racial integration, and the suggestion of colonization was therefore a tactical measure to get such communities on side. For others, blacks were so intellectually inferior that they would not cope living alongside whites.[11] Whether colonization was supported as a tactical measure or as a matter of principle, we can see how these opponents of slavery did not embrace the idea of racial equality, and contributed to the entrenchment of racial prejudices. The American Anti-Slavery Society staked this position in 1834 when it declared that it did not favor granting civil rights to blacks, and opposed admitting blacks into white society beyond what their "intellectual and moral worth" deserved.[12] Yet other opponents of slavery – referred to by some as "non-extensionists" – were merely opposed to the spread of slavery, seemingly content to see bondage remain in areas where it was already legal.[13]

"Abolitionists" had a distinctly different mindset. They tended to be inspired by religious and humanitarian impulses, and issued polemical denunciations of the moral wrong of slavery. Abolitionists opposed gradualism, and took the view that abolitionism must encompass not just the physical freedom of blacks, but also the granting of equal rights and opportunities in a post-emancipation America. They were radical in that they tied the problem of slavery to broader social injustices, drawing attention to issues such as women's rights, and thus called for a radical overhaul of the constitutional and social order.

Scholars have tended to identify the period around 1830 as the time when "abolitionism" came to the fore, noting the moment in January 1831 when William Lloyd Garrison published the first issue of the abolitionist newspaper, *The Liberator*.[14] Garrison understood the limitations of the law and took issue with William Goodell's view that since slavery was a legal institution, its abolition depended on "nothing more nor less than the repeal of these slave laws".[15] Garrison argued that mere repeal of the law would be meaningless "without transformation of the spirit that the law reflected."[16] Lydia Maria Child expressed this sentiment well in 1842, when she remarked: "Great political changes may be forced by the pressure of external circumstances, without a corresponding change in the moral sentiment of a nation; but in all cases, the change is worse than useless; the evil reappears, and usually in a more exaggerated form."[17]

The radical abolitionists recognized the importance of transforming the consciences of the general public, to shake them out of their support for, or apathy towards, slavery. This tactic – referred to as "moral suasion" – was exemplified by the actions of Theodore Dwight Weld, one of the movement's most effective orators. As well as undertaking innumerable public lectures on the subject of slavery, Weld organized the first nationwide petition campaign, seeking to convert large swathes of people to the abolitionist cause.[18] This was a far cry from the PAS's emphasis on focusing on society's so-called elite. In contrast to the PAS's "distinctly conservative style of activism",[19] Garrison and his followers were radical in their outlook and actions, jettisoning the composed, conciliatory tone of the likes of the PAS. "I will be as harsh as truth, and uncompromising as justice", Garrison wrote in the first issue of *The Liberator*, "… I am in earnest, I will not equivocate, I will not excuse, I will not retreat a single inch, and I will be heard."[20]

When Garrison called for the immediate abolition of slavery, he did not literally mean that slavery could be abolished overnight as a practical matter. His concern was with the effects that the rhetoric of gradualism had on the mindsets of Americans. Condoning gradualism, he believed, would necessarily prolong slaves' suffering, and would lead to complacency among abolitionists who would think their work was done upon the enactment of a gradual emancipation law. He was also concerned that the premises of gradualism entrenched the belief that black people were somehow inferior to whites and unable to live as free whites did.

Garrison was explicitly inspired by the black abolitionist David Walker, who in 1829 had argued against gradualism and other conservative anti-slavery measures. Walker claimed that white anti-slavery activists who championed gradualism and colonization contributed to, rather than diminished, the subjugation of black people.[21] In this sense, it is perhaps Walker and other black abolitionists who should be attributed with the birth of immediatism as a strategy, and the historian Manisha Sinha has recently emphasized that black abolitionists were central to the radicalism of the movement.[22] Either way, "immediatism" should be understood as a slogan or a mindset which conveyed the urgency and importance of emancipation. In the words of Garrison: "We have never said that slavery would be overthrown by a single blow; that it ought to be, we shall always contend."[23]

A further aspect of "abolitionism" that rendered it a radical movement was the recognition that slavery was the worst of a range of sins that plagued American society. Slavery, the abolitionists understood, could not be conceptually divorced from other issues such as the mistreatment of free blacks, the subjugation of women, and the degrading treatment of those convicted of criminal offenses, for example. They therefore challenged the institutions that supported slavery and these other sins, as well as the structure and ideology of contemporary conceptions of liberal democracy and the existing constitutional order.[24] Some, such as Garrison, went so far as to call for an outright rejection of the US Constitution, which he considered to be inherently pro-slavery and thus an insurmountable barrier to the goals of radical abolition.

Recently, Manisha Sinha and Ira Berlin have provided accounts of abolition that emphasize continuity within anti-slavery and abolitionist efforts, eschewing the suggestion that the period around 1830 marked a fundamental change in the history of efforts to end involuntary bondage.[25] Garrison's views certainly did not develop overnight, and both authors are correct to point out that enslaved and free blacks had claimed since the Revolutionary era that slavery should end immediately and that black people should have equal standing to whites. The abolition of slavery was a long process, stretching from the earliest days of the American Revolution through to 1865, and at no point in this process did one approach to abolition exist to the exclusion of other approaches. Regardless of *when* radical abolitionism emerged, or who was responsible for developing radicalism as an ideology, what matters for our purposes is that radical abolitionism differed from other types of anti-slavery efforts.

III. Distinguishing between "death penalty abolitionism" and "anti-death penalty activism"

Using the outline above, it does not take much of an intellectual leap to identify similar, albeit not identical, differences in the ideologies and proposed tactics among the women and men who today oppose state-sanctioned executions. We saw in the previous chapter that following the decision in *McCleskey v. Kemp*, the anti-death penalty movement has tended to frame the case against capital punishment in terms that are unique to the phenomenon of state-sanctioned executions, just like the PAS framed the issue of slavery in narrow terms. We also saw that the narratives of innocence and costs eschew moral argumentation, rendering contemporary anti-death penalty discourses rather distinct to the discourses of the radical slavery abolitionists. The prominence of life without parole in current anti-death penalty discourses likewise mirrors the prominence of colonization in anti-slavery efforts: both involve either a tactical compromise, or a principled belief that "undesirables" should be permanently excluded from "our" society.

I think it is inaccurate, though, to characterize today's anti-death penalty movement as conservative, or moderate and merely "anti-death penalty." For a number of reasons, today's movement is better understood as an iteration of the radical slavery abolitionists. To begin with, almost all opponents of capital punishment advocate for the immediate, rather than gradual abolition of the death penalty in the spirit of Walker and Garrison. Even though legislative repeal in the likes of New Mexico have been prospective only, in a manner comparable to the Pennsylvania gradual emancipation law, abolitionists today are still immediatists as a point of principle. Moreover, though, the allegedly conservative and moderate frames of innocence, costs, and LWOP all operate under the banner of a radical framework that situates the moral wrong of capital punishment within broader concerns with a criminal justice system that does not take the idea of dignity seriously. The rest of this chapter sets out the idea of dignity in moral and political philosophy, and in US constitutional law, so that we can better understand the centrality of dignity to radical abolitionism.[26]

IV. Abolitionism and dignity

The notion that human beings have dignity is a popular one in moral and political philosophy. Hugo Adam Bedau was of the view that "[h]uman dignity is perhaps the premier value underlying the last two centuries of moral and political thought."[27] The idea has taken root in legal orders across the world too. In 2013, Christopher McCrudden suggested that "[t]he concept of human dignity has probably never been so omnipresent in everyday speech, or so deeply embedded in political and legal discourse."[28] The idea of human dignity is at the heart of instruments of international human rights law, with the Universal Declaration of Human Rights stating that "the inherent dignity and… the equal and inalienable rights of all members of the human family is the foundation of freedom, justice and peace in the world".[29] Dignity also forms the basis of several domestic legal systems. Article 1 of the German Basic Law reads: "Human dignity shall be inviolable. To respect and protect it shall be the duty of all state authority." Article 7 of the Constitution of the Republic of South Africa explains that human dignity is the basis of that country's Bill of Rights: "This Bill of Rights is a cornerstone of democracy in South Africa. It enshrines the rights of all people in our country and affirms the democratic values of human dignity, equality and freedom." Article 10 reads: "Everyone has inherent dignity and the right to have their dignity respected and protected."

In contrast, the word "dignity" does not appear at all in the text of the US Constitution. For some commentators, this means that dignity is not protected in US law, and that the US Supreme Court should not base judgments on the idea of dignity.[30] James Whitman has suggested that the absence of dignity as a controlling value in the US constitutional order explains the propensity of Americans to support "harsh justice" – including the death penalty – relative to Germany and France.[31] For this reason, it might seem pointless for anti-death penalty advocates to frame the case against capital punishment in dignitarian terms. Daniel LaChance makes this point when he says that "[a]rguing that the death penalty is an affront to human dignity just doesn't work."[32] However, not only has the US Supreme Court repeatedly stated that the idea of dignity is central to the Eighth Amendment prohibition on "cruel and unusual punishments",[33] it is precisely the idea of dignity that renders abolitionism radical in the sense outlined above. Although the idea of dignity is jurisprudentially and philosophically fraught, we can use both slavery and death penalty abolitionist argumentation to understand not just *how* abolitionism centers on the idea of dignity, but also why efforts to end capital punishment *must* center on such an idea. As explained below, today's death penalty abolitionists recognize, just as the slavery abolitionists recognized, that the practice in question engages the dignity of the people involved, the dignity of the wider community, and the dignity, or integrity of the broader constitutional and legal order that permits such practices.

A. Human dignity

i. Definitions of human dignity

At a very rudimentary level, we can say that "dignity" refers to the quality that makes a human being "human". This is not meant solely in a biological sense, though. That is, it is not simply a means of differentiating humans from other entities for the purposes of classification in a positive, morally neutral sense. Rather, the term dignity reflects the widely held moral view that human beings occupy a special place in the strata of living and non-living things. Thus, we afford more importance to humans, and protect human beings in ways, and to extents, that we do not necessarily protect non-human animals, the environment, or inanimate property. To treat a person without respect for their human dignity, then, is to "dehumanize" them, or to degrade them to the status of something other than a member of the human community.

This basic account will not suffice, though, for it still does not provide a philosophical or legal grounding for what respect for dignity actually entails, other than the vague notion of treating a person as a human being. Some questions that need addressing are: What is it about human beings that mean we have dignity? Is dignity a principle that guides our moral conduct, in the sense that we should "act with dignity"? Or is it a right that we can assert against others, to dictate their conduct towards us? Can a person "lose" their dignity, perhaps because of their immoral (undignified) conduct, or perhaps because another person "breaches" or "violates" their dignity by inflicting pain, suffering, or humiliation upon them? Do people only have dignity in a legal sense if there is a positive law granting a "right to dignity", as in the German Basic Law or the South African Constitution, or does the possession of dignity pre-exist the development of the law, thus rendering laws such as the Eighth Amendment to the US Constitution in the service of protecting dignity? Can legal officials remove, or curtail, a person's dignity in light of their moral attributes and conduct, or some other characteristic such as skin color? A failure to satisfactorily address these questions, especially given the absence of the term "dignity" form the text of the US Constitution, gives credence to the view of Raoul Berger, who has condemned judges who invoke the term dignity in constitutional interpretation. "Respect for 'human dignity'", Berger writes, "clearly is spun out of thin air; it is an evangelistic exhortation rather than a constitutional mandate."[34] Berger's concern is that, because of the vagaries of the term, judges who invoke the idea of dignity are simply imposing their own personal moral preferences when deciding cases, rather than interpreting the law.

The etymology of dignity is a helpful point of departure for grappling with philosophical accounts of dignity, which in turn deepen legal understandings of dignity and the way in which abolitionist discourses center around this idea. The word derives from the Latin "dignitas", which referred to the higher social rank of Senators and other noblemen in ancient Rome.[35] Such people, it was believed, should be treated with a certain degree of honor and respect that other people – commoners – did not necessarily deserve. This belief continues in a modified form today – we often speak of "dignitaries" when referring to statesmen and stateswomen, or other people such as the Pope, who have a particular social standing that warrants treatment not normally afforded to "ordinary" people. Generally, though, the idea of dignity has evolved since the era of ancient Rome, and has come to encompass respect for all people by virtue of them belonging to the human community, regardless of social status. During the Enlightenment era, as Europeans turned away from monarchies and towards democratic rule, societies came to believe that all human beings have inherent worth, and thus should be treated equally respectfully. They rejected the special status given to some, but not to others. To be sure, their view of equality was different from contemporary accounts, in that women, non-whites, and non-propertied men were generally considered to be inferior. However, the Enlightenment nonetheless represented a break from the past in this respect.

This account of dignity – the requirement to treat each person as worthy in and of themselves – is usually associated with Immanuel Kant. In the *Groundwork for Metaphysics of Morals*, first published in 1785, Kant proposed that human beings are marked by their capacity for rational thought, and the ability to act as free autonomous agents.[36] As such, they can never be used as a means to an end. That is, every person must treat every other person with respect for each other's rationality and autonomy. Importantly for Kant, people do not differ in their worth, and they are to be respected and treated equally. This is what he means when he says that every person has inherent dignity.

Kant's conception of human dignity requires every person to treat every other person with both positive respect, and negative respect. That is, respect for dignity requires the provision of circumstances to enable another to act autonomously, as well as refraining from inflicting treatment that is contrary to the other's autonomy and rationality.[37] It is clear, then, that dignity as "inner worth" can be implicated in a number of different situations, including the infliction of physical or psychological pain and suffering (such as treatment during bondage or time on death row), and the denial of free will (such as being executed, or being held in bondage). It is in this sense that Kant's ideas resonated in the proclamations of those radical slavery abolitionists who insisted that abolition encompass not just physical freedom, but also the provision of legal rights and political and social opportunities to black people.

Ronald Dworkin develops this idea of dignity as something that is inherent in all human beings, and his conception of dignity matches the twin demands of the slavery abolitionists: liberty and equal treatment. Dworkin writes that dignity entails two principles, the first being the "intrinsic and objective importance of how a human life is lived."[38] His second principle is that of personal responsibility: "the responsibility to make and execute ultimate decisions about what life would be a good one to lead. We may not subordinate ourselves to the will of other human beings in making those decisions; we must not accept the right of anyone else to force us to conform to a view of success that but for that coercion we would not choose."[39] Taken together, we can say that dignity entails the ideals of equality (all human lives are intrinsically and objectively important) and liberty (all humans should have freedom to determine the direction of one's own life).

Not everybody will be convinced by Kant or Dworkin. Ruth Macklin complains that "appeals to dignity are either vague restatements of other, more precise notions or mere slogans that add nothing to the understanding of the topic." In her view, "[d]ignity is a useless concept. It means no more than respect for persons or their autonomy."[40] In a similar vein, Gerhold Becker has suggested that dignity is nothing more than a "rhetorical device" which people adopt when they are attempting to strengthen some moral argument.[41] For example, in debates about abortion, the person who is intuitively in favor of a woman's right to choose will focus on the "dignity" of the woman, whereas a person who is intuitively in favor of a fetus' right to life will emphasize the "dignity" of the fetus in the same debates. In such cases, the term dignity serves no useful purpose for resolving moral dilemmas.

In political and legal debates about slavery and capital punishment, the idea of dignity has similarly been invoked by anti-abolitionists as well as by the abolitionists themselves. Slavery was both attacked as an affront to the dignity of those enslaved, and justified as necessary to protect the dignity of white people. When capital punishment is criticized for violating the dignity of the condemned person, it is often defended as a means of respecting the dignity of the victim of the crime that has attracted a death sentence in the first place. Louis Pojman has expressed this point of view: "the use of capital punishment respects the worth of the victim in calling for an equal punishment to be exacted from the offender."[42] Moreover, Pojman writes, "[h]uman beings have dignity as self-conscious rational agents who are able to act morally. One could maintain that it is precisely their moral goodness or innocence that bestows dignity and a right to life on them. Intentionally taking the life of an innocent human being is so evil that absent mitigating circumstances, the perpetrator forfeits his own right to life. He or she deserves to die."[43] Kant would disagree that a person can forfeit their dignity through immoral conduct. In fact, Kant argued that the death penalty was actually required for those who commit murder in order to respect the inherent dignity of the murderer. His support for proportionate retribution – the ius talionis – led him to believe that "whatever undeserved evil you inflict upon another within the people, that you inflict upon yourself".[44] In Kant's view a murderer must be executed, because they have willed the taking of life into universal law.[45]

It is not self-evident, then, that respect for dignity actually requires abolition of capital punishment. That is, the idea of dignity is not axiomatically helpful for eradicating values or practices that some people consider to be antithetical to liberalist notions of human rights. Michael Rosen explains how the idea of dignity has been used as "a Trojan horse for religiously inspired attacks on equality", citing the example of 19th-Century Catholics using dignity to problematize the concepts of popular sovereignty and equality that were central to the French Revolution.[46]

It is important to turn to another concern with Kant's account of dignity. This lies in his emphasis on rationality and the capacity to determine one's own moral choices. Mary Ford Neal points out that, under this account, babies and certain categories of mentally ill people cannot be said to have "dignity" since they lack the ability to make decisions for themselves. Almost nobody would adhere to the view that it would be permissible to inflict pain on a baby, or to treat a baby without respect for their status as a human being, solely on the basis that a baby cannot think rationally. Indeed, a baby's vulnerability is often cited as a reason for providing extra care when it comes to their treatment. Building on Martha Fineman's work, Neal suggests that it is a person's vulnerability that endows them with dignity. All human beings are vulnerable in at least two ways. First, their well-being depends, to varying extents, on other people. Second, every person is at risk of harm from other people. In her words: "even the *least* vulnerable human being is still fundamentally, and inescapably, vulnerable in the negative sense, since none of us can meet her basic needs and satisfy her core desires without the co-operation of others; and even the most capable adult is vulnerable to hurt and harm, both physical and emotional."[47] Neal points out that we not only commit ourselves to respecting the dignity of those who cannot assert their own responsibility or moral choices, such as babies, but we also take steps to ensure that those people's dignity is not at risk by providing them with, for example, shelter and food.

The point to take from the above account is that we ascribe dignity to all human beings in recognition of every human being's inherent worth, whether that worth derives from rationality, autonomy, or vulnerability. This takes us back to the rudimentary account that I offered above: that the idea of dignity reflects the moral view that human beings occupy a more important place in the strata of all living and non-living things, regardless of their social status within the human community. As an inherent characteristic, it is not something that a person can lose, as such. To say that a person does not have dignity – perhaps because of their conduct or skin color – is to say that that person is not a human being, yet while we might figuratively describe a person as an "animal" or a "monster", such exhortations do not literally turn that person into an animal or other non-human entity. Justice Thomas has made this point in the context of criticizing the invocation of dignity in constitutional interpretation. In *Obergefell v. Hodges*, decided in 2014, the Court held that state prohibitions on marriages of people of the same sex were contrary to the Fourteenth Amendment to the Constitution, with Justice Kennedy stating that "[Petitioners] ask for equal dignity in the eyes of the law. The Constitution grants them that right."[48] Dissenting, Justice Thomas wrote that "[t]he flaw in that reasoning, of course, is that the Constitution contains no 'dignity' Clause". Even if the Constitution did contain such a Clause, Thomas opines, "the government would be incapable of bestowing dignity" because dignity is innate and cannot be granted or taken away from the person. Thomas uses the example of slavery to make this point: "Slaves did not lose their dignity (any more than they lost their humanity) because the government allowed them to be enslaved."[49] Thomas's criticism is important here for two reasons. First, it reflects the view that all human beings, regardless of their perceived moral status, have dignity. Second, Thomas betrays a lack of understanding of how, even if dignity is innate and cannot be "lost", it is still plausible for a person or government to treat another person *without respect* for this dignity. That is, Thomas's criticism inadvertently reveals the importance of *respect* for another's dignity. It is in this sense, then, that dignity refers to more than the intrinsic worth of the individual, but also to the way in which other individuals – or a community of individuals – treat that person.

Today, it seems almost axiomatic that antebellum slavery was contrary to the requirement to respect the dignity of all persons, whichever account of dignity we hold – dignity as autonomy, or rationality, or vulnerability. One of the leading historians of slavery, David Brion Davis, has described the "basic 'problem of slavery'" as the "paradox of trying to reduce a human being to salable chattel". It was a paradox, Davis writes, because treating a slave as property was fundamentally incompatible with "the irreducible human dignity of the slave."[50] Ronald Dworkin writes that "the cruelest aspect of slavery, for the abolitionists… was its failure to recognize a slave's right to decide issues of value for himself or herself." As such, Dworkin writes, "[t]he most powerful arguments against slavery before the Civil War, and for equal protection after it, were framed in the language of dignity".[51]

Although the contention that slavery is incompatible with respect for dignity is something we take for granted today, this was not the case in antebellum America, just as it is contemporaneously not the case that capital punishment is contrary to the requirement to respect dignity.[52] We can use contemporary understandings of how slavery was incompatible with respect for dignity, though, to understand how the death penalty is similarly incompatible with respect for dignity. This will give an indication of how abolitionism can and should be, to use Dworkin's words, "framed in the language of dignity."

ii. Human dignity, slavery, and the death penalty

A popular pro-slavery argument was that bondage was a "positive good" for blacks, since they were innately uncivilized and therefore unable to care for themselves without descending into savagery.[53] In this sense, slavery was a response to the particular vulnerability of black people. Just as Mary Ford Neal's account of dignity is premised on protecting those who are vulnerable, so the pro-slavery lobby claimed to be concerned with the vulnerability of black people. Of course, the so-called "scientific" studies on which the "positive good" argument was based were incontrovertibly wrong, and it is simply baffling today to think that slavery was in any way premised on a genuine concern for the welfare or vulnerability of black people. The point remains, though, that at that time, it was claimed that slavery was compatible with respect for dignity, on account of black people's vulnerability.

Slavery was not always portrayed as a positive good, though, and in many circumstances defenders of bondage implicitly accepted the incompatibility of slavery with dignity by simply refusing to countenance the idea that black people belonged to the human community. That is, they emphasized the innate inferiority and physiological difference of black people. An example of this approach to pro-slavery discourses is J. H. Van Evrie's *Negroes and Negro 'Slavery': The First an Inferior Race: The Latter its Normal Condition*, published in 1861.[54] In this book, Van Evrie took abolitionists to task for claiming that black people were equal to whites. He does this by asserting that black people are biologically distinct to the superior white race, and although he does not use the word dignity, Van Evrie nonetheless couches his argument in the language of dignity that we find in the likes of Kant and Dworkin. He notes, for example, that it is an entity's innate capacities that dictate how they are to be treated:

> If the Creator had designed Horse for food, He would have created him differently, and, instead of the tough and stringy muscles so appropriate to strength and swiftness, would have constructed him with reference to human digestion. And if He had designed the Negro for the same purpose as the white or Caucasian man, He would have given him the same faculties – or rather we should say, he would not have been created at all.[55]

Van Evrie does not literally equate "Negroes" with animals – indeed, he specifically states that black people share more in common with white people than with animals. However, he asserts that all life on earth can be placed on an ascending scale, with white people at the top of the scale since they are "the most elaborate in his structure, and therefore the highest endowed in his faculties".[56] Since "Negroes" do not share these faculties, they are not to be treated as the equals of whites. Van Evrie goes so far as to say that the natural order will be dangerously upended if abolitionists were to succeed in their aim:

> if their monstrous crusade against the harmony of nature as well as the progress of society could be successfully carried out, the nation would not only go back to the anti-progressive and brutalizing 'system' of Europe, and the masses degenerate again into the wretched serfs or slaves of kings and aristocrats, but, intermingling their blood with an inferior race…, they would become the most degraded and contemptible assemblage of mongrels – of monster women and emasculated men – ever known upon the face of the earth.[57]

Van Evrie's beliefs were common in the antebellum era, with a range of so-called "scientific" studies detailing the ways in which black people were biologically and physiologically inferior to whites, and therefore undeserving of the same respect that was to be shown to whites. Black people and slaves were not just compared to animals, though. They were also construed as inanimate property, or "chattel personal". Harriet Beecher Stowe, for example, explained that the slave codes of the South were "designed to keep millions of human beings in the condition of chattels personal".[58] George Stroud made similar remarks: "the cardinal principle of slavery", he wrote, is the idea "that the slave is to be regarded as a thing,–is an article of property,–a chattel personal".[59]

Since they were treated as something other than a fully-fledged member of the human community, slaves were compelled to claim that they should not be treated as such. It was this feature of slavery, Bernard Boxhill writes, that illustrates the incompatibility of bondage with the idea of dignity. The institution of "slavery mocked the human dignity of the slaves", Boxhill writes,[60] because it treated slaves' claims to natural rights as "absurd, or beneath serious consideration."[61] In other words, it was not so much the *treatment* of slaves per se that violated their dignity, but rather it was the *response* of the pro-slavery lobby to the slaves' *claims* of how they should be treated. Slavery was a violation of dignity because it compelled slaves to argue that they should be treated with equal respect and concern, even though white communities assumed such respect and concern for themselves. In Boxhill's words: "the person who has human dignity will take it for granted that – without any question, hesitation, or need for the merest argument – he is entitled to every fundamental moral consideration any society assumes for its members."[62] By not being able to take this entitlement for granted, slaves were made to feel undignified, even if we accept Justice Thomas's claim that their inherent dignity could not be taken away.

Boxhill's comments resonate with one of the central tenets of critical race theory, which is that the formal legal recognition of racial equality under the Fourteenth Amendment is insufficient because in a cultural sense black people have to meet the pre-ordained standard of "whiteness" in order to enjoy equality. That is, "whiteness" is the default standard that black people have to abide by before being accepted as equals.[63] Black people, then, have to make claims about their moral attributes, conduct, and quality that white people are assumed to possess. We see this acutely in the context of modern day shootings of black people by police officers. In almost every case, claims are made about the moral attributes of the deceased person in order to explain why that person should not have been killed.[64] At this juncture, we can tentatively see how the assault on black people's dignity reflects the lack of integrity in the legal and social institutions that demands black people today, like slaves in the antebellum era, to *claim* that they are entitled to moral consideration, before being granted such consideration. This is a theme returned to below.

Frederick Douglass – perhaps the most famous of all former slaves who played a leading role in the abolitionist movement – emphasized in his memoirs how he and other slaves were treated like animals:

> We were all ranked together at the valuation. Men and women, old and young, married and single, were ranked with horses, sheep, and swine. There were horses and men, cattle and women, pigs and children, all holding the same rank in the scale of being, and were all subjected to the same narrow examination.... We had no more voice in that decision than the brutes among whom we were ranked.[65]

Other writers used similar imagery in their slave narratives, and this imagery illustrates the lack of respect for the dignity of slaves in two ways. First, it comports with the definition of dignity that depends on the fundamental biological differences between humans and non-human animals ("all holding the same rank in the scale of being"). Second, it comports with the definitions of dignity that are connected with the concept of autonomy ("We had no more voice in that decision...").

In the context of the death penalty, we find similar sentiments in the writings of those who have been on death row. Nick Yarris, who spent 13 years on death row in Pennsylvania before being exonerated, writes about his wait for a potential transfer to a prison that was notorious for the violence inflicted on prisoners by the guards: "I was shivering as I stood there in my handcuffs and leg irons, dressed only in a prison-issue yellow jumpsuit, lined up in the cold night air like a farm animal ready to be transported to the slaughter house."[66] Yarris also describes the day-to-day conditions of life on death row: "we are only allowed out on weekdays for our 30 minutes of exercise in these dog kennel-like cages behind the Death Row building – although I wouldn't put a full-sized animal in a cage like the ones they make us use."[67] Another exoneree – Anthony Graves – has also described "12 years of having my meals slid through a small slot in a steel door like an animal."[68]

Some might retort that the testimonies of slaves and death row prisoners are subjective, and cannot be used to determine whether such people were actually treated as less-than-human. In response, we can turn to the opinion of Chief Justice Roger Taney in *Dred Scott v Sandford* in 1857, and to the words of a Californian judge in a death penalty case from 2013. Addressing the alleged tension between a Declaration of Independence that proclaimed that all men are created equal, with a practice that involved the subjugation of one race by another, Taney declared that the Founders did not intend black people to be part of the human family to which the Declaration of Independence was addressed: "it is too clear for dispute, that the enslaved African race were not intended to be included, and formed no part of the people who framed and adopted this declaration."[69] In Taney's view, black people were "so far inferior, that they had no rights which the white man was bound to respect… [Africans were] bought and sold, and treated as an ordinary article of merchandise and traffic, whenever a profit could be made of it."[70] The legal construction of black people as more akin to property than to human beings illustrates how slaves were, in legal terms, treated without respect for their human dignity. Likewise, when sentencing Osman Canales to death in 2008, Honorable Steven R. Van Sicklen said to him: "To call you an animal would be an insult to the animal kingdom. The only word that comes to mind when I think of you is the word 'monster'."[71] Here, Sicklen is stating that Canales is not only non-human, but is also not worthy of the respect given to non-human animals. Unlike Taney, Sicklen was not suggesting that the legal system does not recognize Canales's status as a human being for the purposes of legal rights, but it is clear that Sicklen – in his capacity as a legal official – was construing Canales as a non-human entity in order justify the imposition of a death sentence.

Sicklen's words would have troubled the late Justice Brennan, who in *Furman v. Georgia* provided perhaps the most comprehensive outline of how the American death penalty contravenes the constitutional requirement to respect the dignity of the person. Brennan argued that "the deliberate extinguishment of human life by the State is uniquely degrading to human dignity"[72] because such a punishment treats "members of the human race as nonhumans, as objects to be toyed with and discarded. [Capital punishment is] thus inconsistent with the fundamental premise of the [Eighth Amendment] that even the vilest criminal remains a human being possessed of common human dignity."[73] Thus, whereas Chief Justice Taney stated that slaves have no constitutional right to liberty and equality because they do not belong to the human family, Justice Brennan stated that it is precisely the Constitution that forbids the construction of a human being as anything other than a fully-fledged member of the human community.

On the face of it, there appears to be a fundamental difference between slavery and the death penalty – at least when considered from the vantage point of the legal protection of dignity. In many ways, the law explicitly recognizes the dignity of the person facing execution, and the constitutionality of the death penalty actually depends on this recognition. Justice Kennedy in particular has based his death penalty decisions on whether or not the imposition of capital punishment in any given case comports with respect for dignity.[74] The law only allows the death penalty for those who are considered moral rational agents in the Kantian sense, with the Court imposing categorical bans on executing those who lack capacity to be morally blameworthy. Trials must be individualized, so that the person's unique circumstances and personality can be taken into account by the sentencing jury. The convicted have constitutional rights to challenge their death sentences in ways that animals condemned to death do not. Dogs that have been deemed dangerous, for example, are put down without any trial process to determine their guilt or blameworthiness. To be sure, in medieval times certain animals were indeed put on trial before being killed, but such practices have been long abandoned, partly on the grounds that animals lack moral agency.[75] And in the moments before execution, inmates are granted a last meal, last words, and a seemingly "humane" death. As Daniel LaChance has written, "[t]hrough these individualizing procedures, inmates are portrayed as autonomous actors endowed with free will and distinct personalities, in possession of both a kind of agency and authenticity."[76] In contrast, the constitutionality of slavery depended on the legal system's denial of slaves' claims to equal concern and respect. That is, the death penalty depends on the construction of the person as a rational moral agent who deserves death, whereas slavery depended on the refusal that black people were rational moral agents. However, this distinction is more apparent than real. On closer analysis, it becomes clear that capital punishment, like slavery, depends on the *dual* status of those condemned. This point requires some elucidation, as it is central to the idea of radical abolitionism.

In the context of the death penalty, Hugo Adam Bedau has explained that the legality of the death penalty depends on the assumption that the person being executed is a morally rational agent who deserves condemnation for their choice to commit a heinous crime, yet simultaneously involves the denial that that person belongs to the human community, with the intrinsic worth, or dignity, that attaches to all human beings. Bedau explains why this is problematic: "It is conceptually impossible… for a person in a given act to deserve condemnation by the law for the criminality of that act *and* for the person to have proved by this act that he is no longer a person at all – but only a creature who now lacks any moral standing in the community of persons."[77] This contradiction lay at the heart of slavery too. The legal construction of slaves as more akin to animals or property ran counter to the fact that slaves were, in other legal and non-legal respects, treated as human beings. We know that slaveowners regularly sexually assaulted slaves, but there is no record that these same slaveowners sexually assaulted animals or inanimate property. That is, at some level even slaveholders recognized the human qualities of slaves. From the colonial era, through the Revolutionary and antebellum eras, legislators and courts routinely placed limits on the ways in which, and the extent to which, slaveowners and third parties could treat or punish slaves. The wording of these statutes, and the reasoning of the courts, appeared to be based on the fact that slaves were human beings.[78] Slaves were to be counted as persons for the purposes of the Electoral College, and were indeed referred to as "persons" throughout the text of the US Constitution. Animals and property were not.

The dual, fluid status of slaves and death row inmates can lead to several conclusions. First, it might be concluded that this status illustrates the inherent hypocrisy of both institutions. Kenneth Stampp, for example, argued that "the slave's status as property was incompatible with his status as a person."[79] In legally-orientated abolitionism, highlighting this hypocrisy can serve to strip the practice in question of its underlying rationale. This is what Bedau did when he argued that the characterization of certain people as no longer worthy of life was incompatible with the retributive and deterrent rationales for capital punishment.[80]

A second possible conclusion is that the systems in question actually *depend on the appearance* of the dual status of its subjects. In short, whenever we see instances of the law of slavery, or the law of capital punishment, appearing to treat a person with respect for their dignity, the law is actually masking the underlying inhumanity of the practice in question. Put another way, isolated incidents of apparent respect for dignity draw attention away from the structural denial of dignity. Andrew Fede makes this point with regards to slavery. Fede suggests that the legal recognition of the "humanity" of slaves served to mask the very inhumanity of the system of slavery in two ways: "First, it protected the public interest and the owner's interest, and second, it burdened slaves with special legal duties and obligations that marked the complete oppression of the system."[81] This was because all limitations on the master's power over their slaves were concerned primarily with protecting the institution of slavery, rather than with protecting the person condemned to bondage. The power to maim, kill, starve, or even free a slave, Fede writes, threatened the practice of slavery, since the slave would not be economically profitable. Thus, even though the statutes and the courts referred to the humanity of slaves in such cases, such references only served to legitimize and vindicate the very inhumanity of slavery in the abstract. Similarly, the law's apparent recognition of the "humanity" of those facing capital punishment – whether through the individualized sentencing procedure, or approaches to methods of execution – serves to legitimize and vindicate the structural and underlying inhumanity of the death penalty as a conceptual matter. When the law regulates the groups of people who can be executed, or the way in which they are executed, it gives a veneer of acceptability to capital punishment. This is particularly the case in the context of "humane" executions. It has long been noted that the shift away from visibly brutal executions towards executions that appear to be relatively pain-free, such as lethal injections, "may have had little to do with humanitarian concerns, but much to do with identifying a method that would temper opposition to the death penalty and reduce if not eliminate court challenges by the condemned."[82] Similarly, excluding certain groups from capital punishment serves to further legitimize the executions of those not excluded, just as the law's ostensible recognition of the humanity of slaves legitimized human bondage.

Alexander Reinert makes the connection between the "humane" treatment of slaves, and the "humane" treatment of prisoners, clear by illustrating how the Eighth Amendment prohibition on "cruel and unusual punishments" derives from the standards deployed in the treatment of slaves.[83] Reinart documents the local and state laws that used words such as "cruelly",[84] and notes how the pro-slavery lobby pointed to these laws to show that slaves were protected from inhumane treatment. Although Reinart uses this analysis to discuss the contemporary treatment of prisoners, his overarching point remains: the Eighth Amendment was used to regulate a system of subordination. In practice, slaves were rarely spared harsh treatment. As Reinart writes, "the laws themselves may have been a product of a Southern elite's cynical attempt to respond to antislavery critics by demonstrating that slavery could be 'humanize[d]' without altering the underlying brutality of the institution."[85]

It is with this in mind that today's capital punishment, like slavery in the antebellum era, can best be described as a *racialized system of degradation*, as defined in Chapter Two. It is racialized in the sense that racial prejudices guide its application, but it hides this by the occasional sentencing to death of a white person, or the sentencing to death of a person accused of killing a black person. It is a system of degradation in that it gives legal sanction to the moral view that some people can and should be treated as if they are something other than fully human – because of their skin color, their conduct, or both. It hides this, though, by appearing to treat such people as human beings.

The above analysis indicates how respect for the dignity of the person is necessarily intertwined with both the dignity of the community, and of the legal system, since it is the community and the legal system that strive to deny the human being's dignity. Since neither the community nor the legal system are "human beings", though, we need an alternative account of dignity for these contexts.

B. The degradation of the community

Human dignity might well be the "premier value" in moral and political philosophy, and might well be central to constitutional law, but the same cannot be said for the idea of "community" or "societal" dignity. Yet it makes little sense to speak of each individual's dignity as a standalone concept, since individuals invariably live in communities and, in many respects, the contention that each person should respect each other's dignity derives from the interconnectedness of peoples. That is, we cannot conceive of an individual's dignity separate to the moral values of the community in which they belong. Robert Johnson makes this point: "Human beings are endowed with the capacity for a conscious awareness of self that marks the individual as distinct and separate from others …".[86] While this has hallmarks of a Kantian conception of human dignity, Johnson goes further by stating that human beings can only exercise this capacity in a social setting:

"Self-determination is necessarily achieved in the world of other human beings through a process of self-defining social interactions."[87]

The enslavement or condemning to death of persons or groups of persons is predicated on the belief that such people do not belong to the particular community in question, because they do not share the same values or qualities as that "community". This, though, begs a range of questions relating to the identity of that community, and why the excluded people are not perceived to belong to that community. In this respect, Benedict Anderson's concept of "[i]magined [c]ommunities" is useful here. Addressing the phenomenon of nationalism, Anderson defines "the nation" as "an imagined political community… imagined as both inherently limited and sovereign."[88] Nations are "imagined" communities, Anderson writes, in the sense that members of the nation identify with one another even though they "will never know most of their fellow-members, meet them, or even hear of them, yet in the minds of each lives the image of their communion."[89] They are "communities", he goes on to say, in the sense that "regardless of the actual inequality and exploitation that may prevail in each, the nation is always conceived as a deep, horizontal comradeship."[90]

The roots of this comradeship vary. Historically, communities would be bound by a shared religion or dynastic ruler. Comradeship manifests itself in many different ways – national anthems, international sporting events, and the willingness to give one's life to defend one's nation, for example. We can use Anderson's general idea – that communities are made up of individuals who imagine that they share certain values with each other – in order to understand why a community might engage in the degradation of one or more of its members. Put simply, the degrading treatment of a person or persons (that is, the denial of their dignity) in any given situation is premised on the belief that that person or persons do not share the values of said community. In the antebellum era, black people were considered unworthy of living among the community because they allegedly did not share the same values as that community – they were "savage" or "uncivilized"; those convicted of heinous crimes today are likewise considered unworthy of belonging in the community because of their disregard for the victims of their crime.

Radical abolitionists, though, recognize that dignity does not inhere in a person by virtue of their moral attributes, thus counteracting the view of the community set out above. It follows that for a community to deny an individual their dignity is to contradict the very same values that drive members of the community to exclude others in the first place. This assertion requires some unpacking, and we can turn to the work of William Lloyd Garrison for the view that slavery was an affront to the dignity of slaveholders and other free persons because the fact of slavery corrupted their own moral compass. In an article titled "Southern Degradation," published on September 19, 1856, Garrison addressed the pro-slavery argument that bondage was a "positive good" for slaves, and retorted: "However beneficial slavery may have proved to the slaves of the South, it has most fearfully debased and deteriorated the slaveholders, and the entire population of the slave States". This was because slavery "has destroyed in them all sense of justice, all perception of right, all knowledge of virtue, all regard for humanity".[91] The community imagines that its members share the values of justice, right, virtue, and regard for humanity, yet Garrison shows how the practice of slavery rendered these values illusory. It is in this sense that we can say that slavery implicates the dignity of the community at large. Ralph Waldo Emerson expressed this view when speaking against the passage of the Fugitive Slave Law. According to Emerson, "while we reckoned ourselves a highly cultivated nation, our bellies had run away with our brains and the principles of culture and progress did not exist."[92] This is a critique of the impact that the greed and prosperity that had given rise to slavery had had on slaveholding communities.

Frederick Douglass also made the point that, in denying the dignity of some, communities ended up degrading themselves. Douglass described the cruelty of slaveowners towards slaves as "the kick of a jackass, or the barking of a bulldog",[93] to illustrate how slaveowners themselves came to resemble animals rather than humans. To emphasize how slavery degraded those who supported and practiced it, Douglass describes how the wife of one of his masters was initially "a pious, warm, and tender-hearted woman",[94] but came to lose those qualities: "Slavery soon proved its ability to divest her of these heavenly qualities. Under its influence, the tender heart became stone, and the lamblike disposition gave way to one of tiger-like fierceness."[95] While Douglass was focusing on individual human dignity – the dignity of his particular enslavers – his point was applicable to the wider community. Discussing the subjugation of African Americans generally, both during and after slavery, James Baldwin writes: "Our dehumanization of the Negro then is indivisible from our dehumanization of ourselves; the loss of our own identity is the price we pay for our annulment of his."[96] Furthermore, "[i]n overlooking, denying, evading his complexity – which is nothing more than the disquieting complexity of ourselves – we are diminished and we perish; only within this web of ambiguity, paradox, this hunger, danger, darkness, can we find at once ourselves and the power that will free us from ourselves."[97]

It was not just those who held slaves, though, whose dignity was implicated by involuntary bondage. Garrison also argued that the dignity of those who co-operated with slaveowners, or who stood by and let slavery flourish, was implicated. In an article titled "Guilt of New England", published on January 7, 1832, Garrison asked: "what if it should appear, on a candid examination, that we are as guilty as the slave owners? that we uphold and protect a system which is full of cruelty and blood? that the chains which bind the limbs of the slaves have been riveted by us? Let us see whether we are indeed implicated in this bloody business."[98]

The recognition that slavery implicated the dignity of the whole of society has already been cited as a reason for abolishing capital punishment. Writing shortly after the Civil War, when anti-death penalty activities were at their lowest ebb, Edmund Clarence Stedman wrote that the death penalty has a "demoralizing effect upon society". In his words:

> We would put an end to Capital Punishment, for the sake of the law-abiding classes; just as the abolition of Slavery was wisely urged *for the benefit of the*

> *white man*. Death may be a murderer's desert, but for the sake of the community let us reconsider this usage of inflicting it. Whether "the worst use you can put a man to" is, or is not, "to hang him," the worst use to which Society can put itself is the office of the executioner.[99]

Justice Marshall expressed a similar view when finding the death penalty unconstitutional in 1972. Marshall stated that "the Eighth Amendment is our insulation from our baser selves",[100] and went on to explain that since capital punishment is not necessary, it degrades the society that continues to use it.

In recent years, abolitionists have markedly drawn attention to the indignity of complicity with executions, and to the degrading effect of executions on the wider community. The Texas After Violence Project (TAVP), for example, describes itself as an initiative that is "focused on cultivating deeper understandings of the widespread impacts of interpersonal and state violence on individuals, families, and communities."[101] The founder of TAVP, Walter Long, writes that the death penalty is a "public health issue" because of its far-reaching effects on society,[102] and the American Public Health Association has called for abolition on the grounds that "State executions have a direct adverse effect on the public's health by tending to increase homicides and social disruption, and diminish society's respect for human life".[103] As we will see in Chapter Eight, pharmaceutical companies have made it clear that, for ethical reasons, they refuse to provide state authorities with the drugs needed to carry out lethal injections, recognizing that they would be complicit in diminishing respect for life. For now, we can consider how capital punishment, like slavery, threatens the integrity of the legal system.

C. The integrity of the institution

A hallmark of radical slavery abolitionism was the contention that slavery was symptomatic of a constitutional order that was lacking in integrity. Abolitionists differed, though, over whether a fundamental overhaul of the constitutional order was required. Indeed, the question of whether the Constitution was pro- or anti-slavery was often at the heart of anti-slavery debates. William Lloyd Garrison considered the Constitution to be a pro-slavery document, describing it as "a covenant with death, and an agreement with hell."[104] In line with this, he believed that those opposed to slavery had to call for a fundamental change in the institutional structures that not only legalized slavery, but also legitimized the values that underpinned support for slavery. Lewis Tappan, James G. Birney, and Gerrit Smith, on the other hand, all believed that the American Anti-Slavery Society should focus on slavery and racial justice, but stay silent on other issues such as women's rights. Indeed, so deeply held was the view that slavery abolitionists should not address these "ultraisms" that the AASS split in 1840 between Garrisonians and non-Garrisonians, largely on the issue of the breadth of issues that the movement should address.[105] That is, Garrison recognized that the plight of the black person was intricately connected to other issues such as women's rights and, indeed, capital punishment.

As outlined in the previous chapters, racism is not an issue that rears its head in the death penalty on a case-to-case basis, to be dealt with ad hoc when it appears in isolated, distinct cases, but rather it is embedded within the social, legal, and political system that upholds capital punishment. A concern for institutional dignity, then, can be classed as a concern with the values that the institution is perpetuating by upholding a particular practice such as bondage or executions. As indicated in the sections on human dignity and communitarian dignity, the issue is the perpetuation of the belief that some people are entitled to treat other people as if they do not belong to the human family.

James Acker notes the deleterious effect of capital punishment on the very legitimacy of the legal system, mainly because of the disjoint between the law on paper, and the law in practice. He writes: "the law's legitimacy is undermined by the substantial gulf between the rules constructed in fulfillment of the constitutional mandates that govern the death penalty's administration and how those same rules operate in practice."[106] Moreover, "[t]he vast chasm between death-penalty laws as written and their operation in practice – a practice that remains rife with inequities the laws were designed to cure, including systemic arbitrariness, racial discrimination, putting innocent persons at risk, and more – cannot help but cast a dark shadow on the laws' legitimacy."[107] In a similar vein, Justice Sotomayor called into question the integrity of Alabama's death penalty statute, which at the time allowed a judge to over-ride a jury's sentencing decision. Between 2000 and 2013, judges in trial courts in Alabama over-rode a jury's recommendation to sentence an offender to life rather than to death on 26 occasions. Sotomayor asked: "What could explain Alabama judges' distinctive proclivity for imposing death sentences in cases where a jury has already rejected that penalty?" The reason, she said, was that "Alabama judges, who are elected in partisan proceedings, appear to have succumbed to electoral pressures". Sotomayor concluded that the political influence on judicial determinations in death penalty cases "casts a cloud of illegitimacy over the criminal justice system."[108] According to his official biographer, Justice Powell condemned the death penalty in part because the "delay and seemingly endless litigation in every capital case brought the law itself into disrepute."[109]

While Acker and Sotomayor have spoken about the death penalty in practice, or a specific aspect of the death penalty in one particular jurisdiction, Austin Sarat highlights how the death penalty in the abstract undermines the integrity of the legal system as a whole: "The question to be asked about state killing is not what it does for us, but what it does *to* us.... State killing diminishes us by damaging our democracy, legitimating vengeance, intensifying racial divisions, and distracting us from the challenges [that America faces]."[110] The US Supreme Court has often noted the potential for the death penalty to degrade the legal system. In *Deck v. Missouri*, petitioner complained that his due process rights under the Fifth and Fourteenth Amendments had been violated because he had been compelled to wear shackles during the sentencing phase of his capital trial. The jury's impartiality, he argued, would be tainted by the appearance of shackles since it would sway them to assume his dangerousness, and thus sentence him to death. In an amicus curiae brief, the Bar Human Rights Committee of England and Wales, and the National Association of Criminal Defense Lawyers argued that shackling offended the "dignity of the court and of the parties."[111] The Supreme Court agreed. Writing for a 7–2 majority, Justice Breyer emphasized that the "judicial process... is a dignified process." As such, the "courtroom's formal dignity, which includes the respectful treatment of defendants, reflects the importance of the matter at issue". The use of shackles at trial, the majority said, "affronts the dignity and decorum of judicial proceedings."[112]

In *Wellons v. Hall*, petitioner complained that his death penalty trial had been unconstitutionally tainted by unreported and improper contacts between the jury, the judge, and a bailiff during the trial. In particular, some jurors had presented the judge and the bailiff with gifts. In a per curium opinion upholding petitioner's complaint, the Court reiterated that "[f]rom beginning to end, judicial proceedings conducted for the purpose of deciding whether a defendant shall be put to death must be conducted with dignity and respect."[113] The Supreme Court referred to the "integrity not just of one jurist, but of the larger institution" in *Williams v. Pennsylvania*.[114] In *Baze v. Rees*, concerning the constitutionality of a particular lethal injection protocol, the Court expressed concern with the "dignity of the procedure".[115]

It was in *Kennedy v. Louisiana*, decided in 2008, that the Court most forcefully explained how the death penalty might implicate the dignity of the legal institution. In outlawing the death penalty for crimes that do not result in death, Justice Kennedy wrote: "When the law punishes by death, it risks its own sudden descent into brutality, transgressing the constitutional commitment to decency and restraint."[116]

V. Conclusions

It might be argued that the legacy of slavery lends itself not to the inherent immorality of capital punishment, but to the practical problems with its administration. That is, a focus on race discrimination, it might be argued, is no different to the focus on innocence: both are concerned with the way in which the death penalty works in practice, rather than with the contention that capital punishment is always an affront to human dignity. We need to be clear, then, about the wrong of race-based discrimination and subjugation in order to understand the related wrong of capital punishment. Put simply, the radical slavery abolitionists understood that the wrong of slavery lay in the belief that black people were not as worthy as whites. They framed the case against slavery within the language of dignity: the idea that every person, regardless of the color of their skin, is equal in worth and should be treated as such. Thus, when the death penalty treats black people as though their lives are less important than their non-black counterparts, it reveals the broader wrong of the death penalty. In all cases, capital punishment treats a person as not worthy of belonging to the moral and political human community because of that person's moral attributes.

As we have seen in this chapter, though, abolitionism requires more than the focus on the dignity of the person. A recent dissenting opinion from the Eighth

Circuit Court of Appeals encapsulates this view. In April 2017, the State of Arkansas attempted to carry out eight executions over the course of 11 days, on the grounds that the state's supply of drugs needed for lethal injections was due to expire at the end of that month. A multi-pronged legal battle ensued, with lawyers arguing variously that some of the condemned men suffered from mental illnesses, had valid claims of innocence, and that the proposed lethal injection protocol posed a risk of severe and unconstitutional pain.[117] A district court stayed all executions pending further consideration of these claims, but on April 17, 2017, the Eighth Circuit Court of Appeals vacated these stays. Dissenting, Judge Kelly wrote:

> Successive execution denies all involved the dignity to which he is entitled. Grouped together to face execution, the eight appellees are no longer treated as individuals in the criminal justice system. The dignity of prison administrators and the staff involved in the execution is also at stake. They are made to repeatedly suffer the stresses of the execution environment without the time for debriefing or reflection. With back-to-back executions set barely more than an hour apart, the family members of the victims, particularly those who wish to witness the execution, are denied the time to grieve and find closure in the viewing room. Finally, inflicting the penalty of death en masse risks eroding the public's trust in the judicial process and the fairness of the execution process.[118]

Judge Kelly's statement is useful for present purposes because she identifies the multiple dignity concerns. Although she was writing with respect to the particular issue of multiple executions, we will see over the following chapters that her comments are applicable more broadly across the death penalty. Moreover, we will see that today's emphases on issues such as innocence, costs, and the availability of life without parole, all feed into the radicalism of death penalty abolitionism, at least when we accept the definition of radical abolitionism that I have offered in this chapter.

Notes

1 Ira Berlin, *The Long Emancipation: The Demise of Slavery in the United States* (Harvard University Press 2015) 1.

2 For the view that slavery was a benign, compassionate institution, see Ulrich Bonnell Phillips, *American Negro Slavery: A Survey of the Supply, Employment and Control of Negro Labor as Determined by the Plantation Regime* (first published 1918, LSU Press 1966). Also see James G. Randall, 'The Blundering Generation' (1940) 27 The Mississippi Valley Historical Review 3. There have also been disagreements over monuments to slavery, particularly those that reinforce the view that slaves were content with slavery. See Paul A. Shackel, 'Heyward Shepherd: The Faithful Slave Memorial' (2003) 37 Historical Archeology 138.

3 Aileen S. Kraditor, *Means and Ends in American Abolitionism: Garrison and His Critics on Strategy and Tactics, 1834–1850* (Pantheon Books 1969); James L. Huston, 'The Experiential Basis Of The Northern Antislavery Impulse' (1990) 56 The Journal of Southern History 609, 611–612.

4 Manisha Sinha, *The Slave's Cause: A History of Abolition* (Yale University Press 2016).
5 Andrew Delbanco, *The Abolitionist Imagination* (with commentaries by John Stauffer, Manisha Sinha, Darryl Pinckney, and Wilfred M. McClay) (Harvard University Press 2012); Thomas Fleming, *A Disease in the Public Mind: A New Understanding of Why We Fought the Civil War* (Da Capo Press 2013) (It should be noted that Fleming's argument is not "new" at all. See the texts in n 2 above.)
6 Richard S. Newman, *The Transformation of American Abolitionism: Fighting Slavery in the Early Republic* (University of North Carolina Press 2002) 27.
7 ibid 31.
8 PAS to Washington, Pa., Abolition Society, April 20, 1790, Acting Committee Minutes, PAS Papers, reel 1, referenced in ibid 61.
9 The Act rendered future children born to slaves as "indentured servants", meaning that they would work for their mother's master until the age of 28.
10 Berlin (n 1) 83, 90–92.
11 The subject of colonization, and its modern-day parallels in discourses of life without parole as an alternative punishment to the death penalty, are considered in Chapter Seven.
12 Gerald Sorin, *Abolitionism: A New Perspective* (Praeger Publishers 1972) 108.
13 Stanley Harrold, *American Abolitionists* (Routledge 2001) 4–5.
14 William E. Cain (ed), *William Lloyd Garrison and the Fight Against Slavery: Selections from The Liberator* (Bedford 1994). For the view that "abolitionism" thus defined emerged around 1830, see Ronald G. Walters, *The Antislavery Appeal: American Abolitionism After 1830* (John Hopkins University Press 1976) (stating at xi that "Opposition to slavery in North America did not suddenly begin on January 31, 1831… Yet during the 1830s the *Liberator* and similar instruments of propaganda changed abolitionism so dramatically as virtually to make it new".); Daniel J. McInerney, *The Fortunate Heirs of Freedom: Abolition and Republican Thought* (University of Nebraska Press 1994) 3 (arguing that "In terms of goals, tactics, and sectional support, the post-1831 movement stands as a distinct unit of study.").
15 Kraditor (n 3) 163.
16 ibid.
17 Lydia Maria Child, 'Dissolution of the Union', reprinted from *The National Anti-Slavery Standard* in *The Liberator*, May 20, 1842 (quoted in Kraditor (n 3) 23).
18 Sorin (n 12) 49.
19 Newman (n 6) 16.
20 William Lloyd Garrison, 'To the Public' *The Liberator* (1 January 1831) reprinted in Cain (n 14) 72.
21 David Walker, *Walker's Appeal, in Four Articles: Together with a Preamble, to the Coloured Citizens of the World, but in Particular, and Very Expressly, to Those of the United States of America* (first published 1829, University of North Carolina Press 2011) For a recent vindication of this view, see Nicholas Guyatt, *Bind Us Apart: How Enlightened Americans Invented Racial Segregation* (Basic Books 2016).
22 Sinha (n 4).
23 Quoted in Louis Filler, *The Crusade Against Slavery, 1830–1860* (Harper 1960) 61 n 28.
24 Kraditor (n 3) 8.
25 Sinha (n 4); Berlin (n 1).
26 Much of the following draws upon, and develops, the ideas put forward in Bharat Malkani, 'Dignity and the Death Penalty in the United States Supreme Court' (2017) 44 Hastings Constitutional law Quarterly 145.
27 Hugo Adam Bedau, 'The Eighth Amendment, Human Dignity, and the Death Penalty' in Michael J. Meyer and W. A. Parent (eds) *The Constitution of Rights: Human Dignity and American Values* (Cornell University Press 1992) 145.

28 Christopher McCrudden, In Pursuit of Human Dignity: An Introduction to Current Debates' in Christopher McCrudden (ed) *Understanding Human Dignity* (OUP 2013) 1.
29 Universal Declaration of Human Rights (adopted 10 December 1948) UNGA Res 217 A(III) (UDHR) Preamble.
30 Raoul Berger, 'Justice Brennan, 'Human Dignity', and Constitutional Interpretation' in Meyer and Parent (eds) *The Constitution of Rights* (n 27) 129.
31 James Q. Whitman, *Harsh Justice: Criminal Punishment and the Widening Divide between America and Europe* (OUP 2003) (although the title of Whitman's book refers to Europe, his study focuses on Germany and France).
32 Daniel LaChance, 'What Will Doom the Death Penalty?' *New York Times* (8 September 2014) http://www.nytimes.com/2014/09/09/opinion/what-will-finally-doom-the-death-penalty.html?.
33 On the ways in which the US Supreme Court has referred to these three ideas of dignity in its death penalty jurisprudence, see Malkani (n 26).
34 Berger (n 30) 134.
35 Jeremy Waldron, 'Citizenship and Dignity' in McCrudden, *Understanding Human Dignity* (n 28) 327.
36 Immanuel Kant, *Groundwork for the Metaphysics of Morals* (Thomas E. Hill and Arnulf Zweig eds., Arnulf Zweig trans., OUP 2003) AK 4:434 – AK 4:436.
37 Alan Gewirth, 'Human Dignity as the Basis of Rights' in Meyer and Parent (eds) (n 27) 15.
38 Ronald Dworkin, *Is Democracy Possible Here? Principles for a New Political Debate* (Princeton University Press 2008) 11.
39 ibid 17.
40 Ruth Macklin, 'Dignity is a Useless Concept' (2003) 237 British Medical Journal 1419.
41 Gerhold K. Becker, 'In Search of Humanity: Human Dignity as a Basic Moral Attitude' in Matti Häyry & Tuija Takala (eds) *The Future of Value Inquiry* (Brill 2001) 53, 53.
42 Louis Pojman, 'Why the Death Penalty is Morally Permissible' in Hugo Adam Bedau and Paul G. Cassell (eds) *Debating the Death Penalty: Should America Have Capital Punishment? The Experts on Both Sides Make Their Best Case* (OUP 2004) 61.
43 ibid 56.
44 Immanuel Kant, *The Metaphysics of Morals* (first published 1797, 2nd edn Cambridge University Press 1996) 6:332.
45 For an account of Kant's views on the death penalty, see Nelson Potter, 'Kant and Capital Punishment Today' (2002) 36 The Journal of Value Inquiry 267.
46 Michael Rosen, 'Dignity: The Case Against' in McCrudden (n 28) 147.
47 Mary Neal, "Not Gods but Animals': Human Dignity and Vulnerable Subjecthood' (2012) 33 Liverpool Law Review 177, 187 (italics in original). For an account of Martha Fineman's work on vulnerability, see Martha Fineman, 'The Vulnerable Subject: Anchoring Equality in the Human Condition' (2008) 1 Yale Journal of Law & Feminism 20.
48 Obergefell v. Hodges, 135 S. Ct. 2584 (2015).
49 ibid 2639 (Thomas, J., dissenting) (citation omitted) (footnote omitted).
50 David Brion Davis, *Inhuman Bondage: The Rise and Fall of Slavery in the New World* (OUP 2006) 35.
51 Ronald Dworkin, *Freedom's Law: The Moral Reading of the American Constitution* (OUP 2006) 111.
52 Even though contemporary international human rights law considers the death penalty to be contrary to the requirement to respect human dignity, Immanuel Kant argued that respect for dignity requires capital punishment. See Kant (n 44).
53 John C. Calhoun, 'Slavery is a Positive Good' Speech to U.S. Senate, 6 February 1837, reprinted in Jolyon P. Girard, Darryl Mace, and Courtney Smith (eds) *American*

History Through its Greatest Speeches: A Documentary History of the United States (ABC CLIO 2017) 44–45.

54 J. H. Van Evrie, *Negroes and Negro 'Slavery': The First and Inferior Race: The Latter its Normal Condition* (Van Evrie, Horton & Co. 1861).

55 ibid 9.

56 ibid 2.

57 ibid 10–11.

58 Harriet Beecher Stowe, *The Key to Uncle Tom's Cabin* (first published 1853, Arno Press and The New York Times 1968) 132 (quoted in Andrew Fede, *People Without Rights: An Interpretation of the Fundamentals of the Law of Slavery in the US South* (first published 1992, Routledge 2011) 3.

59 George M. Stroud, *A Sketch of the Laws Relating to Slavery* (first published 1856, Negro Universities Press 1968) 11 (quoted in Andrew Fede, *People Without Rights: An Interpretation of the Fundamentals of the Law of Slavery in the US South* (first published 1992, Routledge 2011) 4.

60 Bernard R. Boxhill, 'Dignity, Slavery, and the Thirteenth Amendment' in Meyer and Parent (eds) (n 27) 115.

61 ibid 108.

62 ibid 116.

63 On this point, see James Baldwin, *The Fire Next Time* (first published 1963, Penguin 1990).

64 When Philandro Castile was shot dead by a police officer during a routine traffic stops, much of the subsequent media coverage emphasized that he was a good role model. See, for example, Melissa Chan, 'Philandro Castile was a Role Model to Hundreds of Kids, Colleagues Say' *Time Magazine* (7 July 2016). On the problems with focusing on the character of those shot by police, see Colin Lee, 'The Trouble with the Philandro Castile Case' *Medium* (7 July 2016).

65 Frederick Douglass, *Narrative of the Life of Frederick Douglass, An American Slave, Written by Himself* (first published 1845, David Blight ed., Bedford Books 1993) 64.

66 Nicholas Yarris, *Seven Days to Live* (HarperCollins 2008) 60.

67 ibid 76.

68 Anthony Graves, 'When I Was on Death Row, I Saw a Bunch of Dead Men Walking. Solitary Confinement Killed Everything Inside Them,' (*Blog of Rights, American Civil Liberties Union*, 23 July 2013) https://www.aclu.org/blog/prisoners-rights-capital-punishment/when-i-was-death-row-i-saw-bunch-dead-men-walking-solitary.

69 Dred Scott v Sandford, 60 U.S. 393, 407 (1857).

70 ibid 407.

71 People v Canales (Osman), Supreme Court of California, Case No. YA069639–01 (3 January 2013) Trial Tr. Vol.48, 012202 (on file with author).

72 Furman v. Georgia, 408 U.S. 238, 291 (1972).

73 ibid 272–73. For a useful account of Justice Brennan's approach to dignity in constitutional interpretation, see Stephen J. Wermiel, 'Law and Human Dignity: The Judicial Soul of Justice Brennan' (1998) 7 William & Mary Bill of Rights Journal 223.

74 This is discussed in depth in Chapter Five.

75 E.P. Evans, *The Criminal Prosecution and Capital Punishment of Animals* (first published 1906, Lawbook Exchange 2009). Also see Piers Beirnes, 'The Law is an Ass: Reading E.P. Evans' *The Criminal Prosecution and Capital Punishment of Animals*' (1994) 2 Society and Animals 27. A number of reasons are offered for why animals were put on trial, usually when such animals had caused the death of a human. Literal translations of the Bible influenced some trials. Other trials were held in order to deter human owners of animals from letting their stock run free.

76 Daniel LaChance, 'Last Words, Last Meals, and Last Stands: Agency and Individuality in the Modern Execution Process' (2007) 32 Law and Social Inquiry 701, 704.

77 Hugo Adam Bedau, 'The Eighth Amendment, Human Dignity, and the Death Penalty' in Meyer and Parent (eds) (n 27) 176 (emphasis in original).
78 Fede (n 58) 11.
79 Kenneth Stampp, *The Peculiar Institution: Slavery in the Antebellum South* (Vintage Books 1956) 192.
80 Bedau (n 77).
81 Fede (n 58) 11.
82 Timothy V. Kaufman-Osborn, *From Noose to Needle: Capital Punishment and the Late Liberal State* (University of Michigan Press 2002) 180.
83 Alexander A Reinart, 'Reconceptualizing the Eighth Amendment: Slaves, Prisoners, and "Cruel And Unusual" Punishment' (2016) 94 North Carolina Law Review 817.
84 ibid 834–839.
85 ibid 848–849.
86 Robert Johnson, 'Reflections on the Death Penalty: Human Rights, Human Dignity, and Dehumanization in the Death House' (2014) 13 Seattle Journal for Social Justice 583, 584.
87 ibid 585.
88 Benedict Anderson, *Imagined Communities: Reflections on the Origin and Spread of Nationalism* (Revised edition, Verso 2006) 6.
89 ibid 6.
90 ibid 7.
91 William Lloyd Garrison, 'Southern Degradation' *The Liberator* (19 September 1856) reprinted in Cain (ed) (n 14) 147.
92 Quoted in Dwight McBride, *Impossible Witnesses: Truth, Abolitionism, and Slave Testimony* (NYU Press 2002) 70.
93 Douglass (n 65) 195–196.
94 ibid 59.
95 ibid 59–60.
96 James Baldwin, *Notes of a Native Son* (first published 1955, Pluto Press 1985) 25.
97 ibid 15.
98 William Lloyd Garrison, 'Guilt of New England' *The Liberator* (7 January 1832) reprinted in Cain (n 14) 84.
99 Edmund Clarence Stedman, 'The Gallows in America' *Putnam's Magazine* (February 1869) 225–235 (reprinted in Philip English Mackey, *Voices Against Death: American Opposition to Capital Punishment, 1787–1975* (Burt Franklin & Co. 1976) 133).
100 Furman v. Georgia, 408 U.S. 238, 345 (1972).
101 See the website of the Texas After Violence Project: http://texasafterviolence.org/.
102 Walter C. Long, 'The Death Penalty as a Public Health Problem' in Ivan Šimonovic (ed) *Death Penalty and the Victims* (United Nations Office of the High Commissioner for Human Rights 2016).
103 'Abolition of the Death Penalty' Policy No. 8611, adopted by the American Public Health Association, January 1, 1986 https://www.apha.org/policies-and-advocacy/public-health-policy-statements/policy-database/2014/07/14/13/50/abolition-of-the-death-penalty.
104 Speech of William Lloyd Garrison, 'On the Dissolution of the Union' (at the New England Anti-slavery Convention, 31 May 1855) reprinted in *The Liberator* (Vol. XXV, No. 24 15 June 1855).
105 Sorin (n 12) 58.
106 James R. Acker, 'The Death Penalty: Killing What We Could Be' in Ivan Šimonovic, *Death Penalty and the Victims* (United Nations Office of the High Commissioner for Human Rights 2016) 296.
107 ibid 299.
108 Woodward v. Alabama. 134 S.Ct. 405. (2013). (See Acker [n 106], 300.)

109 John C. Jeffries Jr., *Justice Lewis F. Powell Jr: A Biography* (Charles Scribner's Sons 1994) 452.
110 Austin Sarat, *When the State Kills: Capital Punishment and the American Condition* (Princeton University Press 2001) 250.
111 Br. of *Amici Curiae* Bar Human Rights Committee of England and Wales et al, p.6 for Petitioner, Deck v. Missouri, 544 U.S. 622 (2005).
112 Deck v. Missouri, 544 U.S. 622, 656 (2005) (internal quotations and citations omitted).
113 Wellons v. Hall, 558 U.S. 220, 220 (2010).
114 Williams v. Pennsylvania, 136 S. Ct. 1899, 1902 (2016).
115 Baze v. Rees, 553 U.S. 35, 57 (2008).
116 Kennedy v. Louisiana 554 U.S. 407, 420 (2008).
117 This incident is considered in more detail in Chapter Eight.
118 McGehee v. Hutchinson, 854 F.3d 488, 507 (8th Cir. Ark., 17 April 2017) (Kelly J, dissenting).

5 Radical abolitionist constitutionalism

I. Introduction

Since the over-arching strategy of the anti-death penalty movement is geared towards securing a ruling from the US Supreme Court that the death penalty is contrary to the Eighth and Fourteenth Amendments to the Constitution, it makes sense to explore the ways in which the constitutional case against capital punishment is framed. While the US Supreme Court's death penalty jurisprudence has usually been interpreted as requiring a conservative approach to constitutional argument, focusing on the unworkability rather than the immorality of the punishment, the literature on anti-slavery constitutionalism suggests that the Court's case-law can and should be read as encouraging a more radical anti-death penalty constitutionalism.

A radical abolitionist constitutionalism involves invoking the idea of dignity, and encouraging a jurisprudence that can be used to tackle broader social injustices. A feature of what historian William Wiecek describes as "radical anti-slavery constitutionalism" was its appeal to a "higher law" when countering the claim that the text of the Constitution expressly permitted slavery. In Wiecek's words, the radical constitutionalists "were the antebellum era's leading exponents of a theory of natural-law limitations on governmental power".[1] Although the radical constitutionalists never succeeded in convincing a majority of the Supreme Court to find slavery unconstitutional, they did succeed in laying the groundwork for addressing other injustices. Justin Buckley Dyer takes this view: "The legacy and heritage of the antislavery constitutional tradition is perhaps most evident in the civil rights legislation passed immediately after the Civil War and in the Constitution's Fourteenth Amendment, which sought to enshrine the basic tenets of antislavery constitutionalism in the nation's fundamental law."[2] Ever since it was adopted in 1868, the Fourteenth Amendment has been used to address a whole range of inequalities and injustices,[3] illustrating the importance of promoting a language that aspires to more than just an end of the practice in question. I do not mean to suggest that death penalty abolitionists should be aiming to inspire a new amendment when framing the constitutional case against capital punishment, but we will see that the death penalty jurisprudence of Justices Kennedy and Sotomayor in particular provide the framework for a comparable radical anti-death penalty constitutionalism. This constitutionalism draws on the idea of dignity (which I argue is a modern iteration of the radical anti-slavery constitutionalists' invocation of a "higher law"), and can be, and has been, used to challenge other unjust punishments, such as the imposition of sentences of life without the possibility of parole on young offenders, and the use of solitary confinement. Although constitutional lawyers have tended to refrain from using the idea of dignity when arguing that the death penalty is contrary to the Eighth and Fourteenth Amendments, the history of anti-slavery constitutionalism suggests that the idea of dignity should be placed front and center of anti-death penalty constitutionalism.

II. Barriers to radical abolitionist constitutionalism

In terms of the constitutional strategy, the anti-death penalty movement faces the same challenges that were faced by the antebellum abolitionists: the text of the US Constitution appears to contemplate the legality of the practice in question, thus foreclosing any argument that the practice is unconstitutional. In the context of slavery, William Wiecek labels this assumption as the "federal consensus." The twin tenets of this consensus were "(1) only the states could abolish or in any way regulate slavery within their jurisdictions; (2) the federal government had no power over slavery in the states."[4] This consensus was subject to the few issues that were, by virtue of the text of the Constitution, within the federal government's hands, such as the international slave trade, the subject of fugitive slaves, and the problem of slave insurrections.

A similar "federal consensus" applies in the context of the modern death penalty.[5] The Fifth Amendment provides that "[n]o person shall be held to answer for a capital … crime, unless on a presentment or indictment of a Grand Jury," and that no person shall be "deprived of life…without due process of law." The Fourteenth Amendment clarifies that no state shall "deprive any person of life, liberty, or property, without due process of law." It follows that the federal government can only intervene in the administration of capital punishment when there has been a failure to follow due process. The view that the Constitution otherwise immunizes capital punishment from interference by the federal judiciary was articulated clearly by Justice Scalia in 1994, when he asserted that the Fifth Amendment "clearly permits the death penalty to be imposed, and establishes beyond doubt that the death penalty is not one of the 'cruel and unusual punishments' prohibited by the Eighth Amendment."[6] Scalia repeated this in *Glossip v. Gross*, decided in 2015: "It is impossible to hold unconstitutional that which the Constitution explicitly contemplates."[7]

The federal consensus is one reason why judges in the antebellum era often decided cases against the slave, and in favor of the pro-slave lobby. The 1857 decision in *Dred Scott v. Sandford* is notorious today for its holding that black people did not enjoy the same constitutional protections as whites, and the author of that decision – Chief Justice Taney – has sometimes been characterized as pro-slavery.[8] Yet Taney has been defended by some writers on the grounds that he was bound by the constitutional limits within which he was working.[9] Even those judges who openly complained that they found slavery to be morally repugnant nonetheless issued opinions that condemned persons to bondage, because they considered themselves restrained by the limits on the judicial power. In *Justice Accused*, Robert Cover identifies the "moral-formal dilemma" that anti-slavery judges faced, and writes that these judges invoked a variety of "responsibility-mitigation mechanisms"[10] in order to justify their decision to apply the law in a formal manner that was contrary to their moral disposition. One such mechanism was the "elevation of the formal stakes". The judge would emphasize the grave risks that a departure from the application of legal rules would have on the democratic order or the life of the Union.[11] Another mechanism was the "[r]etreat to mechanistic formalism." This involved the judge proclaiming that they were bound by clear rules of precedent, or separation of powers, or some other formal mechanism that dictated the bounds of the judicial function.[12] A third device for justifying the marginalization of anti-slavery impulses was to ascribe responsibility for the rules and decision elsewhere. In addition to saying that he was bound to follow a particular rule, the judge would emphasize that the responsibility for that rule lies elsewhere, perhaps with Congress or previous members of the judiciary.[13]

The use of these three devices had the overall effect of entrenching and legitimizing slavery. Cover is withering in his analysis: "In these cases, time and again, the judiciary paraded its helplessness before the law; lamented harsh results; intimated that in a more perfect world, or at the end of days, a better law would emerge, but almost uniformly, marched to the music, steeled themselves… and [collaborated] in a system of oppression – Negro slavery."[14] Justice Story's tenure on the Court, Cover argues, was characterized by such parades of "helplessness before the law". After writing opinions in *Prigg v. Pennsylvania* and the *Latimer* case which were in favor of slaveholders,[15] he tried to justify his actions to a friend: "You know full well that I have ever been opposed to slavery. But I take my standard of duty as a judge from the Constitution."[16]

We see these "responsibility-mitigation mechanisms" being utilized by judges who are morally opposed to capital punishment. Dissenting in *Furman v. Georgia* in 1972, Justice Blackmun wrote: "I yield to no one in the depth of my distaste, antipathy, and, indeed, abhorrence, for the death penalty, with all its aspects of physical distress and fear and of moral judgment exercised by finite minds."[17] He went on: "I, perhaps alone among the present members of the Court, am on judicial record as to this."[18] However, Blackmun nonetheless voted to uphold the constitutionality of capital punishment on the grounds that, as a judge, he was institutionally incapable of striking down a law for moral reasons or because of his personal predilections. In his words: "We should not allow our personal preferences as to the wisdom of legislative and congressional action, or our distaste for such action, to guide our judicial decision in cases such as these."[19] After setting out why legislative and congressional action pointed in the direction of permitting the death penalty, Blackmun wrote: "Although personally I may rejoice at the Court's result, I find it difficult to accept or to justify as a matter of history, of law, or of constitutional pronouncement. I fear the Court has overstepped. It has sought and has achieved an end."[20]

Justices Brennan and Marshall joined Blackmun in denouncing the immorality of the death penalty in *Furman*, but no sitting justice has since been explicit about their moral distaste for capital punishment. This is in contrast to the antebellum era, when it was relatively common for judges on the highest courts to express anti-slavery sentiments. It is widely accepted today, though, that nominees to the Supreme Court would not be confirmed by the Senate if they expressed strong moral opposition to capital punishment.[21] Consider, for example, Senator Hatch's remarks during Judge Kennedy's confirmation hearing in December 1987. Discussing the desirability of, and in his view the constitutional requirement for judicial restraint, Senator Hatch made a pointed reference to *Furman:* "judges have overturned capital punishment laws in 34 States – even though the Constitution itself, in four or five instances, mentions the death penalty – and this is known generally as judicial activism. In my mind, judges who take upon themselves to overrule the people's laws without clear warrant from the Constitution, overstep their authority."[22] More recently, Justice Sotomayor faced sustained questioning on her position on the death penalty during her confirmation hearings in 2009. As a Board member of the Puerto Rican Legal Defense Fund, Sotomayor had signed a memorandum outlining the racism inherent in capital punishment schemes, prompting Senator Graham to ask: "What's your view of the death penalty, in terms of personally?" Sotomayor chose not to reveal her personal views, answering instead: "The issue for me with respect to the death penalty is that the Supreme Court, since *Gregg*, has determined that the death penalty is constitutional under certain situations."[23] She likely recognized that an anti-death penalty declaration would work against her nomination, but was equally unwilling to proclaim that she supports capital punishment. She thus ascribed responsibility for the issue elsewhere – namely, to the *Gregg* Court.

Judges on lower courts have also been dissuaded from expressing anti-death penalty views. In 1986, the Chief Justice of the California Supreme Court – Rose Bird – was voted out of office after a vigorous campaign by her opponents that focused on her tendency to decide death penalty cases in favor of the defendant.[24] As a result, judges have refrained from expressing moral opposition to capital punishment, either in extra-judicial statements, or in their judicial capacity. We can see, then, why the text of the Constitution, and the nature of confirmation hearings and the judicial appointments process, might present a barrier to the development of a radical anti-death penalty constitutionalism. Yet as outlined below, in many respects the constitutional strategy of the anti-death penalty movement today is inherently radical.

III. Radical abolitionist constitutionalism

In his study of anti-slavery constitutionalism, William Wiecek identifies three types of constitutional attacks on slavery: Garrisonian, moderate, and radical. Garrisonians – following the lead of William Lloyd Garrison – took the view that the Constitution was inherently pro-slavery and thus could not be used to advance the cause of abolition. Garrison saw the Constitution as "a covenant with death, and an agreement with hell",[25] and abolitionism therefore involved a tearing up of the Constitution. Moderate constitutionalists, on the other hand, believed that even though the Constitution was pro-slavery, it implored the federal government to refrain from actively supporting or defending human bondage. Their hope was that "the removal of federal support, coupled with vigorous antislavery political involvement... would render slavery so vulnerable that the states would abolish it of their own accord."[26] These constitutionalists saw the Constitution's slavery-clauses as concessions that were made to Southern states in order to secure the forming of the Union, rather than (as Garrison did) a normative endorsement of the institution. This reading of the framers' intentions led the likes of Salmon P. Chase to declare that Congress could not establish slavery in the District of Columbia, nor protect slavery in the territories. He also asserted that the Constitution forbade the provision of federal assistance for the recapture of escaped slaves.[27] In other words, the Constitution tolerated slavery as a local institution, but it was not a part of the national government.[28] Moderate constitutionalists thus implored federal authorities to allow slavery to gradually wither away, as they believed it inevitably would.

Radical constitutionalists, Wiecek writes, differed in that they read the Constitution to *demand* the federal government to bring about an end to bondage. These abolitionists were "'radical' because they rejected the [federal] consensus, 'constitutionalists' because they sought to abolish slavery through constitutional action."[29] The starting point for their lines of argument lay in an adherence to a Blackstonian understanding of natural law.[30] Whereas Garrison was strictly positivist in his approach to reading the Constitution, radial constitutionalists claimed that the validity of all man-made laws had to be assessed against the law of nature. It was hardly controversial to make this claim: the Declaration of Independence had been signed just over a half century ago, and was replete with references to natural law limitations on governmental power. Governments were formed, the Declaration stated, to secure the "unalienable Rights [of] Life, Liberty, and the pursuit of Happiness." More pertinently, the Declaration proclaimed that it was a "self-evident" truth "that all men are created equal". To show that the drafters of the Constitution recognized the incompatibility of slavery with natural law principles, these abolitionists pointed to the fact that the word "slavery" did not appear at all in the Constitution. During the constitutional debates, Northern opponents of slavery objected to the use of the term "slavery". James Madison asserted that it would be "wrong to admit in the Constitution the idea that there could be property in men".[31] The delegate from North Carolina – James Iredell – explained after the Convention that "[t]he word slave is not mentioned" because "the northern delegates, owing to their particular scruples on the subject of slavery, did not choose the word slave to be mentioned."[32] Recognizing that Northern delegates would not ratify a document that referred explicitly to "slaves", the Southern delegates accepted the use of "euphemisms and circumlocutions".[33] Indeed, the absence of the word "slavery" from the Constitution was the focus of George W.F. Mellon's 1841 book, *An Argument on the Unconstitutionality of Slavery.*[34]

Alvan Stewart is generally considered to be the one who sowed the seeds of radical anti-slavery constitutionalism in 1837, when he proclaimed that the Fifth Amendment actually empowered the federal government to abolish slavery nationwide.[35] The Due Process Clause of the Amendment, Stewart argued, had a substantive dimension as well as a procedural one. Since all persons had a substantive right to liberty, only those who had been formally declared a slave by judicial proceedings could be kept in servitude. There were flaws with Stewart's arguments, not least of all his mistaken assumption that the Fifth Amendment could be asserted against the states.[36] Even within the anti-slavery community, his ideas were rejected. Adopting his stance would have required the American Anti-Slavery Society to reject the federal consensus, but the members who were committed to working with the Constitution to initiate political action were reluctant to do this. Although Stewart's arguments were rejected by his contemporaries, they nonetheless spawned further radical approaches to anti-slavery constitutionalism, including Mellon's 1841 book, and William Goodell's *Views on American Constitutional Law*, published in 1844. Perhaps the most widely known radical anti-death penalty argument came in 1845, titled *Unconstitutionality of Slavery*, written by Lysander Spooner.[37]

It is with this in mind that we might argue that modern death penalty abolitionism is inherently radical. It is radical because it is premised on the claim that capital punishment is prohibited by the Cruel and Unusual Punishments clause, and that the federal judiciary must impose abolition upon the states. The constitutional strategy is not "moderate", because abolitionists do not restrict their claim to the argument that the federal government should not lend support to the death penalty, and should let it wither away in the states. Contemporary anti-death penalty constitutionalism is also radical in the sense that it draws on the idea of dignity that was outlined in the previous chapter. This idea of dignity bears the hallmarks of the principles of natural law that were invoked by the radical anti-slavery constitutionalists. To understand why, we need to understand how anti-slavery lawyers invoked principles of natural law.

A. From "eternal principles of justice" to "dignity"

A useful example of the anti-slavery constitutionalists' invocation of natural law can be found in John Quincy Adams's submission in *La Amistad*, decided in 1841.[38] A group of Africans were found aboard a Spanish ship just off the US coast, and were subjected to a claim by Spanish slave-traders who sought the return of their "property." During oral arguments before the Supreme Court, Adams referred to Chief Justice Marshall's opinion in *The Antelope*, which had been decided in 1825 on remarkably similar facts. A key difference was that between the dates of the two cases, Spain had outlawed the slave trade. In *The Antelope*, Marshall had condemned the immorality of slavery but held that Spain's sanction of the slave trade contributed to a finding that the law of nations permitted such trade and thus decided in favor of the Spanish slaveholders: "Whatever might be the answer of a moralist to this question," Marshall wrote, "a jurist must search for its legal solution, in those principles of action which are sanctioned by the usages, the national acts, and general assent, of that portion of the world in which he considers himself as a part, and to whose law the appeal is made."[39]

Arguing in *La Amistad*, Adams summarized Marshall's opinion: "To the moral principle the Chief Justice opposes general usage – fact against right."[40] Throughout his oral arguments, Adams emphasized the tension between the natural law principles of America's founding, with the political fact of slavery. He recognized various levels of what Dyer labels "a constitutional disharmony."[41] On one level, there was a discord within the text of the Constitution itself, which struggled to balance the principle of liberty with the fact of slavery. On another level, there was disharmony between the natural law principles that underpinned the Declaration of Independence, and the actual practice of slavery. On yet another level, there was a philosophical tension: regardless of constitutional text or structure, how could men and women be treated as property when they were, as a matter of fact, human? Adams thus implored the Court to bring political practice into line with the natural law aspirations that undergirded the Declaration of Independence and thus the entire constitutional order. To be clear, Adams did not think that the moral attack on slavery *depended* on the Declaration of Independence, for in his view principles of natural law transcended any such written text. Dyer describes Adams's constitutional theory thus: "the principles of the Declaration of Independence provided the normative foundation for subsequent constitutional politics."[42]

In *La Amistad*, Justice Story decided in favor of the liberty of the Africans partly because Spain had outlawed the slave trade. However, even though he rested his decision on "the eternal principles of justice", Story nonetheless indicated that had there existed any positive law to the contrary, such law would have prevailed. It thus cannot be said that Adams and other anti-slavery litigators succeeded in convincing the US Supreme Court to determine the outcome of cases solely on the basis of natural law principles as they understood them. Nonetheless, the constitutionalism that they developed still had far-reaching ramifications. Perhaps most significantly, their natural law-infused constitutionalism influenced the drafting and adoption of the Fourteenth Amendment.

The references to equal protection, birth citizenship, and due process in the Fourteenth Amendment bore a striking resemblance to the natural law philosophies of Adams, and the exhortations of the radical abolitionists who insisted that abolition required more than just physical freedom. During the congressional debates, it became clear that the Amendment was considered to be merely declaratory of rights that already existed, but which had been wrongly denied to black people. Iowa Congressman James Wilson asserted that Congress was "establishing no new right, declaring no new principle."[43] Lyman Trumbull took the view that national legislation was needed in order to ensure that such existing rights were granted to the "millions of the African race in this country who were ground down and degraded and subjected to a slavery more intolerable and cruel than the world ever before knew."[44] Throughout the debates, references to natural rights abound. John Bingham explained that "the rights for which America has contended were the rights of human nature."[45] Of importance to us for contemporary purposes, these debates reflected a concern not just with the enslavement of people, but also with broader issues that the abolitionists had drawn attention to. Consider the thoughtful speech of Jacob Howard in the Senate, who said that the Fourteenth Amendment protected not just African Americans, but also the poor and marginalized. Howard proclaimed that the Amendment "establishes equality before the law, and it gives to the humblest, the poorest, the most despised of the race the same rights and the same protection before the law as it gives to the most powerful, the most wealthy, or the most haughty."[46]

Inevitably, many Congressmen of the time still adhered to the view put forward by Chief Justice Taney in *Dred Scott*, and by Stephen Douglas in his debates with Lincoln. Garrett Davis, for example, said that "this is a white man's Government… it was not to establish a government in which [the Negro] was to be a party or a power that the Declaration of Independence was enunciated to the world."[47] These views were defeated, though, illustrating how the opposite view – that the Declaration of Independence did indeed extend to black people – was effectively constitutionalized by virtue of the Fourteenth Amendment. Another way of putting this is to say that John Quincy Adams's bold claim in *La Amistad* some 20 years earlier took a hold in the constitutional order.[48] Thus, Jacobus tenBroek writes of "the antislavery origins of the Fourteenth Amendment",[49] and Howard Jay Graham likewise states that the Fourteenth Amendment was "the outcome of the organized antislavery movement in the United States".[50] William E. Nelson has also explained that the Fourteenth Amendment finds it roots in the libertarian and egalitarian principles that had been articulated by the slavery abolitionists.[51] This is not to say that the drafters and the Amendment merely mimicked the idea of the abolitionists – Nelson explains how antebellum ideas were slightly transformed during the course of the debates and in the subsequent interpretation and application of the Amendment – but nonetheless, it was their rhetoric that inspired the broad principles of the Amendment

It might be argued that natural law-based arguments are absent from contemporary constitutional challenges to capital punishment because such principles have been discredited since the antebellum era. In an article published in the Harvard Law Review in 1918, Oliver Wendell Holmes, who was an Associate Justice of the US Supreme Court and veteran of the Civil War, attacked the idea of natural law as then understood. In Holmes's view, "[t]he jurists who believe in natural law seem to me to be in that naive state of mind that accepts what has been familiar and accepted by them and their neighbors as something that must be accepted by all men everywhere."[52] Holmes's concern lay with the difficulty of deciding which of any two competing visions of justice was "correct" in any given case, leading him to conclude that "[t]he life of the law has not been logic; it has been experience."[53] For him, the Declaration of Independence and the US Constitution did not ground any moral truths that could be deciphered through constitutional interpretation, and Holmes's view has taken root in the subsequent jurisprudence of the US Supreme Court.[54]

The shift away from giving consideration to the "eternal principles of justice" was illustrated in the decision in *Stanford v Kentucky*, in which moral preferences were located in the polity, rather than in the judiciary's interpretation of the text or principles of the Constitution.[55] Since *Stanford*, the anti-death penalty movement has grounded constitutional challenges in the language of "evolving standards of decency", which is premised on public opinion as expressed through the decisions of juries and state legislatures.[56] And in *McCleskey v. Kemp*, the Court expressed concern with discrediting the death penalty on grounds that would be applicable across the criminal justice system.[57] As outlined in Chapter Three, these cases have compelled abolitionists to pursue pragmatic and conservative styles of argumentation – both in the courtroom, and in the public sphere. As such, it might be said that contemporary anti-death penalty constitutionalism is far from the radicalism of the likes of Adams and other radical anti-slavery constitutionalists. As we will see, though, despite the appearance of conservativism and pragmatism, since the turn of the 21st Century anti-death penalty constitutionalism has been infused with the idea of dignity that was set out in the previous chapter.

In the 2002 case of *Atkins v. Virginia*, Justice Stevens repudiated the *Stanford* approach to Eighth Amendment analysis, and set in motion the development of a radical anti-death penalty constitutionalism.[58] The *Atkins* Court reversed *Penry v. Lynaugh*, decided 13 years earlier, and held it unconstitutional to impose the death penalty on persons suffering from what it then termed "mental retardation."[59] Writing for a 6–3 majority, Justice Stevens continued to place primacy on national opinion, and focused on changes in state legislation and the reducing number of such persons being sentenced to death. However, with respect to "objective evidence" of public opinion, Stevens noted that it was not just the number of states that had outlawed the practice that was relevant, but "the consistency of the direction of change." Since the Court last heard the issue in 1989, 16 states had enacted prohibitions, and no states had moved the other way. Similarly, the numbers of persons executed since 1989 had been relatively small. Stevens did not stop at legislative enactments and the decisions of juries. He also considered the weight of the views of professional organizations that condemned such a punishment, and he noted that religious groups had broadly renounced the death penalty for those suffering from an intellectual disability. Albeit only a footnote, Stevens noted that "within the world community, the imposition of the death penalty for crimes committed by mentally retarded offenders is overwhelmingly disapproved."[60] This was a clear departure from 1989, when a plurality of the Court in *Stanford* held: "We emphasize that it is American conceptions of decency that are dispositive, rejecting the contention of petitioners and the various amici (accepted by the dissent…) that the sentencing practices of other countries are relevant."[61]

Even though Stevens insisted that these other indicators of societal opinion were not dispositive of the issue, and served instead to confirm the reasonableness of state legislative developments and the decisions of juries, he nonetheless received a stinging rebuke from the dissenting justices. Chief Justice Rehnquist chastised the "defects in the Court's decision to place weight on foreign laws, the views of professional and religious organizations, and opinion polls in reaching its conclusion."[62] The dissenters did not just take issue with Stevens' approach to determining public opinion. They also expressed concern with the reintroduction of the Court's "independent evaluation of the issue". After setting out the national consensus, Stevens explained that "the Constitution contemplates that in the end our own judgment will be brought to bear on the question of the acceptability of the death penalty under the Eighth Amendment", and proceeded to explain why the death penalty did not serve retributive or deterrent purposes when imposed on persons suffering from mental retardation. In response, Justice Scalia proclaimed that "[s]eldom has an opinion of this Court rested so obviously upon nothing but the personal views of its members."[63]

The decision in *Atkins*, then, heralded a return to the Court's interventionist position in death penalty cases. Three years later the Court outlawed the death penalty for offenders under the age of 18. In *Roper v. Simmons*, Justice Kennedy followed Stevens's lead in taking a broad approach to measuring national opinion on the propriety of the juvenile death penalty.[64] Only five states had moved to outlaw the juvenile death penalty since *Stanford* had been decided, but Kennedy emphasized that the sheer numbers did not determine the issue. Rather, the direction of change did.[65] Kennedy also developed the Court's approach to proportionality analysis, accepting evidence from the fields of social sciences and child psychiatry when reaching the conclusion that the death penalty is disproportionate when imposed on young offenders because it serves no retributive or deterrent purposes.[66] Perhaps more strikingly, Kennedy devoted nearly four pages of his opinion to a discussion of the relevance of international law and opinion to Eighth Amendment analysis. Although not determinative of whether or not a punishment is cruel and unusual, such opinion, Kennedy said, is helpful for confirming the reasonableness of the Court's finding.[67]

Kennedy also invoked the idea of the dignity. Justice Stevens did not mention the word in *Atkins*, but Kennedy emphasized in *Roper* that "[b]y protecting even those convicted of heinous crimes, the Eighth Amendment reaffirms the duty of the government to respect the dignity of all persons."[68] He went on to state that "[t]he Constitution… sets forth, and rests upon, innovative principles original to the American experience, such as broad provisions to secure individual freedom and preserve human dignity."[69] Even in her dissent, Justice O'Connor accepted the relevance of respect for human dignity to Eighth Amendment analysis, referring to "this Nation's evolving understanding of human dignity".[70] In some respects, Kennedy's invocation of dignity was hardly surprising. As he noted, the Court has actually long held that the idea of dignity is central to the constitutional order. It was in 1958 that the Court in *Trop v. Dulles* stated that "[t]he basic concept underlying the Eighth Amendment is nothing less than the dignity of man. While the State has the power to punish, the Amendment stands to assure that this power be exercised within the limits of civilized standards."[71] In 2008, Kennedy once again referred to the idea of dignity when narrowing the scope of capital punishment to crimes that result in death: "Evolving standards of decency must embrace and express respect for the dignity of the person, and the punishment of criminals must conform to that rule."[72] In 2011, in *Brown v. Plata*, Kennedy again confirmed that "[p]risoners retain the essence of human dignity inherent in all persons. Respect for that dignity animates the Eighth Amendment prohibition against cruel and unusual punishment."[73] And in *Hall v. Florida* in 2014, Kennedy reiterated that respect for dignity animates the Eighth Amendment: "No legitimate penological purpose is served by executing a person with intellectual disability. To do so contravenes the Eighth Amendment for to impose the harshest of punishments on an intellectually disabled person violates his or her inherent dignity as a human being." Writing for the majority, Justice Kennedy asserted that "[t]he Eighth Amendment's protection of dignity reflects the Nation we have been, the Nation we are, and the Nation we aspire to be."[74]

Kennedy has not only highlighted the dignity of the person facing execution. He acknowledged in *Kennedy v. Louisiana* that "[w]hen the law punishes by death, it risks its own sudden descent into brutality, transgressing the constitutional commitment to decency and restraint."[75] In doing so, he recognized the ways in which capital punishment implicates the dignity of the wider community, and of the legal institution itself. Thus, even though his usage of dignity is not a mirror image of the natural law philosophies of the anti-slavery constitutionalists, and even though he does not refer to "eternal principles of justice", Kennedy nonetheless adopts an approach that is akin to Ronald Dworkin's aspirational theory of the Constitution. Dworkin extols "a fusion of constitutional law and moral theory",[76] and urges judges to "find the best justification they can find, in principles of political morality, for the structure as a whole."[77] In *Freedom's Law: The Moral Reading of the American Constitution*, Dworkin explains:

> Judges must not read their own convictions into the Constitution. They may not read the abstract moral clauses as expressing any particular moral judgment... unless they find it consistent in principle with the structural design of the Constitution as a whole, and also with the dominant lines of past constitutional interpretation by other judges. They must regard themselves as partners with other officials, past and future, who together elaborate a coherent constitutional morality, and they must take care to see what they contribute fits with the rest.[78]

It is in this sense that Sotirios Barber and James Fleming identify aspirationalism within Dworkin's approach. Constitutional interpretation, they write, must "reflect critically upon our aspirations in striving for the interpretation that makes the Constitution the best it can be."[79] In this, we can hear the echoes of anti-slavery constitutionalism, which sought to bring constitutional interpretation into line with the visions and aspirations of the Declaration of Independence. Although this approach is not exactly echoed in Kennedy's opinion in *Roper* and subsequent cases, it is close. Kennedy enjoined his view with that of the polity, but also ensured that this view fit with the constitutional structure.

It is not just Justice Kennedy who has encouraged a radical anti-death penalty constitutionalism. Recently, Justice Sotomayor has developed a comparable dignity-based death penalty jurisprudence. Dissenting from a denial of certiorari in *Arthur v. Dunn*, a case concerning the constitutionality of a particular lethal injection protocol, Sotomayor writes that "States have designed lethal-injection protocols with a view toward protecting their own dignity, but they should not be permitted to shield the true horror of executions from official and public view. Condemned prisoners… might find more dignity in an instantaneous death rather than prolonged torture on a medical gurney."[80] Although it is contentious to say that an instantaneous death is a death that is respectful of dignity, Sotomayor at least highlights the relevance of dignity to Eighth Amendment analysis.[81] This line of thinking led her to reject Justice Alito's contention in *Glossip v. Gross* that because the death penalty is constitutional, there must be some way of imposing it. In her words: "If all available means of conducting an execution constitute cruel and unusual punishment, then conducting the execution will constitute cruel and usual punishment. Nothing compels a State to perform an execution."[82] While not explicitly mirroring the constitutionalism of the anti-slavery litigators, Sotomayor pointed out that the principle behind the Eighth Amendment was "higher" in the strata of constitutional principles than the permission granted by the Fifth and Fourteenth Amendments to inflict death as a punishment.

Even those justices who have issued pro-death penalty opinions have nonetheless invoked the term dignity in their opinions. In *Baze v. Rees* (2008), concerning the constitutionality of a lethal injection protocol, Chief Justice Roberts emphasized the need to respect the "dignity of the procedure".[83] And in *Glossip v. Gross* (2015), concerning an alternative lethal injection procedure, Justice Alito recounted how, when executing Clayton Lockett, the execution team had "covered the injection access point with a sheet, in part to preserve Lockett's dignity during the execution."[84]

To better appreciate why this dignity-infused death penalty jurisprudence encourages a radical anti-death penalty constitutionalism comparable to that of the slavery abolitionists, we can consider how this jurisprudence has been used to address other issues in the criminal justice system. For decades, the Court has adhered to the doctrine of "death-is-different", which means that the Court applies different modes of constitutional analysis to death penalty cases, on account of the uniqueness of the punishment. Since 2010, though, the Court has intimated that its approach to capital cases can and should be used to address other issues such as sentences of life without parole for young offenders, and the problem of solitary confinement.

B. Death is (not so) different

In *Furman v. Georgia*, Justice Stewart explained why death penalty cases should be treated differently from other punishments: "The penalty of death differs from all other forms of criminal punishment, not in degree but in kind. It is unique in its total irrevocability. It is unique in its rejection of rehabilitation of the convict as a basic purpose of criminal justice. And it is unique, finally, in its absolute renunciation of all that is embodied in our concept of humanity."[85] In *Woodson v. North Carolina*, Justice Stewart reiterated this perception: "the penalty of death is qualitatively different from a sentence of imprisonment, however long. Death, in its finality, differs more from life imprisonment than a 100-year prison term differs from one of only a year or two." Because of the uniqueness of death as a punishment, Stewart went on to say, "there is a corresponding difference in the need for reliability in the determination that death is the appropriate punishment in a specific case."[86] Put another way, the death penalty is to be treated as analytically distinct to other punishments, with a correspondingly distinct approach to constitutional analysis. The resulting jurisprudence over the last four decades, though, has tended to draw attention away from the very significant problems that pervade other aspects of the criminal justice system. As Carol Steiker and Jordan Steiker have written, "the settled acceptance that 'death is different' may obscure or normalize pathologies that afflict non-capital criminal punishment."[87] We can see this in the way in which the Court has limited proportionality analysis and heightened review to death penalty cases only.

In 1977, one year after the constitutionality of guided-discretion death penalty schemes was upheld in *Gregg*, the Court ruled in *Coker v. Georgia* that the death penalty is unconstitutional for the crime of the rape of an adult because it is "excessive" to the gravity of the crime.[88] We saw above that, since then, the Court has also outlawed capital punishment for offenses that do not result in death, and has imposed categorical bans on sentencing to death those who are not considered to be sufficiently morally blameworthy.[89] Over the same period, though, the Court has declined to apply a similar proportionality test in non-capital cases, and has generally avoided categorical bans in non-capital cases. In 1980, just three years after *Coker* was decided, the Court held in *Rummel v. Estelle* that in cases involving terms of imprisonment, "the length of the sentence actually imposed is purely a matter of legislative prerogative."[90] In *Solem v. Helm*, decided in 1983, Justice Powell seemed to row back from this position, holding that a sentence of life without the possibility of parole for issuing a fraudulent check was excessive and thus unconstitutional.[91] Although Powell did not explicitly mimic the Court's capital proportionality analysis, he introduced a test that was substantively the same: the Court was to consider the gravity of the crime in relation to the harshness of the punishment. However, in 1991, just two years after the Court emphatically rejected proportionality analysis in the capital cases *Stanford* and *Penry*, the Court ruled in *Harmelin v. Michigan* that non-capital sentences would only be unconstitutional when they were "grossly" disproportionate to the severity of the crime.[92]

In the mid-1990s, then, non-capital cases were only subject to a very narrow type of proportionality analysis. When the Court expanded proportionality analysis in the capital context in *Atkins v. Virginia* in 2002 and *Roper v Simmons* in 2005, it simultaneously reiterated the narrowness of such analysis in non-capital contexts. In the 2003 case of *Ewing v. California*, the Court upheld a sentence of 25 years-to-life for a repeat offender convicted under California's "three-strikes-you're-out" law. Ewing had been caught attempting to steal some golf clubs from a shop, but this was not considered to be "the rare case in which a threshold comparison of the crime committed and the sentence imposed leads to an inference of gross disproportionality."[93]

While litigators have generally felt compelled to treat capital and non-capital cases as analytically distinct for the purposes of constitutional challenges, the rationale of *Roper* has been applied to the issue of juveniles facing sentences of life without the possibility of parole for non-homicide offenses, and it is in these cases that the Court has begun to dismantle the wall that it had previously put in place between capital and non-capital punishments. In 2006, Terrance Graham was sentenced to a term of life imprisonment without parole (LWOP) for a non-fatal crime that he had committed when 16 years old. Following the decision in *Roper*, he challenged the constitutionality of such a punishment. His lawyers asserted that "[t]he argument that 'death is different' does not... cabin *Roper* to capital cases. In both capital and non-capital cases, the Court also has examined the offender's characteristics to determine whether a sentence is grossly disproportionate." Graham's attorneys explained that the *Roper* Court had rejected the contention that a "juvenile offender's future characteristics as an adult could be accurately determined on a contemporaneous, individualized basis at sentencing", thus requiring a categorical ban.[94] In another case, Joe Sullivan's lawyers agreed: "The constitutional logic of *Roper v. Simmons*", the Brief began,

> controls this case and requires the invalidation of a sentence of life imprisonment without parole imposed on a 13-year-old child. To be sure, *Roper* dealt with a death sentence, and death is different from lesser sentences in many ways that are relevant to Eighth Amendment analysis. But life without parole is also different from lesser sentences in important ways.[95]

In the conjoined cases of *Graham v. Florida* and *Sullivan v. Florida*, decided in 2010, the Supreme Court agreed with these contentions, outlawing the sentence of LWOP for juveniles convicted of non-homicides.[96] This was the first time the Court applied its death penalty jurisprudence to a non-capital case, suggesting that death is not so different after all.[97] The issue of whether abolitionists should support life without parole as an alternative sentence even for adult offenders is given separate attention in Chapter Seven, but for now we can turn to Kennedy's separate concurring opinion in the death penalty case *Davis v. Ayala* in 2015 to see a second way in which his dignity-based jurisprudence has been applied to other issues of criminal justice. Petitioner had not raised the issue of solitary confinement, but Kennedy nonetheless took it upon himself to write of the ways in which solitary confinement on death row does not comport with respect for that person's dignity. He described how solitary could cause a person to "lapse in and out of a mindless state with almost no awareness or appreciation for time or his surroundings." He went on to say that "[a] considerable number of the prisoners fell, after even a short [solitary] confinement, into a semi-fatuous condition ... and others became violently insane; others, still, committed suicide."[98] Similarly, in *Kennedy v Louisiana*, Kennedy appeared to question the normativity of retribution, urging instead that punishments be designed for more rehabilitative purposes: "In most cases justice is not better served by terminating the life of the perpetrator rather than confining him and preserving the possibility that he and the system will find ways to allow him to understand the enormity of his offense."[99] The recognition of the perpetrator's agency bears hallmarks of Kennedy's conception of dignity.

C. Radical anti-death penalty constitutionalism in lower courts

Radical anti-death penalty constitutionalism has also appeared in lower courts. In 2015, the Connecticut Supreme Court issued an opinion that, perhaps more than any other death penalty judicial opinion in recent years, reflected Alvan Stewart's radicalism. In 1845, Stewart had put his theory about the unconstitutionality of slavery into practice in a freedom suit in New Jersey, which had enacted gradual emancipation statutes in 1804 and 1820. Under these statutes, people who had been born into slavery prior to July 4, 1804, would remain in bondage for life, but all children born to slaves after that date would serve as apprentices to their owners until the ages of 25 if they were male, and 21 for females, at which point they would be freed. In two companion cases, *State v. Van Buren* and *State v. Post*, Stewart argued for the freedom of a slave who had been born before the 1804 statute was passed, and for the freedom of a girl who had been born after 1804, but who was still apprenticed to her master. Stewart's argument ran as follows: the new state constitution of 1844 abolished slavery on grounds that had been modeled on Article I of the 1780 Massachusetts Constitution, which itself had been relied upon by Chief Judge Cushing in the Massachusetts Supreme Court to abolish slavery.[100] Put more succinctly, Stewart argued that the 1844 constitution required the emancipation statutes to apply retroactively. This was the first time that radical constitutionalism – the argument that the court must abolish slavery – has been aired in a courtroom.[101] The Court was unimpressed with Stewart's arguments, with Judge Nevius remarking "that much of the argument seemed rather addressed to the feelings than to the legal intelligence of the court."[102]

The parallels between this case and the 2015 case of *State v. Santiago*, decided in the state supreme court of Connecticut, are striking. In 2012, the legislature had repealed Connecticut's death penalty prospectively only, leaving 11 men on death row, much like how the New Jersey emancipation statute had left the already-enslaved untouched. Petitioner claimed that the repeal should apply retroactively, and the Court agreed. It was unconstitutionally arbitrary, the Court held, to subject capital punishment upon those who had committed capital offenses prior to the date of the legislative repeal. If the death penalty was to be imposed at all, the Court observed, it must be reserved for those who were most deserving of death, not those who happened to commit a crime before a particular date.[103]

D. The ambiguity of the US Supreme Court's approach to race and capital punishment

We can see elements of radical constitutionalism in the US Supreme Court's use of dignity; its expansion of its capital punishment jurisprudence to non-capital cases;

and in the decision of the Connecticut Supreme Court to apply the legislative repeal retroactively. However, it is much more ambiguous whether or not the US Supreme Court's approach to race and the death penalty is radical or not. It was noted in the previous chapters that the Court has habitually declined to address issues of racial bias in the administration of the death penalty. Although in recent years the Court has appeared more willing to strike down death sentences on such claims, it has generally refrained from acknowledging that racism is a systemic problem.

In *Miller-El v Dretke*, decided in 2005,[104] the Court applied the *Batson* rule that forbids the use of peremptory challenges to strike off jurors from cases on the basis of their skin color. Writing for the majority, Justice Souter pointed out that "[t]he prosecutors used their peremptory strikes to exclude 91% of the eligible African-American venire members… Happenstance is unlikely to produce this disparity."[105] Souter was correct that the pattern of excluding black jurors was not coincidental, but he was not willing to hold that the death penalty is systemically biased against minorities. In *Foster v. Chatman*, decided in 2016, the Court once again ruled in favor of petitioner, who claimed that the trial jury was racially biased.[106] Foster, an African American, had been sentenced to death by an all-white jury for the murder of an elderly white woman. At trial, the prosecuting attorney had used their peremptory strikes on all four of the eligible black jurors. The Court held by a 7–1 margin that a *Batson* violation had occurred. It was noted that the prosecutor's copy of the jury venire list had the names of all potential black jurors highlighted in green, with a note indicating that the highlighting "represents Blacks." An investigator had also been tasked with specifying which black person should be accepted to sit on the jury "[i]f it comes down to having to pick one of the black jurors." In the prosecution's notes, all black jurors were identified with the terms "B#1", "B#2" and so on. The reasons offered by the prosecution for striking these black jurors were also held to be unsatisfactory. One was removed on the grounds that he worked at a hospital that dealt with mentally ill people, thus making them "more sympathetic to the underdog." However, the same attorney did not express any concerns about a white prospective juror who worked at the same hospital. The white juror ended up serving on the jury.[107]

The courts have also tackled the pervasiveness of racial discrimination in the sentencing stage of capital trials. In 1997, Duane Buck was sentenced to death in Texas for the double homicide of his ex-girlfriend and her friend, in part because the jury considered that, because of his gender and race, he posed a future threat to society. At Buck's trial, the prosecutor posed the following question to a psychologist who had been called to testify on Buck's behalf: "You have determined that the sex factor, that a male is more violent than a female because that's just the way it is, and that the race factor, black increases the future dangerousness for various complicated reasons; is that correct?" The psychologist answered in the affirmative. The testimony had clear overtones of the "scientific" studies that were used in the 18th and 19th Centuries to justify slavery on the grounds that black people were biologically prone to violence, and thus needed to be kept in captivity.[108]

Buck appealed his sentence, but in 2011 the US Supreme Court refused to intervene in the case. Dissenting from the denial of certiorari, Justices Sotomayer and Kagan highlighted that the "death sentence [was] marred by racial overtones," and asserted that "our criminal justice system should not tolerate" racial discrimination.[109] When the Court finally agreed to hear the case, it ruled in 2017 that the "testimony appealed to a powerful racial stereotype – that of black men as 'violence prone.'" Chief Justice Roberts described such evidence as "a particularly noxious strain of racial prejudice", concluding that Buck had been unconstitutionally sentenced to "death on the basis of race."[110]

Although Buck's case was unique because of Texas's "future dangerousness" statute, similar examples can be found in other parts of the country. In November 2016, the Court of Appeals for the Fourth Circuit upheld a decision to overturn the death sentence of a black man named Johnny Bennett in South Carolina because his trial had been marred by racially-charged statements from the prosecutor, Donald Myers. In front of an all-white jury, Myers repeatedly referred to Bennett as "King Kong", a "caveman," a "mountain man," a "monster," a "big old tiger," and "[t]he beast of burden." Myers made the reference to King Kong when telling the jury what would happen if they did not return a death sentence: "You give him life, the real Johnny will come back. You give him life and he'll come back out. Meeting him again will be like meeting King Kong on a bad day." Myers also brought the jury's attention to the unfounded and irrelevant allegation that Bennett had been having a sexual relationship with a white woman.[111] Together with the references to King Kong, the court considered this to be part of Myers's attempt to influence the all-white jury about the dangerousness of Bennett, based on the color of his skin, by touching on concerns with inter-racial relationships: "Likening Bennett to King Kong in particular stoked race-based fears by conjuring the image of a gargantuan, black ape who goes on a killing spree and proceeds to swing the frail, white, blonde Fay Wray at the top of the Empire State Building." As the Court noted, "in context, the prosecutor's comments mined a vein of historical prejudice against African-Americans, who have been appallingly disparaged as primates or members of a subhuman species in some lesser state of evolution."[112] Again, it is impossible to separate this sentiment from the issues that underpinned slavery: a belief that black people were not as "human" as white people, and could therefore be treated as property or animals.

Despite these rulings, the courts have generally refused to countenance the systemic nature of racism. In 1999, Justice Handler of the New Jersey Supreme Court issued a strongly-worded dissent in which he implored his colleagues to act on the evidence of racial discrimination in the administration of the death penalty. In *State v. Loftin*, Handler argued that New Jersey's death penalty was unconstitutional because of "a long and relentless history of racism that has not only the capacity to cause a disproportionate impact on blacks in the administration of the death penalty, but has indeed done so from the era of slavery in this country, and, many argue, to the present."[113] His colleagues did not share his concerns, though.

A striking exception to the judicial reluctance to address systemic racism can be found in *State v. Santiago*, in which the Connecticut Supreme Court referred to the pervasiveness of racism in the administration of capital punishment.[114] The Court stated that the death penalty "appears to be inescapably tainted by caprice and bias", focusing particularly on "racial and ethnic discrimination."[115] Remarkably, the court had not been presented with statistical evidence of such discrimination, and the issue was not before the court to consider. Similarly, there was no allegation in the pertinent case of racial bias by individual prosecutors, jurors, or judges.[116] In this sense, the observation of the systemic racism in death penalty systems was a radical departure from the *McCleskey* position. The court also referred to the "striking" disparity in the use of the death penalty in the northern states and in "the thirteen states that comprised the Confederacy", making the point that the former Confederate states "were last to abandon slavery and segregation, and ... were most resistant to the federal enforcement of civil rights norms."[117] Justices Fleming Norcott and Andrew McDonald explained the link between the wrong of slavery and the wrong of capital punishment, and although they did not use the word "dignity", their judgment nonetheless invoked the idea of dignity. In their words:

> We strongly emphasize that the fact that a charging or sentencing decision may be based in part on impermissible racial factors does not imply that the prosecutor, judge, or juror making that decision is "racist," as that term is typically used. Statistical studies from other jurisdictions have demonstrated that the most likely explanation for such disparities is the tendency of members of the majority race to be more empathetic to majority victims, who resemble themselves, and less sympathetic to minority perpetrators, with whom they are less able to identify. This conclusion is bolstered by recent scientific studies that now document what has long been recognized: most, if not all, of us exhibit unconscious or implicit bias.
>
> It likely is the case that many, if not most, of the documented disparities in capital charging and sentencing arise not from purposeful, hateful racism or racial animus, but rather from these sorts of subtle, imperceptible biases on the part of generally well-meaning decision makers. Historically, though, it is difficult to refute ... that, at varying times throughout our history, the lives of Native Americans, African–Americans, Asians, Irish, Italians, Jews, Roman Catholics, and Hispanics simply have not been considered to be as innately valuable as those of the cultural majority.[118]

The Connecticut Supreme Court's decision, then, explicitly recognized that the problem of the death penalty is that, at least in some cases, it is premised on the impermissible view that some people are not as "innately valuable" as others.

E. Elements of radicalism in anti-death penalty opinions

Since 1976, 19 justices have served on the US Supreme Court, only six of whom have questioned the constitutionality of the penalty while sitting on the bench.[119] Of those six, only Justices Brennan and Marshall invoked the idea of dignity when holding that state-sanctioned executions are unconstitutional at all times. Justices Blackmun, Stevens, and Breyer (joined by Justice Ginsburg), on the other hand, have issued anti-death penalty opinions which are devoid of any reference to the idea of dignity, and which are based primarily on the unworkability of capital punishment. On the one hand, these decisions provide the framework or roadmap for abolitionists to follow in their quest for a favorable judgement. On the other hand, they promote a conservative approach to abolition that normalizes broader problems with the criminal justice system.

In *Callins v. Collins*, decided in 1994, Justice Blackmun – who had in 1972 upheld the constitutionality of capital punishment notwithstanding his personal opposition to it – opined that he "no longer shall tinker with the machinery of death."[120] His position was shaped by his experience of trying in vain to adequately square the constitutional demand for consistency, with the constitutional demand for individualized sentencing: "Experience has taught us that the constitutional goal of eliminating arbitrariness and discrimination from the administration of death... can never be achieved without compromising an equally essential component of fundamental fairness – individualized sentencing."[121] Blackmun noted that the Court was failing to satisfy either of these competing demands: "[T]his Court," he held, "has engaged in a futile effort to balance these constitutional demands, and now is retreating not only from the *Furman* promise of consistency and rationality, but from the requirement of individualized sentencing as well."[122]

At one point in his decision, Blackmun stated that the death penalty can never be administered in a constitutionally acceptable manner: "It is virtually self evident to me now that no combination of procedural rules or substantive regulations ever can save the death penalty from its inherent constitutional deficiencies." Yet later, he stated: "Perhaps one day this Court will develop procedural rules or verbal formulas that actually will provide consistency, fairness, and reliability in a capital sentencing scheme." He also seemed to explicitly narrow his finding to the death penalty schemes that were in operation at that time when he writes "the death penalty, *as currently administered*, is unconstitutional."[123]

Blackmun was at pains to chastise his colleagues on the Court for "erect[ing] unprecedented and unwarranted barriers to the federal judiciary's review of the constitutional claims of capital defendants",[124] complaining in particular about the rules the Court had created with respect to hearing claims of innocence and racial discrimination. However, he explicitly limited his concerns to the death penalty. He asserted that "[t]here is a heightened need for fairness in the administration of death [because] death truly is different from all other punishments a society inflicts upon its citizens."[125] Moreover, he suggested the risk of error in capital cases raises concerns that are unique to the death penalty:

> While the risk of mistake in the determination of the appropriate penalty may be tolerated in other areas of the criminal law, in capital cases the fundamental respect for humanity underlying the Eighth Amendment ... requires consideration of the character and record of the individual offender and the

> circumstances of the particular offense as a constitutionally indispensable part of the process of inflicting the penalty of death.[126]

Read literally, Blackmun appears to accept the risk of unfairness and error in non-capital contexts, and confines his concern to the death penalty.

Blackmun's dissent from the denial of certiorari in *Callins* thus appears to be replete with conservatism, but it is plausible to identify elements of the idea of dignity in his dissent. Justice Scalia stated that the dilemma identified by Blackmun could be resolved by eliminating the requirements of consistency and individualized sentencing since "[t]hese commands were invented without benefit of any textual or historical support".[127] This brings Blackmun's position into sharp relief: Blackmun could have resolved the dilemma by noting that the Constitution does not demand individualized sentencing, thus paving the way for mandatory death penalty schemes which would satisfy the demand for consistency. Or, he could have noted that the Constitution does not demand consistency. However, underlying Blackmun's position was a recognition that the Constitution must retain integrity (through consistency), and respect must be paid to human dignity (through individualized sentencing). In this sense, his opinion was premised on the idea of institutional and human dignity that was outlined in the previous chapter. It is unfortunate, though, that he was not more explicit about this.

Like Justice Blackmun, Justice Stevens had voted to uphold the constitutionality of capital punishment in *Gregg*. Unlike Blackmun, though, Stevens had not given any clear indication of his personal antipathy towards executions. Thus, when he said in *Baze v. Rees* in 2008 that capital punishment is "excessive and cruel and unusual punishment violative of the Eighth Amendment",[128] it was considered something of a watershed moment. Elisabeth Semel notes that, at least outside the Court, "Justice Stevens's step into the abolitionist camp was wholly unexpected."[129] For our purposes, there are two features of Stevens's opinion that are of interest. The first is that his grounds for ruling the death penalty unconstitutional are generally unique to the phenomenon of capital punishment, thus encouraging the conservative approach to abolition. The second noteworthy feature of Stevens's judgment is that he did not dissent from the holding in *Baze*. Justices Brennan, Marshall, and Blackmun had all announced that they would steadfastly dissent from any case in which a death sentence was affirmed, but Stevens asserted that his conclusion did not "justify a refusal to respect precedents that remain a part of our law."[130] His refusal to dissent not only contributed to the perceived legitimacy of the decision in *Baze*, it also threatened the abolitionist potential of his judgment since, as Robert Cover noted, the adherence to formal legal rules and procedures was a defining characteristic of the judiciary's complicity in slavery. We will first see that despite the apparent conservatism of his opinion, Stevens does illustrate some radical tendencies. However, his decision to not dissent is regrettable.

On August 6, 2005, Justice Stevens addressed the American Bar Association at the Thurgood Marshall Awards Dinner. In his speech, Stevens expressed qualms about the death penalty, but did not indicate that he was prepared to rule the punishment unconstitutional. He noted that Justice Marshall's "rejection of the death penalty rested on principles that would be controlling even if error never infected the criminal process", but he did not proceed to agree with those principles. Instead, he focused specifically on the problem of "error" and the procedural dimensions of capital punishment. Stevens explained that the death-qualification of juries, the permissibility of victim-impact statements, and the fact that sentencing judges in many jurisdictions are affected by considerations of re-election, all combine to "tip the scales in favor of death".[131]

In an article published the next year, James Liebman and Lawrence Marshall described Stevens's death penalty jurisprudence as reflecting a "pragmatic incrementalism" which allowed "for now, at least, to narrow without abolishing the death penalty."[132] Although the authors did not make the connection, we can see echoes of the gradualist philosophy of conservative anti-slavery activists. Given that just two years later Stevens changed course and announced that he considered it constitutionally appropriate to abolish the death penalty, we might describe his position in *Baze* as a conversion to immediatism. A close reading of his opinion, though, suggests that his opinion cannot be read as an endorsement of the radical approach.

In *Baze*, Justice Stevens began by explaining that the punishment serves no penological purposes, stating that "the recent rise in statutes providing for life imprisonment without the possibility of parole demonstrates that incapacitation is neither a necessary nor a sufficient justification for the death penalty."[133] In other words, Stevens began his attack on capital punishment by endorsing the view that some people deserve to be sentenced to die behind prison walls, with no hope of release. It is noteworthy that he begins this section of his opinion with this, as it indicates a deliberate attempt to get skeptics of abolition on side. In fact, the *Gregg* Court had not even considered incapacitation as a primary purpose of the death penalty, focusing instead on deterrence and retribution. In his analysis of deterrence, Stevens again implicitly severs the death penalty from any consideration of the deterrent effect of punishment generally. He highlights the lack of any reliable empirical research that demonstrates that the death penalty deters potential offenders, and states: "In the absence of such evidence, deterrence cannot serve as a sufficient penological justification for this *uniquely severe and irrevocable* punishment."[134] His reference to the uniqueness of the death penalty suggests that even if there is an absence of evidence that deterrence is served by some other non-capital penalty, such as LWOP, his conclusion would not hold because such punishments are not as severe or irrevocable. Finally, his discussion of the retributive rationale for capital punishment betrays support for harsh and painful punishments. At issue in the case was whether a particular lethal injection protocol was "cruel and unusual", and Stevens noted that "our society has moved away from public and painful retribution toward ever more humane forms of punishment,"[135] thus explaining the adoption of lethal injections. However, in his view, humane executions defeat the retributive rationale of capital punishment: "[B]y requiring that an execution be relatively painless, we necessarily protect the inmate from enduring any punishment that is comparable to the suffering inflicted on his victim. This trend, while appropriate and required by the Eighth Amendment's prohibition on cruel and unusual punishment, actually undermines the very premise on which public approval of the retribution rationale is based."[136] Tellingly, Stevens did not go as far as Justice Marshall, who in *Furman* declared that retribution as a goal of punishment was impermissible.[137] Stevens's approach to retribution is thus unclear. He seems to endorse it as a permissible goal, and seems to suggest that retribution is only secured when the painfulness of the punishment is equivalent to the pain inflicted by the defendant. Yet he also notes that the Eighth Amendment demands "relatively painless" punishment. In this respect, Stevens actually opens the door to challenges against harsh retributivism generally, and he hints that the basis of public support for a punishment does not necessarily render that punishment constitutional (noting that the trend towards humane punishment, which is demanded by the Eighth Amendment, "actually undermines the very premise on which public approval of the retribution rationale is based.").

Stevens goes on to note that the *Gregg* Court only sanctioned capital punishment insofar as its application was relatively free from arbitrariness, discrimination, and error.[138] For four reasons, he surmises that death penalty schemes across the nation have failed to live up to the standards demanded by the *Gregg* Court. Three of these four reasons, though, are applicable only to the context of capital punishment. The process of death-qualification, he writes, results in juries that are "biased in favor of conviction".[139] The unique facts of death penalty cases, Stevens suggests, has encouraged policy-makers, judges, and juries to focus more on ensuring that the crime does not go unpunished, rather than on ensuring that the conviction and sentence are fair. To support this, he cites the Court's decisions that permit a mandatory death sentence when a jury finds aggravating and mitigating factors to be in equipoise, and that permit the introduction of victim-impact statements notwithstanding their irrelevance to the moral culpability of the offender. Abolishing the death penalty, though, would not necessarily have an impact on the commission of offenses that currently attract death. Instead, such cases with their "unique" facts will encourage policy-makers and so on to secure sentences of life without parole.[140] Only his third factor – the perniciousness of racial discrimination – is applicable to non-capital contexts. His fourth factor – the risk of executing an innocent person – does nothing to counter the problem of other harsh punishments. Indeed, he explicitly writes: "The risk of executing innocent defendants can be entirely eliminated by treating any penalty more severe than life imprisonment without the possibility of parole as constitutionally excessive."[141]

Perhaps most strikingly, Stevens ultimately agreed to join the opinion upholding the method of execution and lethal injection protocol in question, stating that his finding that the death penalty is likely unconstitutional

> does not, however, justify a refusal to respect precedents that remain a part of our law. This Court has held that the death penalty is constitutional, and has established a framework for evaluating the constitutionality of particular methods of execution. Under those precedents... I am persuaded that the evidence adduced by petitioners fails to prove that Kentucky's lethal injection

> protocol violates the Eighth Amendment. Accordingly, I join the Court's judgment.[142]

He thus deploys what Robert Cover would describe as a "[r]etreat to mechanistic formalism," proclaiming that he is bound by the formal rules of the judicial procedure.

More recently, Justice Breyer's dissenting opinion in *Glossip v. Gross* (2015), joined by Justice Ginsburg, has caught the attention of anti-death penalty activists. Breyer outlined "three fundamental constitutional defects [with the death penalty]: (1) serious unreliability, (2) arbitrariness in application, and (3) unconscionably long delays that undermine the death penalty's penological purpose. Perhaps as a result, (4) most places within the United States have abandoned its use."[143] Several in the anti-death penalty community have argued that Breyer's opinion provides a roadmap towards abolition, with Robert Smith of the Eighth Amendment Project writing that "*Glossip* feels different" to the opinions of Justices Brennan, Marshall, Blackmun, or Stevens, "because it is no longer unthinkable that there are five votes for ending the death penalty."[144] In a statement issued shortly after the decision was handed down, Amnesty International described Breyer's dissent as "a welcome development".[145]

Breyer's dissent derived from his experience of hearing death penalty cases, and he notably did not go as far as Brennan or Marshall in stating the capital punishment is immoral. Instead, he focused on the tension between the constitutional requirement that executions be delayed to ensure that only the "worst of the worst" were being executed, with the penological requirement that executions *not* be delayed so as to serve the retributive and deterrent purposes of capital punishment. Again, this line of argument is unique to the penalty of death, since any other sentence is meted out the moment it is handed down by the sentencer.

Breyer reiterated Stevens's concerns with death-qualified juries and with the chances that the horrific facts of death penalty cases heightened the chances of wrongful convictions. After discussing the risk of error, Breyer then considered the excessive delays in death penalty processes across the country. In his words: "A death penalty system that seeks procedural fairness and reliability brings with it delays that severely aggravate the cruelty of capital punishment and significantly undermine the rationale for imposing a sentence of death in the first place."[146] Breyer concludes that delays are needed in order to ensure that the death penalty is applied fairly and reliably, and that without such delays, the punishment would be contrary to the Eighth Amendment.

Although much of Breyer's opinion appears to be solely focused on the irreversibility of capital punishment, his opinion has hallmarks of a radical approach for at least three reasons. First, he expressly identified the wrong of dehumanizing those on death row through the lengthy stays on death row, describing how prisoners suffer "decades of especially severe, dehumanizing conditions of confinement."[147] Second, he eschewed Justice Stevens' reasons for adhering to precedent, and has since consistently dissented when the Court has denied certiorari in death penalty cases.[148] Third, he also addressed the institutional competency of the Court to strike down the death penalty. Rather than deploy responsibility mitigation mechanisms, he squarely stated that the "lack of reliability, the arbitrary application of a serious and irreversible punishment, individual suffering caused by long delays, and lack of penological purpose are quintessentially judicial matters. They concern the infliction – indeed the unfair, cruel, and unusual infliction – of a serious punishment upon an individual." He concludes with the observation that the Court has "made clear that the Constitution contemplates that in the end our own judgment will be brought to bear on the question of the acceptability of the death penalty under the Eighth Amendment."[149] Breyer is therefore somewhere between Justices Brennan and Marshall on the one hand, and Justices Blackmun and Stevens on the other. He understands that the issue of dignity is relevant to the constitutionality of capital punishment, and he recognizes that abolition is within the bounds of the judicial role, but he focuses primarily on matters that are unique to capital punishment and that do not address the root of the problem.

IV. Conclusions

The radical slavery abolitionists' natural law-based claims regarding equality and liberty for all contributed to the Fourteenth Amendment, which has been used to bring American laws and practice closer into line with the vision of the radical abolitionists. It can therefore be argued that a similar natural law-inspired approach to anti-death penalty constitutionalism might offer a framework for addressing other issues in the criminal justice system. However, to date litigators rarely invoke the term "dignity" in briefs – indeed, despite the *Roper* Court's use of the term in 2005, the Brief for Patrick Kennedy (in *Kennedy v. Louisiana*, three years after *Roper*) did not make reference to this idea at all, and the only reference to the "integrity" of the constitutional system was made in the context of the need to respect the Court's previous case law.[150] In *Baze v. Rees*, respondents, defending the state's lethal injection protocol, asserted that the protocol in question "did not offend the dignity of the condemned or of society as a whole."[151] It was asserted that even petitioners' own expert witnesses accepted that pancuronium bromide "speeds the death process, prevents involuntary muscular movement that may interfere with the proper functioning of the IV equipment, and contributes to the dignity of the death process."[152] Counsel for Baze, on the other hand, referred to the *Roper* Court's reference to dignity, but did not engage with the idea further. Even in *Glossip v. Gross*, in which the issue of methods of execution squarely implicated the dignity of the person facing execution, petitioner did not raise the word at all in his brief.[153] Indeed, Glossip conceded that the proposed lethal injection would be "humane" if it went according to plan, concentrating instead on the risk that the execution would not go as planned. In *Hall v. Florida*, there was again no reference to the idea of dignity or integrity in the Brief for Petitioner.[154]

Advocates have not entirely ignored Kennedy's jurisprudence, though. In *Foster v. Chatman*, the Brief for Petitioner referenced both the dignity of the person, and the integrity of the legal system: "Race discrimination in the selection of jurors offends the dignity of persons and the integrity of the courts."[155] During oral argument in *Buck v. Texas*, Christina Swarns, Counsel for Duane Buck, emphasized the dangers of racism to the integrity of the legal system. She stated that the "racial bias that not only undermined the integrity of his own death sentence, it undermined the integrity of the court's."[156] The Court responded favorably to this submission, with Chief Justice Roberts writing in his opinion that "[r]elying on race to impose a criminal sanction poisons public confidence in the judicial process. It thus injures not just the defendant, but the law as an institution … the community at large, and … the democratic ideal reflected in the processes of our courts."[157] The promises of this sort of decision – one which opens the door to future challenges against practices that likewise damage the "the law as an institution … the community at large, and … the democratic ideal" – should be seized upon by abolitionists, taking into account the fact that comparable radical anti-slavery constitutionalism sowed the seeds for future challenges to a broad array of social injustices.

This is not to say that abolitionism could or should eschew appeals to popular opinion. Even though the Court has shifted its Eighth Amendment analysis away from the rudimentary bean counting that *Stanford* involved, national opinion is still a primary consideration in the Court's analysis. Moreover, though, changing the hearts and minds of the broader public is a central tenet of radical abolitionism. Moral suasion was considered by William Lloyd Garrison, for example, to be far more important than engaging with politicians or the judiciary. It is therefore to abolitionism in the public sphere that we now turn.

Notes

1 William M. Wiecek, *The Sources of Anti-Slavery Constitutionalism in America, 1760–1848* (Cornell University Press 1977) 274.

2 Justin Buckley Dyer, *Natural Law and the Antislavery Constitutional Tradition* (Cambridge University Press 2012) 187–188.

3 Raoul Berger was critical of the US Supreme Court's expansive interpretation of the Fourteenth Amendment, particularly that of the Warren Court. Berger controversially argues, for example, that the Framers of the Amendment never intended it to prohibit segregated schooling. Regardless of one's normative view of how Courts have applied the Amendment, it is widely accepted that successive Courts have adopted an expansive view of the Amendment. See Raoul Berger, *Government by Judiciary: The Transformation of the Fourteenth Amendment* (Harvard University Press 1977).

4 Wiecek, (n 1) 16.

5 Sanford Levinson, 'Wrong, But Legal?' *The Nation* (26 February 1983) 248 ("Any textualist comes up with a devastating problem in regard to the death penalty: both the Fifth and Fourteenth Amendments specifically acknowledge the possibility of a death penalty. They require only that due process of law be followed before a person can be deprived of life.")

6 Callins v. Collins 510 U.S. 1141 (1984).

7 Glossip v. Gross, 135 S.Ct. 2726 at 2747 (2015) (Scalia, J., concurring).

8 Charles Sumner stated that Taney "administered justice at last wickedly, and degraded the judiciary of the country, and degraded the age." *Congressional Globe*, 38 Cong., 2 Sess., 1012 (23 February 1865).

9 For example, see Edward S. Corwin, 'The *Dred Scott* Decision in the Light of Contemporary Legal Doctrines' (1911) 17 American Historical Review 52.
10 Robert Cover, *Justice Accused: Antislavery and the Judicial Process* (Yale University Press 1984) 199.
11 ibid 229–232.
12 ibid 232–236
13 ibid 236–238.
14 ibid 5–6.
15 Prigg v. Pennsylvania, 41 U.S. 539 (1842).
16 Joseph Story to Ezekial Bacon, in William Wetmore Story (ed), *Life and Letters of Joseph Story* (C.C. Little and J. Brown, 1851) 2: 431. Quoted in Cover, (n 10) 119.
17 Furman v. Georgia, 408 U.S. 238, 405 (1972).
18 ibid 406.
19 ibid 411.
20 ibid 414.
21 Kenneth Williams suggests that the "intense ideological screening" of Supreme Court nominees began in 1987 as a result of a campaign by liberal interest groups against the nomination of Robert Bork who was known for his staunchly conservative views. Kenneth Williams, *Most Deserving of Death? An Analysis of the Supreme Court's Death Penalty Jurisprudence* (Ashgate 2012) 177.
22 Statement of Senator Hatch, Hearings on the Nomination of Judge Anthony M. Kennedy to the Supreme Court, Senate Judiciary Committee, December 14, 1987.
23 Transcript of Hearings on the Nomination of Judge Sonia Sotomayor to the Supreme Court, Senate Judiciary Committee, Jul 14, 2009 p.42.
24 See Williams, (n 21) 78–79.
25 Speech of William Lloyd Garrison, 'On the Dissolution of the Union' (at the New England Anti-Slavery Convention, 31 May 1855) reprinted in *The Liberator* (Vol. XXV, No. 24 15 June 1855).
26 Wiecek (n 1) 17.
27 Salmon P. Chase, 'Address of the Southern and Western Liberty Convention, Held at Cincinnati, June 11 and 12, 1845. To the People of the United States,' in Charles D. Cleveland (ed) *Anti-Slavery Addresses of 1844 and 1845* (J.A. Bancroft 1867) 86 (cited in Wiecek (n 1) 210).
28 Sean Wilentz 'Constitutionally, Slavery is no National Institution' *The New York Times* (16 September 2016) http://www.nytimes.com/2015/09/16/opinion/constitutionally-slavery-is-no-national-institution.html.
29 Wiecek (n 1) 16.
30 ibid 38.
31 Jonathan Elliot (ed.) *The Debates in the Several State Conventions on the Adoption of the Federal Constitution*, 5 vols. (Vol. 5, Yale University Press 1911) 478.
32 Paul Finkelman, *Slavery and the Founders: Race and Liberty in the Age of Jefferson* (3rd edn, Routledge 2015) 6
33 Dyer (n 2) 16.
34 Wiecek (n 1) 256.
35 ibid 255.
36 ibid 266.
37 ibid 256–257.
38 United States v. Schooner Amistad, 40 U.S. 518 (1841).
39 The Antelope. 23 U.S. (10 Wheat.) 66, 121 (1825).
40 Dyer (n 2) 75.
41 ibid 77.

42 ibid 85.
43 James Wilson, *Congressional Globe*, 39th Congress, 1st Session, 1117 (1866). See also Howard Jay Graham, 'Our 'Declaratory' Fourteenth Amendment' (1954) 7 Stanford Law Review 3, 38.
44 Lyman Trumbull, *Congressional Globe*, 39th Congress, 1st Session, 474 (1866).
45 John Bingham, *Congressional Globe*, 39th Congress, 1st Session, 1090 (1866).
46 Jacob Howard, *Congressional Globe*, 39th Congress, 1st Session, 2766 (1866).
47 Garrett Davis, *Congressional Globe*, 39th Congress, 1st Session, 528 (1866).
48 Dyer (n 2) 187–191.
49 Jacobus tenBroeck, *The Antislavery Origins of the Fourteenth Amendment* (University of California Press 1951).
50 Howard Jay Graham, 'The Early Antislavery Background of the Fourteenth Amendment' (1950) Wisconsin Law Review 483.
51 William E. Nelson, *The Fourteenth Amendment: From Political Principle to Judicial Doctrine* (Harvard University Press 1988) In particular, see Chapter 4: The Use of Antebellum Rhetoric in the Amendment Debates (noting that "the debates on the Fourteenth Amendment amounted to little more than a rhetorical replay of antebellum antislavery arguments") 64.
52 Oliver Wendell Holmes, 'Natural Law' (1918) 32 Harvard Law Review 41, 41.
53 Oliver Wendell Holmes *The Common Law* (Little, Brown and Company 1881).
54 Dyer (n 2) 25–31; Gary J. Jacobsohn, *The Supreme Court and the Decline of Constitutional Aspiration* (Rowman & Littlefield 1986).
55 Stanford v. Kentucky, 492 U.S. 361 (1989).
56 See the discussion in Chapter Three.
57 McCleskey v. Kemp, 481 U.S. 279, 314–315 (1987).
58 Atkins v. Virginia, 536 U.S. 304 (2002).
59 Penry v. Lynaugh, 492 U.S. 302 (1989). The Court now uses the term "intellectually disabled" instead. See 134 S. Ct. 1986 (2014).
60 Atkins (n 58) 316, n. 1.
61 Stanford (n 55) 369 n 1.
62 Atkins (n 58) 322.
63 ibid 338 (Scalia J., dissenting)
64 Roper v. Simmons, 543 U.S. 551 (2005).
65 ibid 566.
66 ibid 568–575.
67 ibid 575–578.
68 ibid 560.
69 ibid 578.
70 ibid 605.
71 Trop v. Dulles, 356 U.S. 86, 100 (1958) (plurality opinion).
72 Kennedy v. Louisiana, 554 U. S. 407, 420 (2008).
73 Brown v. Plata, 563 U.S. 493, 510 (2011).
74 Hall v. Florida, 134 S. Ct. 1986, 1992 (2014) (internal references omitted).
75 Kennedy (n 72) 420.
76 Ronald Dworkin, *Taking Rights Seriously* (Harvard University Press 1978) 149.
77 Ronald Dworkin, 'Natural Law Revisited' (1982) 34 University of Florida Law Review 165, 165.
78 Ronald Dworkin, *Freedom's Law: The Moral Reading of the American Constitution* (OUP 2006) 10.
79 Sotirios Barber and James Fleming, *Constitutional Interpretation: The Basic Questions* (OUP 2007) 160.
80 Arthur v. Dunn, 137 S. Ct. 725, 734 (2017) (Sotomayor J., dissenting from denial of certiorari).

81 For more discussion about the role of dignity in methods of executions, see Imogen Jones and Bharat Malkani, 'Beastly Humans: The Welfare Model of Executions' (2017) Law, Culture, and the Humanities 1 [online first version].
82 Glossip v. Gross, 35 S. Ct. 2726, 2795 (2015) (Sotomayor J., dissenting).
83 Baze v Rees, 553 U. S. 35, 57 (2008).
84 Glossip (n 82) 2734.
85 Furman (n 17) 306 (Justice Stewart, concurring).
86 Woodson v. North Carolina, 428 U.S. 280, 305 (1976).
87 Carol S. Steiker and Jordan M. Steiker, 'Opening a Window or Building a Wall? The Effect of Eighth Amendment Death Penalty Law and Advocacy on Criminal Justice More Broadly' (2008) 11 Journal of Constitutional Law 155, 177.
88 Coker v. Georgia, 433 U.S. 584 (1977).
89 Steiker and Steiker, 'Opening a Window' (n 87) 178–184.
90 Rummel v. Estelle, 445 U.S. 263, 274 (1980).
91 Solem v. Helm, 463 U.S. 277 (1983).
92 Harmelin v. Michigan, 501 U.S. 957 (1991).
93 Ewing v. California, 538 U.S. 11, 30 (2003) (internal quotes and citations omitted).
94 Brief for Petitioner, *Graham v. Florida*, No 08–7412 (filed July 16, 2009) at 24–25.
95 Brief for Petitioner, *Sullivan v. Florida,* No 08–7621 (filed July 16, 2009) at 5.
96 Graham v. Florida, 560 U.S. 48 (2010).
97 Mary Berkheiser, 'Death Is Not So Different After All: *Graham v. Florida* and the Court's 'Kids Are Different' Eighth Amendment Jurisprudence' (2011) 36 Vermont Law Review 1. Adult offenders are still eligible for LWOP for a range of offenses, but see Sarah F. Russell and Tracy L. Denholtz, 'Procedures for Proportionate Sentences: The Next Wave of Eighth Amendment Noncapital Litigation' (2016) 48 Connecticut Law Review 1121.
98 Davis v. Ayala, 135 S. Ct. 2187, 2209 (2015) (Kennedy J. concurring in judgment).
99 Kennedy (n 72) 447.
100 See John D. Cushing, 'The Cushing Court and the Abolition of Slavery in Massachusetts: More Notes on the "Quock Walker Case"' (1961) 5 American Journal of Legal History.
101 See Wiecek (n 1) 256–57; Cover (n 10) 55–60
102 Cover (n 10) 56–57.
103 State v. Santiago, 122 A.3d 1 (Conn. 2015).
104 Miller-El v. Dretke, 545 U.S. 231 (2005).
105 ibid 241 (internal citations and quotations omitted).
106 Foster v. Chatman, 136 S. Ct. 1737; 195 L. Ed. 2d 1 (2016).
107 ibid 1742–1744.
108 See Brief of *Amicus Curiae* Lawyers' Committee for Civil Rights Under Law, Buck v. Texas No. 15–8049. Also see Maurice Chammah, 'The Case of Duane Buck' *The Marshall Project* (22 February 2017) https://www.themarshallproject.org/2016/04/20/what-you-need-to-know-if-the-supreme-court-takes-the-case-of-duane-buck#.S4BZoxk7k.
109 Buck v. Thaler, 565 U.S. 1022, 1025 (2011) (Sotomayor J., dissenting from denial of certiorari).
110 Buck v Texas, 137 S. Ct. 759, 776 (2017).
111 Bennett v. Stirling, 842 F.3d 319; 2016 U.S. App. LEXIS 20789 (21 November 2016).
112 ibid 324–325.
113 State v. Loftin, 724 A.2d, 129, 206 (N.J. 1999) (Handler, J., dissenting).
114 State v. Santiago, 122 A.3d 1, 66–8 (Conn. 2015).
115 Ibid.
116 ibid 85 (Norcott & McDonald, JJ., concurring) ("[W]e cannot end our state's nearly 400 year struggle with the macabre muck of capital punishment litigation without

speaking to the persistent allegations of racial and ethnic discrimination that have permeated the breadth of this state's experience with capital charging and sentencing decisions.").

117 ibid 52.

118 ibid 95–66 (Norcott & McDonald, JJ., concurring). See also McCleskey (n 57) 332 ("[A]mericans share a historical experience that has resulted in individuals within the culture ubiquitously attaching a significance to race that is irrational and often outside their awareness.").

119 Justice Powell admitted his reservations about capital punishment after retiring. See John C. Jeffries Jr., *Justice Lewis F. Powell Jr: A Biography* (Charles Scribner's Sons 1994) 451.

120 Callins v Collins, 510 U.S. 1141, 1144 (1994) (Blackmun J. dissenting from denial of cert.).

121 ibid.

122 ibid.

123 ibid 1159 (emphasis added).

124 ibid 1158 (internal quotations and citations omitted).

125 ibid 1141.

126 ibid 1149–1150.

127 ibid 1142.

128 Baze (n 83) 83 (Stevens J., concurring in judgment).

129 Elisabeth Semel, 'Reflections on Justice John Paul Stevens's Concurring Opinion in *Baze v. Rees*: A Fifth *Gregg* Justice Renounces Capital Punishment' (2010) 43 U.C. Davis Law Review 783, 786.

130 Baze (n 83) 87 (Stevens J., concurring in judgment).

131 Justice John Paul Stevens, 'Address to the American Bar Association' (Thurgood Marshall Awards Dinner, Chicago, 6 August 2005) https://www.supremecourt.gov/publicinfo/speeches/viewspeech/sp_08-06-05.

132 James S. Liebman and Lawrence C. Marshall, 'Less Is Better: Justice Stevens and the Narrowed Death Penalty' (2006) 74 Fordham Law Review 1607, 1611–1612.

133 Baze (n 83) 78 (Stevens J., concurring in judgment).

134 ibid 79 (emphasis added).

135 ibid 80.

136 ibid 80–81(internal citations omitted).

137 Furman (n 17) 344 (Marshall, J., concurring) ("It is plain that the view of the *Weems* Court was that punishment for the sake of retribution was not permissible under the Eighth Amendment … . To preserve the integrity of the Eighth Amendment, the Court has consistently denigrated retribution as a permissible goal of punishment.").

138 Baze (n 83) 84 (Stevens J., concurring in judgment).

139 ibid 85.

140 ibid 84–85.

141 ibid 86.

142 ibid 87.

143 Glossip (n 82) 2756 (2015) (Breyer J. dissenting).

144 Robert Smith, 'The End of the Death Penalty?' *Slate* (1 July 2015) http://www.slate.com/articles/news_and_politics/jurisprudence/2015/07/death_penalty_at_the_supreme_court_kennedy_may_vote_to_abolish_capital_punishment.html.

145 Amnesty International, 'USA: Supreme Court Upholds Use of Execution Drug, but two Justices Question Constitutionality of Death Penalty Itself' *AI* AMR 51/1976/2015 (29 June 2015) https://www.amnesty.org/en/documents/amr51/1976/2015/en/.

146 Glossip (n 82) 2772.

147 ibid 2765.

148 Reed v. Louisiana 580 U. S. ____ (2017); Ruiz v. Texas 580 U. S. ____ (2017); Sireci v. Florida 580 U.S. ___ (2017).
149 Glossip (n 82) 2776 (internal quotations and citations omitted).
150 Brief for Petitioner, *Kennedy v. Louisiana*, No 07–343 (filed Feb. 14 2008) at 27.
151 Brief for Respondents, *Baze v. Rees,* No 07–5439 (filed Dec. 3 2007) at 25.
152 ibid 52 (quoting Workman v. Bredesen, 486 F.3d 896, 909 (6th Cir. 2007)).
153 Brief for Petitioner, *Glossip v. Gross,* No 14–7955 (filed Mar. 9 2015).
154 Brief for Petitioner, *Hall v. Florida,* No 12–10882 (filed Dec. 16 2013).
155 Brief for Petitioner, *Foster v. Chatman* No 14–8349 (filed Mar. 24 2015) at 50.
156 Transcript of Oral Argument, *Buck v. Texas* No 15–8049 (Oct 5, 2016) at 10–11.
157 Buck (n 110) 778 (internal quotations and citations omitted).

6 The experiential abolitionist

I. Introduction

The anti-death penalty movement has historically been led by lawyers, and the prevailing view is that it will be lawyers who secure nationwide abolition through the United States Supreme Court. Yet a key part of the movement's litigation strategy includes what we can term "political abolitionism," since the Supreme Court has made it clear that popular opinion plays a role in its determination of which punishments contravene the Eighth Amendment prohibition on cruel and unusual punishments. It follows that grassroots campaigners and organizers play a vital role in abolitionist efforts. Indeed, much of the recent progress towards abolition has been attributed to the work of political activists, who have helped bring about legislative repeal in five states since 2007, and have encouraged the governors of four more states to impose moratoria on executions pending reviews of their death penalty systems. Political and public-facing abolitionist efforts have also led to a sharp decline in popular support for capital punishment.[1]

The orthodox view is that pragmatic and conservative anti-death penalty discourses have spread distaste with capital punishment among the broader public and lawmakers. Several commentators have surmised that the decline in political and public support for executions is due to an increasing awareness of the risk of executing an innocent person.[2] Others have highlighted how the argument relating to the costs of capital punishment has pushed some towards the abolitionist position.[3] Yet others have said that states would not repeal the death penalty if abolitionists did not accept, or actively encourage, the use of life in prison without the possibility of parole (LWOP) as an alternative punishment.[4] These views support the contention of social movement theorists such as David Snow, who argue that reform movements are more likely to be successful if they adopt the approach of "frame alignment." This involves framing the case for or against a particular practice in terms that align with the existing interests and values of the movement's target audience.[5] Abolitionists will quote scripture when speaking to religious audiences; highlight race discrimination when speaking to those with an interest in racial justice; and emphasize the incompatibility of capital punishment with standards of international human rights law when speaking to proponents of human rights at home and abroad. It would make little sense to frame the case in such terms, however, when speaking to those who do not share these starting points. According to these social movement theorists, to appeal to supporters of capital punishment, or those who are apathetic about state-sanctioned executions, the anti-death penalty movement should instead focus on issues such as innocence, the high costs of capital punishment, and the availability of LWOP.

The usual criticism of these approaches is that they legitimize other wrongs, such as the degrading treatment of those factually guilty of crimes, and the assumption that harsh retributivism should be the over-arching response to criminality. Some writers have been critical of how the shift towards pragmatic and conservative anti-death penalty discourses have tended to marginalize the issue of race, contending that it is not feasible to condemn capital punishment in America without acknowledging the centrality of racial prejudices to the administration of the death penalty.[6]

The history of slavery and abolition sheds a distinctive light on this debate. It is generally acknowledged that the involvement of those with experience of slavery in anti-slavery efforts imbued the movement with a degree of radicalism. It was black people and former slaves who understood most vividly that moderate anti-slavery discourses would merely entrench the deeper illness of racial subjugation, and that abolitionist efforts had to encompass broader social injustices that stemmed from the values that underpinned support for slavery. Thus, we find that these experiential abolitionists necessarily adopted a radical approach to abolitionism that was centered on the idea of dignity. Over the last 15 years or so, the anti-death penalty movement has similarly come to encompass more and more experiential abolitionists, such as exonerees from death row, and former executioners and corrections officials. Even though these voices have sometimes spoken in the language of innocence, we will see that, like the experiential slavery abolitionists did before them, they nonetheless operate under a broader radical framework that is centered on the idea of dignity. In her book on racial differences within the anti-death penalty movement, Sandra Jones reveals that black abolitionists – in other words, those who understand the relationship between capital punishment and broader forms of racial subjugation – are the ones who advocate the radical rather than conservative approach to abolition. In Jones's words:

> One of the questions I asked of the activists is whether they feel that the movement would be more effective if it narrowed or broadened its focus. Of all the questions I asked them regarding their framing strategies, it was this question that yielded the largest racial divide. While a majority of the white activists (65 percent) feel that it is best to maintain a narrow focus exclusively on the death penalty, most of the black activists (75 percent) feel that in order to build a stronger, more effective movement, the message must be broadened to include concerns about other issues of social justice.[7]

Put another way, if we accept that it is important to take the voice of experience seriously, and the voice of experience advocates a radical approach, then we can see why experiential abolitionists will necessarily shift the anti-death penalty movement towards a more radical position.

To explain all this, we must first appreciate the challenges that the anti-death penalty movement has historically faced in the public and political arenas. Like the slavery abolitionists, they have been accused of lacking credibility and authenticity because they do not have first-hand experience of the issues in question. In response to these accusations, anti-death penalty activists – like the slavery abolitionists before them – have increasingly placed emphasis on those with such experience. Just as former slaves played an important role in efforts to eradicate slavery, so people who have spent time on death row; former executioners and corrections officials; and the families of murder victims in whose name the death penalty is sought, have come to play an important role in contemporary abolitionist efforts.

II. The charge against the abolitionists

The anti-death penalty movement faces the same problem that the anti-slavery movement faced: the direct beneficiaries of abolition are in captivity and do not have the physical capability to lead a movement. It follows that a common anti-abolitionist refrain is that the leaders and rank-and-file members of the abolitionist movements in question lack credibility because they do not really understand the issues, and are not personally affected by the practice. The director of the National Coalition for the Abolition of the Death Penalty, for example, is not somebody who has spent time on death row, or who speaks from experience of homicide. This stands in contrast to many other reform movements, such as the gay-rights movement that has historically been led by those who can speak from experience of homophobia and discrimination, and will benefit from changes such as legislation permitting same-sex marriage.[8] Women tend to lead the feminist movement, and African Americans tend to lead civil rights movements for similar reasons. The gun-control lobby also has people with direct experience of gun crime at its forefront. The Brady Campaign to End Gun Violence, for example, was founded and is led by victims of gun crime, and is named after Jim Brady – the press secretary who suffered a severe gunshot wound in 1981 during an assassination attempt on President Ronald Reagan, and who went on to become a prominent advocate for stricter gun control laws.[9]

William J. Grayson – a Southern politician, planter, and poet – explained why, in his view, opponents of slavery should not be listened to because they did not understand the nature of slavery, or the benefits of involuntary servitude for free persons and slaves alike. In the Preface to his pro-slavery poem *The Hireling and the Slave,* Grayson writes: "The malignant abuse lavished on the slaveholders of America by writers of this country and England can be accounted for but in one way consistently with any degree of charitable consideration for the slanderers. They have no knowledge of the thing abused. They substitute an ideal of their own contriving for the reality."[10] Put another way, it is slaveowners who have first-hand knowledge of the realities of slavery and of the moral depravity of black people, thus superseding the spurious and abstract moral assertions of opponents of slavery. Grayson goes further, arguing that the detachment of abolitionists from the actual practice of slavery, and from black people, betrays the abolitionists' true motivations: "What have the Abolitionists done, what have they given, for the Negro race? They use the slave for the purposes of self-glorification only, indifferent about his present or future condition. They are ambitious to bring about a great social revolution – what its effects may be they do not care to inquire." In contrast, according to Grayson, "[u]nder the master's care, the miserable black savage has been fed, clothed, [and] instructed in useful arts."[11]

In a similar vein, Joshua Marquis has criticized death penalty abolitionists for advocating the forgiveness of those who have committed grievous crimes, contending that they cannot speak with credibility about such issues: "It's much easier to be forgiving if someone you love hasn't been butchered by some sociopath. But since very few murder victims come from the upper strata of our society, murder rarely hits home with society's elite."[12] Taken with Herbert Haines's description in 1999 of the anti-death penalty movement as "mostly … middle-class white people with professional backgrounds and liberal politics",[13] Marquis's argument is clear: opponents of the death penalty are generally from "society's elite," they therefore have no experience of the gruesome homicides that warrant the death penalty, and this means that their arguments against the death penalty are not as credible as the arguments of those who have experienced violent crime and support capital punishment. Marquis also states that "[o]pponents of the death penalty often refer to it as 'state-sanctioned murder,' a phrase that betrays how little they know."[14] This is an explicit claim that death penalty opponents lack authenticity and credibility because they do not have first-hand experience or knowledge of the violent crime that, in his view, justifies the imposition of death sentences.

Paul Cassell has echoed these concerns, stating that "nowhere [in abolitionists's arguments] do we find a clear discussion of the crimes at issue."[15] Cassell's point is that we cannot form opinions on the death penalty without first getting to grips with the sorts of crimes that the death penalty is a response to. He goes on to recount the details of the crimes of Kenneth Allen McDuff in order to justify capital punishment. Cassell's coup de grâce is that he can speak with credibility about the need for the death penalty because he has overseen numerous death penalty cases in his capacity as a judge. Cassell states that he is "haunted" by the stories of victims of crimes, thus implying that his first-hand knowledge of the effect of violent crimes on the wider community supersedes the allegedly baseless claims of death penalty opponents.[16] Justice Scalia of the US Supreme Court adopted a similar position. In *Callins v. Collins*, he admonished Justice Blackmun's critique of the death penalty because, according to Scalia, Blackmun conveniently ignored the suffering of homicide victims.[17] Elsewhere, Scalia argued that Supreme Court justices should not impose their opposition to the death penalty on the broader public because "we federal judges live in a world apart from the vast majority of Americans. After work, we retire to homes in placid suburbia or to high-rise co-ops with guards at the door… We are not confronted with the threat of violence that is ever present in many Americans' everyday lives."[18]

The implications of these sorts of statements are clear: abolitionists cannot appreciate the suffering of victims, the depravity of offenders, and the resulting need for the death penalty, because they are too far removed from the facts of such cases. This anti-abolitionist stance must be understood in conjunction with the Marshall Hypothesis. Justice Marshall hypothesized that if people learned about how the death penalty actually works in practice, they would disavow the punishment.[19] If we accept the contention that education will push people towards the abolitionist position (though there is some evidence that this is not always the case),[20] then we can see why attacks on the credibility of abolitionists are vital to the survival of capital punishment. We can also see why the anti-death penalty movement would make efforts to ward off such attacks.

III. Repudiating the anti-abolitionist claims

Abolitionists have responded to the anti-abolitionist position by framing the case against capital punishment in terms that will resonate with the likes of Marquis and Cassell. Regardless of our opinions on how to respond to the sorts of crimes that they discuss, we can all agree that we should not execute an innocent person, and we can all agree that in times of fiscal crisis, public money is better spent on things such as education and crime prevention. To align the case against the death penalty with the existing moral framework of the likes of Marquis and Cassell, abolitionists have also resisted condemning life without parole as an alternative punishment. Since these issues have been addressed at length elsewhere, they are given relatively brief attention here.[21] Instead, the focus will be on the ways in which the anti-death penalty movement has amplified the voices of those with experience of capital punishment, in order to counter the claim that they lack authenticity and credibility. This feature of abolitionism draws heavily on the experience of slavery abolitionism, and reveals the underlying radical premise of contemporary anti-death penalty discourses.

A. Framing the case against capital punishment

After the US Supreme Court affirmed the constitutionality of capital punishment in 1976, the National Coalition for the Abolition of the Death Penalty (NCADP) was formed with the aim of coordinating state and nationwide abolitionist efforts. A year later, Amnesty International announced that abolition of capital punishment worldwide was to be a central aim of the human rights organization, and alongside the American Civil Liberties Union, these non-governmental organizations spearheaded public and political-facing efforts in America throughout the 1980s and 1990s.

These groups have tended to frame the case against the death penalty in the language of human rights, but more recently anti-death penalty groups have eschewed moralistic arguments in favor of more pragmatic and conservative discourses. We saw in Chapter Three, for example, that the National Conference on Wrongful Convictions and the Death Penalty, which took place in Chicago,

Illinois, in November 1998, propelled the issue of innocence towards the forefront of anti-death penalty discourses. At the time of the conference, 74 people had been exonerated from death rows across America. As of December 2017, that number stands at 160.[22] These incidents have undoubtedly influenced public and political opinion. In January 2000 – just over a year after the conference in Chicago – the Governor of Illinois, George Ryan (a Republican and supporter of capital punishment) cited the risk of executing an innocent person when imposing a moratorium on Illinois's death penalty. In Ryan's words: "I now favor a moratorium, because I have grave concerns about our state's shameful record of convicting innocent people and putting them on death row".[23] Thirteen people had been exonerated from death row in Illinois in the space of a few years, leading Ryan to state: "Until I can be sure that everyone sentenced to death in Illinois is truly guilty, until I can be sure with moral certainty that no innocent man or woman is facing a lethal injection, no one will meet that fate".[24] Ryan appointed a Commission to study the state's death penalty, which outlined 85 recommendations for reform.[25] In light of this, he commuted the sentences of all 167 death row inmates on January 10, 2003. No further executions took place and, in 2011, Governor Quinn signed a repeal bill into law. In Maryland, it was reported that legislators who gave reasons when voting in favor of abolition in 2013 cited innocence as the main reason for their decision.[26] On February 13, 2015, Governor Wolf of Pennsylvania imposed a moratorium on executions, citing the fact that six people have been exonerated from Pennsylvania's death row.[27] The issue of innocence has also had an impact on judicial decisions relating to capital punishment. In 2002, federal trial court judge Jed Rakoff struck down the federal death penalty primarily because of the risk of executing an innocent person: "We now know, in a way almost unthinkable even a decade ago, that our system of criminal justice, for all its protections, is sufficiently fallible that innocent people are convicted of capital crimes with some frequency."[28]

It would be a mistake, though, to assume that the issue of innocence has been the primary cause of the nationwide shift towards abolition, or that the issue inevitably pushes people towards the abolitionist position. States that have seen the highest number of exonerations from death row nonetheless resist abolitionist efforts and continue to sentence relatively high numbers of people to death. Florida currently has the most exonerations from death row since 1973, with 27 people having been exonerated. Yet Florida also currently has the second largest death row population, and has executed 48 people since 2000. Only Texas and Oklahoma have executed more.[29] To compound matters, in 2013 the Florida legislature passed the Timely Justice Act, which was designed to accelerate the appeals process. Even though it was known that innocent people have been sentenced to death at a remarkable rate in Florida, it was still considered prudent to clamp down on prisoners' opportunities to challenge their death sentences. In his study of whether the "decline in death sentences is statistically correlated with the states that have the most exonerations," Brandon Garrett finds that "the more death sentences a state has, the more exonerations it has." It follows, he argues, that "[e]xonerations do not seem to be driving the decline in death sentences at all."[30]

Even if the discourse of "innocence" has contributed to the decline in the death penalty, there are at least three concerns with the focus on innocence. First, the issue of innocence has inevitably been accompanied by discussions of DNA evidence, with such evidence being used to incontrovertibly prove 20 death row inmates' innocence.[31] In turn, the increasing faith placed in DNA evidence has strengthened the conviction of others. That is, just as DNA evidence can prove innocence, it can also prove guilt. In these cases, it is difficult to use the innocence frame to argue for abolition, and the discussion sometimes collapses into discussions about reforms instead. For example, the pro-death penalty lobby can argue that the death penalty can be retained for cases involving DNA evidence that proves a person's guilt. This, however, misses the point that the death penalty is not just about guilt or innocence: it is also about moral culpability and dignity. Proving that someone committed a crime does not say anything about that person's moral blameworthiness, and thus if we do have a system whereby only the incontrovertibly guilty are eligible for death, we will still have the problems of determining who, if anyone, deserves to die.

A second way in which the focus on innocence buttresses conservative values is that it reinforces conservative support for prohibiting abortions. A number of conservatives support the death penalty but oppose abortion, and they often justify this difference by stating that the fetus is innocent, whereas the death row inmate has forfeited his or her right to life because of their criminal act. The anti-death penalty movement's focus on innocence plays into this narrative by suggesting that the lives of the "innocent" are more important than the lives of the guilty.[32] This, of course, would not be problematic if death penalty abolitionists were also pro-life, but many abolitionists follow the liberalist tradition of advocating for women's rights to exercise control over their own bodies.

Another problem with emphasizing innocence is that it implies that it is permissible to treat the factually guilty without respect for their human dignity. Silvia Federici describes this as an "ontological apartheid": "capital punishment postulates the existence of two, almost ontologically different humanities: on the one side the 'rational' citizens, for whose benefit executions are allegedly carried on, on the other, the beastly criminals, to whom anything can be done, since by their actions – we are told – they have placed themselves outside the boundaries of our humanity."[33] Once we accept that some people are "outside the boundaries of our humanity", we can conceivably subject these "entities" to treatments and punishments that we would not impose on human beings. Such punishments include solitary confinement, life without parole, and other lengthy sentences of imprisonment in inhumane conditions.

These problems with the innocence frame highlights the conservative, pragmatic nature of the discourse of innocence. It situates the problem with the death penalty in isolation to other issues of social justice. This is not to say that anti-death penalty activists should not continue to emphasize the risk of an innocent person being executed. As outlined above, it cannot be denied that the specter of an innocent person coming close to execution is a powerful one that should be utilized by the anti-death penalty movement for its efficacy in changing people's hearts and minds. However, such messages should be delivered within an overarching narrative of the moral wrong of a criminal justice system that permits the permanent exclusion of a human being from the political and moral community. Below, we will see that those who have been released from death row, as well as former executioners and corrections officials, do indeed situate the problem of innocence within a wider dignitarian framework, but this is often underappreciated.

In addition to the narrative of innocence, the costs-argument has been effective in rescinding support for capital punishment.[34] Study after study has revealed that capital cases are far more expensive than non-capital cases. A 2017 report on Oklahoma's death penalty estimated that at a minimum, capital cases cost $110,257 more than non-capital cases.[35] In Oregon, a 2016 study suggested that death penalty cases are, on average, 3.5 to 4 times more expensive per case than similar non-death penalty cases.[36] Research in other states has led to similar conclusions, with an investigation in Pennsylvania revealing that the cost of sentencing 408 people to death between 1978 and 2008 was approximately $816 million higher than had those people been sentenced to life without parole instead.[37]

It would appear that the high costs associated with capital punishment may be a factor in the decline in death sentences. Prosecutors in small, relatively poor counties have stopped seeking death sentences because of the financial strain it places on local budgets.[38] Between 2005 and 2016, just seven out of 95 counties in Virginia imposed death sentences, most of which were wealthy.[39] However, as a 2013 report by the Death Penalty Information Center reveals, in reality these counties do not bear the brunt of the costs. The report states that "the dramatically higher appellate costs instigated by a decision to proceed capitally are mainly triggered by the small set of counties that impose [the] most death sentences and are largely subsidized by state and federal taxpayers".[40] As such, it remains tempting for abolitionists to draw attention to the huge financial burden that taxpayers across the country are shouldering in order to maintain a death penalty that is used by an ever-decreasing number of counties.

These findings have played a role in convincing conservatives to oppose capital punishment. In October 2017, Conservatives Concerned About the Death Penalty (CCATDP) issued a report detailing the extent to which Republican lawmakers – not usually associated with anti-death penalty sentiments – have sponsored repeal bills since the organization was formed in 2013. "From 2000 to 2012," the report notes, "the number of Republican state lawmakers sponsoring death penalty repeal bills never rose above single digits in any year." However, in 2013, no fewer than 20 Republican lawmakers sponsored repeal bills. The number has stayed in double-digits ever since, with 40 Republican repeal sponsors in 2016.[41] Although CCATDP have not expressly lobbied each of these lawmakers to sponsor such bills, the Report argues that "CCATDP's 2013 launch and subsequent expansion have shined a spotlight on conservative opposition to the death penalty, creating opportunities for people to learn and consider the conservative case against the death penalty for the first time. Lawmaker activity is a reflection of this growing trend."[42] Put another way, it is the conservative voice against capital punishment – focused on issues such as costs, rather than the dignity of the person facing execution – that has propelled the introduction of repeal bills across America. In a study published in 2014 of abolitionist efforts in five states that had recently outlawed the penalty, Jolie McLaughlin found that the costs argument played a significant role in persuading legislators to vote for repeal: "Although the cost argument has not been a 'magic bullet' for ending the death penalty in America, it has proven more successful than any of the moral arguments that the anti-death penalty movement has used in the past."[43]

If we accept that the costs argument has been effective, we must be aware that the argument is conservative in nature, and does not address the root of the problem. CCATDP distances itself from liberalist-based human rights concerns with the dignity of the offender, explaining instead that the system of capital punishment "makes mistakes, fails to keep us safe, and wastes millions of dollars."[44] In other words, it is the incompatibility of capital punishment with conservative values of limited government and tight fiscal policy that forms the basis of CCATDP's opposition to state-sanctioned executions. The website of CCATDP lists five concerns with capital punishment: innocence, cost, victims, public safety, and fairness.[45] The issue of race discrimination and prejudice does not appear in this list, not even under the heading "fairness".[46] CCATDP also expressly endorses the use of LWOP in death's stead. It was outlined above how the costs argument is usually framed to emphasize how much cheaper sentences of life without parole are. This is given separate treatment in the next chapter, but suffice to say that although some commentators have identified the option of LWOP as crucial to the advancement of abolition,[47] others have argued that abolitionists should not be promoting or acquiescing in the sentencing of people to spend the rest of their natural lives behind bars, with no hope of release. Indeed, life sentences are only cheaper because they do not attract the same level of political or judicial scrutiny, yet we know that there are many innocent people serving sentences of LWOP who need the sort of appeals opportunities that are only available to death row inmates.[48] This alone illustrates the problem with the costs-argument. At a more basic level, critics of LWOP have pointed out that the permanent casting away of a person from society is the very problem that abolitionists are trying to eradicate in the first place.[49]

Even if the focus on innocence, costs, and the availability of LWOP have been factors in shifting America towards abolition, we can see how these discourses appear to be antithetical to a central tenet of radical abolitionism, which involves centering abolitionist discourse on the idea of dignity. William Lloyd Garrison, we saw in Chapter Four, excoriated conservative anti-slavery activists who did not place racial equality front and center of abolitionism, and he emphasized "moral suasion" – the tactic of changing the hearts and minds of those who believed in white supremacy, rather than appealing to their existing moral framework.[50] Indeed, this was one reason why Garrison rejected political abolitionism. The political system, he believed, was innately pro-slavery and ought to be renounced.[51] The current deployment of pragmatic and conservative anti-death penalty discourses as a result of the shift towards political abolitionism appears to vindicate to some extent Garrison's concerns: the system has led abolitionists to entrench the root of the problem.

It is not accurate, though, to describe contemporary political abolitionism as predominantly pragmatic and conservative. When we use understandings of slavery abolitionism to interrogate the larger abolitionist context in which these discourses operate, we see that these anti-death penalty messages actually do promote a much more radical agenda. This is largely because of *who* delivers these messages, rather than the discourses themselves. However, abolitionists could and should be more explicit about this.

B. The voice of experience

The emergence of apparently conservative and pragmatic anti-death discourses cannot be separated from the issue of race, with Austin Sarat asserting that "the rhetorical center of abolitionist argument has come to focus less on race and more on claims of actual innocence."[52] Some abolitionists have heeded Sarat's warning that the question of race should not be marginalized, and have made a concerted effort to frame the case against capital punishment within the context of racial justice.[53] Writing in November 2017, Fatimah Loren Muhammad acknowledges that the anti-death penalty movement has not prioritized the issue of race, but also makes the point that "[w]ithin the last 10 years, [Equal Justice USA] has made a commitment to exploring race, and has demonstrated that campaigns become stronger when they include not only the voices of crime survivors but also the voices of communities of color specifically."[54] Khalilah Brown-Dean and Ben Jones have also argued that the participation of murder victims' families and communities of color was vital to successful abolitionist efforts in Connecticut in 2012, outlining the role of those with "authentic power".[55] They had "authentic power", Brown-Dean and Jones write, because they could speak from experience of the issues.

The participation of these groups should be understood as an extension of the way in which the slavery abolitionists brought experiential abolitionists into the fold. As outlined above, attacks on the credibility of both slavery and death penalty abolitionists have been instigated by a belief that opponents of the practice in question cannot speak from experience of the issues. Slavery abolitionists responded to such attacks by giving voice to those with first-hand experience of involuntary bondage. To be sure, as James Huston has argued, "white Northern abolitionists" such as William Lloyd Garrison, Benjamin Lundy, and William Henry Seward, who all appeared to be far removed from slavery, did tend to witness slavery before advocating for abolition.[56] However, as the pro-slavery lobby recognized, the voices of those with actual experience of bondage presented the gravest danger to its survival. Such persons included former slaves who had been manumitted, and those who had illegally escaped captivity. Former slaveholders also provided an important voice. In a letter to John C. Calhoun, James Henry Hammond wrote: "A Slave holder then or Southern man who falters, who apologizes, much less who denounces Slavery & regards abolition as inevitable is in my opinion *our very worst enemy*, the man who saps our strength at the core & does more to destroy us than a brigade of abolitionists could."[57] J. Brent Morris writes that "[o]nce-committed slaveholders who embraced abolitionism often became some of the most effective antislavery reformers because of their unique insight into the mind of the master class."[58] It was for these reasons why, as Benjamin Quarles explains, "the white Southerner had to ignore the Negro as abolitionist wherever possible, for to do otherwise would have been to unhinge a cardinal tenet of the Southern faith – the concept of the contented slave and the impassive black."[59] The Grimké sisters and James G. Birney (who actually endorsed the principle of gradualism) are perhaps the most famous anti-slavery activists who at some point held people in bondage.[60] During the presidential campaign of 1844, a newspaper editor remarked that "Should [Birney] die this day, he has achieved more for the liberty and welfare of his country than all the presidents of other candidates for the presidency, that have lived since Washington died."[61] In her comprehensive account of the abolitionists, Manisha Sinha states that "[f]ugitive slaves created an authentic, original, and independent critique of slaveholding, one which made their narratives potent antislavery material. No longer could slaveholders claim that their northern critics had no idea about the actual conditions of southern slaves." Fugitive slaves, Sinha explains, were of central importance to advancing abolitionism.[62]

Given the generally accepted view that "experiential abolitionists" were vital to the successes of the slavery abolitionists, it makes sense for today's anti-death penalty movement to place the voice of experience front and center of abolitionist efforts. While crime victims and "communities of color" are indeed such voices, exonerees from death row have been particularly adept at advancing the abolitionist cause, and more recently former executioners and corrections officials have taken up a more visible role in anti-death penalty efforts. Having said this, there are at least two potential pitfalls with placing people with experience front and center of abolitionist efforts. The first lies in the trauma that such people have invariably suffered, and the second lies in the prevailing political and cultural context in which these men and women undertake abolitionist activities. Yet as outlined below, it is precisely these two issues that inject radicalism into anti-death penalty arguments, just as they did in slavery abolitionism.[63]

i. Asserting one's dignity

At one point during the National Conference on Wrongful Convictions and the Death Penalty in Chicago, in 1998, 31 exonerees from death row solemnly walked across the stage of the Thorne Auditorium at Northwestern University, and each one placed a sunflower in a vase to symbolize each life that had been spared. Media reports of the conference invariably focused on this, with the *New York Times*' headline reading: "Survivors Make the Case Against Death Row."[64] At the time, 74 people had been exonerated nationwide since 1972, but not all of them accepted the invitation to the conference. According to the organizer, Lawrence Marshall, "[t]he pain was too intense" for some of them. Adjusting to a life of freedom after spending time on death row is often immensely challenging and several have either been imprisoned on other charges, or taken their own lives since being released.[65] Since the conference, survivors of death row have continued to make the case against capital punishment. The abolitionist organization Witness to Innocence (WTI), which was set up in 2003 and comprises exonerees from death row who wish to speak out against capital punishment, currently has 33 members.[66] However, this is a small percentage of the 160 people who have been exonerated from death row since 1973. Many more have been released on the grounds that their convictions do not stand up to scrutiny, even though they have not been formally exonerated.[67] As was the case with the 1998 conference, many exonerees and former death row inmates refrain from getting involved in abolitionism because of the trauma that they have suffered. Ron Keine – who was exonerated in 1976 after spending two years on death row and who is a member of WTI – writes that "when they talk about it, exonerees actually retraumatize themselves. It puts them right back on death row."[68] Important as it is to get stories of experience into the public domain, this must clearly be achieved without subjecting the person to further trauma.

While speaking publicly might be difficult, though, it can also be part of the healing process. It is in this sense that elevating the place of those with experience can constitute a recognition of that person's dignity, and thus place abolitionist efforts under a dignitarian framework. Frederick Douglass famously used his biographies to demonstrate his status as a human being, and not just to inform his readers of how slavery operated in practice. In *Narrative of the Life of Frederick Douglass*, he describes how, after initially accepting abuse at the hands of his overseer Mr Covey, he eventually resisted further beatings. Douglass tells his audience: "You have seen how a man was made a slave; you shall see how a slave was made a man."[69] With these sorts of passages in mind, David Blight notes that the act of writing was liberating for Douglass, and that "through Douglass's writing and speaking he desperately sought a secure social identity."[70]

We see elements of this in the writings of those released from death row, too. In *Life After Death*, Damien Echols explains how his identity was destroyed in prison: "The whole purpose was to rob everyone of their identity. Dress everyone exactly alike, give them the same haircut, take away their name, and give them a number. To the prison system, I am not Damien Echols. I am inmate SK931."[71] Even after being released, Echols is "often plagued by thoughts that people will think of me only as either someone on Death Row or someone who used to be on Death Row."[72] Furthermore: "Sometimes it seems as if I live in a world where I have no identity outside the case. That I am the case and the case is me."[73] Thus, Echols publishes his memoir with the aim not just of educating the public about life on death row, but also to restore his identity as Damien Echols. He writes that he does not want people to read the book "out of a morbid sense of curiosity"[74] about death row, and he does "not want to be an oddity, a freak, or a curiosity [or]... the car wreck that people slow down to gawk at."[75] Echols writes to show that he is more than just a former death row inmate, and he writes in order to emphasize the moral agency that had been denied to him by prison.

Whereas Douglass's memoir used concepts of masculinity to reassert his identity, Harriet Jacobs focused on the idea of motherhood to assert hers in *Incidents in the*

Life of a Slave Girl.[76] Jacobs's memoir is notorious for its depiction of the sexual abuse of female slaves, but Jean Fagan Yellin explains that Jacobs

> does not characterize herself conventionally as a passive female victim, but asserts that – even when young and a slave – she was an effective moral agent. She takes full responsibility for her actions: "I will not try to screen myself behind the plea of compulsion from a master; for it was not so. Neither can I plead ignorance or thoughtlessness … I knew what I did, and I did it with deliberate calculation."[77]

We can see how the assertion of moral agency plays an important part in Jacobs's telling of her story. Yellin also outlines the difficulty that Jacobs had in securing a publisher for her narrative, since she was concerned that she would lose editorial control. White abolitionists could be patronizing towards blacks, sometimes assuming that former and fugitive slaves were incapable of contributing to the abolitionist movement without assistance.[78] Since many former and fugitive slaves were illiterate, they were dependent on white amanuenses, and thus slave narratives were often influenced by the beliefs and agendas of white abolitionists. When writing about his attempts to tell his story, Frederick Douglass noted the paternalism of some white abolitionists and expressed a determination to take control of his own narrative. He recounts an incident when he was told by a white abolitionist to: "Give us the facts… we will take care of the philosophy."[79] That is, white abolitionists believed that Douglass should stick to recounting the facts of his experiences, and leave the philosophical case against slavery to the allegedly more educated, and more articulate, white people. Douglass resisted these pressures, and in doing so asserted his autonomy and dignity, two qualities that had not been respected during his periods of enslavement. In Douglass's words: "I could not always obey, for I was now reading and thinking… It did not entirely satisfy me to *narrate* wrongs; I felt like *denouncing* them."[80]

While some leaders of the anti-slavery movement were paternalistic and condescending of blacks, others such as Gerrit Smith and John Brown were particularly sensitive to the importance of ensuring that those most affected by slavery had their voice heard during anti-slavery struggles. Smith accepted the proclamation of his friend, the black physician James McCune Smith, that "[t]he heart of the whites must be changed, thoroughly, entirely, permanently changed," before racial equality could be secured.[81] It was not just white supporters of slavery who needed to put themselves in the shoes of black people, though. Opponents of slavery, Smith asserted, would also be doomed to fail if they did not respect the position of black people, and if they did not overcome their own racial prejudices. The failure of the slavery abolitionists to fully grasp the importance of advocating racial equality, we have seen elsewhere in this book, contributed to the persistence of racial difficulties in America. Today's abolitionists should therefore ensure that they also respect the views of those most affected by capital punishment. Many in the anti-death penalty movement already do so, illustrating the undercurrent of radicalism that runs through the movement. As noted above, EJUSA has acknowledged the imperative to place the voices of crime victims and communities of color front and center.[82] The mission statement of Witness to Innocence (WTI) – the organization comprised of death row exonerees – reads: "The mission of WTI is to abolish the death penalty by *empowering* exonerated death row survivors and their loved ones to become *effective leaders* in the abolition movement."[83] The Campaign to End the Death Penalty – a grassroots organization with chapters in California, Texas, Delaware, and New York – states explicitly that "[w]e believe that those who have experienced the horrors of death row first hand – death row prisoners themselves and their family members – should be at the forefront of our movement. Their experiences help to shape our strategies."[84] We will see in the next chapter the importance of those with experience in debates about alternatives to capital punishment, but for now we can explore how those with experience can further contribute to the radicalism of the abolitionists.

ii. Advancing radicalism

Even when the trauma that "experiential abolitionists" have suffered is taken into consideration, there remains the problem of how they frame their stories. Dwight McBride observes that even though slaves were empowered by the opportunity to contribute to abolitionism in the ways described above, they were also restricted by contemporaneous discourses of abolitionism.[85] Using *Narrative of the Life of Frederick Douglass* as an example, McBride shows how slave narratives were often shaped by the potential reader. This reader, McBride writes, "is a confluence of political, moral, and social discursive concerns that animate, necessitate, and indeed make possible slave testimony itself."[86] In fact, McBride suggests that the reader is comparable to Benedict Anderson's *Imagined Communities*, discussed in Chapter Four. The reader's imagination has been shaped by existing pro-slavery and abolitionist discourses, and thus Douglass is compelled to deploy rhetorical strategies that will resonate with the existing frame of mind of the reader.

With McBride's observation in mind, we can see why those with experience of capital punishment have tended to focus on the issue of innocence, and other conservative and pragmatic discourses, since it is these issues that make it possible for exonerees and former executioners to have their voice heard at all. Some of the most famous writings from death row are from those who have maintained their innocence. Mumia Abu-Jamal, described in 2001 as "perhaps the world's best known death-row inmate",[87] has resolutely maintained his innocence, as did Caryl Chessman, whose memoir *Cell 2455, Death Row*, was a bestseller. Perhaps more obviously, exonerees from death row – who play an exceptionally visible and effective role in abolitionism – speak in the language of innocence. Kirk Bloodsworth, who spent nine years in prison in Maryland for the murder of a nine-year-old girl called Dawn Hamilton, two of which were on death row, was integral to successful abolitionist attempts in that state in 2013. Bloodsworth met with legislators and served as the physical embodiment of the abstract claims being made about the wrong of capital punishment. When the Senate spent four days debating the bill, an opponent of the measure – Senate Minority Leader E.J. Pipkin – accused supporters of abolition of invoking Bloodsworth's name 53 times.[88] A journalist covering the debates described Bloodsworth as "Exhibit A" for repeal,[89] and Delegate Barbara A. Frush explained that even though she supported capital punishment, she voted for abolition because of the discussion that she had with Bloodsworth.[90]

It is not just exonerees such as Bloodsworth who appear to perpetuate conservative anti-death penalty discourses. In 2016, several current and former corrections officials joined forces with prosecutors and law enforcement officials to form Public Safety Officials on the Death Penalty (PSODP). Although the name does not specify opposition to capital punishment, their stated mission is to "share concerns about the fairness and efficacy of the death penalty in America."[91] PSODP offers a valuable perspective for anti-death penalty efforts since they bring credibility due to their involvement in the process, and are relatively immune to pro-death penalty attacks on any alleged "softness on crime." At first glance, though, it would appear that law enforcement personnel who speak out against capital punishment are reinforcing conservative values of being "tough" on crime. The PSODP website states that the group brings together "current and former law enforcement, prosecutors and corrections officials who do not support the death penalty on a variety of pragmatic or moral grounds, as well as those who continue to support capital punishment, but recognize that the death penalty directs needed resources away from policing and community safety."[92] Put another way, attention is drawn away from the moral question of state killing, and towards the economic and resources argument. Although PSODP does not take an official stance on life without parole, some members have emphasized that such sentences are cheaper than death sentences, thus implicitly lending support for LWOP.[93] And as with the testimonies of death row exonerees, we find that former executioners in particular have emphasized the issue of innocence.[94] Yet when we interrogate the testimonies and actions of these experiential abolitionists – both exonerees and former corrections officials – further, we see that their discourses shed light not just on the moral wrong of capital punishment, but also on the idea that the death penalty is merely a symptom of a broader problem with the criminal justice system.

Only a handful of examples can be given here, but we can start with that of Clarence Brandley. In 1981, Brandley was sentenced to death for the rape and murder of a 16-year-old white girl named Cheryl Dee Fergeson in a high school in Conroe, Texas, where Brandley worked as a janitor. According to reports, Texas Ranger Wesley Styles, who was investigating the murder, considered it likely that a janitor had committed the crime given that the perpetrator must have had access to the building, and told a group of janitors that one of them would hang for the crime. Speaking to Brandley, he said: "Since you're the nigger, you're elected". Brandley was exonerated nine years later, and his public talks invariably focus on race and the criminal justice system.[95]

John Thompson was sentenced to death in Louisiana in 1985 for the death of Raymond Liuzza, who had been killed during the course of an armed robbery. In April 1999, 30 days before Thompson's scheduled execution, an investigator discovered that the prosecution had deliberately withheld evidence that exculpated

Thompson from the crime. At a retrial in 2003, a jury acquitted Thompson in just 35 minutes. After being released, Thompson not only spoke out against the death penalty, but he also founded the non-profit Resurrection After Exoneration, which offers support to exonerees as they reintegrate into society. In addition to helping exonerees with the challenges of adapting to a life of freedom, Thompson was also awarded a prestigious Soros Fellowship in 2011 to "create a public education and advocacy campaign to demand accountability for prosecutorial misconduct."[96] Thompson made immense contributions to efforts to address the issue of overzealous prosecutors who make the decision whether to seek death sentences or not.[97] It is perhaps no surprise to find that in recent years prosecutors who have been renowned for seeking death sentences have either voluntarily left office after unwanted public scrutiny, or have been voted out of office for the same reason. In 2015, in Caddo Parish, Louisiana, District Attorney Dale Cox declined to re-run for office after a national outcry over his call for the death penalty to be used more often. And in 2016, Angela Corey was resoundingly beaten in elections in Florida because voters had become embarrassed with the attention that her use of capital punishment brought to the area.[98]

Kirk Bloodsworth has not just limited his advocacy to abolition efforts either. His name adorns the federal "Kirk Bloodsworth Post-Conviction DNA Testing Grant Program",[99] which helps states with the costs associated with post-conviction DNA testing in capital and non-capital cases alike. This program was included in the broader Justice For All Act 2004, which was inspired by concerns with wrongful convictions more generally.

Former executioners have also proven adept at using the innocence frame to shine a light on how capital punishment implicates the dignity and interests of others. Don Cabana presided over three executions when he was warden at Mississippi State Penitentiary, and then published a memoir detailing the detrimental effects of capital punishment on executioners and society at large.[100] Testifying before the Judiciary Committee of the Minnesota House of Representatives in 1995, Cabana drew particular attention to how the risk of a wrongful execution implicates the humanity of the executioner: "…in the name of justice, in the name of law and order, in the name of retribution, you, and when I say you, I mean, generically, Americans, do not have the right to ask me, or any prison official, to bloody my hands with an innocent person's blood."[101] Jerry Givens, who carried out 62 executions over 17 years in Virginia, has also used the issue of innocence as a doorway towards a broader critique of capital punishment. An interview with *Newsweek* begins with the assertion that "[o]nly a fellow executioner like 59-year-old Jerry Givens would know how crushingly hard it will continue to be for those who put Troy Davis to death last week even as he continued to insist on his innocence." Givens explains the toll that the execution of an innocent person has on an executioner: "You take an innocent life – that means I committed murder." The interview does not solely dwell on the issue of innocence, though, as Givens describes the detrimental effect of working on death row notwithstanding the guilt or innocence of inmates. He explains "the executioner high", a state of mind that enables the executioner to emotionally distance him- or herself from the reality of taking another human life, noting that he "had to transform [him]self into a person who would take a life… That transformation might linger for a while. You might be on that for three weeks."[102]

In September 2011, Allen Ault made public his attempts to persuade the Governor of Georgia to stay the impending execution of Troy Davis.[103] Davis's case had attracted national and international attention because of the significant evidence that he was innocent,[104] and Ault had served as commissioner of the Georgia Department of Corrections between 1992 and 1995, during which time he oversaw five executions. In a joint letter with five other former corrections officials, he wrote:

> We write to you today with the overwhelming concern that an innocent person could be executed in Georgia tonight. We know the legal process has exhausted itself in the case of Troy Anthony Davis, and yet, doubt about his guilt remains… Living with the nightmares is something that we know from experience. No one has the right to ask a public servant to take on a lifelong sentence of nagging doubt, and for some of us, shame and guilt. Should our justice system be causing so much harm to so many people when there is an alternative?[105]

As with Givens, though, Ault does not limit his concerns to innocence. Notably, he has prefaced his anti-death penalty tracts with the words: "Having witnessed executions firsthand, I have no doubts: capital punishment is a very scripted and rehearsed murder".[106] This serves to counter Joshua Marquis's claim that "[o]pponents of the death penalty often refer to it as 'state-sanctioned murder,' a phrase that betrays how little they know."[107] Ault, more than Marquis, knows what it means to execute a person.

Ault also emphasizes that the death penalty is brutalizing regardless of the guilt or innocence of the individuals involved. He provides anecdotal evidence of how the first two people he executed "were entirely different people" at the point of execution from when they first entered prison, thus countering one of the rationales for capital punishment, namely, that some people are beyond all hope for redemption. He then explains how he attempted to rationalize the act of killing another human being, only to realize that such an attempt was futile. He defends executioners and other death row officials as people who "do their best to perform the impossible and inhumane job with which the state has charged them", but asserts that the job ultimately damages them: "Those of us who have participated in executions often suffer something very much like posttraumatic stress. Many turn to alcohol and drugs. For me, those nights that weren't sleepless were plagued by nightmares. My mother and wife worried about me. I tried not to share with them that I was struggling, but they knew I was."[108]

Although the number of persons involved in administering capital punishment, either as prosecutors or corrections officials or executioners, who now speak out against the death penalty is increasing, there are still many who have not converted to abolitionism. This, however, does not mean that those officials who support capital punishment do not offer anything to the abolitionist movement. Based on extensive interviews with those who work on death row, Robert Johnson explains that prison officials adopt a range of measures to ensure that they are desensitized to executions, thus enabling them to carry out such a job. As Johnson points out, "[o]fficers become expert at denial of the humanity of prisoners – especially condemned prisoners – a process of dehumanization"[109] which serves the purposes of enabling the commission of an act that the guard would not normally inflict on a fellow human being. Johnson recounts how "[o]ne executioner described himself as 'a normal John Doe that walks the streets every day. I work and live a normal social life.' How ironic that this person would characterize himself as a John Doe – an anonymous man, often a corpse – as if in subconscious recognition that it takes a nameless, dehumanized entity – dead to others – to kill other men in cold blood for a living."[110] It is not just the execution that implicates the dignity of those who work on death row, though. The nature of death row requires routine safety checks involving strip-searches, and officers have "protested that their own dignity was undermined by the obligation to look at 'one naked inmate after another' all day."[111] These observations lead Johnson to conclude: "We should abolish the death penalty, then, not so much to save executioners from stress, even disabling and dehumanizing stress. We should abolish the death penalty to put an end to an institution that kills empathy and compassion, and ultimately corrupts us all."[112] Using research methods from social cognitive theory, Michael J. Osofsky, Albert Bandura, and Philip G. Zimbardo find that the institutional structure behind death rows and executions enables officials to suppress the usual processes of moral self-regulation that would normally prevent them from killing a fellow human being. In their words, "the execution process is institutionally professionalized and dignified, but the offenders tend to be dehumanized by those who have to take a human life."[113] When these studies are added to the statements of the likes of Ault and Givens, we can see how former executioners and corrections officials necessarily invoke the idea of dignity in anti-death penalty discourses.

Yet another group of experiential abolitionists are those whose loved ones have been murdered, and in whose name the death penalty is carried out. These groups also include those whose loved ones have been executed by the state. Murder Victims' For Reconciliation (MVFR) was established as long ago as 1976, and seeks to give a voice to families of murder victims who do not wish to see the death penalty imposed in their name. Their "vision statement" is unequivocal: "MVFR envisions a future where the death penalty is nonexistent, where families of homicide and execution receive care and support, and where restorative justice is common practice."[114] We saw in Chapter Three that discourses of victims' rights have tended to stymy abolitionist efforts, and Marie Gottschalk in particular has been critical of this. However, in 2002, MVFR issued a report that highlights the radicalism in the "victim's" voice in two distinct ways. First, they expressly draw on the work of Sojourner Truth to highlight that discussions of victims' rights must include the voice of those who oppose the death penalty too. Second, they expressly invoke the idea of dignity. In *Dignity Denied*, the authors begin with the question "Ain't *I* a Victim?" As the footnote to the text explains, it was the former slave Sojourner Truth who asked "Ain't I a Woman?" at the 1851 Women's Convention in Akron, Ohio. Truth was challenging the Convention to take into account the rights of black women as well as those of whites. As Renny Cushing and Susannah Sheffer put it, "Truth's challenge to the broader community parallels the challenge that homicide survivors who oppose the death penalty are posing here."[115] As well as drawing on the ideas of a slavery abolitionist, Cushing and Sheffer squarely frame their case within the language of "dignity". They take issue with the problem of prosecutors ignoring their wishes when deciding whether to seek a death sentence or not, drawing attention to the fact that the federal Victims of Crime Act 1984 concretizes the right of victims "to be treated with fairness and with respect for the victim's dignity and privacy".[116]

IV. Conclusions

The sheer number of local, statewide, and nationwide anti-death penalty groups that are focused on energizing supporters and converting others to the abolitionists' cause makes it difficult to comprehensively cover all public-facing activities, but we can see that today's abolitionists do, and should continue, to draw on what I have termed "experiential abolitionists", bearing in mind the experiences of those former slaves and slaveholders who joined the abolitionist ranks in the antebellum era. If we accept that, ultimately, opinions about capital punishment turn on instincts and emotions, rather than on rational cost-benefit analyses and concerns with arbitrary and discriminatory application,[117] then we can see why human stories will have considerable impact. But we have also seen that not all experiential abolitionists explicitly frame their stories within the framework of dignity, and the narratives of some of those outlined above appear to feed into the conservative and pragmatic framework. Abolitionists should heed the words of Gerrit Smith – it is imperative for those without experience of the issues to place the voice of those with experience front and center. And abolitionists should heed the warning from the history of emancipation and its aftermath – a failure to forthrightly frame the case against the death penalty in the language of dignity risks the entrenchment of the very problems that the abolitionists are trying to eradicate.

Notes

1 Since 2007, New Jersey (2007), New Mexico (2009), Illinois (2011), Connecticut (2012), and Maryland (2013) have legislatively abolished capital punishment. The Governors of Oregon (2011), Colorado (2013) Washington (2014), and Pennsylvania (2015) have imposed moratoria. For the decline in public support, see Gallup Polling, *Death Penalty*http://www.gallup.com/poll/1606/death-penalty.aspx.

2 See Lawrence C. Marshall, 'The Innocence Revolution and the Death Penalty' (2004) 1 Ohio State Journal of Criminal Law 573 and n 22 below and accompanying text.

3 See Jolie McLaughlin, 'The Price of Justice: Interest-Convergence, Cost, and the Anti-Death Penalty Movement' (2014) 108 Northwestern University Law Review 675 and n 34 below and accompanying text.

4 See Andy Hoover and Ken Cunningham, 'Framing, Persuasion, Messaging, and Messengers: How the Death Penalty Abolition Movement Succeeded in New Jersey' (2014) 38 Humanity & Society 443 and n 47 below and accompanying text.

5 David Snow, E. Burke Rochford Jr, Steven K. Worden, and Robert D. Benford, 'Frame Alignment Process, Micromobilization, and Movement Participation' (1986) 51 American Sociological Review 464; Herbert Haines, *Against Capital Punishment: The Anti-Death Penalty Movement in America, 1972–1994* (OUP 1999).

6 See, for example, Austin Sarat, 'The Rhetoric of Race in the 'New Abolitionism'' in Charles J. Ogletree Jr and Austin Sarat (eds), *From Lynch Mobs to the Killing State: Race and the Death Penalty in America* (NYU Press 2006) 263, 277.

7 Sandra J Jones, *Coalition Building in the Anti-Death Penalty Movement: Privileged Morality, Race Realities* (Lexington 2010) 204.

8 At the time of writing, for example, Chad Griffin is President of Human Rights Campaign, which is the largest national lesbian, gay, bisexual and transgender civil rights organization in America. See http://www.hrc.org/staff/profile/chad-griffin1.

9 For an outline of the history of the Brady Campaign see http://www.bradycampaign.org/jim-and-sarah-brady.

10 Willam J. Grayling, *The Hireling and the Slave* (McCarter & Co 1856) iv.

11 ibid xi.

12 Joshua K Marquis, 'Truth and Consequences' in Hugo Adam Bedau and Paul G. Cassell (eds) *Debating the Death Penalty: Should America Have Capital Punishment? The Experts on Both Sides Make Their Best Case* (OUP 2005) 120–121.

13 Haines (n 5) 103.

14 Marquis (n 12) 121.

15 Paul G Cassell, 'In Defense of the Death Penalty' in Bedau and Cassell (eds) (n 12) 183.

16 ibid 185.

17 Callins v. Collins, 510 U.S. 1141, 1143 (1994) (Scalia J. concurring in denial of certiorari).

18 Glossip v. Gross, 135 S.Ct. 2726, 2749 (2015) (Scalia, J., concurring).

19 For an outline of Justice Marshall's hypothesis, see Carol S Steiker, 'The Marshall Hypothesis Revisited' (2009) 52 Howard Law Journal 525.

20 John K Cochran and Mitchell B Chamlin, 'Can Information Change Public Opinion? Another Test of the Marshall Hypotheses' (2005) 33 Journal of Criminal Justice 573 (finding that death penalty supporters tended to be less well-informed about the mechanics of capital punishment than abolitionists, but that those who support capital punishment for retributive reasons will generally not change their minds even after learning about how the punishment works in practice).

21 For a recent outline of the various factors that have propelled America towards abolition, see Brandon Garrett, *End of its Rope: How Killing the Death Penalty Can Revive Criminal Justice* (Harvard University Press 2017).

22 The Death Penalty Information Center keeps an up-to-date record of those who have been released from death row. See 'Innocence and the Death Penalty' at https://deathpenaltyinfo.org/innocence-and-death-penalty.

23 Office of the Governor, 'Governor Ryan Declares Moratorium On Executions, Will Appoint Commission To Review Capital Punishment System' (31 January 2000) https://www2.illinois.gov/pages/news-item.aspx?ReleaseID=359.

24 ibid.

25 *Report of the Governor's Commission on Capital Punishment* (Governor's Commission on Capital Punishment, Illinois 2002).

26 David A. Love, 'Abolition in Maryland,' *The Nation* (3 June 2013) http://www.thenation.com/article/174309/exonerated-prisoners-are-winning-fight-against-death-penalty.

27 Wallace McKelvey, 'Gov. Tom Wolf declares moratorium on death penalty in Pa.' *PennLive* (13 February 2015) http://www.pennlive.com/politics/index.ssf/2015/02/gov_tom_wolf_declares_moratori.html.

28 US v Quinones, 196 F. Supp. 2d 416, 420 (2002).
29 These numbers are correct as of 10 December 2017, See Death Penalty Information Center, 'Innocence and the Death Penalty' https://deathpenaltyinfo.org/innocence-and-death-penalty#inn-st.
30 Garrett (n 21) 44.
31 For a sortable database on information relating to exonerations from death row, see 'Innocence Database', Death Penalty Information Center https://deathpenaltyinfo.org/innocence?inno_name=&exonerated=&state_innocence=All&race=All&dna=All&order=dna&sort=desc.
32 Colleen Eren, 'The Right Anti-Death Penalty Movement? Framing Abolitionism for the Twenty-first Century' (2015) 15 New Politics 95, 97.
33 Silvia Federici 'Why Feminists Should Oppose Capital Punishment' (Untitled blog) https://www.ocf.berkeley.edu/~marto/adpp/federici.htm.
34 McLaughlin (n 3).
35 See 'The Report of the Oklahoma Death Penalty Review Commission' (March 2017) http://okdeathpenaltyreview.org/the-report/ p.207, Table 3. Also see Appendix 1B for post-conviction costs.
36 Aliza B. Kaplan and Peter A. Collins, 'Oregon's Death Penalty: A Cost Analysis' (Lewis & Clark Law School, 16 November 2016) https://law.lclark.edu/live/files/22888-oregons-death-penalty-a-cost-analysis-2016.
37 Nicole C. Brambila and Liam Migdail-Smith, 'Executing Justice: A Look at the Cost of Pennsylvania's Death Penalty' *Reading Eagle* (19 June 2016) (finding that Pennsylvania has spent $272 million on each execution since 1978) See generally 'Costs of the Death Penalty' Death Penalty Information Center https://deathpenaltyinfo.org/costs-death-penalty#financialfacts.
38 Garrett (n 21) 143 ("The smaller, poorer counties do not bother seeking the death penalty anymore", relying on data collated by the author).
39 ibid 142–143.
40 Richard C. Dieter, 'The 2% Death Penalty: How a Minority of Counties Produce Most Death Cases At Enormous Costs to All' (Death Penalty Information Center, October 2013) https://deathpenaltyinfo.org/documents/TwoPercentReport.pdf p.2 (quoting James S. Liebman and Peter Clarke, 'Minority Practice, Majority's Burden: The Death Penalty Today' (2012) 9 Ohio State Journal of Criminal Law 255, 312).
41 Conservatives Concerned About the Death Penalty, 'The Right Way: More Republican Lawmakers Championing Death Penalty Repeal' (October 2017) 6 https://conservativesconcerned.org/wp-content/uploads/2017/10/The-Right-Way-Online.pdf.
42 ibid 9.
43 McLaughlin (n 3) 710.
44 See the homepage of the website of Conservatives Concerned About the Death Penalty: https://conservativesconcerned.org/.
45 Conservatives Concerned About the Death Penalty, 'Why We're Concerned' http://conservativesconcerned.org/why-were-concerned/fairness/.
46 Conservatives Concerned About the Death Penalty, 'Fair and Equal Under the Law?' http://conservativesconcerned.org/why-were-concerned/fairness/.
47 Adam Liptak, 'Serving Life, with No Chance of Redemption' *New York Times* (5 October 2005) http://www.nytimes.com/2005/10/05/us/serving-life-with-no-chance-of-redemption.html?_r=0 (quoting James Liebman as endorsing the use of LWOP for abolitionist purposes); Hoover and Cunningham (n 4) 445 (based on an interview with Pete McDonough, a public relations expert who had been hired by New Jerseyans for Alternatives to the Death Penalty).
48 See Chapter Seven for a more detailed outline of the problems with advocating life without parole as an alternative to capital punishment.
49 Marie Gottschalk, *The Prison and the Gallows: The Politics of Mass Incarceration in America* (Cambridge University Press 2006) 198.

50 On the role of "moral suasion" in abolitionism, see Manisha Sinha, *The Slave's Cause: A History of Abolition* (Yale University Press 2016) particularly Chapter 7; Gerald Sorin, *Abolitionism: A New Perspective* (Praeger Publishers 1972) Chapter 4. For an outline of how and why "moral suasion" should not be solely equated with Garrison, see Tunde Adeleke, 'Afro-Americans and Moral Suasion: The Debate in the 1830s' (1998) 83 The Journal of Negro History 127.

51 See Ronald G. Walters, *The Antislavery Appeal: American Abolitionism after 1830* (John Hopkins University Press 1976) 12–14. (Noting that Garrison's rejection of the political process stemmed from his belief in "non-resistance", which was a form of Christian anarchism that preferred God's rule to the rule of legislators.)

52 Austin Sarat, 'The Rhetoric of Race in the 'New Abolitionism'' in Charles J. Ogletree Jr and Austin Sarat (eds), *From Lynch Mobs to the Killing State: Race and the Death Penalty in America* (NYU Press 2006) 263.

53 Fatimah Loren Muhammad, 'Justice from Within: The Death Penalty and a New Vision for Criminal Justice through a Racial Justice Lens' *Nonprofit Quarterly* (28 November 2017) https://nonprofitquarterly.org/2017/11/28/justice-within-death-penalty-new-vision-criminal-justice-racial-justice-lens/.

54 ibid.

55 Khalilah Brown-Dean and Ben Jones, 'Building Authentic Power: A Study of the Campaign to Repeal Connecticut's Death Penalty' (2017) 5 *Politics, Groups, and Identities* 321.

56 James L. Huston, 'The Experiential Basis of the Northern Antislavery Impulse' (1990) 56 The Journal of Southern History 609.

57 Letter from James Henry Hammond to John C Calhoun, 26 September, 1845, in Clyde N Wilson (ed) *The Papers of John C. Calhoun, 1845–1846* (Vol 22, University of South Carolina Press 1995) 172. Emphasis in original.

58 J. Brent Morris, ''We are Verily Guilty Concerning our Brother': The Abolitionist Transformation of Planter William Henry Brisbane' (2010) 111 The South Carolina Historical Magazine 118, 118.

59 Benjamin Quarles, *Black Abolitionists* (OUP 1969) ix.

60 Betty Fladeland, *James Gillespie Birney: Slaveholder to Abolitionist* (Greenwood Press 1969).

61 ibid v.

62 Sinha (n 50) 421.

63 Bharat Malkani, 'Voices of the Condemned: A Comparative Study of Slave Narratives and the Testimonies of Death Row Exonerees' (2014) Law, Culture and the Humanities 1–21 (online first version).

64 Don Terry, 'Survivors Make the Case Against Death Row' *The New York Times* (16 November 1998) http://www.nytimes.com/1998/11/16/us/survivors-make-the-case-against-death-row.html.

65 Laurie Aucoin, 'Righting Wrongful Convictions' *Northwestern Magazine* (Spring 1999) http://www.northwestern.edu/magazine/northwestern/spring99/convictions.htm.

66 There have been four more members who have passed away: John Thompson, Dave Keaton, Delbert Tibbs, Greg Wilhoit.

67 For a list of persons freed from death row but not exonerated, see 'Additional Innocence Information' Death Penalty Information Center https://deathpenaltyinfo.org/additional-innocence-information. There are a number of reasons why people might be released from death row but not officially exonerated. Some, like Damien Echols, accept what is known as an Alford plea. This involves the person maintaining their innocence, but accepting that on the weight of evidence against them, a court would likely convict them. In other words, there is no evidence of innocence.

68 Ron Keine, 'Exoneree initiatives and innocence reform: Witness to Innocence' in Marvin Zalman and Julia Carrano (eds) *Wrongful Conviction and Criminal Justice Reform: Making Justice* (Routledge 2013) 117.

69 Frederick Douglass, *Narrative of the Life of Frederick Douglass, An American Slave, Written by Himself* (David Blight ed., first published 1845, Bedford Books 1993) 75.
70 David Blight, 'A Psalm of Freedom' in Douglass, *Narrative* (n 69) 19.
71 Damien Echols, *Life After Death: Eighteen Years on Death Row* (Atlantic Books 2013) 351–352. Slaves were also deprived of their real names, being forced to adopt the names of their owners.
72 ibid 2.
73 ibid 388.
74 ibid 2.
75 Ibid.
76 Harriet A. Jacobs, *Incidents in the Life of a Slave Girl, Written by Herself* (Jean Fagan Yellin ed, Harvard University Press 1987) xxvi.
77 ibid xxx.
78 August Meier and Elliot Rudwick, 'The Role of Blacks in the Abolitionist Movement' in John H Bracey Jr, August Meier, and Elliot Rudwick (eds) *Blacks in the Abolitionist Movement* (Wadsworth Publishing 1971) 108, 115; Jane H. Pease and William H. Pease, 'Ends, Means, and Attitudes: Black-White Conflict in the Antislavery Movement' (1972) 18 Civil War History 117–128.
79 Frederick Douglass, *My Bondage and My Freedom* (first published 1855, Dover Publishing 1969) 367.
80 Ibid.
81 John Stauffer, *The Black Hearts of Men: Radical Abolitionists and the Transformation of Race* (Harvard University Press 2002) 1
82 See 'Our Mission', Witness to Innocence, at https://www.witnesstoinnocence.org/.
83 Emphasis added.
84 See 'About Us', Campaign to End the Death Penalty, at http://nodeathpenalty.org/about-us Also see Emile DeWeaver, 'The Prison Reform Movement Must Center The Voices of Incarcerated People' *Colorlines* (31 October 2017) https://www.colorlines.com/articles/prison-reform-movement-must-center-voices-incarcerated-people-opinion.
85 Dwight McBride, *Impossible Witnesses: Truth, Abolitionism, and Slave Testimony* (NYU Press 2002) 5 (noting that the content and form of the slave narratives were determined by the "context of their presentation… [but] even as the discursive terrain enables these articulations, it also restricts them.").
86 ibid 151.
87 Sara Rimer, 'Death Sentence Overturned in 1981 Killing of Officer' *The New York Times* (19 December 2001) http://www.nytimes.com/2001/12/19/us/death-sentence-overturned-in-1981-killing-of-officer.html?pagewanted=all.
88 'As Maryland Votes on Repeal, Exonerated Man Becomes a Living Reminder' *Washington Post* (14 March 2013) https://www.washingtonpost.com/local/md-politics/as-maryland-votes-on-death-penalty-repeal-exonerated-man-becomes-a-living-reminder/2013/03/14/8fb87e84-8ca8-11e2-9838-d62f083ba93f_story.html?utm_term=.18811747147e.
89 ibid.
90 Scott Shane, 'A Death Penalty Fight Comes Home,' *The New York Times* (5 February 2013) http://www.nytimes.com/2013/02/06/us/exonerated-inmate-seeks-end-to-maryland-death-penalty.html (Bloodsworth was released from prison in 1993, but was not formally exonerated until 2003).
91 See the website of Public Safety Officials On the Death Penalty, at http://psodp.org/.
92 See http://psodp.org/who-we-are/.
93 Gerald Galloway, 'Public Safety Officials on the Death Penalty' (2016) 42 ABA Human Rights Magazine (noting that "compelling evidence indicates that the death penalty is considerably more expensive than life without parole". Galloway does not

go on to discuss the propriety of LWOP, though, implying support, or acquiescence, in harsh retributivism.).

94 See n 101 below and accompanying text.

95 For an example, see Brandon K. Scott, 'Clarence Brandley Helps Attorneys Confront History of Racism in Montgomery County' *Houston Chronicle* (11 March 2015).

96 For information, see the website of the Open Society Foundation, https://www.opensocietyfoundations.org/about/programs/us-programs/grantees/john-thompson.

97 For an overview of the various ways in which John Thompson engaged in reform efforts after his release, see John Simerman and Katy Reckdahl, 'Former death row inmate John Thompson, who became advocate for the exonerated, dies at 55' *The New Orleans Advocate* (3 October 2017) http://www.theadvocate.com/new_orleans/news/article_ffc7f03a-a8a3-11e7-9321-bf5918f03592.html.

98 Zach Beaird, 'Dale Cox Brings Bad Press to Caddo' *Shreveport Times* (15 July 2015) http://www.shreveporttimes.com/story/news/local/2015/07/15/dale-cox-brings-bad-press-caddo/30223399/ Jessica Pishko, 'Voters Have Ousted Notorious Florida Prosecutor Angela Corey' *The Nation* (August 31, 2016) https://www.thenation.com/article/voters-have-ousted-notorious-florida-prosecutor-angela-corey/.

99 42 U.S. Code § 14136e.

100 Donald Cabana, *Death at Midnight: The Confession of an Executioner* (New edition, Northeastern University Press 1998).

101 Quoted in Bruce Weber, 'Donald Cabana, Warden Who Loathed Death Penalty, Dies at 67' *The New York Times* (13 October 2013).

102 Michael Daly, 'I Committed Murder' *Newsweek* (25 September 2011).

103 Tony Rehagen, 'Q and A with Allen Ault' *Atlanta Magazine* (1 December 2011) http://www.atlantamagazine.com/culture/qa-with-allen-ault1/ (describing him as "re-entering the fray").

104 Jenny Marlowe, Martina Davis-Correia, and Troy Davis, *I Am Troy Davis* (Haymarket Books 2013).

105 Letter from Allen Ault et al to Governor Nathan Deal, 21 September 2011 (available at the website of the Southern Center for Human Rights, https://www.schr.org/action/resources/corrections_officials_sign_on_for_troy_davis).

106 Allen Ault, 'Ordering Death in Georgia Prisons' *Newsweek* (25 September 2011).

107 Marquis (n 12) 121.

108 Ault (n 106). Mark Earley, Jeanne Woodford, and several other former corrections officials have also lent their voice to the anti-death penalty cause. For an insightful account into how former corrections officials are best placed to rebut the retributive justification for capital punishment, see Susan A. Bandes, 'What Executioners Can – and Cannot – Teach Us About the Death Penalty' (2016) 35 Criminal Justice Ethics 183.

109 Robert Johnson, 'Executioners At Work: Collateral Consequences of Executions for Officers Working on Death Row and in the Death House' in *Death Penalty and the Victims* (United Nations, Office of the High Commissioner for Human Rights 2016) 261, 272.

110 ibid 270.

111 ibid 265 (citing Walter C. Long and Oliver Robertson 'Prison Guards and the Death Penalty' (Briefing Paper, Penal Reform International 2015).

112 ibid 278.

113 Michael J. Osofsky, Albert Bandura, and Philip Zimbardo 'The role of moral disengage-ment in the execution process' (2005) 29 Law and Human Behavior 371, 387.

114 Murder Victims' Families for Reconciliation http://www.mvfr.org/vision_statement.

115 Renny Cushing and Susannah Sheffer, *Dignity Denied: The Experience of Murder Victims' Family Members Who Oppose the Death Penalty* (Murder Victims' Families for Reconciliation 2002) n 2.

116 Also see Charles F. Baird and Elizabeth E. McGinn, 'Re-Victimizing the Victim: How Prosecutorial and Judicial Discretion Are Being Exercised to Silence Victims Who Oppose Capital Punishment' (2004) 15 Stanford Law and Policy Review 447.

117 David R. Dow, 'Death Penalty Survives In California, But Three-Strikes Law Cut Back' *The Daily Beast* (9 November 2012) ("when you throw the death penalty into the mix, moral considerations rule. Economic arguments matter at the margins, but at its core, the debate over the death penalty is never really about dollars and cents – rather, it turns on our idea of what it means to be a human being.").

7 Abolitionism and "alternatives"

I. Introduction

One of the central issues that emerged from the previous chapter is the extent to which "new voices" in the anti-death penalty movement have either explicitly endorsed, or at least not actively opposed, the suggestion that death sentences should be replaced with sentences of life in prison without the possibility of parole (LWOP). This warrants further scrutiny because these voices rarely acknowledge the scale of life without parole, and what such sentences actually entail. At the end of 2016, there were 53,290 people living behind bars without any hope of release, compared to the roughly 3,000 that are currently on death rows across the US.[1] There are many reasons that account for the numbers serving LWOP, including the mandatory imposition of such sentences for some crimes in some jurisdictions, and the lengthy list of crimes that are punishable by such a sentence. Marie Gottschalk has suggested that the anti-death penalty movement's lack of objections to LWOP have also contributed to the proliferation of such sentences, although some other scholars have cast doubt on the extent to which advances towards abolition have any correlation with the advancing numbers of those sentenced to LWOP.[2] It is not my intention in this chapter to determine whether death penalty abolitionism has significantly contributed to the rise of LWOP, and I take as a starting point the view that a substantial section of the anti-death penalty movement believes that endorsing or offering LWOP as an alternative is a necessary, or at least useful, weapon in the abolitionists' arsenal, notwithstanding any statistical evidence relating to LWOP's actual use as an alternative to death. These views are countered by those who consider LWOP to be just as morally abhorrent as the death penalty. My intention, therefore, is to use the history of slavery abolitionism to enquire into how anti-death penalty activists should, if at all, situate the use of LWOP within abolitionist discourses.[3]

We will start with an outline of how a similar dilemma plagued the anti-slavery movement. There were some who considered it necessary to advocate an alternative to bondage in order to secure emancipation, and thus proposed the colonization of freed blacks. This would involve freeing blacks from bondage on the condition that they would be sent to live away from white communities, beyond the shores of America. While some in the movement adopted this position for tactical purposes, to placate those who opposed slavery but could not abide the thought of racial integration or assimilation, others genuinely believed that blacks and whites could not live together. Yet others, though, took the view that the principles behind colonization were objectionable. These abolitionists insisted that black people should be considered equal to whites, and be given the opportunity to live in freedom in the country that was their home.[4]

We will then map these debates on to the current debates surrounding LWOP and the death penalty in contemporary abolitionist circles. The same three-sided debate emerges, between those who accept LWOP for tactical purposes; those who genuinely support LWOP as a normative matter; and those who consider such sentences to be just as objectionable as capital punishment. It is with this in mind that we will then use historians' understandings of the effects of colonization on race relations in America today, to set out why today's abolitionists should be wary of advocating LWOP. In *Bind Us Apart: How Enlightened Americans Invented Racial Segregation*, Nicholas Guyatt argues that the rhetoric of colonization helped entrench and perpetuate racial injustices that have continued to this day. Ibram X. Kendi similarly highlights how the suggestion of colonization as an alternative to slavery perpetuated assumptions about black inferiority that have had a pervasive and long-lasting effect on American laws and policies.[5] It is tempting to use these texts to conclude that death penalty abolitionists should not explicitly or implicitly endorse a practice such as LWOP, since it perpetuates and institutionalizes the idea that some people are beyond all hope for reform, and can be treated without respect for their human dignity. Such a conclusion, though, would unhelpfully ignore the empirical evidence about the role of LWOP in advancing the abolition of capital punishment. A more nuanced conclusion, one taken from the works of Guyatt, Kendi, and others, is that the anti-death penalty movement should couch the language of "alternatives" within the framework of dignity that was outlined in Chapter Four. This, we will see, will help future activists continue the work of the abolitionists.

II. The role of "alternatives" in progressing abolition

A. Slavery and colonization

Thomas Jefferson is renowned for his moral ambiguity. At once a leading figure in the anti-slavery movement, he also fathered six children through a coercive relationship with Sally Hemings, who was just one of the many slaves that he kept.[6] And while Jefferson provided radical abolitionists with their most potent weapon – the statement in the Declaration of Independence that "all men are created equal" – he also endorsed the agenda of conservative anti-slavery activists who were reluctant to grant equal political and social status to freed blacks upon emancipation. In *Notes on the State of Virginia*, published in 1785, Jefferson outlined his view that blacks were inferior to whites, and that even though slavery should be abolished, the two races should not live side-by-side. Jefferson struggled with the causes of such perceived inferiority – he was aware that the differences might be the product of enslavement, and that white racists might have denigrated the conditions of blacks, but he was also open to the view that blacks were innately inferior to whites. He wrote that black people were "improved" during enslavement, and this observation led him to conclude that racial differences were not merely a consequence of circumstances: "The improvement of the blacks in body and mind, in the first instance of their mixture with the whites, has been observed by every one, and proves that their inferiority is not the effect merely of their condition of life."[7] It followed, for Jefferson, "that the blacks, whether originally a distinct race, or made distinct by time and circumstances, are inferior to the whites in the endowments both of body and mind."[8] This, for Jefferson, rendered post-emancipation plans problematic. To make his point, Jefferson alluded to Roman slavery, which had not been predicated on race. Romans could thus emancipate their slaves and allow them to live in the community, but this option was not open to American slaveholders: "Among the Romans emancipation required but one effort. The slave, when made free, might mix with, without staining the blood of his master. But with us a second is necessary, unknown to history. When freed, he is to be removed beyond the reach of mixture."[9] He outlined the reasons why blacks and whites could not mix in a post-emancipation era: "Deep rooted prejudices, entertained by the whites; ten thousand recollections, by the blacks, of the injuries they have received; new provocations; the real distinctions which nature has made; and many other circumstances, which divide us into parties, and produce convulsions which will probably never end but in the extermination of the one or the other race."[10]

Jefferson was not the only high-ranking public figure to endorse the view that racial separation was desirable in a post-emancipation America, and in 1816, a society was formed that was devoted to promoting the resettlement of freed slaves to West Africa. This organization – the American Colonization Society – came to dominate abolitionist discourses for the next couple of decades. Among its members were such luminaries as James Monroe, Andrew Jackson, Henry Clay, and James Madison. Even William Lloyd Garrison initially supported the aims of the ACS, which was "the colonizing of the free people of colour, with their consent, in Africa or such other place as Congress may deem most expedient". In 1821, the state of Liberia was founded in West Africa for the purposes of colonization, and approximately 10,000 black people migrated there from the US over the next four decades. In the 1850s, when Abraham Lincoln attempted to re-energize the colonization scheme, he accepted that sending people to Liberia was impracticable, and instead looked to the Caribbean and Central America.[11] Nevertheless, Lincoln's thinking was shaped by Jefferson: it was not possible for the races to co-exist, and the most expedient way of ending slavery was to promise slaveholders and white racists that freed slaves would not live amongst them in a post-emancipation America. Consider, for example, the words of Henry Clay during the inaugural meeting of the ACS in 1816. Clay described the purpose of the ACS: to "rid our country of a useless and pernicious, if not dangerous portion of the population."[12]

The proposal to transport free blacks to Africa or some other place outside the US was supported by another group of people. In addition to those who felt uneasy about slavery but who genuinely believed that black people were not worthy or capable of living alongside whites, there were those who believed that, notwithstanding the abstract ideal of racial equality, colonization was a strategically sensible way of promoting abolition because it met proponents of slavery and racial prejudice half way. The idea was that slaveholders would voluntarily manumit their slaves if they could be convinced that they would not have to live alongside them in a post-emancipation America. James Madison, for example, was moved towards colonization partly because of the potential for expediting abolition. A "settlement of freed blacks on the coast of Africa," he wrote, "might prove a great encouragement to manumission in the southern parts of the U.S., and even afford the best hope yet presented of putting an end to the slavery in which not less than 600,000 unhappy negroes are now involved."[13]

Whatever one's views are today on the stance of the ACS towards black people, it is not difficult to understand why some abolitionists would endorse such a position at that time. Any calls for emancipation had to contend with the question of what would be done with the freed population. Even if we reject the view that black people were, or are, "inferior" to whites, slaves had nonetheless been denied any sort of education that would help them make their way in life, and it was not wholly objectionable for people to worry that there would therefore be a degree of chaos in the aftermath of abolition. And even if we reject the idea put forward by defenders of slavery that black people were, or are, fundamentally immoral and unable to control their violent and sexual impulses, we can still see why the likes of Jefferson might fear that freed blacks would be hostile to the people who had kept them in bondage for so long.[14]

B. Capital punishment and life without parole

In the contemporary anti-death penalty community, we similarly find two groups of people who either actively support, or at least passively accept, the use of life without parole as an alternative to capital punishment. First, there are those who genuinely believe that LWOP is a morally justifiable and practically appealing sentence because it serves the penological purposes of retribution, deterrence, and public protection, while avoiding the practical problems that plague capital punishment, such as the risk of executing innocent persons, or the high costs associated with the capital process. Second, there are those who find LWOP morally objectionable in principle, but who believe that endorsing the punishment, or at least not actively opposing it, will expedite the abolition of capital punishment.

In the former category, the group Conservatives Concerned About the Death Penalty explains why LWOP is a morally justifiable and practically appealing punishment. They list four main reasons for opposing the death penalty, none of which is applicable, in their view, to LWOP. The first reason offered is the incompatibility of "small government" with the death penalty, "especially when we compare the high costs of capital punishment to life without possibility of release." The second ground for opposing executions lies in their distrust in the state's ability "to get it right. We already know that some innocent people have been sentenced to death, and for others it may already be too late." In contrast, innocent people sentenced to LWOP do not face the risk of being executed while appealing their conviction. Third, "[s]ome of us are disturbed by the roller coaster for family members of murder victims, or wonder why we're investing so much in a system that doesn't keep us any safer than the alternatives." Fourth, "[s]ome of us believe that the death penalty contradicts our values about protecting life."[15]

In the latter camp, we find those who abhor the idea of locking a person behind bars for the rest of their natural life, but who seek to appeal to the existing values and concerns of their target audience – supporters of, and those apathetic about, state-sanctioned executions. In this sense, the acceptance, if not outright endorsement, of LWOP is tied to the other non-radical tropes that such abolitionists have used, which were discussed in the previous chapter: the risk of a wrongful execution, and the high costs of death sentences. Evi Girling explains how the use of LWOP in death penalty abolitionism can be traced to the rational and non-emotive argumentation that has informed anti-death penalty discourses in recent years. In her words, death penalty abolitionists' "appeal to restraint [risk of executing the innocent] and rationality [the high costs of capital punishment] contributed to the ascendance of LWOP as an alternative to the death penalty; LWOP provided a logical, practical, tested and… satisfying, alternative to the death penalty for offenders convicted of capital crimes."[16]

It is not always easy to distinguish between those in the former camp, and those in the latter. While groups such as Conservatives Concerned About the Death Penalty are explicit about their support for harsh retributivism, and are clear that their opposition to executions stems from their particular political philosophy, there are other instances of abolitionists extolling the virtue of LWOP even though we might expect them to abhor such sentences for the same reasons they abhor capital punishment. In 1990, the director of the American Civil Liberties Union National Capital Punishment Project stated that the ACLU would "acquiesce, but not support" sentences of life without parole if it were offered as an alternative to the death penalty, because such sentences were qualitatively similar to death sentences.[17] On an undated webpage, though, the Northern California branch of the American Civil Liberties Union states that "[l]ife without parole provides swift, severe, and certain punishment" whereas "[t]he death penalty costs more, delivers less, and puts innocent lives at risk."[18] Similarly, the actor and activist Mike Farrell has claimed to oppose capital punishment because he disagrees with the notion that some people are dispensable: "We have determined that some human beings are not human, are not worthwhile or capable, and that we can just do away with them… If you set up that belief system in a society, you can justify torture, assassinations by drone, just about anything."[19] Yet in September 2015, Farrell signed the letter that proposed a statewide ballot initiative in California that would have replaced the death penalty with LWOP, and in this letter Farrell set out the benefits of such sentences: "Life in prison without the possibility of parole ensures that the worst criminals stay in prison forever and saves money."[20]

Notwithstanding the difficulties in determining whether any particular activist accepts LWOP on principled or tactical grounds, it is clear that the availability of

LWOP enables political leaders to further the anti-death penalty cause. In 2004, the Governor of Kansas – Kathleen Sebelius – signed a law permitting LWOP, as a means of signaling her opposition to capital punishment without attracting accusations of being "soft" on crime.[21] This was a remarkable step because at the time, Kansas had only nine people on death row, and had not carried out any executions since 1965. In other words, support for the death penalty was not particularly strong, yet Governor Sebelius still felt it necessary to assure the public that those found guilty of the most serious crimes would be subject to the punishment of LWOP. This mirrored the strategy of Governor Mario Cuomo of New York in the early 1990s. An ardent opponent of the death penalty, Cuomo not only called for the use of LWOP, but also offered to sign away his clemency powers in order to sway the public towards his position.[22] Cuomo's electoral defeat in 1994 has been attributed to his stance on capital punishment, but this has not deterred other governors such as Sebelius from following his lead.

These governors have most likely been responding to polling data on the use of LWOP in death's stead. In January 2017, Public Policy Polling surveyed voters in Utah and found that 47 percent of respondents preferred life in prison without parole, plus a requirement that the convicted person work in prison to pay restitution to the victims (LWOP plus restitution), compared to just 29 percent who preferred the death penalty. The pollsters found that the preference for LWOP plus restitution held firm across race, gender, age, religion, and political party affiliation. 53 percent of Utahns also said they would strongly or somewhat support a bill to replace the death penalty with life without parole, compared to 41 percent of respondents who would oppose such a bill.[23] Polling by Craig Haney in Florida in 2016 revealed similar results: 57 percent of respondents expressed a preference for LWOP.[24] The American Values Survey in 2015 yielded similar results: "When asked which punishment they prefer for people convicted of murder, a majority (52%) of Americans say they prefer life in prison with no chance of parole, compared to 47% who say they prefer the death penalty."[25]

The experience of Texas illustrates the effect that LWOP has on people's minds about the death penalty. In 1994, the US Supreme Court ruled that jurors had to be told of the availability of LWOP, if it existed, in cases in which the prosecutor relied on "future dangerousness" as a reason for seeking a death sentence.[26] In Justice Blackmun's words: "where the defendant's future dangerousness is at issue, and state law prohibits the defendant's release on parole, due process requires that the sentencing jury be informed that the defendant is parole ineligible."[27] However, the Court did not say that trial courts were obliged to tell jurors of the availability of sentences of life *with* parole. For many years, then, jurors in Texas – which did not have LWOP until 2005 – were not necessarily informed of alternatives to the death penalty at the sentencing stage of capital trials.[28] Even when they were informed that the defendant would be sentenced to 40 years imprisonment before they would be eligible for parole, which was the next most severe punishment in Texas until 2005, the very possibility of parole led some juries to opt for a death sentence. Senator Eddie Lucio Jr made this point in 2004: "Oftentimes, jurors are conflicted about whether to sentence dangerous offenders with mental retardation or a mental illness to death, yet they must do so because there is no assurance that the defendant will remain behind bars."[29] For years, prosecutors discouraged legislators from introducing a life without parole statute, because they feared that if such a statute existed, there would be a decline in the number of death sentences handed down.[30] Texas only introduced LWOP in 2005, after the US Supreme Court outlawed the death penalty for offenders under the age of 18. Worried that juveniles henceforth, and those already on death row, would be eligible for parole in their late 50s or early 60s under the existing law, the legislature rushed through a law that permitted LWOP.[31]

Outside the political realm, it is understandable why a lawyer might not oppose LWOP in specific cases. Working within the confines of the legal system, she or he might agree to LWOP as part of a plea bargain, to avoid a death sentence. The lawyer might convey the severity of LWOP when trying to convince a jury to spare their client's life. And in post-conviction appeals too, or requests for clemency, the alleged virtues of LWOP might be extolled in order to prevent an execution. Judges who have set out their opposition to capital punishment have also felt it necessary to assure those who read their opinions that life without parole serves the same penological purposes as capital punishment, but without the same constitutional defects. In *Glossip v. Gross*, Justice Breyer explained the constitutional defects with capital punishment, and asserted that "whatever interest in retribution might be served by the death penalty as currently administered, that interest can be served almost as well by a sentence of life in prison without parole".[32]

It is no surprise, then, to see that as support for capital punishment has declined, so the use of LWOP has proliferated.[33] In the mid-1990s, just 16 states permitted life without parole. Today, that number stands at 49, with Alaska the sole exception.[34] Indeed, Alabama, Illinois, and Louisiana all enacted statutes allowing for the imposition of life without parole as an immediate response to the US Supreme Court's decision in *Furman v. Georgia* in 1972, indicating the role of LWOP as a replacement for death sentences. Similarly, the state legislatures that have recently repealed their death penalty statutes have fallen back on LWOP as an alternative sanction. In Connecticut, for example, the legislature replaced "capital felony" crimes – which would attract the death penalty – with "murder with special circumstances", which automatically results in the imposition of LWOP.[35] Since the state supreme court outlawed the death penalty in Delaware, persons convicted of capital murder are automatically sentenced to a term of life without parole. In Maryland, which abolished the death penalty in 2013, LWOP is now the harshest sentence available.

On the basis of polling data, legislative action to repeal death penalty statutes and replace them with LWOP, and the general decline in the numbers of death sentences handed down, James Liebman writes that the availability of "[l]ife without parole has been absolutely crucial to whatever progress has been made against the death penalty."[36] Andy Hoover and Ken Cunningham, who led efforts to abolish capital punishment in New Jersey, asserted that "emphasizing LWOP as an alternative to the death penalty was key to the success of the movement for abolition of the death penalty in New Jersey."[37] Richard Dieter, the former

Executive Director of the Death Penalty Information Center, has said of LWOP: "It's a practical alternative to the death penalty that the public may be willing to accept. Having a stated alternative that sounds tough makes a big difference."[38]

This is not to say that the likes of Dieter support LWOP, but rather these quotes illustrate the view that if people are willing to disavow their support for capital punishment on the proviso that LWOP is imposed instead, then it becomes almost unbearably tempting for abolitionists to either actively champion such sentences, or at least refrain from criticizing such sentences, in the same way that many opponents of slavery championed, or passively accepted, colonization. Indeed, even those who have qualms about the morality of LWOP might take the view that such sentences are not as bad as death sentences. In looking at the effect of punishment on the families of those being punished, Michael Radelet notes that death sentences and executions have a qualitatively different effect than life sentences on the families of offenders. With executions, families have to contend with the "roller coaster" of emotions that accompany appeals and last minute stays of execution. They may witness their loved one being executed, and many have expressed feelings of guilt, believing that they could have said something during the sentencing phase of the trial which would have convinced the jury to spare the individual their life.[39] Radelet describes these impacts on family members, and writes that "the incremental (added) retributive effects of the death penalty often punish a greater number of innocent people than life imprisonment."[40] In *Woodson v North Carolina*, Justice Stewart noted that "[d]eath, in its finality, differs more from life imprisonment than a 100-year prison term differs from one of only a year or two".[41] The irrevocability of an execution, and the moral magnitude of casting a human being to be positively killed by an agent of the state, signifies the qualitative difference between sentences of death, and all other sentences, including life without parole. Having said this, we find that just as abolitionists' support for LWOP mirrors the anti-slavery support for colonization, so the objections to LWOP mirror the objections that were leveled at colonization.

III. The problems with discourses of alternatives

Almost no historian today extols the virtues of colonization. Yet at the time, colonization was not just viewed as a necessary compromise, or as a means of preventing irreconcilable racial divisions in a post-emancipation America. It was also not purely cast as a measure designed to preserve the welfare of whites. Colonization was also advertised as a positive good for blacks. That is, some abolitionists thought that anti-black racism would stifle any realization of the potential capabilities of black people.[42] John Parrish – a Pennsylvania reformer – suggested that removal from America would enable former slaves to enjoy "liberty and the rights of citizenship" in their own country. Parrish also predicted that their example would inspire emancipation elsewhere: "many persons of humanity, who continue to hold slaves, would be willing to liberate them on condition of their so removing."[43] It was in this sense that the ACS could present themselves as progressive and liberal in their outlook. But opposition to colonization from within the anti-slavery community was strong from the outset, and these opponents highlighted two problems with such a measure. First, black Americans in particular took the ACS to task for perpetuating racial prejudices and for denigrating non-whites. Second, they argued that colonization actually stifled progress towards abolition. For these reasons, it became clear to opponents of colonization that a more radical type of abolitionism was needed, and that black Americans themselves would need to spearhead efforts to ensure that emancipation was accompanied by efforts to ensure equal rights and opportunities for black people.

A study of the problems with LWOP reveals two similar ways in which abolitionist endorsement of such sentences perpetuate the wrong of capital punishment, and stifle progress towards abolition. First, the endorsement of such sentences perpetuates the view that some people should be permanently cast away from the political and moral human community. Second, notwithstanding the views outlined above, it has been argued that the endorsement of such sentences has not led to a significant decline in the use of capital punishment, and has thus simply created another problem that needs addressing. Indeed, just as those most affected by colonization took a lead in speaking out against it, so we find that death row inmates today sometimes speak out against the abolitionist tactic of acquiescing in the imposition of LWOP.

A. Perpetuating the wrong in question

Incensed by the premises of colonization, David Walker issued an abolitionist tract in September 1829 entitled *Appeal to the Colored Citizens of the World*, which caught the attention of William Lloyd Garrison and gave impetus to the radical wing of slavery abolitionism. In his *Appeal*, Walker highlighted the shortcomings of colonization specifically, and of conservative approaches to abolition generally. Walker's *Appeal* warrants a close reading, for in it he identifies dehumanization and the denial of dignity as the roots of the problem with slavery, and he highlights the importance of placing respect for dignity at the center of abolitionist efforts. Proponents of slavery and racial subjugation, Walker said, inflicted "insupportable insult" on blacks by claiming that blacks were not part of the "human family", and descended instead from "Monkeys or Orang-Outangs."[44] Directing his attention at Thomas Jefferson, Walker highlights the injury that colonization inflicted on black people, stating that Jefferson's belief in the inferiority of blacks had "in truth injured us more, and ... been as great a barrier to our emancipation as any thing that has ever been advanced against us". This was because Jefferson's views had "sunk deep into the hearts of millions of the whites and never will be removed this side of eternity."[45]

Walker went further. He also claimed that the motivations behind members of the ACS were invidious. He suggested that the real aim of the ACS was to strengthen the system of slavery by removing the most vociferous opponents of the institution from America. Free blacks were active in the anti-slavery movement, and provided considerable assistance to those in bondage. It was people such as Harriet Tubman, for example, who led the Underground Railroad. The more free blacks that left America, then, the less help there was for the enslaved, thus strengthening the institution of slavery: "The real sense and meaning of the [ACS] is," Walker wrote, "get the free people of colour away to Africa, from among the slaves, where they may at once be blessed and happy, and those who we hold in slavery, will be contented to rest in ignorance and wretchedness, to dig up gold and silver for us and our children."[46] Walker repeats this accusation a little later: "Here is a demonstrative proof, of a plan got up by a gang of slave-holders to select the free people of colour from among the slaves, that our more miserable brethren may be the better secured in ignorance and wretchedness, to work their farms and dig their mines, and thus go on enriching the Christians with their blood and groans."[47]

In 1833, James Cropper surmised that colonization actually hindered progress towards emancipation, since it "perpetuate[d] that abomination" of prejudice against black people.[48] Colonization, in Cropper's view, normalized the belief that black people should be subjugated. The year before, William Lloyd Garrison had published *Thoughts on African Colonization*, in which he rescinded his earlier support for the ACS.[49] His objections to colonization encompassed an objection to the principle of "gradualism", which had dominated anti-slavery strategies and tactics. "Gradualists" took the view that the abolition of slavery should be achieved in a piecemeal fashion in order to ensure the smooth transition from slave society to free society. Instead of "gradualism", Garrison promoted the principle of "immediatism."[50] This was not to be taken literally, in that Garrison did not think that slavery could be, or even should be, abolished overnight. Rather, "immediatism" was to be understood as a slogan that emphasized the urgency with which slavery needed to be abolished. Gradualism, he complained, rendered abolitionists complacent and self-satisfied with their apparent "successes", even though it left people in bondage.

In all, Garrison made it clear that he considered "the colonization scheme [to be] inadequate in its design, injurious in its operation, and contrary to sound principle."[51] Similar criticisms have been leveled at the anti-death penalty movement's endorsement of LWOP. Such "alternative" sentences are problematic as a matter of substance, and as a matter of procedure. Taking these two problems together, such sentences also become problematic as a matter of principle, since they compound and perpetuate the idea that some people can be treated as mere objects, and cast aside from the moral and political human community.

As a matter of substance, a number of death penalty abolitionists have raised concerns comparable to those raised by David Walker in his *Appeal*, and Garrison in his *Thoughts*. Put bluntly, it has been said that the proposed solution is just as morally abhorrent as the problem. David Dow – a death penalty defense lawyer based in Texas – claims that "[s]ending a prisoner to die behind bars with no hope of release is a sentence that denies the possibility of redemption every bit as much as strapping a murderer to the gurney and filling him with poison." As such, in Dow's view, "[t]he justifications given by death penalty opponents who have embraced life without parole reveal the extent to which abolitionists have surrendered the moral basis of their position."[52] For Sharon Dolovich, LWOP "most effectively captures the central motivating aim of the contemporary American carceral system. LWOP promises permanent exclusion. In one move, it guarantees that the targeted offender will never reemerge, never reintegrate, never again move freely in the shared public space."[53] Put another way, LWOP mimics the purposes of capital punishment: to permanently remove an undesirable person from the moral and political community. In the words of Marie Gottschalk,

> a number of leading abolitionists have ardently supported LWOP. They have uncritically accepted LWOP as a viable alternative to the death penalty and thus have helped to legitimize the wider use of a sentence that has many features in common with capital punishment. These abolitionists have helped normalize a sanction that, like the death penalty, is way out of line with human rights and sentencing norms in other developed countries.[54]

Outside America, authorities have recognized that LWOP, like the death penalty, is incompatible with the duty to respect human dignity. In *Hutchinson v. United Kingdom*, decided on January 17, 2017, the European Court of Human Rights stated that "respect for human dignity requires prison authorities to strive towards a life sentenced prisoner's rehabilitation."[55] Thus, the Court held that the prohibition on "inhuman or degrading treatment or punishment" in Article 3 of the European Convention on Human Rights outlawed sentences of life without parole – or "irreducible life sentence[s]" in the Court's parlance.[56] The pertinent part of the judgment reads:

> The Convention does not prohibit the imposition of a life sentence on those convicted of especially serious crimes, such as murder. Yet to be compatible with Article 3 such a sentence must be reducible de jure and de facto, meaning that there must be both a prospect of release for the prisoner and a possibility of review. The basis of such review must extend to assessing whether there are legitimate penological grounds for the continuing incarceration of the prisoner. These grounds include punishment, deterrence, public protection and rehabilitation.[57]

The Pope, too, has described life without parole as a "hidden death penalty",[58] and has recognized the incompatibility of such sentences with the requirement to respect human dignity.[59]

In many ways, then, the term "life without parole" is misleading. Such sentences are perhaps better termed as a sentence to die behind bars, in the same way that the death penalty is a sentence to die in state custody. It is death by natural causes, rather than death by lethal injection. Some commentators have gone further, claiming that life sentences with no hope of release are actually more repugnant than death sentences. Cesare Beccaria – the Italian philosopher whom contemporary abolitionists usually regard as the founder of the anti-death penalty movement – wrote: "It is not the terrible but fleeting sight of a felon's death which is the most powerful brake on crime, but the long-drawn-out example of a man deprived of freedom, who having become a beast of burden, repays the society which he has offended with his labour."[60] When New Mexico abolished capital punishment in 2009, Governor Bill Richardson announced that his decision to sign the bill into law was premised on the risk of executing an innocent person, coupled with the reassurance that life without parole sentences would keep the public safe and satisfy demands for retribution because such sentences were "worse than death." Speaking about a visit to the state penitentiary, Richardson said: "My conclusion was those cells are something that may be worse than death,… I believe this is a just punishment."[61] In 1928, Lewis E. Lawes, warden of Sing Sing prison in New York in the 1920s and 1930s, wrote: "Death fades into insignificance when compared with life imprisonment. To spend each night in jail, day after day, year after year, gazing at the bars and longing for freedom, is indeed expiation."[62]

It has not just been lawyers, judges, politicians, religious leaders, and academics who have highlighted the comparisons between death sentences and LWOP though. Gottschalk has noted that over half of death row inmates in Tennessee who were surveyed about the matter believed LWOP to be harsher than execution.[63] Kenneth E. Hartman, who is serving a term of LWOP in California, founded an organization called "The Other Death Penalty Project" which, as the name suggests, seeks to educate the public and policy-makers about how life sentences are merely another type of death sentence. The Project has published an anthology of inmates' writings that highlights how those sentenced to life feel as though they have been sentenced to death.[64] During efforts to outlaw the death penalty in California in 2012, the Campaign to End the Death Penalty sent surveys on Proposition 34 to more than 200 death row inmates in the Golden State. Fifty inmates responded, 47 of whom opposed the measure because they did not want to spend decades behind bars with no hope of release.[65] The same pattern emerged when the death penalty was again on the ballot in 2016. Of the 46 death row prisoners who responded to a survey, 21 stated that they opposed replacing death sentences with life without parole, and only 17 declared support for the measure.[66]

It might be plausible for a death penalty abolitionist to claim that these concerns – that LWOP is substantively the same as a death sentence – are better left to be tackled another day, after capital punishment has been abolished. However, the way in which support for LWOP has been situated within abolitionist discourses is problematic, and cautions against this assumption. As explained above, LWOP is usually offered as an alternative on the grounds that it avoids the risk of an innocent person being executed, and that it saves taxpayers money. That is, LWOP is being championed in its current form and procedure. However, if death sentences were to be abolished without any corresponding change to the administration of LWOP, we would see the perpetuation and proliferation of problems within the criminal justice system. Put simply, if sentences of LWOP really are comparable to the death penalty in a substantive sense – and abolitionists and supporters alike agree that, in many respects, they are – then it follows that such sentences should be subject to similar limitations and safeguards. However, the scope of applicability, and the procedural regulations, that accompany LWOP fall far short of those that accompany the use of capital punishment. And, if we accept Carol Steiker and Jordan Steiker's view that the death penalty is being "regulated" out of existence by virtue of these limitations and safeguards,[67] then we can surmise that LWOP is not being regulated to the point of abolition. In this sense, it will be even more difficult to abolish LWOP than it has been to abolish the death penalty.

We saw in Chapter Five that the restrictions on the use of capital punishment are designed to ensure that death sentences are only imposed when such sentences are considered proportionate to the gravity of the crime and the moral culpability of the offender. We also saw, though, that the Court has not applied the same proportionality analysis to non-capital cases. Sentences of life without parole are therefore available for a wide range of offenses including non-violent property offenses. In 2005, the US Supreme Court outlawed the death penalty categorically for offenders under the age of 18, but such persons can still be sentenced to life without parole in 31 states, if convicted of murder.[68] In fact, as noted above, legislators in Texas specifically introduced LWOP in 2005 in order to ensure that the young offenders spared from execution under *Roper v. Simmons* would never be eligible for parole.[69] And, as Marie Gottschalk has documented, "[i]n a pattern familiar in other states, the list of qualifying crimes for LWOP expanded in Texas" after it was introduced in 2005.[70]

In addition to the lack of any rigorous proportionality analysis, LWOP is also free from individualized sentencing procedures, except in cases involving juveniles. In *Woodson v. North Carolina*, the US Supreme Court explained why death sentences must be individualized. Defendants, the Court ruled, must be allowed to introduce mitigating evidence in order to ensure that only the most morally depraved are executed. And in *Hurst v. Florida*, the Court explained that death sentences could only be imposed by a jury, and not by a judge.[71] When we look at LWOP schemes around the country, though, we see mandatory schemes abound. Even in some jurisdictions where the penalty is not mandatory, we see the potential for individuals to be sentenced to LWOP at the discretion of a judge rather than a jury. Consider, for example, the schemes in the seven jurisdictions that have outlawed capital punishment since 2007. In five of these states, LWOP is mandatory for some crimes. In Connecticut, in 2012, a jury-imposed, discretionary death penalty for "capital felonies" was replaced with a mandatory LWOP for offenses of "murder with special circumstances."[72] When the Delaware Supreme Court invalidated the state's death penalty, it left LWOP as the only punishment available upon a finding of guilt for capital crimes. In Illinois, which abolished the death penalty in 2011, LWOP is mandatory when certain aggravating factors are found, as is the case in New Mexico and New York. Even though LWOP is not mandatorily imposed in Maryland, which abolished the death penalty in 2013, it is nonetheless a decision for a judge to make, rather than a unanimous jury.

In addition to the mandatory application of LWOP in some states, such sentences also lack the sort of procedural safeguards that are applicable in capital cases to ensure that convictions are free from error. Thus, when anti-death penalty advocates encourage the use of LWOP on the grounds that it is a cheaper punishment, they are by implication contributing to what Gottschalk calls "the carceral state", because prisoners sentenced to LWOP will have less chance of having their sentence reviewed or overturned. In this sense, we can draw parallels with David Walker's criticism of the American Colonization Society. Walker suggested that the true motives of the ACS were to strengthen the subjugation of black people by removing those who worked most hard for abolition and equality. While it might be implausible to argue that anti-death penalty advocates who champion LWOP are purposively entrenching harsh punishments, the underlying concern is comparable: such an "alternative" has the effect of subjugating the very people it is supposed to help. In some respects, if you are innocent it is better to be sentenced to death and take advantage of the heightened review procedures available, than it is to be sentenced to a lesser-reviewed sentence of LWOP.

By advocating for the imposition of LWOP in its current form (that is, without heightened procedural safeguards), anti-death penalty advocates are normalizing and institutionalizing harsh retributivism. Consider, for example, the reversal rate for capital cases. It currently stands at 68 percent, because of the heightened review procedures. In non-capital cases – including LWOP – the reversal rate is between 10–20 percent, in part due to the relatively weaker safeguards and fewer opportunities for review.[73] Capital defendants currently have a right to have their case reviewed by the state's highest court; but non-capital defendants – even those serving a term of LWOP – do not. Also, as noted above, if a prosecutor wishes to rely on "future dangerousness" as a reason for seeking a death sentence, the jury must be informed of the availability of LWOP as an alternative punishment.[74] In other words, the defendant benefits from the jury being informed of alternative, allegedly lesser, punishments. However, in cases where LWOP is the maximum available sentence, juries are not required to be told of alternatives. Thus, there is more scope for a jury to be inclined to sentence someone to LWOP, unaware that there is a less harsh, but just as effective, alternative available.[75]

The endorsement of LWOP can also contribute to the institutionalization of racism in the criminal justice system. For example, North Carolina's Racial Justice Act, which has now been repealed, mandated the replacement of a death sentence with a sentence of life without parole in cases in which a prisoner successfully showed that race had impermissibly played a role in the imposition of their death sentence. As a result, it gave legitimacy to sentences of LWOP in cases that had been affected by racial prejudice.

Death penalty abolitionists who criticize life without parole have also pointed to the counter-productivity of those who endorse such sentences, either for moral or strategic purposes. Such sentences are often touted as cheaper than death sentences, but Roger Hood and Carolyn Hoyle highlight the "enormous cost implications of housing increasing numbers of elderly people in prisons who will inevitably need medical and geriatric care."[76]

Perhaps more startling than the substantive and procedural shortcomings of LWOP, though, is the observation that even if there has been some decrease in the use of capital punishment as a result of the use of LWOP, this is nothing compared to the increased use of LWOP instead of lesser punishments. That is, it is arguable that people who would ordinarily have been sentenced to a term of imprisonment *with* the possibility of parole have instead been sentenced to LWOP as the latter has become acceptable. Ashley Nellis has found that "[b]etween 1992 and 2016, there was a 12.7 percent increase in the number of people on death row while over the same period the LWOP population rose 328 percent."[77] It is highly unlikely that all those sentenced to LWOP in that period would have been sentenced to death had the former not been available, and as Carol Steiker and Jordan Steiker note, "...even if the entire decline in death sentencing were (implausibly) attributed to LWOP, the number of capital defendants affected by LWOP's introduction would still be dwarfed by the number of noncapital defendants affected by its widespread adoption and use."[78] That is, even if the promotion of LWOP has led to a small decline in death sentences, this has been nothing compared to the startling increased use of LWOP instead of lesser sentences. In Nellis's words: "LWOP's widespread use in both capital and noncapital crimes has had a normalizing effect on extreme sentences and places an upward pressure on sentences across the spectrum."[79] Indeed, as of 2016, nearly half of all LWOP sentences have been passed in just four states. Florida accounts for 16.7 percent of all LWOP sentences; Pennsylvania 10.1 percent , California 9.6 percent , and Louisiana 9.1 percent .[80] All except Louisiana also appear in the list of the five most populous death rows.[81]

To paraphrase William Lloyd Garrison, then, "the [promotion or acceptance of LWOP] is inadequate in its design, injurious in its operation, and contrary to sound principle."[82] It is inadequate because it fails to account for the problems inherent in LWOP in its current form; it is injurious because it has normalized the use of such sentences in cases that might have otherwise attracted lesser sentences, and subjects people to a lifetime behind bars with no hope of release; and it is contrary to principle because it normalizes and institutionalizes the belief that some people can be permanently excluded from the human community, which is the very wrong that death penalty abolitionists are trying to eradicate in the first place.

B. Taking the views of the condemned seriously

The American Colonization Society was also criticized for the way in which it failed to take seriously the views of those it was (ostensibly) trying to help. Of course, if members of the ACS really did believe that blacks were "inferior", then this explains why only whites were involved in the establishment of the Society. A key component of human dignity is agency and autonomy, and the exclusion of blacks from abolitionism betrayed a belief that black people were not capable of exercising agency. Had white abolitionists taken the dignity of black people seriously, they would have realized that many of them had come to view America as their home – indeed, by this time many blacks had been born in America – and so they rejected the notion of moving overseas. A similar concern can be raised in the context of promoting LWOP as an alternative to capital punishment. While those who are guilty of committing horrific crimes should not dictate the terms of their punishment, the point remains that abolitionists should consider whether those on death row will actually welcome having their sentences commuted to life in the wake of abolition, especially considering the substantive nature of the punishment, and the lack of procedural safeguards available to those serving such sentences. Put another way, both the ACS, and the pro-LWOP death penalty abolitionists display a type of paternalism that is at odds with the premise of radical abolitionism: the inviolability of the dignity of every person, regardless of their skin color or moral attributes.[83]

IV. Resolving the dilemma

The dilemma facing death penalty abolitionists is a difficult one to resolve. On the one hand, those who claim that abolitionists should not support LWOP for the reasons given in this chapter can be accused of an idealism that threatens to derail the progress of the anti-death penalty movement, since there is some, albeit inconclusive, evidence that suggests that avoiding criticism of LWOP is vital for bringing about an end to executions. On the other hand, it can be argued that a conservative approach that does not take the dignity of the person facing punishment seriously risks not only degrading that person, but also contributing to, and strengthening, the carceral state.

The history of slavery abolitionism and post-emancipation America offers a potential resolution for this dilemma. The anti-slavery activists who championed colonization actively encouraged the idea of racial segregation, and it was the lack of any assertion of racial equality in these discourses that paved the way for post-emancipation racism to take root.[84] It can therefore be surmised that if death penalty abolitionists actively champion a dignity-free abolition, this will pave the way for dignity-free punishments such as LWOP to take root. The issue, then, is not a stark choice between accepting or denouncing LWOP. It is, rather, how to construe life sentences within anti-death penalty discourses in a way that takes the idea of dignity seriously. At present, LWOP is portrayed as an affirmative answer to the ills of the death penalty, because the ills of the death penalty are construed on non-dignitarian grounds.[85] However, if complaints against the death penalty were centered on discussions of dignity, then it would be plausible for abolitionists to reluctantly accept LWOP as an alternative, while laying the groundwork for a post-abolition assault on such sentences.

Jonathan Simon has argued that anti-death penalty discourses should begin a "dignity cascade" which can be used to challenge and eliminate other harsh punishments, such as LWOP.[86] Drawing on the work of David Garland and Marie Gottschalk, Simon emphasizes the role of capital punishment in infusing the entire criminal justice system with discourses of violence and dehumanization. That is, the existence of capital punishment, and the vociferous debates that take place around the topics of murder and state-sanctioned executions, has "infused criminal justice policy generally, helping to transform even the most pedestrian criminal matters into a subject of drama and emotion, and, inevitably, harsh punishment".[87] As Simon points out, it is in discussions about capital punishment that we find the idea of literal equivalence between crimes and punishment – a life for a life. In no other penal context do we speak of literally equivalent punishment. We do not contemplate raping rapists, or stealing from thieves. The presence of the death penalty, though, bends discussions of punishments *towards* the idea of literal proportionality. Perhaps, as Simon contemplates, "removing the one anchor that holds the metaphoric structure of crimes to that of punishments [would] destabilize the entire logic of equivalence, which both legitimizes penal justice and bends it toward harshness".[88] Simon acknowledges that this is an "optimistic scenario", but hopes that "abolition, even with the terms on offer [i.e., LWOP], will deepen an existing shift in that context away from reliance on extreme punishments as anchors of public safety and back toward the broader mix of social control (and one hopes social justice) tools that include policing and probation, but also health insurance, social services, mental health care, and housing support."[89]

In many ways, this shift away from equivalence between crime and punishment has already been happening in the US Supreme Court. We saw in Chapter Five and above that ever since *Furman v. Georgia* was decided in 1972, the Court has developed what has come to be known as its "death is different" jurisprudence. Put crudely, given the uniqueness of death as a punishment, the Court applies a unique approach when deciding capital cases. This is particularly true of its Eighth Amendment case law, in which the Court applies a considered proportionality analysis in capital cases, but not in other cases. Yet it was in the context of a life without parole case that the Court for the first time applied its death penalty jurisprudence to a non-capital context. In *Graham v. Florida*, decided in 2010, the Court applied its death penalty proportionality analysis to outlaw sentences of life without parole for juvenile offenders convicted of non-fatal offenses. The *Graham* Court's reasoning, and its progeny, offer hope for a "dignity-cascade."

Terrance Graham was 16 years old when, in July 2003, he unsuccessfully attempted to rob a restaurant in Jacksonville, Florida, with three other teenagers. The prosecutor elected to charge Graham as an adult rather than a juvenile, and charged him with attempted armed burglary. Graham avoided a custodial term by pleading guilty, but within a year was back in court for violating the terms of his probation. He had been arrested in connection with a home-invasion robbery, and was charged for that crime and for evading arrest, possession of a firearm, and associating with persons engaged in criminal activity. The trial judge had little hesitation in sentencing him to life in prison without parole. Although Graham was 19 at the time of sentencing, he was 17 when he was arrested for violating his probation. He therefore appealed his sentence on the grounds that it was unconstitutionally "cruel and unusual" to sentence him to life without parole for a crime committed when he was under the age of 18.

Writing for the Court, Justice Kennedy began by observing that "[t]he concept of proportionality is central to the Eighth Amendment. Embodied in the Constitution's ban on cruel and unusual punishments is the 'precept of justice that punishment for crime should be graduated and proportioned to [the] offense.'"[90]

Kennedy noted, though, that the Court has developed two streams of proportionality jurisprudence: "The first involves challenges to the length of term-of-years sentences given all the circumstances in a particular case. The second comprises cases in which the Court implements the proportionality standard by certain categorical restrictions on the death penalty."[91] On the one hand, since *Graham* did not involve the death penalty, the Court could have applied the first type of proportionality analysis. A leading case of this type is *Harmelin v. Michigan*, in which the Court held that the Eighth Amendment contains only a "narrow proportionality principle," which "does not require strict proportionality between crime and sentence". Instead, it "forbids only extreme sentences that are 'grossly disproportionate' to the crime."[92] In *Harmelin*, petitioner's sentence of LWOP for possession of a large quantity of cocaine was upheld. Similarly, in *Ewing v. California*, the Court rejected a challenge to a sentence of 25 years for a minor theft, under California's three-strikes scheme for punishing recidivists. In light of these decisions, we might have expected the Court to uphold Graham's sentence.

The *Harmelin*-line of cases – which permit the bend towards harsh punishments – survives because the death penalty both legitimizes harsh punishments, and also distracts the public and policy-makers from questioning the appropriateness of such punishments. As Ashley Nellis has observed, "it is more difficult to have an LWOP case examined because of the perception advanced that less is at stake compared to a death sentence."[93] Through its decision in *Graham*, though, the Court has instigated a conversation about the appropriateness of such punishments. This is because the Court declined to apply the *Harmelin*-standard in this case. Instead, it decided *Graham* under the second stream of proportionality cases that, up until now, had been reserved for death penalty cases given the uniqueness of death as a punishment. In death penalty cases, the Court has been willing to consider categorical bans on the punishment based either on the nature of the offense, or on the culpability of the offender. Thus, the Court has ruled the death penalty unconstitutional when imposed for non-fatal offenses, because the purposeful infliction of death as a punishment is only proportionate when the crime in question involves the intentional causing of death. Likewise, those who lack capacity to be morally blameworthy, by virtue of insanity, intellectual disability, or under-developed brains, will be categorically exempt from capital punishment on grounds of proportionality. *Graham*, the Court reasoned, was suited to this second type of proportionality analysis because petitioner was calling for a categorical ban on sentences of LWOP for those under the age of 18 who did not cause death.

Drawing on the 2005 death penalty case *Roper v. Simmons*, in which the Court had outlawed capital punishment for offenders under the age of 18, Kennedy explained why young offenders lack the same levels of moral culpability as their adult counterparts, and thus warrant a categorical exemption from the punishment of life without the possibility of parole, at least in cases not involving homicide.[94] Central to Kennedy's decision was the argument that, because of their youthfulness, young offenders are more amenable to rehabilitation and change: "[D]evelopments in psychology and brain science continue to show fundamental differences between juvenile and adult minds. For example, parts of the brain involved in behavior control continue to mature through late adolescence." Therefore, because "[j]uveniles are more capable of change than are adults…[f]rom a moral standpoint it would be misguided to equate the failings of a minor with those of an adult, for a greater possibility exists that a minor's character deficiencies will be reformed."[95]

Graham has been followed by two other cases in which the Court has outlawed mandatory sentences of LWOP for young offenders convicted for homicide, and clarified that all inmates currently serving mandatory sentences of LWOP for crimes committed when under the age of 18 must have their sentences reconsidered.[96] In both cases, the Court affirmed the use of its death penalty jurisprudence notwithstanding that these cases did not involve capital punishment. What is of interest here is that in *Roper* – the case on which the *Graham* Court relied – the Court invoked the idea of respect for dignity as a reason for outlawing the death penalty for young offenders. As Kennedy said in *Roper*, "[b]y protecting even those convicted of heinous crimes, the Eighth Amendment reaffirms the duty of the government to respect the dignity of all persons."[97] We can see, then, how a dignity-inspired death penalty decision has been used to address the imposition of life without parole, and the problem of approaches to punishing young offenders. We saw in Chapter Five that the US Supreme Court's death penalty jurisprudence encourages a radical approach to abolitionism precisely because the Court has in recent years invoked the idea of respect for "dignity" in its capital cases.

V. Conclusions

It is the uncritical endorsement of LWOP as an alternative punishment, then, that shares problems with the promotion of colonization as an alternative to slavery. Although it has proven effective in the short term in convincing members of the public to reject capital punishment, and has enabled state legislators to repeal death penalty statutes without fear of electoral backlash, the endorsement of LWOP poses many ethical and practical problems. It is not just that the punishment of LWOP will be entrenched, it is that the principles underpinning support for, and the operation of, LWOP normalize other harsh sentences. The focus on death and LWOP draws attention away from issues such as mandatory terms of 99 years imprisonment, which operates in the non-death penalty and non-LWOP state of Alaska.[98] Other harsh sentences abound, including terms of life with parole but where parole is only granted some 80 or 90 years into the sentence.[99] It also does not help that the worldwide community has been slow to place LWOP in the same category as the death penalty. The European Union – which has a formal death penalty abolitionist position – implicitly endorses the use of LWOP in America by allowing member states to extradite individuals to the US when LWOP is a potential sanction, but not when the death penalty is.[100] For the international community to mirror its role in anti-slavery efforts, it should be more vocal in opposing the use of LWOP as well.

It has been noted that the promotion of LWOP involves "a strange pairing of death penalty abolitionists with pro-incarceration activists and legislators",[101] and it is this strange pairing that serves to perpetuate the values that abolitionists are trying to eradicate. That is, proponents of LWOP, like proponents of colonization, cannot be described as "radical", since they endorse the very values that underpin the challenged practices in the first place: the belief that some people, either by virtue of their skin color or their conduct, do not deserve to ever live among "our" community. This is the main reason why abolitionists should be wary of endorsing LWOP: they may well leave a legacy of the very issue that they are objecting to.

Notes

1 Ashley Nellis, 'Still Life: America's Increasing Use of Life and Long-Term Sentences' Report issued by *The Sentencing Project* (3 May 2017) available at http://www.sentencingproject.org/wp-content/uploads/2017/05/Still-Life.pdf. The National Association for the Advancement of Colored People Legal Defense Fund issues quarterly statistics of the national death row population, and as of 1 April 2017, there were 2,843 inmates known to be sentenced to death across the USA. See NAACP LDF, 'Death Row U.S.A., Spring 2017' available at http://www.naacpldf.org/files/about-us/DRUSASpring2017.pdf. Also see http://www.naacpldf.org/death-row-usa for historical and more recent data. For a general collection of essays about life without parole, see Charles J. Ogletree Jr and Austin Sarat (eds) *Life Without Parole: America's New Death Penalty?* (NYU Press 2014).

2 Marie Gottschalk, 'No Way Out? Life Sentences and the Politics of Penal Reform' in Ogletree Jr and Sarat (n 1) 259. For the view that the decline in the death penalty has no, or little, causal relationship with the rise in LWOP, see Nellis 'Still Life' (n 1) 24 ("While some proponents of LWOP contend that it serves as an effective alternative to the death penalty, a causal relationship between the two is not evident. Between 1992 and 2016, there was a 12.7 percent increase in the number of people on death row while over the same period the LWOP population rose 328 percent. With 53,290 people serving LWOP as of 2016, it is not plausible that all, or even most, would be on death row if not for LWOP as the alternative." Also see Carol S. Steiker and Jordan M. Steiker, *Courting Death: The Supreme Court and Capital Punishment* (Belknap Press 2016) 286.

3 For a discussion of the role of life without parole in anti-death penalty discourses, see Steiker and Steiker (n 2) 296–297; Brandon Garrett, *End of its Rope: How Killing the Death Penalty Can Revive Criminal Justice* (Harvard University Press 2017) Chapter 7 (noting that "while the evidence is strong that LWOP did little to hasten the demise of death penalty cases, the evidence is overwhelming that its scope has expanded tremendously. Tens of thousands of people who never could or never would have been sentenced to death now get the 'other death penalty.'" At 167).

4 For an account of the role of colonization in anti-death penalty efforts, see Nicholas Guyatt, *Bind Us Apart: How Enlightened Americans Invented Racial Segregation* (Basic Books 2016).

5 ibid; Ibram X. Kendi, *Stamped From the Beginning: The Definitive History of Racist Ideas in America* (The Bodley Head 2017).

6 See Annette Gordon-Reed, *Thomas Jefferson and Sally Hemings: An American Controversy* (University of Virginia Press 1999).

7 Thomas Jefferson, *Notes on the State of Virginia* (2nd American edn, Philadelphia 1794) 205.

8 ibid 209.

9 ibid 209–210.

10 ibid 200.
11 For views on Lincoln's plans for colonization, see Charles H. Wesley, 'Lincoln's Plan for Colonizing the Emancipated Negroes' (1919) 4 Journal of Negro History, 7; Warren A. Beck, 'Lincoln and Negro Colonization in Central America' (195) 6 Abraham Lincoln Quarterly 162; Michael Vorenberg, 'Abraham Lincoln and the Politics of Black Colonization' (1993) 14 Journal of the Abraham Lincoln Association 22.
12 Quoted in Donald Przebowski, *The Rise and Fall of the United States* (Xlibris 2009) 286.
13 Quoted in Guyett (n 4) 216.
14 To be clear, I am *not* suggesting that it would be fair to blame freed black people for any resulting societal problems. Rather, I am merely noting that it was not beyond the bounds of reasonableness for some non-blacks to express concerns with post-emancipation plans.
15 See http://conservativesconcerned.org/who-we-are/.
16 Evi Girling, 'Sites of Crossing and Death in Punishment: The Parallel Lives, Trade-offs and Equivalencies of the Death Penalty and Life Without Parole in the US' (2016) 55 The Howard Journal of Crime and Justice 345, 350.
17 Marie Gottschalk, 'No Way Out?' (n 2) 261. Also see Mary E. Medland and Craig Fischer, 'Life without Parole Offered as Alternative to Death Penalty' *Criminal Justice Newsletter* (January 16, 1990) 4.
18 'The Truth About Life Without Parole: Condemned to Die in Prison' ACLU of Northern California (Undated) https://www.aclunc.org/article/truth-about-life-without-parole-condemned-die-prison.
19 Jazmine Ulloa, 'How "MASH" Actor Mike Farrell Became a Leading Voice Against the Death Penalty in California' *Los Angeles Times* (11 October 2016) http://www.latimes.com/politics/la-pol-ca-mike-farrell-death-penalty-20161011-snap-htmlstory.html.
20 Letter from Mike Farrell to Ashley Johansson, Initiative Coordinator, Office of the Attorney General, 'Request for Title and Summary for The Justice That Works Act of 2016' (15 September 2015) available at http://yeson62.com/wp-content/uploads/2016/08/Prop-62-Full-Text.pdf.
21 Ashley Nellis, 'Tinkering With Life: A Look at the Inappropriateness of Life Without Parole as an Alternative to the Death Penalty' (2013) 67 University of Miami Law Review 439, 445–446.
22 Herbert Haines, *Against Capital Punishment: The Anti-Death Penalty Movement in America, 1972–1994* (OUP 1999) 179
23 See 'Utah Survey Results' (9 February 2017) available at http://www.deathpenaltyinfo.org/files/pdf/UtahResults2017.pdf.
24 Craig Haney, 'Floridians Prefer Life Without Parole over Capital Punishment for Murderers' *Tampa Bay Times* (16 August 2016) http://www.tampabay.com/opinion/columns/column-floridians-prefer-life-without-parole-over-capital-punishment-for/2289719.
25 Robert P. Jones, Daniel Cox, Betsy Cooper, and Rachel Lienesch, 'Anxiety, Nostalgia, and Mistrust: Findings from the 2015 American Values Survey' Public Religion Research Institute (17 November 2015) 47 https://www.prri.org/wp-content/uploads/2015/11/PRRI-AVS-2015-1.pdf.
26 Simmons v. South Carolina, 512 U.S. 154 (1994).
27 ibid 156.
28 Gottschalk, 'No Way Out?' (n 2) 262; Danya W. Blair, 'A Matter of Life and Death: Why Life without Parole Should Be a Sentencing Option in Texas' (1994) 22 American Journal of Criminal Law 191.
29 Press Release: 'Senator Lucio Files Life-Without-Parole Bill' (27 October 2004) http://www.senate.texas.gov/press.php?id=27-20041027a.
30 Gottschalk, 'No Way Out?' (n 2) 262.

31 I. Bennett Capers, 'Defending Life' in Ogletree Jr and Sarat (n 1) 167, 171 (noting that "What caused the balance to shift decidedly in favour of the [LWOP] bill was a death penalty decision. In 2005, the Supreme Court decided *Roper v. Simmons*, ruling that the execution of individuals for crimes committed before the age of eighteen was inconsistent with evolving standards of decency. Faced with the contraction of the death penalty, Texas prosecutors softened their opposition to the LWOP bill, ensuring its passage.").

32 Glossip v. Gross, 135 S. Ct. 2726, 2769 (2015) (Breyer J dissenting). Also see Baze v. Rees, 553 U.S. 35, 78 (Stevens, J., concurring in the judgment) ("the recent rise in statutes providing for life imprisonment without the possibility of parole demonstrates that incapacitation is neither necessary nor a sufficient justification for the death penalty.").

33 But see n 2 for the view that there is no correlation between the decline of capital punishment, and the proliferation of LWOP.

34 This is correct as of December 2017.

35 See the website of the Death Penalty Information Center: https://deathpenaltyinfo.org/lwop-post-repeal.

36 Quoted in Adam Liptak, 'Serving Life, with No Chance of Redemption' *New York Times* (5 October 2005) http://www.nytimes.com/2005/10/05/us/serving-life-with-no-chance-of-redemption.html?_r=0.

37 Andy Hoover and Ken Cunningham, 'Framing, Persuasion, Messaging, and Messengers: How the Death Penalty Abolition Movement Succeeded in New Jersey' (2014) 38 Humanity & Society 443, 445 (based on an interview with Pete McDonough, a public relations expert who had been hired by New Jerseyans for Alternatives to the Death Penalty).

38 Sasha Abramsky, 'Lifers' *Legal Affairs* (March 2004) https://www.legalaffairs.org/issues/March-April-2004/feature_abramsky_marpar04.msp.

39 See, for example, the account given by Marilyn Shankle-Grant about her experiences as the parent of a person sentenced to death, in Maurice Chammah, 'A Mother Visits Her Son, Who's Condemned to Die in April' *The Marshall Project* (February 16, 2017) https://www.themarshallproject.org/2017/02/16/draft-life-inside#.xtz7ZSBTg.

40 Michael L. Radelet, 'The Incremental Retributive Impact of a Death Sentence Over Life Without Parole' (2016) 49 University of Michigan Journal of Law Reform 795, 796.

41 Woodson v. North Carolina, 428 U.S. 280, 305 (1976).

42 Guyatt, *Bind Us Apart* (n 4) 247 ("Liberal reformers in the North and the Upper South had identified two rationales for black colonization. It would persuade slaveholders to part with their slaves, and it would enable free blacks to fulfill their potential without the deadening effects of white prejudice."

43 See Nicholas Guyatt, 'The American Colonization Society: 200 Years of the "Colonizing" Trick' *Black Perspectives: African American Intellectual History Society* (22 December 2016) http://www.aaihs.org/the-american-colonization-society-200-years-of-the-colonizing-trick/ Also see Guyatt, *Bind Us Apart* (n X) 248–249.

44 David Walker, *Walker's Appeal, in Four Articles: Together with a Preamble, to the Coloured Citizens of the World, but in Particular, and Very Expressly, to Those of the United States of America* (first published 1829, University of North Carolina Press 2011) 16 Also see Manisha Sinha, *The Slave's Cause: A History of Abolition* (Yale University Press 2016) 205–206.

45 Walker (n 44) 31–32.

46 ibid 52.

47 ibid 55.

48 James Cropper, *The Extinction of the American Colonization Society: The First Step to the Abolition of American Slavery* (S. Bagster Publishing 1833) 3.

49 William Lloyd Garrison, *Thoughts on African colonization : or, An impartial exhibition of the doctrines, principles and purposes of the American Colonization Society : together with the resolutions, addresses and remonstrances of the free people of color* (Garrison and Knapp 1832).
50 On Garrison and Immediatism, see George Sorin, *Abolitionism: A New Perspective* (Praeger Publishers 1972) Chapter 3.
51 Garrison (n 49) 2.
52 David R. Dow, 'Life Without Parole: A Different Death Penalty' *The Nation* (26 October 2012) https://www.thenation.com/article/life-without-parole-different-death-penalty/.
53 Sharon Dolovich, 'Creating the Permanent Prisoner' in Ogletree, Jr. and Sarat (n 1) 96
54 Gottschalk, 'No Way Out?' (n 2) 259.
55 Hutchinson v. United Kingdom [2017] ECHR 65 [43].
56 ibid [33].
57 ibid [42].
58 Agence France-Presse, 'Pope Francie Blasts Life Sentences as "Hidden Death Penalty"' *The Guardian* (23 October 2014) https://www.theguardian.com/world/2014/oct/23/pope-francis-life-sentence-hidden-death-penalty-torture.
59 Meritxell Abellán Almenara and Dirk van Zyl Smit 'Human Dignity and Life Imprisonment: the Pope Enters the Debate' (2015) 15 Human Rights Law Review 369.
60 Cesare Beccaria, *On Crimes and Punishments and Other Writings* (ed Richard Bellamy) (Cambridge University Press 2003) 67.
61 Associated Press, 'New Mexico Repeals Death Penalty' *The Los Angeles Times* (19 March 2009) http://articles.latimes.com/2009/mar/19/nation/na-newmexico-death19.
62 Lewis E. Lawes, 'Why I Changed My Mind' in Philip English Mackay, *Hanging in the Balance: The Anti-Capital Punishment Movement in New York State, 1776–1861* (Garland Publishing 1982) 192, 194.
63 Gottschalk, 'No Way Out?' (n 2) n.48, citing Julian H. Wright, Jr., 'Life without Parole: The View from Death Row' (1991) 27 Criminal Law Bulletin 348.
64 See http://www.theotherdeathpenalty.org/ and Kenneth E. Hartman (ed) *Too Cruel, Not Unusual Enough* (The Steering Committee Press 2013).
65 Dow (n 52).
66 See Campaign to End the Death Penalty http://nodeathpenalty.org/voices-californias-death-row-2. (Also noting that seven death row inmates said they were ambivalent about the ballot measure, and one inmate responded by saying that they were in favor of capital punishment.)
67 Steiker and Steiker (n 2) 4.
68 This information is correct as of December 2017, and the data is taken from The Campaign for the Fair Sentencing of Youth, which keeps track of such developments. See http://fairsentencingofyouth.org/reports-and-research/sentenceeliminated/.
69 Nellis (n 21) 446.
70 Gottschalk (n 2) 262.
71 Hurst v. Florida, 136 S. Ct. 616 (2016).
72 This information is taken from the Death Penalty Information Center: https://deathpenaltyinfo.org/lwop-post-repeal.
73 Jessica Henry, 'Death-in-Prison Sentences: Overutilized and Underscrutinized' in Ogletree and Sarat, *Life Without Parole* (n 1) 66, 77.
74 See footnote 26 and accompanying text.
75 Nellis (n 21) 449.
76 Roger Hood and Carolyn Hoyle, *The Death Penalty: A Worldwide Perspective* (5th edn OUP 2015) 490.
77 Nellis (n 1) 24.
78 Steiker and Steiker (n 2) 286.

79 Nellis (n 1) 24.
80 ibid 10.
81 This is correct as of December 2017. See the Death Penalty Information Center: https://deathpenaltyinfo.org/death-row-inmates-state-and-size-death-row-year.
82 Garrison (n 49) 2.
83 David Brion Davis, *Inhuman Bondage: The Rise and Fall of Slavery in the New World* (OUP 2006) 258 ("Black abolitionists in the 1810s and 1820s ... rejected the paternalism of ACS leaders and showed how the colonizationists' alleged concern for blacks actually accentuated and legitimated racism – particularly the bedrock assumption that that the blacks' degradation in America was irremediable and permanent.").
84 Of course, the fault with post-emancipation racial inequalities is to be laid at the feet of those who actively subjugated the non-white population to degrading and discriminatory treatment.
85 See, for example, Letter from Mike Farrell to Ashley Johansson (n 20).
86 Jonathan Simon, 'The Cruelty of the Abolitionists' (2014) 6 Journal of Human Rights Practice 486, 489.
87 ibid 494–495 (citing David Garland, *Peculiar Institution: American Capital Punishment in an Age of Abolition* (Harvard University Press 2012) and Marie Gottschalk, *The Prison and the Gallows: The Politics of Mass Incarceration in America* (Cambridge University Press 2006)).
88 Simon (n 86) 495.
89 ibid 500.
90 Graham v. Florida, 560 U.S. 48, 59 (2010) (citing Weems v. United States, 217 U. S. 349, 367 (1910)).
91 ibid 59.
92 Harmelin v. Michigan, 501 U.S. 957, 997, 1000–1001 (1991) (Kennedy J., concurring in part and concurring in judgment).
93 Nellis (n 21) 450.
94 Roper v. Simmons, 543 U. S. 551 (2005).
95 Graham (n 90) 68 (internal citations and quotations omitted).
96 Miller v. Alabama, 567 U.S. 460 (2012); Montgomery v. Louisiana, 136 S. Ct. 718 (2016).
97 Roper (n 94) 560.
98 Alaska Statutes Title 12. Code of Criminal Procedure § 12.55.125. Sentences of imprisonment for felonies (defining the circumstances in which a "defendant convicted of murder in the first degree shall be sentenced to a mandatory term of imprisonment of 99 years").
99 Rachel E. Barkow, 'Life Without Parole and the Hope for Real Sentencing Reform' in Ogletree Jr and Sarat (n 1) 190, 193.
100 See Harkins v. United Kingdom [2017] ECHR 239.
101 Note, 'A Matter of Life and Death: The Effect of Life-without-Parole Statutes in Capital Punishment' (2006) 119 Harvard Law Review 1839, 1839.

8 Non-complicity and abolitionism

From fugitive slaves to lethal injections

I. Introduction

Harriet Tubman escaped from slavery in 1849, and like many other fugitive slaves went on to play a leading role in abolitionist efforts. While some of these men and women delivered public lectures and written accounts of slavery for propaganda purposes, Tubman actually returned to slave states in order to help other slaves flee from captivity. The network of passages and safe houses that activists used to help slaves escape from captivity is often referred to as the Underground Railroad,[1] and William McFeely has compared today's network of death penalty defense lawyers to the Underground Railroad, on the grounds that they also help free people in a practical sense. Although this comparison is flawed because lawyers today do not surreptitiously help inmates flee in secrecy,[2] the reaction of the pro-slavery lobby to the issue of fugitive slaves sheds light on an important aspect of contemporary death penalty abolitionism. Slaveholders and their agents went to great lengths to recapture fugitive slaves, resulting in abolitionists and the authorities of free states adopting the principle of non-complicity. William Lloyd Garrison explained why abolitionists and Northerners should not be complicit in slavery: "what if it should appear, on a candid examination, that we are as guilty as the slave owners? that we uphold and protect a system which is full of cruelty and blood? that the chains which bind the limbs of the slaves have been riveted by us? Let us see whether we are indeed implicated in this bloody business."[3] To this extent, abolitionists undertook a range of actions to ensure that they were not complicit in the enslavement of others, including the boycott of slave produce. But perhaps the most striking and ultimately effective course of non-complicity came in the context of fugitive slaves. Abolitionists and free states would refuse to assist slaveholders recapture escaped slaves, and the ensuing saga is widely believed to have been a central factor in converting people to the abolitionists' cause and bringing about an end to slavery.[4] Today, the anti-death penalty movement has likewise developed a principle of non-complicity that, in practical terms, is assisting efforts to stop executions. Authorities in non-death penalty states have refused to hand over suspects to face trial unless assurances are received that the death penalty will not be sought, and abolitionists have collaborated with pharmaceutical companies to prevent states from acquiring the drugs needed for executions. This has ensured that such companies are not knowingly or unwittingly complicit in the administration of capital punishment, while simultaneously ensuring that those opposed to the death penalty are not "implicated in [the] bloody business" of capital punishment, to paraphrase Garrison.

We will first set out how the slavery abolitionists refused to be complicit in the return of fugitive slaves, and how the pro-slavery lobby reacted to this. The passage of the Fugitive Slave Act in 1850 – which was designed to strengthen the rights of slaveholders – was used by abolitionists to highlight the threat that the pro-slavery lobby posed to the civil liberties and self-interest of Northerners. We will then explore how non-death penalty states have similarly refused to hand over suspects if there is a risk that they will face capital punishment. The focus, though, will be on the ways in which the pro-death penalty lobby has reacted to the refusal of abolitionists to be complicit in the supply of drugs needed for lethal injections. Just as the pro-slavery lobby did not give up on recapturing fugitive slaves, the pro-death penalty lobby has not been content to let people live. In their haste to carry out executions, a number of states have acquired drugs from dubious sources, and have exposed individuals to excruciatingly painful executions. Legislatures have enacted secrecy laws so that abolitionists cannot identify the source of the drugs used, and some states have introduced alternative methods of execution in the event that lethal injections become impossible to carry out. But just as ante-bellum abolitionists proved adept at highlighting how the backlash of the pro-slavery lobby threatened the interests of those otherwise unconcerned with slavery, so the current lethal injection saga might have greater abolitionist potential if the pro-death penalty response can be construed as an attack on the civil liberties and self-interest of those not already within the abolitionist camp. This is not to endorse the pragmatism of appealing to an audience's self-interest, though. As Garrison emphasized, the issue must be framed as a moral imperative to not be complicit in a moral wrong.

II. Non-complicity and non-rendition in the context of slavery

At the Constitutional Convention in 1787, the Framers acknowledged the tension that arose whenever slaves escaped captivity and travelled to free states.[5] On the one hand, slaveholders demanded that their property be returned to them, but on the other hand those who opposed slavery were reluctant to knowingly hand over an individual to a life of servitude and probable punishment for fleeing from captivity in the first place. At the Constitutional Convention, the Framers assumed that free states would cooperate with slaveholders in the return of slaves, and so the issue of runaway slaves was given little debate. The Framers had reason to believe that free states would cooperate, since even those territories that had abolished slavery, or that were moving towards abolition, initially accepted that slaves should be returned to their owners. For example, the Act for the Gradual Abolition of Slavery in the Commonwealth of Pennsylvania in 1780 allowed for the return of fugitive slaves, as did comparable acts in Rhode Island and Connecticut in 1784.[6] Therefore, the Fugitive Slave Clause that was included in Article 4, Section 2 of the Constitution was quite brief: "No Person held to Service or Labour in one State, under the Laws thereof, escaping into another, shall, in Consequence of any Law or Regulation therein, be discharged from such Service or Labour, But shall be delivered up on Claim of the Party to whom such Service or Labour may be due."[7]

The Fugitive Slave Clause appears just after the Extradition Clause, which addresses the issue of fugitives from justice crossing state lines. The proximity of these two clauses in the Constitution is of little surprise since both issues were concerned with "a similar procedural question and with the important constitutional issue of interstate comity."[8] That is, the Framers considered the issues of fugitive slaves and fugitives from justice to be two sides of the same coin, and assumed that both issues would be resolved through comity and cooperation between the states. As such, the Extradition Clause reads: "A person charged in any state with treason, felony, or other crime, who shall flee from justice, and be found in another state, shall on demand of the executive authority of the state from which he fled, be delivered up, to be removed to the state having jurisdiction of the crime." In many ways, the proximity of the Fugitive Slave and Extradition Clauses in the Constitution lends weight to the argument that today's criminal justice processes are bound up with the legacy of slavery, and that death penalty opponents can learn from the actions of the anti-slavery movement.

Ultimately, the Framers were mistaken in their belief that states would cooperate with each other. A dispute between Virginia and Pennsylvania shortly after the adoption of the Constitution provides an illustration of the difficulties surrounding claims involving both fugitives from justice and fugitive slaves, and is an early example of an act of non-cooperation. The dispute revolved around a black man by the name of John Davis who, in 1788, was forcibly taken from Pennsylvania to Virginia, where he was enslaved.[9] Governor Mifflin of Pennsylvania took the view that Davis had attained freedom under that state's 1780 Act for the Gradual Abolition of Slavery, and thus sought the extradition from Virginia of the three men who had, in his view, unlawfully kidnapped Davis. Governor Randolph of Virginia, though, took a different view. Randolph asserted that Davis was actually a fugitive slave who had unlawfully escaped from Virginia, and asserted that the three Virginians had, if anything, only committed a minor trespass when entering Pennsylvania to recapture Davis. Since Virginia authorities had no legal right to arrest these three men for a minor trespass, Randolph opined that he could not order Virginia law enforcement agents to arrest and extradite the three men to Pennsylvania. The case, then, began as one involving alleged fugitives from justice, and highlights how different attitudes towards slavery created conflicts between the states.

Governor Mifflin eventually sought the assistance of President Washington, and it became clear to the federal government that Article 4, Section 2 of the Constitution was inadequate because fugitive slaves and fugitives from justice would not necessarily be returned or extradited by the relevant states out of comity and cooperation. Congress responded to this case by passing the Fugitive Slave Act in 1793, which was aimed at preventing future stand-offs between states. Since this Act was a response to a factual situation that involved both fugitive slaves and fugitives from justice, the Act, like the Constitution, linked the extradition of fugitives from justice with the rendition of fugitive slaves. We can see, therefore, why the contemporary issue of extraditing individuals to face the death penalty might at least be conceptually linked to the historical issue of the rendition of fugitive slaves.

The 1793 Act proved to be less favorable to Pennsylvania and other free states than to Virginia and slaveholders in general. With regards to the extradition of fugitives from justice, the Act stated that state authorities receiving an extradition request would have to arrest and detain the suspect. That is, the asylum state would have to actively assist in the capturing of the suspect. On the face it, this was favorable to Pennsylvania in the John Davis case, but the Act provided no procedure to deal with instances of state authorities refusing to comply with an extradition request. In other words, under this Act, Governor Randolph could quite easily have refused to hand over the three Virginians, and Governor Mifflin would have had no legal recourse. With regards to fugitive slaves, an earlier version of the Bill included a comparable provision for the authorities of free states to assist in the capture and rendition of such individuals. However, many Northerners did not want to be compelled to act as slave-catchers,[10] and thus this provision was removed from the final Act. This had the effect, though, of making it lawful under the 1793 Act for a slaveholder, or their agents, to enter a free state and capture the alleged fugitive slave directly and unilaterally. Although the Act imposed a duty to bring the slave before a magistrate's court in order to prove that the individual was in fact a slave, and that the capturer was in fact the owner of the slave, the standard of proof was set very low. Sworn affidavits would suffice, but there was no means of testing the reliability of such affidavits.[11] The Act also did not permit accused fugitive slaves to testify in their own defense.

It did not take long, then, for Northerners to realize that their desire to not be complicit in slavery had resulted in an Act that actually strengthened the institution of slavery and made it relatively easy for slaveholders to capture blacks and take them into servitude. Northerners and abolitionists balked at this unintended consequence of their policy of non-cooperation, fearing that lawfully free blacks might be wrongfully captured and taken into servitude by slave-catchers and slaveholders.

Northerners and opponents of slavery soon identified loopholes in the 1793 Act and enacted anti-kidnapping laws and Personal Liberty Laws that were either in direct conflict with the federal law, or placed considerable hurdles to the rendition process under the 1793 statute.[12] For example, although the Act placed a duty on slaveholders and slave-catchers to have their case heard before a magistrate's court, it did not impose a duty on state judges to hold such hearings. Some free states therefore enacted laws that excluded fugitive slave cases from the jurisdiction of the state courts,[13] meaning that slaveholders could not have their case heard and thus could not remove alleged fugitive slaves from free states. Some states also denied aid to claimants, making it more difficult for slaveholders to successfully take blacks into servitude. In Indiana, the state legislature passed a law that required removal hearings to be heard in front of a jury, and gave the accused fugitive slave an opportunity to testify. This process served to ensure that the rendition of fugitive slaves went through a robust procedure that would protect free blacks and also, in some cases, prevent fugitive slaves from being taken back into servitude.

It was the Pennsylvania legislature, though, that really tested the limits of the 1793 Act. In 1826, a law was passed that made it an offence for any individual to unilaterally attempt to use the federal law to capture an alleged fugitive slave, directly contradicting the "self-help" provisions of the 1793 Act. Under Pennsylvania law, a claimant would have to first obtain a warrant from a state judge before seeking the alleged fugitive slave, and even then an alleged fugitive slave could only be arrested by a law enforcement officer. Even if a judge granted a warrant in the first instance, and even if the alleged slave was captured, the claimant would then have to obtain a second certificate from the judge to authorize the removal of the alleged slave from the state of Pennsylvania. To add to this, the alleged slave was permitted to present evidence that he or she was not a fugitive, whereas the claimant was barred from testifying. Put quite simply, the Pennsylvania law was designed to make it as hard as possible for slaveholders to take a person across state lines and into servitude.

These personal liberty laws, which were examples of acts of non-cooperation, antagonized slave states. Such states retaliated by refusing to extradite those suspected of kidnapping free blacks from Northern states. This was the issue in *Prigg v. Pennsylvania*, decided by the US Supreme Court in 1842.[14] Edward Prigg, a slave-catcher from Maryland, obtained a warrant to have alleged fugitive slaves arrested in Pennsylvania, but the state judge then refused to issue the second certificate that was required to take them over the border into Maryland. Prigg therefore forcibly took his captives across the border, and when Pennsylvania sought the extradition of Prigg to be tried for kidnapping, Maryland refused to hand him over. The states agreed to hand the case over to the Supreme Court for resolution, where Pennsylvania argued that the Personal Liberty Laws were designed to protect free residents of Pennsylvania from being mistaken for fugitive slaves. The Court, though, ruled the statute unconstitutional. Writing for the majority, Justice Story held that the Fugitive Slave Clause of the Constitution prioritized the property rights of slaveholders over the rights of states to protect their residents. According to Story, the Clause "manifestly contemplates the existence of a positive, unqualified right on the part of the owner of the slave, which no state law can in any way qualify, regulate, control, or restrain."[15]

Even though the decision strengthened the rights and ability of slaveholders to capture alleged fugitive slaves, the decision led to further acts of non-cooperation, which in turn contributed to the downfall of slavery. Crucially, although the Court ruled that free states had no authority to place additional procedural barriers to the return of fugitive slaves, the judgment maintained that the federal government could not compel state authorities to assist in the return of fugitive slaves. In other words, the Court accepted that Northern states could passively refrain from cooperating in the return of fugitive slaves. The scope of this element of the ruling was soon tested by free states, especially when controversial cases based on *Prigg* came to light. In Massachusetts in 1842, for example, there was an outcry over the use of *Prigg* to detain an alleged fugitive slave by the name of George Latimer.[16]

Latimer was kept in the city jail for two weeks while the claimant was given permission by Justice Story to gather enough evidence to prove that Latimer was a fugitive slave. This did not sit easily with Bostonians, with *The Liberator* commenting: "Thus is Boston, made the slave-hunting ground of the South, and thus does the city consent to aid and abet the vilest of Kidnappers!"[17] Public opinion eventually forced the sheriff to order the transfer of custody of Latimer from the city jail to the claimant, who then freed Latimer as he feared that he would not be able to hold on to him without assistance. Latimer was freed, and a personal liberty law was passed in Massachusetts in 1843 which prohibited state judges from accepting jurisdiction in cases under the 1793 Act, and which prohibited state officials from aiding claimants in the locating and detaining of alleged fugitive slaves.

Pennsylvania also took steps to ensure compliance with *Prigg* to the minimum extent possible. It followed the Massachusetts model of prohibiting state officials from assisting in the rendition of alleged fugitive slaves, and prohibited the use of state detention facilities to hold alleged runaway slaves. The 1847 Act also prohibited the use of violence in the seizure of fugitive slaves, taking on board Justice Story's condemnation of the use of "illegal violence" by Edward Prigg. The Act also enabled state judges to issue writs of habeas corpus so that they could inquire into the legality of the detention of any individual within the state, such as the detention of alleged fugitive slaves by slaveholders. It is not hard to see why Thomas Morris described the 1847 law as "an experiment in the possibilities left open by the case, as well as an effort at containment."[18]

Although the decision in *Prigg* prohibited free states from actively deciding how fugitive slave cases should be adjudicated, it permitted such states to "disassociate themselves from slavery and thereby confine all action to the narrowest limits that would satisfy the Constitution."[19] Slaveholders and Southern states inevitably complained about the action, or rather inaction of Northern states, claiming that the personal liberty laws made a mockery of the Constitution.[20] Taking their grievances to Congress, it was proposed that the 1793 Act be modified in light of the free states' failure to enforce the law. In 1850, a new Fugitive Slave Act was passed which was weighted even more in favor of slaveholders. The 1850 Act set up a body of federal Fugitive Slave Commissioners, whose job was to help slaveholders with the rendition of fugitive slaves. These Commissioners were responsible for adjudicating fugitive slave cases, and for ensuring that fugitive slaves did not escape custody when captured. Federal marshals could now be compelled to execute warrants for the capture and detention of alleged slaves, and any person who prevented a slaveholder from capturing an alleged fugitive slave could be fined $1000. Remarkably, these Commissioners were to be paid $10 when they found in favor of the claimant, but only $5 if they found against the claimant and set free the alleged fugitive slave. Thus, there was a financial incentive for Commissioners to side with slaveholders. Section 6 of the Act prohibited captured individuals from testifying in their own defense. Once again, the attempts of Northerners and abolitionists to resist complicity in slavery resulted in a Congressional statute that strengthened the institution of slavery, and that put even more free blacks at risk of being wrongfully captured and subjected to servitude.

Inevitably, the 1850 Act drew stinging rebukes from Northerners. The Supreme Court of Wisconsin went so far as to rule the Act unconstitutional,[21] although unsurprisingly the US Supreme Court overruled this decision because state courts had no authority to rule on the constitutionality of federal statutes.[22] In many cases, juries across Northern states signaled their opposition to the law by acquitting defendants who were accused of violating the federal law even when there was overwhelming evidence against such defendants.[23]

Although the policies of non-cooperation described above were often defeated in the courts, and although the pro-slavery backlash meant that the chances of people being taken into servitude increased, such policies nonetheless satisfied the abolitionists' moral imperative to refrain from being complicit in a practice that they objected to. These policies also served propaganda purposes, reminding the populace of the reasons why slavery was opposed, and the ways in which slavery implicated the civil liberties of all persons. The case of Anthony Burns is an example. In 1853, Burns escaped from captivity in Virginia, and fled to Boston, Massachusetts. He was captured under the 1850 Act, but popular resentment of the Act was so strong that the federal government ended up spending $40,000, and mobilizing four platoons of marines and 22 companies of state militia in order to enforce the law. This only served to strengthen the abolitionists' resolve. Theodore Parker used the affair to rally Northerners to the abolitionist cause: "A few years ago they used to tell us 'Slavery is an abstraction, we at the North have nothing to do with it!'" and Bronson Alcott noted that "[t]he question 'What has the North to do with slavery?' is visibly answered."[24] As George Sorin has noted, "[i]t was only when slavery became associated with civil liberties and sectional pride that the tiny abolitionist movement which was interested in increasing the freedom of blacks grew into the larger antislavery movement which was interested in reducing the political power and prestige of Southern slaveholders."[25] Louis Menand concurs: "The new Fugitive Slave Law… radicalized the North. It pushed many previously passive unionists into active animosity toward the South – not because they considered the law an encroachment on the liberties of black Americans, but because they considered it an encroachment on the liberties of Northern Whites."[26] As explained below, the tactic of illustrating how the pro-slavery lobby threatened the civil liberties of Northerners offers valuable lessons for how today's abolitionists can highlight the threat that the death penalty poses to those who support, or are apathetic about, capital punishment.

III. Non-rendition in the context of capital punishment

It is rare to find authorities of death penalty free jurisdictions within the US adopting similar measures of non-rendition in death penalty cases. The only ones that I have been able to locate are those involving Jason Pleau and Thomas Grasso.[27]

On September 20, 2010, Jason Pleau murdered David Main in Rhode Island during the course of a robbery. He pled guilty to relevant charges under Rhode Island law, and accepted a term of life imprisonment without the possibility of parole. Notwithstanding this, federal authorities sought custody of Pleau under the Interstate Agreement on Detainers (IAD)[28] so that he could be tried for federal offences relating to the same set of facts.[29] The Governor of Rhode Island at the time – Lincoln Chafee – refused to transfer Pleau, citing the possibility that Pleau would be subjected to the federal death penalty. Explaining his position, Governor Chafee said: "As a matter of public policy, Rhode Islanders have long opposed the death penalty, even for the most heinous crimes. To voluntarily let Mr. Pleau be exposed to the federal death penalty for a crime committed in Rhode Island would be an abdication of one of my core responsibilities as governor: defending and upholding the legitimate public-policy choices made by the people of this state."[30]

The case received little national or international attention – at least when compared to cases such as Troy Davis, or Mumia Abu-Jamal – but Pleau's case was "very unusual", as one legal commentator put it, because it is rare for a governor to refuse detainer requests from either federal or state authorities, at least since the Interstate Agreement on Detainers was introduced in 1970.[31] Since the death penalty was restored in 1976, only Governor Cuomo of New York has adopted a similar position to Chafee. In 1992, a New York court sentenced Thomas Grasso to 20 years imprisonment for a murder and robbery. Grasso not only confessed to the crimes, but he also confessed to another murder and robbery that he had committed in Oklahoma some six months prior to the New York crime. Governor Keating of Oklahoma therefore requested custody of Grasso under the IAD so that he could be prosecuted. When Grasso was sentenced to death in the Oklahoma court, Keating asked Governor Cuomo to waive New York's right under Art V(e) of the IAD to have Grasso serve his 20-year sentence in New York before being sent back to Oklahoma for execution. Even though Grasso also expressed a desire to be executed rather than serve out his prison sentence in New York first,[32] Cuomo refused to waive the New York sentence, and ordered Grasso's return to New York.[33] Cuomo's moral opposition to capital punishment was well known, and was the reason why he fought Keating's request.

The two cases had remarkably different conclusions. The federal government successfully challenged Governor Chafee's refusal to transfer custody of Pleau, but the US Attorney General ultimately agreed to not seek the death penalty. In contrast, a legal challenge to Governor Cuomo's position was defeated, but the affair became the focal point of the 1994 gubernatorial election in New York. George Pataki successfully used the Grasso affair to oust Cuomo from office, and one of Pataki's first acts as Governor was to transfer Grasso to Oklahoma, where he was executed in 1995.

Despite these contrasting conclusions, both Chafee and Cuomo's actions fed into a broader international tactic of refusing to co-operate with the administration of capital punishment. In the ninth quinquennial report on the use of capital punishment worldwide, covering the period 2009–2013, the Secretary-General of the United Nations noted that "[a]ll fully abolitionist States [have] a policy of denying extradition to States where the death penalty might be imposed unless assurances were given that the individual concerned could not be sentenced to death or, if sentenced to death, the penalty would not be carried out."[34] The

European Court of Human Rights has moved from permitting extradition in death penalty cases provided that the implementation of a death sentence does not violate the prohibition in the European Convention on Human Rights on inhuman treatment, to prohibiting extradition on the grounds that the death penalty per se violates the right to life. In 2000, the European Union included the following provision in the Charter of Fundamental Rights: "No one may be removed, expelled or extradited to a State where there is a serious risk that he or she would be subjected to the death penalty…."[35] The UN Human Rights Committee has likewise prohibited abolitionist countries from extraditing suspects without obtaining assurances that a death sentence will not be imposed, and the Supreme Court of Canada has issued a comparable judgment.[36]

There has been little in the way of controversy here. Death penalty jurisdictions both in America and elsewhere have routinely issued assurances that the death penalty will not be sought in such cases, so as to ensure that the person concerned stands trial. Nonetheless, it is worth pointing out that these policies of non-extradition have contributed however marginally to the declining rate of death sentences, and have satisfied a moral and legal imperative on the parts of abolitionists to refrain from aiding the use of the death penalty elsewhere.[37] Far more controversial has been abolitionists' attempts to stem the supply of drugs that are needed for executions. Not only have these actions prevented executions from being carried out, they have also drawn attention to the inherent brutality of capital punishment in the same way that the fugitive slave saga drew attention to the brutality of slavery.

IV. Non-complicity in lethal injections

Over the last decade, states have found it increasingly difficult to acquire the drugs needed for lethal injections, resulting in a significant decline in executions. The difficulties have arisen in part because of a collaborative approach between anti-death penalty campaigners and pharmaceutical companies, who have worked together to stop drugs from being used in executions. On the one hand, this practical interference with the machinery of death is playing a significant role in bringing about an end to capital punishment. Not only are the numbers of executions declining, but public awareness about the inherent cruelty of state killing is also growing. On the other hand, just as the pro-slavery lobby redoubled its efforts to capture escaped slaves, the pro-death penalty lobby has intensified its attempts to carry out executions (leading in some cases to botched executions that subject the individual to considerable pain and suffering). In the context of this book, another potentially problematic feature of the lethal injection saga is its inherent conservatism, in the sense that it is focused solely on ending the phenomenon of state-sanctioned executions, and does not situate the problems with capital punishment within the wider problems with the criminal justice system identified in earlier chapters.

We will see over the remainder of this chapter though that death penalty abolitionists can draw inspiration from how the slavery abolitionists responded to the pro-slavery backlash in the context of fugitive slaves. As noted earlier, abolitionists drew attention to the threat posed by the pro-slavery lobby to the civil liberties and self-interest of Northerners and others who hitherto considered slavery to be of no concern to them. In particular, death penalty abolitionists can draw, and have drawn, attention to the threat to First Amendment rights posed by secrecy laws; to the issue of states stockpiling drugs that could be used in medical treatment; and to how the whole issue of complicity with executions draws attention to the fact that the death penalty is not about a person being executed, so much as it is about the community and legal system engaging in the killing of another human being.

A. The adoption of lethal injections

In 1977, Oklahoma became the first state to adopt lethal injections as a primary method of execution.[38] A sequence of three drugs would be injected intravenously: sodium thiopental (to render the person unconscious), followed by pancuronium bromide (to paralyze the person), and then potassium chloride (to bring about cardiac arrest). Over the ensuing four decades, lethal injections have become the primary method of execution in all death penalty jurisdictions.

Policy-makers have tended to justify the use of lethal injections on the grounds that it is a "humane" method of execution, in that it brings about death while allegedly inflicting minimal suffering on the part of the person being killed.[39] The US Supreme Court has consistently demanded that methods of execution be humane, and has defined such executions as those which do not involve "unnecessary cruelty" and which bring about a "quick, certain death."[40] Despite the rhetoric of "humaneness", though, medical personnel and anti-death penalty activists have expressed concern with the three-drug protocol, and with lethal injections in general, from the outset. Some opponents of capital punishment have said that lethal injections only provide the appearance of serenity, and that the true purpose behind the adoption of such a method has been to make the death penalty more palatable to people who are queasy about state-sanctioned executions, thus stifling any latent abolitionist sentiment.[41] Several medical practitioners have expressed concern with the medicalization of executions, claiming that healthcare professionals should not in any way be associated with the taking of life for the purposes of punishment.[42] With respect to the specific three-drug protocol, there have been concerns that a failure to properly sedate the prisoner with the first drug would result in an excruciatingly painful death. The prisoner would be conscious while slowly suffocating, but unable to express that pain because of the paralytic agent.[43]

Although these concerns were expressed from the moment lethal injections were first proposed, they became more pronounced during the 2000s. The internationally-renowned British medical journal *The Lancet* published an article in 2005 that proclaimed: "Methods of lethal injection anaesthesia are flawed and some inmates might experience awareness and suffering during execution."[44] Two years later, a similar article was published in *Public Library of Science Medicine*, edited by Harvard Medical School.[45] With these concerns gaining traction, the US Supreme Court agreed to consider the constitutionality of the three-drug protocol.

The Court granted certiorari in *Baze v. Rees* in September 2007, leading to a moratorium on executions pending the outcome of the case. When the Court announced its decision in 2008, it held that the protocol under review did not violate the Eighth Amendment prohibition on "cruel and unusual punishments" because petitioners had not demonstrated that the combination of drugs presented a "substantial" or "objectively intolerable" risk of "serious harm"[46] compared to "known and available alternatives."[47] The decision was in some ways unsurprising: the Court has never found a method of execution, or a particular execution protocol, to be contrary to the Eighth Amendment.[48]

Although it was generally believed that executions would resume at a rapid pace, as states sought to carry out the backlog of executions that had been put on hold pending the outcome of the case, it transpired that *Baze* did not settle the constitutionality of lethal injections. Not only were the Justices split on their reasoning, but states were also soon to discover that they could not acquire sodium thiopental. That is, not long after the Court approved the three-drug protocol, states found that they could not adopt that protocol anyway. Just as the slavery abolitionists tested the limits of *Prigg v. Pennsylvania* and sought to stifle its effect, so death penalty abolitionists have done the same with respect to *Baze*.

B. A domestic shortage of a vital drug

The shortage of sodium thiopental arose because outside the context of the death penalty, medical practitioners had generally turned to newer types of anesthetic, leading drug manufacturers to cease production of the drug. In 2009, Hospira – the sole US-based producer of sodium thiopental – announced that it would stop producing the drug in the US because of a shortage of raw materials with which to carry out the manufacturing process. Hospira planned to transfer the manufacturing of thiopental to its plant in Italy, and to import it into the US. In the meantime, though, states sought alternative suppliers of sodium thiopental. On September 26, 2010, Jeffrey Landrigan was executed in Arizona using drugs that had been imported from Dream Pharma – a British-based company that had also sold sodium thiopental at inflated prices to prisons in Georgia, California, South Carolina, and Arkansas.[49] Two days later, Brandon Rhode was executed in Georgia using drugs from the same British supplier. Although at this point Dream Pharma had not been identified as the supplier to these states, lawyers acting for Edmund Zagorski in Tennessee had learned that he was also to be executed using British-sourced drugs.[50] They contacted Reprieve – a legal charity based in the United Kingdom that assists death row prisoners across the world – and thus began an innovative abolitionist campaign, one which has reduced the numbers of executions, shed light on the brutality of capital punishment, and raised awareness about how the death penalty implicates the dignity of the wider community, in a manner comparable to Garrison and the radical abolitionists of the antebellum era.

C. Foreign complicity in executions

On October 28, 2010, Reprieve – through the law firm Leigh Day & Co. – wrote to the Secretary of State for Business, Innovation and Skills, urging him to impose an immediate ban on the export of sodium thiopental from the UK.[51] Vince Cable, who was then-Secretary of State, provided three reasons for refusing this request.[52] First, he claimed to be powerless to impose the requested measures because European Union regulations prohibiting trade in materials for use in capital punishment did not specify a ban on the trade in chemical substances. This regulation, passed in 2005, does not refer to the idea of non-complicity, but does make it clear that the measure is intended to practically contribute to the end of executions worldwide: "In order to contribute to the abolition of the death penalty in third countries… it is considered necessary to prohibit the supply to third countries of technical assistance related to goods which have no practical use other than for the purpose of capital punishment…"[53] Such goods include "gallows and guillotines", electric chairs, gas chambers, and "[a]utomatic drug injection systems designed for the purpose of execution of human beings by the administration of a lethal chemical substance." As Cable stated, though, the regulation did not prohibit the trade in the actual drugs to be used in lethal injections.

The second reason provided by Cable was that sodium thiopental had legitimate medicinal purposes, and export controls would affect "legitimate trade of medical value". Third, Cable wrote that export restrictions were "unlikely to be effective in preventing any execution from taking place in the United States given that the drug is generally available and traded globally."[54] Cable's reasoning suggests that he was either unaware that a failure to enact controls would amount to British complicity in executions, or that he was aware, but believed that other interests – such as trading interests – superseded any moral or ethical imperative to refrain from complicity. Either way, in early November 2010, at least one then-unidentified British company (Dream Pharma) and the UK government were assisting the imposition of capital punishment in the US.

D. An emerging policy of non-complicity

When Vince Cable's letter was received, Reprieve and Leigh Day sought judicial review of his decision.[55] They argued that sodium thiopental was not widely used for medical purposes, and that in any event, the US Food and Drug Administration prohibited the importation of sodium thiopental from foreign sources, rendering any such trade illegal notwithstanding British trading interests or medicinal interests. Cable's third ground – that a ban would be ineffective because other companies would supply the drug – was also considered to be inappropriate: an immoral action such as complicity with capital punishment does not become acceptable simply because others are behaving immorally.[56]

Faced with these arguments, Cable reversed course on November 29, 2010 and issued the requested controls before the High Court could decide on the matter. In a statement, he wrote: "This move underlines this government's and my own personal moral opposition to the death penalty in all circumstances without impacting legitimate trade."[57] It is tempting to balk at Cable's hypocrisy, but his reversal marked a major step in the emerging doctrine of non-complicity with capital punishment both as a tactic to advance abolition, and as a statement of recognition that moral opposition to capital punishment entails non-cooperation.

During the course of the High Court proceedings, investigators from Reprieve, led by Maya Foa (then Director of the Death Penalty Team), pieced together how British drugs had come to be used in American executions. It emerged that the sodium thiopental which was used in Landrigan's execution had been manufactured by a company called Novartis, based in Austria, and had been marketed in the UK by Archimedes Pharma. Archimedes Pharma had supplied the drug to a small company called Dream Pharma, which operated out of the back of a driving school in West London, which had then exported the drugs to various death penalty states.[58] It soon became apparent that death penalty jurisdictions were reaching out to numerous pharmaceutical companies across the world, and were importing the other two drugs needed for lethal injections too. Accordingly, Reprieve set up the Stop the Lethal Injection Project (SLIP) with the aim of helping such companies ensure that their products are not used in executions.[59] Indeed, Archimedes Pharma did not oppose the application for judicial review, expressing concern that it had unwittingly contributed to executions.[60] Pharmaceutical companies in Austria, Italy, and India were among the first to be identified as potential collaborators – knowingly or unknowingly – in US executions.

On November 5, 2010, Reprieve sent letters to the Austrian Finance Minister, Justice Minister, and Minister for European Affairs, urging them to take measures to ensure that Austrian-produced drugs were not used in executions.[61] Links were made with Hands Off Cain – an Italian non-governmental organization that campaigns against capital punishment across the world – to ensure that Hospira did not follow through with its intention to resume production of sodium thiopental in its Italian plant with a view to exporting the drug to America.[62] Ahead of a press conference to raise public awareness of potential Italian collaboration with capital punishment, the salient point was made that "[w]hile abolitionist countries like Italy and the UK are busy at the UN working towards a worldwide moratorium on executions, they risk becoming complicit in the death penalty in the United States".[63] The Italian government passed a motion committing the government to ensuring that Hospira's medicines were not distributed for use in lethal injection executions and Hospira announced on January 21, 2011, that it would no longer produce sodium thiopental, much less export it to the US.[64]

Hospira's press release noted that the company had "never condoned" the use of its products in capital punishment, but the company's decision to exit the market appears to have been based on pressure from the Italian government, rather than because of any inherent desire to avoid complicity. The company lamented the fact "that our many hospital customers who use the drug for its well-established medical benefits will not be able to obtain the product from Hospira", and made it clear that it was ceasing production because "we cannot take the risk that we will be held liable by the Italian authorities if the product is diverted for use in capital punishment. Exposing our employees or facilities to liability is not a risk we are prepared to take."[65] Thus while Hospira might not have been motivated by a concern with capital punishment per se, the Italian government was clearly of the view that to allow a private company to assist with the administration of the death penalty abroad would be tantamount to illegal complicity with the death penalty. This is not to say that Hospira reluctantly pulled its drugs from the market, for two months later the company wrote to several Departments of Corrections explaining their preference that their drugs not be used in executions.[66]

In April 2011, Kayem Pharmaceuticals – based in India – announced that it would stop providing Nebraska with sodium thiopental. In a public statement, the company put forward ethical reasons for its decision: "In view of the sensitivity involved with sale of our thiopental sodium to various jails/prisons in USA and as alleged to be used for the purpose of lethal injection, we voluntary declare that we as Indian Pharma Dealer who cherish the Ethos of Hinduism (A believer even in non-livings as the creation of God) refrain ourselves in selling this drug where the purpose is purely for Lethal Injection and its misuse".[67] Kayem Pharmaceutical is believed to have also provided South Dakota with the drug, and over the course of 2011 it emerged that a number of death penalty states had been seeking out overseas suppliers with some vigor.

Difficulties with acquiring sodium thiopental had led several states to adopt pentobarbital as an alternative sedative, and at least 11 states had resorted to procuring pentobarbital from foreign suppliers.[68] In July 2011, the Danish-based supplier of the drug – Lundbeck – adopted measures to ensure that its products would not be distributed to prisons for the purposes of carrying out executions. Like Kayem Pharmaceuticals, Lundbeck expressed concern with the prospect of being complicit in the taking of life: "Lundbeck adamantly opposes the distressing misuse of our product in capital punishment."[69] It should be noted, though, that Lundbeck was not initially enthusiastic about enacting distribution controls. Lundbeck's then CEO, Ulf Wiinberg, said in an interview that this created a conundrum for the company.[70] It would have been unethical to stop producing a drug that had legitimate medical uses, but if they sold it off as planned, Lundbeck would be accused of avoiding its responsibilities.

Traditional and social media were energetically engaged every time an execution took place using Lundbeck's drugs, leading shareholders to raise questions at the company's annual general meeting. As a result of the furor, a pension fund sold its shares in the company, and Lundbeck's place on an annual ranking of Denmark's best companies fell from 17 to 40.[71] In an atmosphere of intense scrutiny from investors and the public, Lundbeck went in search of a solution. The company entered a dialogue with Reprieve, and together they developed a new distribution model that would ensure access to the medicine for legitimate medical users, but prevent its use in executions.

In the month before Lundbeck's statement, the federal government of the US had stepped into the matter. The Secretary for Commerce, Gary Locke, asked his German counterpart to assist with the supply of drugs, but the Economics Minister Phillip Rösler declined to help, citing his Catholic faith as a reason for refusing to co-operate with the imposition of capital punishment.[72] Soon, the US Drug Enforcement Agency was taking steps to ensure that Departments of Corrections were not receiving foreign-manufactured thiopental. During 2011, the DEA seized shipments that were being imported into America because, without being approved by the FDA, there was a risk that such drugs were impure, ineffective, and generally unsafe.[73] Towards the end of 2011, under pressure from US-based lawyers and global civil society, the European Union amended its 2005 regulations to ensure that specific drugs could not be exported by Member States to the US for use in lethal injections.[74]

The cat-and-mouse game between state authorities on the one hand, and pharmaceutical companies, foreign governments, and other organizations on the other hand, has continued to mimic that of the fugitive slave saga. In 2012 Missouri became the first state to adopt propofol as the sole drug with which to carry out executions, and this was swiftly followed by the UK government imposing export controls on propofol.[75] The German-based producer of the drug, Fresenius Kabi also took steps to ensure that its products were not used in executions, stating that the use of propofol in executions was contrary to the company's "mission of 'Caring for Life'".[76] Facing the prospect of being unable to import propofol from Europe, the Governor of Missouri halted its use.[77] Since 2012, states have also used midazolam, hydromorphone, rocuronium bromide, and vecuronium bromide in executions, leading to more pharmaceutical companies taking steps to ensure that their products are not used in lethal injections. Working closely with Reprieve, more than two dozen companies, including Hikma, Akorn, Mylan, and perhaps most notably, the pharmaceutical giant Pfizer enacted distribution controls on their products to prevent them from being acquired by prison officials for the purposes of carrying out executions. In a statement on May 13, 2016, Pfizer stated that it "makes its products to enhance and save the lives of the patients we serve. Consistent with these values, Pfizer strongly objects to the use of its products as lethal injections for capital punishment."[78] Pfizer's move meant that every FDA-approved supplier of any current execution drug had blocked the sale of medicines to execution chambers.[79] The adoption of distribution controls led Lincoln Caplan at the *New Yorker* to write that pharmaceutical companies had "closed the open market for the federally approved drugs that have been used for lethal injections."[80] In November that year, the European Union once again amended its regulations to strengthen trade rules against goods that can be used for the purposes of capital punishment.[81]

As access to FDA-approved sources of lethal injection medicines has run out, authorities in several instances have turned to compounding pharmacies when experimenting with lethal injection protocols. Compounding pharmacies mix drugs according to individual needs, and are not regulated by the FDA. Thus, there is little assurance that the drugs used will meet the standards set by the Supreme Court in *Baze*. Nonetheless, numerous executions have been carried out using drugs mixed in compounding pharmacies. In October 2012, South Dakota executed two men using such drugs, and in March 2013, the Director of Colorado Department of Corrections contacted 97 compounding pharmacies in that state seeking "sodium thiopental or other equally or more effective substances to cause death."[82] Texas used pentobarbital from a compounder when executing Michael Yowell on October 9, 2013. In the same month, Ohio announced that it also planned to acquire drugs from compounding pharmacies. In November, Missouri used pentobarbital from a compounder to execute Joseph Franklin. Drugs from an unnamed compounding pharmacy were used by Georgia in 2014, when Mississippi also announced plans to use pentobarbital from a compounding pharmacy. Louisiana, Pennsylvania, Colorado, and Oklahoma have also all at least contacted such pharmacies.[83]

Alarmed with the frequency with which compounding pharmacies were supplying the drugs needed for executions, the International Academy of Compounding Pharmacists issued a statement on March 24, 2015, discouraging "its members from participating in the preparation, dispensing, or distribution of compounded medications for use in legally authorized executions."[84] Although the IACP Board "recognize[d] an individual practitioner's right to determine whether to dispense a medication based upon his or her personal, ethical and religious beliefs," the statement was later updated to note that "[p]harmacy, and compounding in particular, is a profession of healing and care that is focused on individual patients and providing the best and most appropriate medications at all times."[85]

E. The abolitionist potential of non-complicity

It was noted above that the decision in *Prigg v Pennsylvania* prohibited [f]ree states from actively deciding how fugitive slave cases should be adjudicated, but it permitted such states to "disassociate themselves from slavery and thereby confine all action to the narrowest limits that would satisfy the Constitution."[86] The parallels between the reaction to *Prigg* and the contemporary reaction to *Baze* are clear: just as antebellum abolitionists frustrated the intended outcome of *Prigg* by disassociating themselves from slavery and thus preventing slaveowners and their agents from recapturing escaped slaves, so today's abolitionists have frustrated the intended outcome of *Baze* by encouraging disassociation from capital punishment and thus preventing executions from proceeding.

The refusal of pharmaceutical companies and foreign governments to assist states with the acquisition of the materials needed for executions has been incredibly effective in stopping executions. Indiana, Nebraska, and South Carolina have put executions on hold because they have been unable to obtain the required drugs.[87] In other states, executions have been stayed by state and federal courts pending legal evaluations of the proposed drug protocols. Although the challenge to the traditional three-drug protocol failed in *Baze*, the use of alternative drugs and the adoption of new lethal injection protocols have inspired an avalanche of new challenges, which state and federal courts have struggled to grapple with because *Baze* is no longer adequate authority given the factual differences in the drugs used.[88]

The use of midazolam in particular has attracted concern because medical experts have repeatedly testified that the drug is not effective as a sedative, thus creating a very real risk that prisoners will feel excruciating pain when the second and third drugs are administered. Although the US Supreme Court rejected a challenge to the use of midazolam as a sedative in a three-drug cocktail, the ruling in *Glossip v. Gross* in 2015 did not enable executions to proceed nationwide without difficulties. In May 2016, for example, US District Judge Neil Wake stayed all executions in Arizona pending a legal challenge to the state's proposed use of midazolam, citing factual differences between the protocol under review in *Glossip*, and the instant case.[89] In Louisiana, the state both lacks the drugs required, and is judicially barred from conducting executions until 2018. Louisiana's protocol stipulates that executions are to be carried out using either a single dosage of pentobarbital, or a combination of midazolam and hydromorphone, but executions have been stayed at the request of the state Attorney General.[90] Executions in Montana and Oklahoma are also on hold as a result of court orders.

It is clear, then, that these principles and practices of non-complicity have contributed to a sharp decline in the number of executions being carried out. The expected surge in executions following the decision in *Baze* in 2008 has never materialized, and in 2016 there were just 20 executions nationwide – the lowest annual number since 14 people were executed in 1991.[91] In light of these developments, a number of observers have suggested that the fate of the American death penalty lies in the hands of pharmaceutical companies and foreign governments. On May 21, 2016, Lincoln Caplan wrote in *The New Yorker*: "The campaign to halt lethal injections as a mode of capital punishment by restricting access to the lethal drugs has not yet ended the death penalty. But it may very well have accelerated the end game".[92]

V. The pro-death penalty backlash

It is not axiomatic, though, that the campaign to stop the supply of drugs needed for lethal injections will result in the demise of capital punishment, and it can reasonably be argued that recent developments point to the entrenchment of capital punishment in law, politics, and local culture. As already seen, the pro-death penalty lobby has gone to great lengths to procure the drugs needed for lethal injections, but authorities have also enacted secrecy measures to prevent abolitionists from identifying the source of such drugs, thus preventing practical or legal challenges to executions. Some states have also introduced alternative methods of execution; and, in the case of Oklahoma, have constitutionalized capital punishment so that it is immune from legal challenges in the state courts. As a result of these measures, a number of "botched" executions have taken place, thus raising ethical dilemmas for abolitionists.

The parallels with slavery – particularly the issue with fugitive slaves – are stark. When free states harbored fugitive slaves to protect them from recapture, the reaction of the pro-slavery lobby initially appeared to entrench slavery and make matters worse. We saw above, for example, how the enactment of the Fugitive Slave Law of 1850 put free blacks at risk of kidnapping, just as – we will see below – recent measures have put people at risk of botched executions. We also saw how the decision in *Prigg*, like those in *Baze* in *Glossip*, was considered to be an anti-abolitionist decision, and legitimated the anti-abolitionist position. But we also know that the actions of the pro-slavery lobby ultimately invigorated abolitionism. Antebellum activists used the pro-slavery reaction to draw attention to the multifarious ways in which slavery implicated the civil liberties, self-interest, and dignity of the Northern communities that otherwise did not consider slavery to be an issue of concern to them. We can thus use this chain of events to see how the comparable laws, policies, and Supreme Court decisions can be used by today's abolitionists to further their cause.

A. Entrenching capital punishment

In November 2016, the electorate in Oklahoma voted to amend the state constitution so that Section 9 to Article II now reads: "…Any method of execution shall be allowed, unless prohibited by the United States Constitution… The death penalty provided for under such statutes shall not be deemed to be, or to constitute, the infliction of cruel or unusual punishments, nor shall such punishment be deemed to contravene any other provision of this Constitution." The ballot measure had been introduced because of fears that Oklahoma's death penalty was under threat from drug shortages and legal challenges to particular lethal injection protocols.[93] The passage of this law was in some ways unsurprising, as Oklahoma has consistently resisted the campaign to stop lethal injections. In April 2015, when signing into law a bill that allows the use of nitrogen gas, Governor Fallin said: "I believe capital punishment must be performed effectively and without cruelty." Critics of the law, though, noted that the use of nitrogen oxide has not been tested on humans.[94] Although other states have legalized alternative methods of execution, they have generally re-introduced methods that have been used in the past. In May 2014, Tennessee introduced a law that mandates the use of the electric chair in the event that lethal injection drugs are unavailable,[95] and on March 23, 2015, Utah enacted a law that permits the use of firing squads if it is not possible to administer lethal injections because of the shortage of drugs.[96]

Oklahoma has also adopted the most expansive "secrecy" statute. Although authorities across the US have long kept secret the identities of execution teams, their attempts to conceal the source of lethal injection drugs are a more recent phenomenon. As of late 2017, 16 states have statutory provisions that allow departments of corrections to withhold information that might reveal the identity of the person or company who has supplied the state's execution drugs.[97] Oklahoma's is the most wide-ranging in the extent to which it prohibits disclosure in almost all circumstances,[98] though other states have adopted similarly wide-ranging measures. In October 2013, the Missouri Department of Corrections declared that the suppliers of lethal injection drugs now constitute the "execution team," which must be kept secret.[99] In early 2016, it was revealed that following the change in policy, Missouri began to pay the execution team in cash in order to limit any paper trail that might reveal their identity. Arizona and Oklahoma Departments of Corrections were also found to have paid execution teams in cash, though unlike Missouri there has been no suggestion that they did not comply with federal tax laws.[100]

The proffered rationale for these confidentiality statutes has been to protect pharmaceutical companies, distributors, and other suppliers from harassment and intimidation. When Georgia adopted the Lethal Injection Secrecy Act in July 2013, a spokesperson for the Department of Corrections asserted: "The purpose of the bill is to protect the safety of the officers, nurses, doctors and pharmacists involved in this process... Identifying these individuals and businesses jeopardizes their safety and makes them a target for harassment and intimidation, simply because of their involvement in court-ordered executions."[101] In 2012, the Texas Department of Criminal Justice issued a strongly-worded letter to the Attorney General of Texas, Greg Abbott, accusing Reprieve of "intimidation and commercial harassment" of the manufacturers of the drugs used in lethal injections. The letter went on to say that Reprieve "crosses the line from social activists dedicated to their cause to authoritarian ideologues who menace and harass private citizens who decline to submit to Reprieve's opinion on the morality of capital punishment by lethal injection". The TDCJ surmised that "Reprieve's unrestrained harassment will escalate into violence against a supplier", and compared the charity to prison gangs by stating that Reprieve's methods "present classic, hallmark practices comparable to practices by gangs incarcerated in the TDCJ who intimidate and coerce rival gang members and which have erupted into prison riots".[102] In May 2015, the Texas legislature amended the state's criminal procedure so that the identity of "any person or entity that manufactures, transports, tests, procures, compounds, prescribes, dispenses, or provides a substance or supplies used in an execution" is concealed.[103]

Notwithstanding these claims, an investigation by the online news organization BuzzFeed suggested that many of these threats had been greatly exaggerated, with no indication that the Federal Bureau of Investigations had ever taken such threats to be a cause for real concern.[104] An investigation by the Associated Press similarly found "scant evidence" that pharmacies that supply the state with execution drugs would be in danger of violence if their identities were made public.[105] Garrett Epps, the Supreme Court correspondent for *The Atlantic*, concluded that Texas was more concerned about the effectiveness of Reprieve's actions, rather than with any threats: "It seems likely that Reprieve's real offense is effectiveness", he wrote.[106] Instead, then, it is more likely that the secrecy measures have been motivated by a desire to stifle legal and practical efforts to stop executions.

The secrecy laws – in isolation and when combined with other actions such as the experimentation with different drug cocktails – have in many ways given rise to the same sorts of problems that were described above in relation to the Fugitive Slave Act 1850. The law now enables executions to be carried out, just like the recapture of alleged fugitive slaves was carried out, with very little judicial oversight. And just as there was an increased risk of free persons being illegally taken into captivity, so there is now a greater risk of individuals suffering an inhumane death.

It is worth emphasizing at this point the conceptual and historical links between these secrecy laws and America's history of racial violence. Brian Kammer – a defense attorney in Georgia – drew the link between Georgia's secrecy law and America's history of racial violence when he said: "The secrecy in this context to me invokes images of lynchings by hooded men – it's very emblematic of an earlier time in the south."[107] We also saw in Chapter One how the privatization of executions in the 1800s contributed to the institutionalization of racially disparate capital punishment processes. In an article for the *Richmond Times-Dispatch* on April 8, 2017, Dale Brumfield proclaimed that "[t]he newly enhanced secrecy behind Virginia's capital punishment protocols underscores a legacy of death born in institutionalized racism".[108] Brumfield recounts how Virginia first moved to keep execution processes from public view in March 1879 because public executions tended to make black defendants into martyrs. When that law proved ineffective at preventing mass gatherings on execution days, the legislature passed another law in 1908, which changed the method of execution from hanging to electrocution, and which moved all executions to take place in the state penitentiary in Richmond. On October 14, 1908, the *Richmond Times-Dispatch* explained that "[t]he publicity, the excitement and the general hurrah-and-holiday air attending the old-time hanging were a positive allurement to the negro.... The electric execution wholly does away with that.... The whole affair is conducted with secrecy and mystery, well calculated to inspire terror in the heart of the superstitious African."[109] Even in the context of secrecy laws, then, we can see the legacy of racial violence rear its head.

B. The challenges posed by the pro-death penalty backlash

The lack of transparency in contemporary executions means that no observer can know whether the drugs used were procured in accordance with legal guidelines set out by the FDA, and thus there is no assurance that the drugs will be effective in bringing about death humanely. These concerns – and a spate of actual botched executions – led the American Bar Association to issue a Resolution in 2015 that urged the relevant authorities to "promulgate execution protocols in an open and transparent manner and allow public comment prior to final adoption".[110] The Report that accompanied the Resolution baldly stated: "When jurisdictions are permitted to operate in secrecy, the courts, legislatures, and the public cannot provide critical oversight to guard against the use of risky and experimental drug protocols and untrained and unqualified execution team members. Botched executions are the predictable result of such practices."[111]

Although botched executions have been a perennial feature of capital punishment,[112] recent botched executions have to be understood within the context of secrecy laws, experimentation, and the rush to carry out executions while drug supplies last. It is also in this context, though, that abolitionists can draw inspiration from the antebellum activists' responses to *Prigg* and the Fugitive Slave Act 1850.

C. Responding to the backlash

It was noted above that it was only when slavery appeared to threaten the civil liberties of Northerners that others joined the ranks of the abolitionists, even if they were not so much concerned with the freedom of blacks as they were with "reducing the political power and prestige of Southern slaveholders."[113] Likewise, the phenomena of botched and rushed executions, in addition to the secrecy laws and the extents to which authorities have stockpiled drugs while able to do so, can all contribute to abolitionism.

The abolitionist potential of botched executions is mixed. On the one hand, detailed accounts of the suffering of people can draw attention to the barbarity of capital punishment. In 2014, three executions in particular attracted national and international attention. On January 16, 2014, Dennis McGuire was executed in Ohio by lethal injection, but it took 26 minutes, rather than the expected five minutes, for McGuire to die. Witnesses to the execution recalled that he struggled "like a fish lying along the shore puffing for that one gasp of air that would allow it to breathe."[114] Lawrence Hummer – a priest who witnessed the execution – described it as "inhumane".[115] On April 29, Clayton Lockett suffered a similar fate in Oklahoma. Lockett was injected with a three-drug cocktail of midazolam, vecuronium bromide, and potassium chloride, but due to the failure of the state to properly access Lockett's veins, he ultimately died of a heart attack 43 minutes after the procedure began. Many witnesses described how Lockett seemed to writhe in agony.[116] Even the White House commented that the execution "had fallen short of humane standards."[117] On July 23, 2014, Joseph Wood was executed in Arizona using the same two-drug protocol that had failed to work as intended in the execution of McGuire just a few months earlier. This time, it took 1 hour and 57 minutes for the drugs to bring about death. One witness asserted that Woods gasped for air 660 times over the two hours.[118]

Abolitionists might intuitively expect "botched" executions to help the anti-death penalty movement, but the specter of a person suffering while being executed has not historically advanced calls to outlaw capital punishment.[119] Many people who are not actively opposed to state-sanctioned executions believe that those who have been convicted of capital offenses deserve to suffer. Robert Blecker has argued that the retributive purposes of capital punishment are better served when the person being executed suffers in a manner comparable to the suffering of the victim of the capital crime: "punishment must be painful to be punishment, and sometimes too, punishment must be very painful to be just."[120] Indeed, the botched executions of McGuire, Lockett, and Wood did not attract unilateral sympathy or outrage. McGuire had been convicted of the rape and murder of a pregnant woman called Joy Stewart, and Joy's sister issued the following statement the day before McGuire was executed: "There has been a lot of controversy regarding the drugs that are to be used in his execution, concern that he might feel terror, that he might suffer. As I recall the events preceding her death – forcing her from the car, attempting to rape her vaginally, sodomizing her, choking her, stabbing her, leaving her to bleed out – I know she suffered terror and pain. He is being treated far more humanely than he treated her."[121] Similar opinions were aired in the wake of Lockett's execution, with some arguing that he deserved to suffer given that he had buried alive a 19-year old girl.[122] The Arizona Attorney General's office flatly denied that Wood had gasped for air,[123] and a relative of Wood's victims said that his final two hours were "nothing compared to what happened on August 7, 1989," when Woods shot and killed his estranged girlfriend Debra Dietz and her father, Eugene Dietz.[124]

A further problem with the focus on botched executions is that they sometimes shift the conversation to one of reform, rather than abolition. As Austin Sarat has outlined, historically, problematic executions have resulted in new technologies being developed which serve not necessarily to make executions *actually* more reliable in minimizing pain, but to give the *appearance* of humaneness so as to stifle any abolitionist sentiment.[125]

Even if "botched" executions did incite sympathy for the prisoner and calls for abolition, the perceived *cause* of botched executions can work against abolitionists. The *Daily Mail* – a UK newspaper – ran a story in 2014 with the headline: "A lethal irony: Are Death Row convicts dying in agony because of the well-meaning efforts of British campaigners fighting to ban executions?" It was surmised that abolitionists – specifically Reprieve – only have themselves to blame for the suffering endured by the likes of McGuire, Lockett, and Woods. In the newspaper's view, "it appears the road to a more hellish form of death has been paved by those with good intentions."[126] Justice Alito of the US Supreme Court has also expressed the view that abolitionists are to blame for any problems with lethal injections. During oral argument in *Glossip v. Gross*, Alito asked: "is it appropriate for the judiciary to countenance what amounts to a guerilla war against the death penalty which consists of efforts to make it impossible for the States to obtain drugs that could be used to carry out capital punishment with little, if any, pain?"[127] Alito seemed to suggest that the allegedly underhand tactics of the abolitionist movement undermined any constitutional claim that petitioners had, and that the pain felt by those being executed was a result of the actions of abolitionists, not of the state authorities who were experimenting with different lethal injection protocols. The Court ultimately ruled against petitioners in *Glossip v. Gross*, upholding a controversial lethal injection procedure and thus enabling executions to go ahead.[128] There are at least two responses to this. The first is that state authorities are not compelled to carry out executions, and as such abolitionists cannot be held responsible for the choice of state authorities to experiment with different protocols. The second is that abolitionists have not exposed individuals to greater risks of pain, but have instead prevented state authorities from hiding the suffering that individuals have felt ever since the adoption of lethal injections in 1977. That is, the traditional execution cocktail was not itself painless and problem-free. It only appeared to be so because it included a paralytic.

Perhaps more fruitful for abolitionists will be the apparent rush towards executions. In 2017, the states of Arkansas and Ohio threatened to reinvigorate the declining institution of capital punishment by carrying out multiple executions over a short period of time. In June 2016, the Arkansas Supreme Court rejected a challenge to the state's lethal injection protocol, seemingly giving the green light for eight scheduled executions to proceed. However, the Court also voted by a 4–3 margin to halt executions until the matter could be determined by the US Supreme Court.[129] On February 21, 2017, though, the Court declined to review the state supreme court's decision, and six days later Governor Asa Hutchinson announced that the eight men would be executed over an 11-day period in April that year. Described as a "killing spree" by both the *New York Times* and the *Washington Post*,[130] the plans attracted controversy. There was no precedent in the modern death penalty era for such a concentration of executions over such a short period, raising fears that mistakes would be made, and that the execution team would suffer a psychological toll. Since 1976, there had been only ten occasions on which multiple executions had taken place in a single state on the same day.[131] In Oklahoma, the Department of Public Safety had recommended that executions be scheduled at least seven days apart, citing the "extra stress" that is suffered by the execution team when carrying out executions close together.[132] In 2016, the Missouri Supreme Court adopted a rule that only one execution could take place in a calendar month.[133] Governor Hutchinson defended the state's actions on the grounds that its supply of midazolam was due to expire at the end of April. Although the state's supply of potassium chloride had already expired in January 2017, authorities announced that they had been able to acquire sufficient supplies to carry out the executions. Abolitionists quickly launched multiple assaults on the planned executions. Activists organized a petition drive and rallies, and lawyers litigated to stay the executions. The Fair Punishment Project issued a report detailing the cases of the eight men awaiting execution, arguing that the prisoners were "defined by mental illness, intellectual disability, and bad lawyering."[134] A letter was sent to Governor Hutchinson signed by 23 former correctional officials, stating that their "first-hand and unique experience with the death penalty compels [them] to share [their] concerns" that "performing so many executions in so little time will impose extraordinary and unnecessary stress and trauma on the staff responsible with carrying out the executions."[135] Damien Echols, who spent 18 years wrongfully convicted on death row in Arkansas, also joined the coalition of voices that spoke out against the planned executions.[136]

On Friday April 14, just three days before the first scheduled executions, Judge Wendell Griffen of the Pulaski County Circuit Court issued an order forbidding Arkansas authorities from using their supply of vecuronium bromide, thus halting the executions.[137] The largest pharmaceutical company in the United States – McKesson Corporation – had issued a complaint that state authorities had procured the drug from them under false pretenses. In its complaint, McKesson noted that the Arkansas Department of Corrections (ADC) had "led McKesson to believe that the order was placed at the request for the benefit of the physician and would be used for a legitimate medical purpose… In fact, ADC intended to use this product in connection with executions, a fact that was never disclosed to McKesson."[138] The complaint details the extraordinary lengths that the ADC went to in order to hide their true intentions from McKesson. For example, when placing the order, the ADC requested that the drugs be shipped to the ADC's healthcare facility. This was because the ADC was aware that McKesson, as a distributor, was prohibited under its agreement with Pfizer, the manufacturer of vecuronium, from selling the drug for the purposes of administering capital punishment. The disingenuous actions of the ADC are not an isolated incident. An investigation in 2015 revealed that at least four states illegally bought drugs from a salesman based in Kolkata, India. The manufacturer – the Swiss company Naari – had been deceived into providing the drugs to Harris Pharma in India in the belief that the drugs were to be supplied to Zambia for medical purposes.[139]

Back in Arizona, on April 15, 2017 the court for the Eastern District of Arkansas issued an order granting a preliminary injunction on the grounds that the prisoners were likely to succeed on an Eighth Amendment claim.[140] The stays of execution, though, were vacated by the Court of Appeals for the Eighth Circuit just two days later.[141] After further legal wrangling, four executions were carried out. The other four were stayed on grounds relating to mental competency and claims of innocence.[142]

A similar chain of events occurred in Ohio. On January 26, 2017, US Magistrate Judge Michael Merz halted all forthcoming executions on the grounds that "midazolam does not have the same pharmacologic effect on persons being executed as the barbiturates thiopental sodium and pentobarbital."[143] Six months later, the US Court of Appeals for the Sixth Circuit vacated Merz's order. By an 8–6 majority, the Court signaled that Ohio could resume executions.[144] Governor Kasich promptly announced that 27 executions would take place between July 2017 and September 2020. Once again, concerns were raised about the effect that repeated executions would have on the execution team, and once again concerns were raised about the prospects of botched executions.[145]

To date, legal challenges to the secrecy laws have been unsuccessful.[146] It has been claimed that such laws violate the Eighth Amendment because it is inherently cruel and unusual to punish a person without telling them how they will be punished, and it has also been argued that secrecy laws violate free speech rights under the First Amendment. These find a parallel in the challenges to the gag rules in the antebellum era. Outside the context of fugitive slaves, abolitionists had swamped Congress with hundreds of thousands of petitions, leading pro-slavery members of the House of Representatives to pass a series of "gag rules" to ensure that the petitions could not be discussed.[147] The rules were in place from 1836 until 1844, during which time abolitionists raised awareness of the threat that the rules posed to the hallowed First Amendment right to free speech. The modern First Amendment cases, even though not successful in the courts, have likewise raised awareness of how capital punishment, like slavery, implicates the rights and freedoms of those not directly affected by the practice.

Abolitionists have also attempted to draw attention to how the actions of departments of corrections in stockpiling drugs that are needed for executions have diverted these drugs from potentially life-saving medical treatment. Dr Joel Zivot, an anesthesiologist at Emory University in Atlanta, Georgia, has said: "The public must realize that when states take these vital drugs and repurpose them as poison and use them to kill, there are serious consequences... People don't appreciate that these drugs might one day be needed for their own medical treatment."[148] According to Dr Zivot, Arkansas has stockpiled sufficient supplies of lethal injection drugs that could instead be used to treat 1,800 patients.

VI. Conclusions

The anti-death penalty efforts to practically interfere with the machinery of death, most notably by preventing authorities from acquiring the drugs needed for lethal injections, has so far proven to be something of double-edged sword. On the one hand, it has led to a decline in executions, it has brought the medical profession into abolitionist circles, and it has kept the issue of the death penalty in the spotlight. On the other hand, the pro-death penalty lobby has adopted measures – particularly the constitutionalization of the death penalty in Oklahoma – that will stifle further abolitionist attempts. However, when it became clear that free blacks were at risk of kidnapping as a result of the Fugitive Slave Act 1850, abolitionists embarked on a vociferous campaign to not only prevent black people from being taken into captivity, but also to draw attention to ways in which the Act implicated the interests of Northerners. In 1851, Charles Beecher published "The Duty of Disobedience to Wicked Laws", which was one of the most influential of all literature that judged the Act unfavorably against the demands of a "higher law".[149] Likewise, when abolitionists draw attention to the rush towards executions, and to botched executions, they are implicitly judging these processes against the requirement that society and the legal system act with dignity, and with respect for the dignity of others. It is in this respect that the practical method of abolitionism is not wholly conservative. While it might appear to be narrowly focused on the phenomenon of executions only, it nonetheless draws attention to the fact that the dignity of the person, of the broader community, and of the legal system generally, are implicated by criminal justice policies and practices.

The policies of non-cooperation satisfied a moral requirement on the part of the slavery abolitionists to refrain from being complicit in a practice that they considered objectionable, and although such policies were often defeated in the courts, and although they sometimes increased the chances of people being taken into servitude, they nonetheless played a role in the downfall of slavery. On December 3, 1860, James Buchanan warned Congress that the Southern states "would be justified in revolutionary resistance to the Government of the Union" if the Personal Liberty Laws of the North were not repealed.[150] Christopher Hitchens suggested that it was the Fugitive Slave Act of 1850 and the *Dred Scott* decision seven years later – both of which were "triumphs" for supporters of slavery – that sounded the death knell for slavery, in part because they radicalized the North, and gave strength to the cause of the abolitionists.[151] It is possible that the events of 2016 and 2017 outlined above are the metaphorical Fugitive Slave Act and *Dred Scott* moments: the pro-death penalty backlash, it can be surmised, is drawing more and more attention to the barbarity of capital punishment. And if we accept Thomas Morris's assertion that the spirit of the Personal Liberty Laws came to be embodied in the Thirteenth and Fourteenth Amendments, then we can surmise that the doctrine of non-complicity with capital punishment will likewise have far-reaching effects.[152]

Notes

1 For an overview of the Underground Railroad, see Larry Gara, *The Liberty Line: The Legend of the Underground Railroad* (University of Kentucky Press 1961). Gara points out that the scope of the Underground Railroad has been exaggerated, and that the network was more ad hoc than systematic. He takes issue with a biographer of Harriet Tubman, who argued that the Underground Railroad "was one of the greatest forces which brought on the Civil War, and thus destroyed slavery" (Earl Conrad, *Harriet Tubman* (Associated Publishers 1943) 43).

2 William S. McFeely *Proximity to Death* (W.W. Norton & Co. 2000) 102; 105. Also see Stuart Banner, *Too Close for Insight (Review of Proximity to Death)* (2000) 28 Reviews in American History 460

3 William Lloyd Garrison, 'Guilt of New England' *The Liberator* (7 January 1832) reprinted in William E. Cain (ed), *William Lloyd Garrison and the Fight Against Slavery: Selections from The Liberator* (Bedford 1994) at 84.

4 Manisha Sinha, *The Slave's Cause: A History of Abolition* (Yale University Press 2016) 500 ("The passage of the Fugitive Slave Act of 1850 crystallized abolitionists' commitment to direct action. The fugitive slave rebellions during this decade of crisis coalesced slave resistance, a tradition of self-defense among black communities, and revolutionary abolition… As popular revulsion against fugitive rendition in the North grew with each minibattle, abolition took a revolutionary turn.")

5 The literature on fugitive slaves is too vast to summarize here, but some selected texts are: Thomas D Morris, *Free All Men: The Personal Liberty Laws of the North, 1780–1861* (John Hopkins University Press 1974); Paul Finkelman, 'Fugitive Slaves, Midwestern Racial Tolerance, and the Value of 'Justice Delayed" (1992) 78 Iowa Law Review 89; Kathryn Grover, *The Fugitive's Gibraltar: Escaping Slaves and Abolitionism in New Bedford, Massachusetts* (University of Massachusetts Press 2001); Steven Lubet, *Fugitive Justice: Runaways, Rescuers, and Slavery on Trial* (Harvard University Press 2010).

6 Paul Finkelman, 'The Kidnapping of John Davis and the Adoption of the Fugitive Slave Law of 1793' (1990) 56 Journal of Southern History 398, 397–422.

7 This Clause was superseded by the Thirteenth Amendment to the Constitution, which outlawed slavery.

8 Finkelman (n 6) 408.

9 For a more detailed account of this dispute, see ibid.

10 ibid 416.

11 ibid 419.

12 Morris (n 5) Chapters 2–6; Scott J. Basinger, 'Regulating Slavery: Deck-Stacking and Credible Commitment in the Fugitive Slave Act of 1850' (2003) 19 Journal of Law, Economics, and Organization 307

13 For example, Pennsylvania's 1820 anti-kidnapping statute prohibited state courts from exercising .jurisdiction in fugitive slave cases. See Morris (n 5) 45.

14 Prigg v. Pennsylvania, 41 U.S. 539 (1842).

15 ibid 540.

16 See Morris (n 5) 109–110.

17 *The Liberator* (28 October 1842).

18 Morris (n 5) 118.

19 ibid 127.

20 Richard K. Calle (ed), *The Works of John C Calhoun* (Vol 6, Appleton 1870) 295 (noting that Calhoun considered that the successful implementation of Personal Liberty Laws had "practically expunged from the Constitution" the duty to return fugitive slaves).
21 In Re: Booth, 3 Wis. 1 (1854).
22 Ableman v. Booth, 62 U.S. 506 (1859).
23 This phenomenon is referred to as "jury nullification". On jury nullification and the Fugitive Slave Act, see Gary Collison, "This Flagitious Offense': Daniel Webster and the Shadrach Rescue Cases, 1851–1852' (1995) 68 New England Quarterly 609.
24 George Sorin, *Abolitionism: A New Perspective* (Praeger Publishers 1972) 108.
25 ibid 107.
26 Louis Menand, *The Metaphysical Club* (Flamingo 2001) 10–11.
27 It should be noted though that non-death penalty jurisdictions in America often complain when the federal government seeks to try a federal death penalty case in an abolitionist jurisdiction. See Eric A. Tirschwell and Theodore Hertzberg, 'Politics and Prosecution: A Historical Perspective on Shifting Federal Standards for Pursuing the Death Penalty in Non-Death Penalty States' (2009) 12 Journal of Constitutional Law 57, 85–94. For example, in 2000 a federal judge ruled that the death penalty could not be sought in a case in Puerto Rico because the death penalty is outlawed there (see U.S v. Acosta Martinez (Acosta Martinez I), 106 F. Supp. 2d 311 (D.P.R. 2000)). The First Circuit Court of Appeals overturned this decision in June 2001 (U.S v. Acosta-Martinez (Acosta Martinez II), 252 F.3d 13 (1st Cir. 2001)) This ruling came in the face of sustained opposition from Puerto Ricans. Thus, when a jury acquitted Acosta-Martinez and Rivera-Alejandro of all charges, commentators surmised that this was an instance of jury nullification, intended to send a message to the federal government to cease seeking to impose the death penalty in Puerto Rico. See Tirschwell and Hertzberg, 93.
28 The IAD provides rules and procedures to be followed when an individual has committed crimes in more than one state or jurisdiction.
29 For an overview of this case, see Patrick Anderson, 'Sentence not the Issue in Pleau Case' *Providence Business News* (10 September 2012) http://www.pbn.com/detail.html?page=1&sub_id=14feba0743c2.
30 Governor Chafee, 'In Pleau Case, I'm Standing up for State's Core Values' *Providence Journal* (19 August 2011) http://news.providencejournal.com/letters-to-the-editor/2011/08/lincoln-d-chafee-in-pleau-case-im-s.html.
31 Michael Mannheimer, 'The (Very) Unusual Case of Jason Pleau' (*Prawfsblawg*, April 4, 2012) http://prawfsblawg.blogs.com/prawfsblawg/2012/04/the-very-unusual-case-of-jason-pleau.html.
32 Indeed, comparisons can be drawn between those who want to be executed and those who wanted to be returned to servitude. On one such fugitive slave case, see Paul Finkelman, 'Legal Ethics and Fugitive Slaves: The Anthony Burns Case, Judge Loring, and Abolitionist Attorneys' (1996) 17 Cardozo Law Review 1793, and Owen M. Fiss, 'Can a Lawyer Ever Do Right' (1996) 17 Cardozo Law Review 1859.
33 See Edward G. Hild, 'The Death Penalty and the Interstate Agreements on Detainers Act: A Proposal for Change' (1996) 29 John Marshall Law Review 499.
34 Report of the Secretary-General, 'Capital punishment and implementation of the safeguards guaranteeing protection of the rights of those facing the death penalty' UN doc E/2015/49, 13 April 2015, Summary and para 57.
35 Charter of Fundamental Rights of the European Union, OJ EC 18 December 2000, 2000/C 364/1, Art 19(2).
36 Judge v. Canada, Comm. No. 829/1998, U.N. Doc CCPR/C/78/D/829/1998 (2003), at [10.3].
37 On the potential legal obligation to refrain from complicity in capital punishment, see Bharat Malkani, 'The Obligation to Refrain from Assisting the Use of the Death Penalty' (2013) 62 International and Comparative Law Quarterly 523.

38 For an account of the adoption of lethal injections as a method of execution, see Deborah W. Denno, 'For Execution Methods Challenges, the Road to Abolition is Paved with Paradox' in Charles J. Ogletree Jr and Austin Sarat (eds) *The Road to Abolition? The Future of Capital Punishment in the United States* (NYU Press 2009) 183, 186–190. Also see Ty Alper, 'Anesthetizing the Public Conscience: Lethal Injection and Animal Euthanasia' (2008) 35 Fordham Urban Law Journal 817.

39 For an outline of how lawmakers have professed to be concerned with the "humanity" of executions, see Jürgen Martschukat, "No Improvement over Electrocution of Even a Bullet': Lethal Injection and the Meaning of Speed and Reliability in the Modern Execution Process' in Ogletree Jr and Sarat (n 38) 252; Imogen Jones and Bharat Malkani, 'Beastly Humans: The Welfare Model of Executions' (2017) Law, Culture, and the Humanities 1 [online first version].

40 Baze v. Rees, 553 U.S. 35, 48, 58 (2007).

41 Denno (n 38) 204 (noting that "Some death penalty opponents believe... that enhancing the humaneness of an execution method may make executions far more acceptable scientifically and politically than ever before.").

42 For an outline of the positions of the medical community – including those who do not consider it unethical for physicians to participate in executions – see Ty Alper, 'The Truth about Physician Participation in Lethal Injection Executions' (2009) 88 North Carolina Law Review 11.

43 See Brief for Petitioners at 41–49, Baze, 553 U.S. 35 (2007).

44 Leonidas G. Koniaris and Teresa A. Zimmers, 'Inadequate Anaesthesia in Lethal Injection for Execution' (2005) 365 Lancet 1412, 1412.

45 Teresa A. Zimmers, Jonathan Sheldon, David A. Lubarsky, Francisco López-Munoz, Linda Waterman, Richard Weisman, and Leonidas G. Koniaris, 'Lethal Injection for Execution: A Chemical Asphyxiation?' (2007) 4 PLoS (Public Library of Science) Medicine 646, 647.

46 Baze (n 40) 50.

47 ibid 61.

48 Wilkerson v. Utah, 99 U. S. 130 (1879) (finding death by firing squad to be constitutional); In re Kemmler, 136 U.S. 436, 446 (1890) (finding death by electrocution to be constitutional); Louisiana ex rel. Francis v. Resweber, 329 U.S. 459 (1947) (permitting a second attempt at electrocution after the first attempt failed to kill Willie Francis Resweber); Baze v. Rees, 553 U.S. 35 (2007) and Glossip v. Gross, 135 S. Ct. 2726 (2015) (both upholding constitutionality of lethal injections per se, and the specific protocols under review).

49 'British Drugs Linked with Third Botched Executed as Jeffrey Landrigan is revealed to have died in Agony in Arizona' (20 February 2011) http://www.reprieve.org.uk/press/2011_02_20_dream_pharma_landrigan/.

50 Reprieve, 'Press Release: High Court Hears Second Day of Arguments in Execution Drug Export Case' (22 November 2010) http://www.reprieve.org.uk/press/2010_11_22_high_court_hearing/.

51 Letter from Leigh Day & Co. to Rt Hon Vince Cable MP (28 October 2010) http://www.reprieve.org.uk/wp-content/uploads/2014/10/2010_10_27_PUB_Leigh_Day_letter_to_V_Cable_re_execution_drug.pdf.

52 Letter from Rt Hon Vince Cable MP to Leigh Day & Co (1 November 2010) http://www.reprieve.org.uk/wp-content/uploads/2014/10/2010_11_01_PUB_DenialFromVinceCable.pdf.

53 Council Regulation (EC) No 1236/2005 concerning trade in certain goods which could be used for capital punishment, torture or other cruel, inhuman or degrading treatment or punishment [2005] OJ L200/1, para 20 http://eur-lex.europa.eu/legal-content/EN/TXT/HTML/?uri=CELEX:32005R1236&from=EN.

54 Letter from Rt Hon Vince Cable MP (n 52).

55 Leigh Day & Co., 'Vince Cable Sued for Refusing to Stop Export of Execution Drug' (2 November 2010) https://www.leighday.co.uk/News/2010/November-2010/Vince-Cable-sued-for-refusing-to-stop-export-of-ex.

56 In Reprieve's words, "if something is immoral, it does not matter that someone else will commit the offence." http://www.reprieve.org.uk/press/2010_11_29_execution_drug_ban/.

57 Peter Walker, 'Vince Cable Restricts Export of Drug Used in US Executions' *The Guardian* (29 November 2010) https://www.theguardian.com/science/2010/nov/29/sodium-thiopental-export-restrictions.

58 R (Zagorski and Baze) v. Secretary of State for Business, Enterprise and Skills & Anor [2010] EWHC 3110 (Admin) [20]-[26].

59 For the full background to Reprieve's Stop the Lethal Injection Project, see http://www.reprieve.org.uk/topic/lethal-injection/ For the view that pharmaceutical companies have generally always objected to the use of their products in lethal injections, but had until now been ineffective in preventing such use, see Ty Alper, 'The United States Execution Drug Shortage: A Consequence of Our Values' (2014) 21 Brown Journal of World Affairs 27.

60 R (Zagorski and Baze) (n 58) [20]-[26].

61 Reprieve, 'Briefing: Lethal Injection Drugs Trade' (11 February 2011) http://www.reprieve.org.uk/wp-content/uploads/2014/10/2011_02_11_Lethal_Injection_Drugs_Trade-_Submission_to_All_Party_Parliamentary_Group.pdf.

62 Hands Off Cain, 'How an Abolitionist Country is Collaborating in Putting People to Death in the United States' (2 December 2010) http://www.handsoffcain.info/chi siamo/index.php?idtema=13316650.

63 Reprieve, 'Reprieve and Hands Off Cain Challenge Italian Trade in Execution Drug Sodium Thiopental' (2 December 2010) http://www.reprieve.org.uk/press/2010_12_02_hospira_italy_press_conference/.

64 Atti della Camera della XVI Legislatura, *Mozione 1–00508* (presented by Elisabetta Zamparutti on November 25 20101), approved on 22 December 2010 http://aic.camera.it/aic/scheda.html?numero=1-00508&ramo=CAMERA&leg=16. Hospira, 'Hospira Statement Regarding Pentothal (sodium thiopental) Market Exit' *Hospira* (21 January 2011) http://phx.corporate-ir.net/phoenix.zhtml?c=175550&p=irol-newsArticle&ID=1518610&highlight=.

65 Hospira (n 64).

66 See, for example, Letter from Hospira to Ohio Department of Corrections, 31 March 2010 https://deathpenaltyinfo.org/documents/HospiraMarch2010Statement.pdf.

67 Kevin O'Hanlon, 'Company Says it No Longer will sell Drug for Lethal Injection' *Lincoln Journal Star* (7 April 2011) http://journalstar.com/news/state-and-regional/nebraska/article_4ec6475d-e308-5647-85e0-78769e6f4c0f.html.

68 John David Duty became the first person to be put to death using pentobarbital in December 2010, in Oklahoma. See Emanuella Grinberg, 'Drug Shortage Leads to Condemned Man Receiving Anesthetic for Animals' *CNN* (17 December 2010) http://edition.cnn.com/2010/CRIME/12/17/oklahoma.execution.drugs/.

69 Lundbeck, 'Lundbeck Overhauls Pentobarbital Distribution Program to Restrict Misuse' (1 July 2011) http://investor.lundbeck.com/releasedetail.cfm?releaseid=605775.

70 Holly Williams, 'Meet the woman behind a shortage of execution drugs' *CBS News* (30 April 2014) https://www.cbsnews.com/news/meet-the-woman-behind-a-shortage-of-execution-drugs/.

71 Raymond Bonner, 'A Prolonged Stay: The Reasons Behind the Slow Pace of Executions' *ProPublica* (22 May 2013) https://www.propublica.org/article/a-prolonged-sta y-the-reasons-behind-the-slow-pace-of-executions.

72 Anon, 'German Minister Denies US Request for Execution Drugs' *Der Spiegal* (9 June 2011) http://www.spiegel.de/international/world/european-opposition-to-death-penalty-german-minister-denies-us-request-for-execution-drugs-a-767613.html.

73 See Deborah W. Denno 'Lethal Injection Chaos Post-*Baze*' (2014) 102 Georgetown Law Journal 1331, 1361. Also see Beaty v. FDA, 853 F. Supp. 2d 30 (D.D.C. 2012), affirmed in part and vacated in part by Cook v. FDA, 733 F.3d 1 (D.C. Cir. 2013).

74 Commission Implementing Regulation (EU) No 1352/2011 of 20 December 2011, amending Council Regulation (EC) No 1236/2005 concerning trade in certain goods which could be used for capital punishment, torture or other cruel, inhuman or degrading treatment or punishment [2011] OJ L.338/31.

75 Juliette Jowit, 'UK to Ban Export of Drug Approved for Use in US Executions' *The Guardian* (10 July 2012) https://www.theguardian.com/world/2012/jul/10/uk-ban-export-drug-us-executions.

76 Statement from Fresenius Kabi concerning the provision of Propofol (August 28, 2012) http://www.deathpenaltyinfo.org/documents/FreseniusPropofolStatement.pdf.

77 Jim Salter, 'Missouri Gov. Halts 1st US Execution by Propofol' *The Washington Post* (11 October 2013) https://www.washingtonpost.com/politics/missouri-gov-halts-1st-us-execution-by-propofol/2013/10/11/559e6af6-32d9-11e3-8627-c5d7de0a046b_story.html?utm_term=.00ab09ef6ade.

78 https://www.pfizer.com/files/b2b/GlobalPolicyPaperLethalInjection.pdf.

79 Erik Eckholm, 'Pfizer Blocks the Use of ist Drugs in Executions' *The New York Times* (13 May 2016) https://www.nytimes.com/2016/05/14/us/pfizer-execution-drugs-lethal-injection.html.

80 Lincoln Caplan, 'The End of the Open Market for Lethal-Injection Drugs' *The New Yorker* (21 May 2016) http://www.newyorker.com/news/news-desk/the-end-of-the-open-market-for-lethal-injection-drugs.

81 Regulation (EU) 2016/2134 of 23 November 2016 amending Council Regulation (EC) No 1236/2005 concerning trade in certain goods which could be used for capital punishment, torture or other cruel, inhuman or degrading treatment or punishment [2016] OJ L.338/1 http://eur-lex.europa.eu/legal-content/EN/TXT/PDF/?uri=CELEX:32016R2134.

82 See International Academy of Compounding Pharmacists, 'IACP Board Updates Position on Compounding for Lethal Injection' (undated) http://www.iacprx.org/page/CC32315LethalIn/IACP-Board-Updates-Position-on-Compounding-for-Lethal-Injections.htm.

83 For an outline of the use of compounding pharmacies, see 'Compounding Pharmacies and Lethal Injection' (Death Penalty Information Center https://deathpenaltyinfo.org/compounding-pharmacies.

84 International Academy of Compounding Pharmacists, 'IACP Adopts Position on Compounding of Lethal Injection Drugs: Board Discourages Practice Among Members' Ball Consulting Group (24 March 2015) http://c.ymcdn.com/sites/www.iacprx.org/resource/resmgr/Media/Press_Release_Compounding_fo.pdf Notwithstanding this, in October 2015, Virginia executed Alfredo Prieto using compounded pentobarbital that it acquired from the Texas Department of Criminal Justice.

85 See International Academy of Compounding Pharmacists, 'IACP Board Updates Position on Compounding for Lethal Injection' (n 82).

86 Morris (n 5) 127.

87 This is correct as of December 2017. The Death Penalty Information Center keeps up-to-date information on the status of execution methods and lethal injection protocols in each state. See 'Death Penalty in Flux' http://www.deathpenaltyinfo.org/death-penalty-flux.

88 See Denno (n 73).

89 First Amendment Coal. of Ariz., Inc. v. Ryan, 188 F. Supp. 3d 940; 2016 U.S. Dist. LEXIS 66113 (D. Ariz., May 18, 2016). Also see Michael Kiefer, 'Federal Court Judge Keeps Arizona Executions on Hold' *AZ Central* (20 May 2016) http://www.azcentral.com/story/news/local/arizona-investigations/2016/05/20/joseph-wood-midazolam-neil-wake-arizona-lethal-injection-execution/84616724/.

90 Della Hasselle, 'Executions in Louisian on Hold Until at least January 2018' *The Lens* (1 June 2016) http://thelensnola.org/2016/06/01/executions-in-louisiana-on-hold-until-at-least-january-2018/.

91 Numbers taken from the Death Penalty Information Center, https://deathpenaltyinfo.org/executions-year.

92 Lincoln Caplan (n 80). Also see: Clare Algar, 'Can Big Pharma end the Death Penalty in the US?' *The New Statesman* (22 October 2013) http://www.newstatesman.com/law/2013/10/could-big-pharma-end-death-penalty Matt Ford, 'Can Europe End the Death Penalty in America?' *The Atlantic* (18 February 2014) https://www.theatlantic.com/international/archive/2014/02/can-europe-end-the-death-penalty-in-america/283790/.

93 Kyle Schwab, 'Oklahoma State Question 776 Would Protect Death Penalty in State Constitution' *New OK* (24 October 2016) (noting that Representative Mike Ritze, who co-authored the initiative, said it was needed in order to clear up "this logjam of the judicial system".) http://newsok.com/article/5523531.

94 Okla. Stat. Ann. tit. 22 § 1014. Associated Press, 'Oklahoma Governor Signs "fool-proof" Nitrogen Gas Execution Method' *The Guardian* (18 April 2015) https://www.theguardian.com/us-news/2015/apr/17/oklahoma-nitrogen-execution-method-death-penalty.

95 Tenn. Code Ann. § 40–23–114.

96 Utah Code Ann. § 77–18–5.5.

97 Arizona (Ariz. Rev. Stat. § 13–757 C); Arkansas (Ark. Code § 5–4-617(g)); Florida (Fla. Stat. § 945.10(l)(g)); Georgia (Ga. Code, § 42–5-36(d)(2)); Louisiana (La. Rev. Stat. §15:570 G); Missouri (Mo. Rev. Stat. § 546.720); North Carolina (N.C. Gen. Stat. § 132–1.2); Ohio (Ohio Rev. Code § 2949.221); Oklahoma (Okla. Stat. tit. 22, § 1015(B)); South Dakota (S.D. Codified Laws § 23A-27A-31.2); Tennessee (Tenn. Code Ann.§ 10–7-504 (h)(1)); Texas (Tex.Gov. Code Ann. § 552.1081); Virginia (Va. Stat. § 53.1–234, ¶ 4); Mississippi (Miss. Stat. § 99–19–51(2) ¶¶ 2–3); Indiana (Ind. Stat. § 35–38–6-1(f)(1)); Wyoming (Wyo. Stat. § 7–13–916).

98 'The Report of the Oklahoma Death Penalty Review Commission' (March 2017) http://okdeathpenaltyreview.org/the-report/ at 183.

99 Missouri Department of Corrections, 'Preparation and Admnistration of Chemicals for Lethal Injections' (available on the website of the Death Penalty Information Center at https://deathpenaltyinfo.org/files/pdf/ExecutionProtocols/MissouriProtocol10.18.2013.pdf.

100 Chris McDaniel, 'Missouri Paid Executioners $250,000 in Cash, Possibly Violating Tax Law' *BuzzFeed* (28 January 2016) https://www.buzzfeed.com/chrismcdaniel/missouri-paid-executioners-in-cash?utm_term=.fv5gXk953#.dfdEqxyWX.

101 'Bill Would Cloak Lethal Injection Information in Secrecy' *The Atlanta Journal-Constitution* (21 March 2013).

102 Ed Pilkington, 'Texas Accuses Anti-Death Penalty Charity Reprieve of Fomenting Violence' *The Guardian* (28 March 2015) https://www.theguardian.com/world/2012/mar/28/death-penalty-texas-reprieve. For a response by the founder of Reprieve, see Clive Stafford-Smith, 'A Response to Texas' Charge of 'Intimidation' Against Reprieve' *The Guardian* (29 March 2012) https://www.theguardian.com/commentisfree/cifamerica/2012/mar/29/texas-charge-intimidation-reprieve.

103 Tex. Code Crim. Proc. Ann § 43.14(b).

104 Chris McDaniel, 'FBI Documents Don't Back Up Claimed Threat to Execution Drug Supplier' *BuzzFeed* (30 August 2016) https://www.buzzfeed.com/chrismcdaniel/fbi-documents-dont-back-up-claimed-threat-to-execution-drug?utm_term=.yrLvYra8r#.ajR3GEQnE.

105 Associated Press, 'Scant Evidence of Threats to Execution Drugmakers' *The Daily Mail* (4 April 2014) http://www.dailymail.co.uk/wires/ap/article-2596442/Scant-evidence-threats-execution-drugmakers.html#ixzz4zdufklRb.

106 Garrett Epps, 'Out of Spite: The Governor of Nebraska's Threat to Execute Prisoners' *The Atlantic* (5 June 2015) https://www.theatlantic.com/politics/archive/2015/06/a-governor-threatens-to-execute-prisoners-out-of-spite/394949/.

107 See Ed Pilkington, 'Georgia Court Blocks Warren Hill Execution as State Acquires New Drugs' *The Guardian* (18 July 2013) http://www.guardian.co.uk/world/2013/jul/18/georgia-blocks-warren-hill-execution-new-drugs.

108 Dale Brumfeld, 'Virginia's Dark Legacy of Secrecy About Executions' (8 April 2017) http://www.richmond.com/opinion/their-opinion/guest-columnists/dale-brumfield-column-virginia-s-dark-legacy-of-secrecy-about/article_2a5ef608-8a3a-55f6-a115-2f7d1fdf9d06.html.

109 ibid.

110 ABA House of Delegates, Resolution 108B (adopted 9 February 2015) ("Urges jurisdictions that imposes capital punishment to promulgate execution protocols in an open and transparent manner.").

111 Virginia E. Sloan et al., ABA, Death Penalty Due Process Review Project, *Report to the House of Delegates* (2015) 1, 6.

112 See Austin Sarat, *Gruesome Spectacles: Botched Executions and America's Death Penalty* (Stanford University Press 2014) for a thorough account of botched executions since 1890.

113 Sorin (n 25) 107.

114 Lawrence Hummer, 'I Witnessed Ohio's Execution of Dennis McGuire. What I saw was Inhumane' *The Guardian* (22 January 2014) http://www.theguardian.com/commentisfree/2014/jan/22/ohio-mcguire-execution-untested-lethal-injection-inhumane.

115 Ibid.

116 For a detailed outline of the circumstances surrounding the execution of Clayton Lockett, see Jeffrey E. Stern, 'The Cruel and Unusual Execution of Clayton Lockett' *The Atlantic* (June 2015) http://www.theatlantic.com/magazine/archive/2015/06/execution-clayton-lockett/392069/.

117 Associated Press, 'White House says Botched Oklahoma Execution not Done Humanely' *New York Daily News* (30 April 2014) http://www.nydailynews.com/news/politics/white-house-botched-oklahoma-execution-not-humanely-article-1.1774283.

118 Mark Berman, 'Arizona execution lasts nearly two hours; lawyer says Joseph Wood was 'gasping and struggling to breathe'' *Washington Post* (23 July 2014) https://www.washingtonpost.com/news/post-nation/wp/2014/07/23/arizona-supreme-court-stays-planned-execution/?utm_term=.edcac96e2929.

119 Sarat (n 112).

120 Robert Blecker, 'Killing them Softly: Meditations on a Painful Punishment of Death' (2008) 35 Fordham Urban Law Journal 969, 993.

121 Jennifer Preston, 'After Slow Execution, Renewed Death Penalty Debate and Threat of Lawsuit' *New York Times* (17 January 2014) https://thelede.blogs.nytimes.com/2014/01/17/after-slow-execution-renewed-death-penalty-debate-and-threat-of-lawsuit/?_r=0.

122 Katie Zezima, 'Clayton Lockett Execution: Oklahomans Left Stunned after Criticism of Botched Execution' *The Independent* (3 May 2014) http://www.independent.co.uk/news/world/americas/clayton-lockett-execution-oklahomans-left-stunned-at-criticism-of-botched-execution-9321366.html.

123 Chris Geidner and Tasneem Nashrulla, 'Arizona Attorney General's Office Pushes Back, Says Inmate "DID NOT Gasp For Air" During Execution' *BuzzFeed* (24 July 2014) http://www.buzzfeed.com/chrisgeidner/arizona-attorney-generals-office-pushes-back-says-inmate-did.

124 'Victims' Family: "Killer Got What He Deserved"' *Sky News* (24 July 2014) http://news.sky.com/story/victims-family-killer-got-what-he-deserved-10395557.

125 Sarat, *Gruesome Spectacles* (n 112).
126 Guy Walters, 'A Lethal Irony: Are Death Row Convicts Dying in Agony Because of the Well-meaning Efforts of British Campaigners Fighting to Ban Executions?' *The Daily Mail* (5 May 2014) http://www.dailymail.co.uk/news/article-2620313/A-lethal-irony-Are-Death-Row-convicts-dying-agony-meaning-efforts-British-campaigners-fighting-ban-executions.html.
127 Transcript of Oral Argument at 14, *Glossip v. Gross*, 35 S.Ct. 2726 (2015).
128 *Glossip v. Gross*, 35 S.Ct. 2726 (2015).
129 Kelley v. Johnson http://www.deathpenaltyinfo.org/node/6509 //http://opinions.aoc.arkansas.gov/WebLink8/0/doc/355663/Electronic.aspx.
130 Editorial, 'Arkansas's State-sponsored Killing Spree' *Washington Post* (April 10, 2017); Meghan McCracken and Jennifer Moreno, 'Arkansas's Cruel and Unusual Killing Spree' *New York Times* (March 20, 2017).
131 Data taken from the Death Penalty Information Center https://deathpenaltyinfo.org/Most_US_Executions_in_Shortest_Time.
132 Oklahoma Department of Public Safety, 'The Execution of Clayton D. Lockett' (undated) at 23 http://s3.amazonaws.com/content.newsok.com/documents/14-0189SI%20Summary.pdf.
133 Mo. S. Ct. R. Rule 30.30 Sentence of Death – Setting Execution Dates. Also see K.K. Rebecca Lai, 'The Legal Battle Over Arkansas' Execution Plans' *New York Times* (17 April 2017) https://www.nytimes.com/interactive/2017/04/13/us/arkansas-executions.html.
134 Fair Punishment Project, 'Prisoners on Arkansas's Execution List Defined By Mental Illness, Intellectual Disability, and Bad Lawyering' (March 2017) http://fairpunishment.org/new-report-arkansass-executions/.
135 'Letter from Former Corrections Officials to Governor Hutchinson' (28 March 2017) https://drive.google.com/file/d/0BxR5nee8pBYQRl12N1J2S0tmZGc/view.
136 Phil McCausland, 'Arkansas Executions: Damien Echols, Ex-Death Row Inmate, Will Speak for Condemned' *NBC News* (11 April 2017) https://www.nbcnews.com/storyline/lethal-injection/arkansas-executions-damien-echols-ex-death-row-inmate-will-speak-n744471.
137 McKesson v Arkansas , No 60cv-17–1921 (Pulaski County Circ. Ct. April 14, 2017).
138 The complaint is available at https://deathpenaltyinfo.org/files/pdf/Arkansas/McKessonComplaint.pdf.
139 Chris McDaniel and Tasneem Nashrulla, 'This Is The Man In India Who Is Selling States Illegally Imported Execution Drugs' *BuzzFeed* (20 October 2015) https://www.buzzfeed.com/chrismcdaniel/this-is-the-man-in-india-who-is-selling-states-illegally-imp?utm_term=.fu3p3GMa7#.coxK2awZN.
140 *McGehee et al v Hutchinson*, 2017 U.S. Dist. LEXIS 57836 (E.D. Ark. 15 April 2017).
141 *McGehee et al v Hutchinson,* 854 F.3d 488; 2017 U.S. App. LEXIS 6544 (8th Cir. Ark., 17 April 2017).
142 For a full outline of the eight cases, and the flurry of legal appeals, see Death Penalty Information Center, 'Background on Arkansas April 2017 Executions' https://deathpenaltyinfo.org/Background_on_Arkansas_April_2017_Executions.
143 In re: Ohio Execution Protocol Litigation, 235 F. Supp. 3d 892; 2017 U.S. Dist. LEXIS 11019 (S.D. Ohio, 26 January 2017).
144 In re: Ohio Execution Protocol Litigation, 860 F.3d 881; 2017 U.S. App. LEXIS 11491; 2017 FED App. 0136P (6th Cir. 28 June 2017).
145 Scott Martelle, 'Ohio has a troubled death penalty system yet intends to resume executions anyway' *Los Angeles Times* (21 July 2017).
146 For example, see Guardian News & Media LLC et al v Ryan, 225 F. Supp. 3d 859; 2016 U.S. Dist. LEXIS 176639 (21 December 2016) (requiring access to view executions, but not disclosure of the source of execution drugs) Also see Kelly A. Mennemeier, 'A Right to Know How You'll Die: A First Amendment Challenge to

State Secrecy Statutes Regarding Lethal Injection Drugs' (2017) 107 Journal of Criminal Law and Criminology 443.

147 Daniel Wirls, '"The Only Mode of Avoiding Everlasting Debate": The Overlooked Senate Gag Rule for Antislavery Petitions' (2007) 27 Journal of the Early Republic 115.

148 Leslie Newell Peacock, 'Doctors object to prison stockpiling of drugs that could be used to save lives' *Arkansas Times* (20 April 2017) https://www.arktimes.com/ArkansasBlog/archives/2017/04/20/doctors-object-to-prison-stockpiling-of-drugs-that-could-be-used-to-save-lives.

149 Sinha (n 4) 442.

150 Morris (n 5) 202.

151 Christopher Hitchens, 'Foreword: Slouching Toward Abolition', in David Dow and Mark Dow (eds), *Machinery of Death: The Reality of America's Death Penalty Regime* (Routledge 2002) v.

152 Morris (n 5) 218.

9 A peculiar abolition

On February 6, 1837, Senator James Calhoun described slavery as the "peculiar institution of the South". Calhoun was defending slavery in the face of, in his words, an abolitionist "crusade" which had drawn attention to the fact that the rest of the country, like the rest of the world, had turned its back on involuntary bondage.[1] His description inspired the title of Kenneth Stampp's monograph on slavery in the antebellum South, published in 1956.[2] Over 50 years later, David Garland co-opted the term "peculiar institution" to describe capital punishment in the US, on the basis that the death penalty is primarily practiced in the Southern and former Confederate states, in contrast to the current national and global trend towards abolition.[3] Garland did not use a phrase associated with slavery for mere rhetorical purposes. As we have seen, America's death penalty is steeped in the country's history of racial subjugation and degradation. Both slavery and the death penalty are institutional manifestations of the belief that some people's lives are worth less than others.

In this book, I have argued that just as slavery and capital punishment were, and are, "peculiar institution[s]", so abolition of the death penalty in America will be "peculiar" because the process and outcome of abolition will be tied to America's particular history of racial subjugation, and efforts to tackle such degradation. It is hardly unusual for a country's path towards the abolition of capital punishment to be paved by that country's unique history. West Germany, for example, repealed its death penalty in the years following World War Two because of the specter of Nazism. There were those who believed that if the country were to cleanse itself of its fascist past, it would have to outlaw all the cogs that had kept the machinery of Nazism turning, which included the death penalty. There were others who were sympathetic to Nazis, and wanted the death penalty abolished so that Nazi officials standing trial for war crimes and crimes against humanity would be spared the punishment of death.[4] Likewise, it is difficult to extricate South Africa's experience of abolition from its experience of racial Apartheid. On February 2, 1990, President F.W. de Klerk announced a moratorium on all executions in the same speech in which he declared an end to Apartheid, and the release of Nelson Mandela.[5] When the South African Constitutional Court ruled the punishment unconstitutional in 1995 – just one year after the first general election in which people of all races were allowed to vote – Justices Chaskalson and O'Regan explicitly referred to the punishment's association with Apartheid.[6]

When America does abolish the death penalty, then, abolition must be understood within the context of the country's historical modes of racial subjugation such as slavery, and historical efforts to eradicate racial subjugation. This history, I have argued, requires contemporary anti-death penalty efforts to be understood as the continuation of the project that was put in place by the radical slavery abolitionists, which was to end practices that are not compatible with the idea of dignity. It is in this sense that I have argued that abolition should be centered on the idea of dignity, rather than on pragmatic and conservative anti-death penalty discourses.

Not all historians or commentators would support the idea that the radical slavery abolitionists are to be emulated. Andrew Delbanco, for example, has recently taken the slavery abolitionists to task for their moral absolutism, claiming that the radicals were not only a significant cause of the Civil War, but also influenced the divisiveness of contemporary political discourses in America.[7] He therefore advocates the path of centrism and compromise in reform efforts, cautioning against the idealism and utopianism of the radical abolitionists. Delbanco, though, fails to acknowledge that the radical abolitionists rejected centrism precisely because they recognized that slavery was a symptom of a greater ill, and that anything short of a radical approach would enable the illness to thrive. The experience of emancipation and its aftermath suggests that the radicals were not wrong to fear this. A number of other scholars have outlined how centrist, moderate anti-slavery voices entrenched racial divisions to the point that they find expression in all features of American life today, including in the country's adherence to capital punishment.[8] It is for these reasons that a radical approach to death penalty abolition is preferable. A non-radical approach risks entrenching the very values that are at the root of the problem with capital punishment. The slavery abolitionists recognized this root to be a failure to regard each and every life as innately valuable, and thus a radical approach to abolition must be centered on the idea of dignity.

In this concluding chapter, I want to address two potential criticisms of my central thesis. First, I imagine that some readers will remain unconvinced about the feasibility of the radical approach to abolition that I have proposed. It might be believed that the US Supreme Court, let alone the broader public, will never embrace the idea that those who commit the most horrific crimes imaginable should be treated with respect for their dignity, or that the imposition of capital punishment demeans the wider community and the legal system. Second, there may be some readers who think that I have not taken the radical approach far enough. Peter Hodgkinson, for example, writes that abolitionism should avoid piecemeal reform of capital punishment. In his words, "when opposition to the death penalty is restricted to some injustice in its administration, usually characterised by such concerns as prosecutorial bias, ineffective assistance of counsel, race, mental illness, mental impairment, youth, physician participation and mode of execution…the 'abolition' activities concentrate on a particular concern and, once corrected, cease."[9] As Hodgkinson argues, this incremental approach to abolition "could considerably delay the process of replacing the death penalty for all crimes in all circumstances and is in any event achieved at the expense of unacceptable compromises. Such a piecemeal approach offers governments an opportunity for delay in confronting the total removal of the death penalty."[10] On both counts, the work of prison abolitionists – who also draw on the ideas of the slavery abolitionists – is instructive.

Angela Davis and other prison abolitionists, such as the organization Critical Resistance, draw explicit connections between slavery, death penalty, and prison abolitionism. Vincenzo Ruggiero, for example, describes the "ancestors of contemporary [prison] abolitionists" as "the women and men who fought against slavery, and after the campaigners who battled, and continue to do so, for the abolition of the death penalty."[11] Prison abolitionists take issue with the widely held assumption that prisons are necessary for dealing with crime, and they lament – like Hodgkinson does in the context of capital punishment – the over-riding focus on "prison reform", rather than abolition. In Davis's view, the idea of reform serves to legitimize imprisonment in the abstract, which therefore perpetuates the legacy of slavery in America, given the historical linkages between enslavement and incarceration.

In response to the claim that the outright abolition of prisons is infeasible, Davis reminds us that it once seemed infeasible to speak about ending slavery.[12] This, in my view, is the crux of radical abolitionism. It is not the contention that wholesale change can or even should be brought about overnight, but rather to develop the mindset and framework for bringing about such changes in the future.[13] We have seen that, in the context of slavery, William Lloyd Garrison himself accepted that immediatism was more a rhetorical device than a practical measure, which was needed to shake anti-slavery activists out of their comfort zone. Discussions of "prison reform" stifle the development of a mindset that helps us look beyond punitiveness. It is only when we think in the language of "abolition", Davis writes, that we can wholeheartedly set about creating "an array of social institutions that would begin to solve the social problems that set people on the track to prison, thereby helping to render the prison obsolete."[14]

In the context of the death penalty, pragmatic and conservative approaches to abolition risk entrenching the very values that drive support for capital punishment in the first place. The radical approach, on the other hand, with its emphasis on the idea of dignity, serves as a constant reminder that although capital punishment today is perhaps the most extreme manifestation of the beliefs that the slavery abolitionists were trying to eradicate, it is just one manifestation. We see examples of these beliefs throughout the criminal justice system. It appears in other harsh punishments such as life without parole, solitary confinement, and lengthy mandatory minimum terms of imprisonment. It is embodied in the phenomenon of mass incarceration – particularly the mass incarceration of black people and the poor. And it manifests itself in the killings of Eric Garner, Tamir Rice, Philandro Castile, Michael Brown, Alton Sterling, and so many other people at the hands of law enforcement personnel.[15]

Throughout this book, we have seen how contemporary anti-death penalty efforts offer the prospect of radical changes to a criminal justice system that currently revolves around the idea that some lives are not as valuable as others. The focus on innocence has shed light on prosecutorial misconduct, leading to the elections and appointments of prosecutors who have argued for lower levels of incarceration, and a retreat from punitiveness.[16] Two such prosecutors, in fact, have vowed never to seek capital punishment during their tenure. On March 16, 2017, Aramis Ayala declared that she would never seek the death penalty while she was District Attorney for Orange and Osceola counties in Florida.[17] After a lengthy court battle instigated by Governor Rick Scott's decision to reassign all capital cases to another attorney, Ayala eventually agreed to seek the death penalty in future cases, but only when a panel of seven prosecutors unanimously agree that the facts of the case warrant such action.[18] On November 7, 2017, Larry Krasner was elected District Attorney for Philadelphia, Pennsylvania, after a campaign in which he vowed to radically reform approaches to criminal justice. In his victory speech, he linked the end of capital punishment to broader reforms: "If you, like us, believe it's time to end the death penalty. If you think it's time to end mass incarceration. If you think it's time to stop making prisoners of poor people by using cash bail…," Krasner said, "We hope to hear from you."[19] Prosecutors such as Krasner will, one hopes, provide much needed institutional overhaul.

The cost argument has meant that the concerns of Murder Victims' Families for Reconciliation that were outlined in Chapter Six have been taken on board. When Maryland abolished the death penalty, the legislature ensured that the money saved would be spent on helping families of homicide victims, going some way to ensure that such families are treated with dignity.[20] We also saw in Chapter Seven that the abolition of capital punishment for offenders under the age of 18 sparked both a political and judicial trend away from imposing sentences of life without the possibility of parole on young persons, with Justice Kennedy invoking the idea of respect for dignity as central to Eighth Amendment analysis. While there appears to be little prospect of abolishing life without parole for adults in the near future, we can forecast the use of anti-death penalty discourses to attack such sentences as incompatible with the constitutional requirement that all persons, even those convicted of the most horrific offenses, are treated with respect for their dignity.

In *End of its Rope*, Brandon Garrett also argues that the fight against the death penalty offers hope for addressing broader issues with the criminal justice system. Death penalty abolitionism, Garrett writes, has drawn attention to issues such as the fallibility of justice, the importance of well-trained and resourced defense teams, and the necessity of checks on prosecutorial power. With this in mind, he calls for "mercy in criminal justice",[21] stating that communities need to "rethink how we treat mentally ill, poor, innocent, and poorly represented defendants generally. We can all share the responsibility – and the credit – for moving past the most punitive era in American history."[22] The subtitle to his book is *How Killing the Death Penalty Can Revive Criminal Justice,* suggesting that contemporary efforts to end capital punishment are thus indeed more radical than conservative.

The legacy of slavery also rears its head beyond the realm of prisons, capital punishment, and the criminal justice system. On August 12, 2017, Heather Heyer was killed by a Neo-Nazi during a "Unite the Right" rally that took place in Charlottesville, Virginia.[23] White supremacists, members of the Ku Klux Klan, and other far-right groups were protesting against the removal of a statue of General Robert E. Lee, who had commanded the Confederate Army of Northern Virginia in the Civil War. They were also opposed to the re-naming of Lee Park, where the statue stood, to Emancipation Park. The rally drew a counter-protest from those opposed to fascism and racism. Heyer, a 32-year old legal assistant with a keen interest in civil rights, was struck by a car that was driven into the crowd of counter-protesters. A 20-year old named James Alex Fields Jr, a known far-right extremist, was arrested on suspicion of causing her death. President Donald Trump's reaction became the subject of intense scrutiny. He took 48 hours to issue a statement, in which he condemned violence on both sides of the protest. When Republicans and Democrats alike urged him not to draw a moral equivalence between Neo-Nazis and anti-racists, he pointedly said: "Racism is evil. And those who cause violence in its name are criminals and thugs, including the KKK, neo-Nazis, white supremacists, and other hate groups that are repugnant to everything we hold dear as Americans."[24] However, on August 15, 2017, he reverted to his original position, stating: "I think there's blame on both sides. And I have no doubt about it". He explicitly condemned the anti-fascists and anti-racists for being "very violent": "And you have – you had a group on one side that was bad, and you had a group on the other side that was also very violent, and nobody wants to say that, but I'll say it right now."[25]

President Trump's comments must be understood in the context of the perennial backlashes that have followed the successes of anti-racists. His election in November 2017 has been explained by some as the inevitable backlash to the election of the first black president, Barack Obama, eight years previously.[26] Trump has repeatedly endorsed white supremacists, and the events in Charlottesville, including his response, are a stark reminder that America is far from achieving the ideals of equality and liberty – or, as Justice Brennan put it, the constitutional aspiration towards respect for dignity of all persons – that the radical slavery abolitionists fought for. The legacy of slavery has its tentacles firmly wrapped around all facets of American life, and although abolishing the death penalty might only unwrap one of those tentacles, if the process and act of abolition is framed in the language of dignity, then it could be the precursor to the unwrapping of many others.

Notes

1 John J Calhoun, 'Speech on the Reception of Abolition Petitions' (delivered to the US Senate, 6 February 1837) (reprinted in John C. Calhoun, *Union and Liberty: The Political Philosophy of John C. Calhoun* (ed. Ross M. Lence, Liberty Fund 1992) 461.

2 Kenneth M. Stampp, *The Peculiar Institution: Slavery in the Ante-Bellum South* (Vintage Books 1956).

3 David Garland, *Peculiar Institution: America's Death Penalty In An Age Of Abolition* (Belknap Press 2010). On the status of the death penalty worldwide, see Roger Hood and Carolyn Hoyle, *The Death Penalty: A Worldwide Perspective* (4th edn, OUP 2008); William Schabas, *The Abolition of the Death Penalty in International Law* (3rd edn, Cambridge University Press 2002); *Death Sentences and Executions 2012*, Amnesty International (2013) *available at* http://www.amnesty.org/en/library/asset/ACT50/001/2013/en/bbfea0d6-39b2-4e5f-a1ad-885a8eb5c607/act500012013en.pdf.

4 Article 102, Basic Law (adopted 1949). Also see Charles Lane, 'The Paradoxes of a Death Penalty Stance' *The Washington Post*, (4 June 2005) http://www.washingtonpost.com/wp-dyn/content/article/2005/06/03/AR2005060301450.html.

5 F.W. de Klerk, ' Speech at the Opening of Parliament' (Cape Town, February 2, 1990).

6 *State v Makwanyane*, [1995] ZACC 3, 1995 (3) SA 391.

7 Andrew Delbanco, *The Abolitionist Imagination* (Harvard University Press 2012). Delbanco suggests that the absolutism of the abolitionists is mirrored in the absolutism of the pro-life movement today. There have been a number of criticisms of Delbanco's thesis, most notably by Manisha Sinha and John Stauffer. Sinha is correct to say that in their opposition to women's rights, the pro-life lobby today is the antithesis of the abolitionists. See John Stauffer, 'Fighting the Devil with His Own Fire', and Manisha Sinha, 'Did the Abolitionists Cause the Civil War?', both printed in *The Abolitionist Imagination* as responses to Delbanco's essay.

8 See, for example, Nicholas Guyatt, *Bind Us Apart: How Enlightened Americans Invented Racial Segregation* (Basic Books 2016).

9 Peter Hodgkinson, 'Capital Punishment: Improve it or Remove it?' in Peter Hodgkinson and William A. Schabas (eds) *Capital Punishment: Strategies for Abolition* (Cambridge University Press 2004) 32.

10 ibid 32.

11 Vincenzo Ruggiero, *Penal Abolitionism* (OUP 2010) 2. For more on the idea of prison abolitionism, see the website of 'Critical Resistance': http://criticalresistance.org/.

12 Angela Y. Davis, *Are Prisons Obsolete?* (Seven Stories Press 2003); Angela Y. Davis, *Abolition Democracy: Beyond Empire, Prisons, and Torture* (Seven Stories Press 2006).

13 See Robin D. G. Kelley, *Freedom Dreams: The Black Radical Imagination* (Beacon Press 2002) ix (stating that the power of reform movements lies not so much in what they achieve, but in the "merits or power of the visions themselves.").

14 Davis (n 12) 96.

15 Jon Swaine, Oliver Laughland, Jamiles Lartey and Ciara McCarthy, 'Young Black Men Killed by US Police at Highest Rate in Year of 1,134 Deaths' *The Guardian* (31 December 2015). The Guardian is currently keeping track of all persons killed by law enforcement personnel in the US. See 'The Counted', https://www.theguardian.com/us-news/series/counted-us-police-killings. Also see Black Lives Matter, http://blacklivesmatter.com/.

16 Maurice Chammah, 'These Prosecutors Campaigned for Less Jail Time – And Won' *The Marshall Project* (9 November 2016) https://www.themarshallproject.org/2016/11/09/these-prosecutors-campaigned-for-less-jail-time-and-won#.fCmPqvBJ6.

17 Dar Kam, 'Prosecutor who won't pursue death penalty replaced on cop killer case' *Palm Beach Post* (16 March 2017) http://www.palmbeachpost.com/news/state–regional-govt–politics/prosecutor-who-won-pursue-death-penalty-replaced-cop-killer-case/btbUuHYUpvN7VVkNURX1AI/.

18 Gal Tziperman Lotan, 'State Attorney Ayala rescinds her death-penalty ban' *Orlando Sentinel* (1 September 2017).

19 Bobby Allyn, 'Krasner routs Grossman, coasting to victory in Philly DA race' *WHYY* (7 November 2017) https://whyy.org/articles/krasner-routs-grossman-coasting-victory-philly-da-race/.

20 National Association for the Advancement of Colored People, 'Maryland Death Penalty Repeal Legislation to use Funds from Savings to the New Maryland Victims Fund'

Press Release (14 February 2013) http://www.ncadp.org/press/entry/maryland-death-penalty-repeal-legislation-to-use-funds-from-savings-to-the. Also see Renny Cushing and Susannah Sheffer, *Dignity Denied: The Experience of Murder Victims' Family Members Who Oppose the Death Penalty* (Murder Victims' Families for Reconciliation 2002).

21 Brandon Garrett, *End of its Rope: How Killing the Death Penalty Can Revive Criminal Justice* (Harvard University Press 2017) 235.

22 ibid 236.

23 The media coverage of these events was extensive. See, for example, Sarah Rankin, '3 Dead, Dozens Injured, Amid Violent White Nationalist Rally in Virginia' *Chicago Tribune* (13 August 2017).

24 'Statement by President Donald Trump' The White House (14 August 2017) https://www.whitehouse.gov/the-press-office/2017/08/14/statement-president-trump

25 See 'President Trump's Q-and-A at Trump Tower' *CNN* (15 August 2017) http://edition.cnn.com/2017/08/15/politics/read-president-trumps-q-and-a-at-trump-tower/index.html.

26 Ta-Nehisi Coates, 'The First White President' *The Atlantic* (September 7, 2017); Ta-Nehisi Coates, *We Were Eight Years in Power: An American Tragedy* (One World Publishing 2017).

Index

References to endnotes refer to their in-text callouts.

abolitionists: backlash to successes of 10, 15, 29, 32–4, 46–9, 187, 192–4, 202–06, 210; conservative/moderate/pragmatic 2, 5–7, 11–14, 56, 65, 67–71, 80–3, 107, 110–12, 115, 125–7, 137–8, 141–6, 150–1, 163, 170, 177, 210, 221–3; radical 2, 11–16, 79–84, 86, 93–98, 100–1, 107–8, 110–18, 121–31, 138–9, 163, 170–1, 221–4
Alabama 24, 39–42, 99, 168
Alexander, Michelle 6n39, 63, 66
American Anti-Slavery Society 81, 98, 112
American Bar Association 67, 126, 205
American Civil Liberties Union 43, 56–7, 70, 141, 166
American Colonization Society 81, 164, 171n48, 175, 176 *see also* colonization
American League to Abolish Capital Punishment 40
Amnesty International 57–8, 129, 141, 220n3
Amsterdam, Anthony 43, 63
Anderson, Benedict 96, 150
anti-racists 50, 79, 224; and anti-death penalty efforts 10–11, 24–9, 33, 37, 41–2, 61–5 *see also* racial discrimination
Anti-terrorism and Effective Death Penalty Act 1996 67
Arkansas 3, 66, 101, 196, 207–210
Arizona 196, 202–03, 206–07, 209
Atkins v Virginia 5n30, 115–16, 119
Ault, Allen 153–4

Baldus Study, The 62–4
Baldwin, James 91n63, 97
Banner, Stuart 1n3, 23n3, 25n23, 29, 39
Batson v Kentucky 61, 122
Baze v Rees 100, 118, 130, 196, 200–02; Justice Steven's concurring opinion 126–9
Beccaria, Cesare 23–4, 172–3
Bedau, Hugo Adam 62n50, 83–4, 93–4, 140n12
BlackLivesMatter movement 63, 72
Blackmon, David 32–4
Blackmun, Justice Harry 67, 109, 125–6, 140, 167
Bloodsworth, Kirk 150–1, 152
Brandley, Clarence 151
Brennan, Justice William 44, 47, 62–3, 224; views on constitutionality of the death penalty 92, 110, 126; views on dignity in the US constitutional order 92n73, 124
Breyer, Justice Stephen 100; views on the constitutionality of capital punishment 100, 125, 129–30, 168
Buck v Texas 122–3, 131
Burns case, The 192
Bush, President George H.W. 66

Cabana, Donald 152
Calhoun, James 33, 89n53, 146, 191n20, 220
California: and the anti-death penalty movement 150, 166; deregulation of capital punishment 3, 110; as a free state 55; and harsh retributivism 119, 179; and lethal injections 196; life without parole 166, 173, 176
Callins v Collins 67, 125–6, 140
Campaign to End the Death Penalty 150, 173
Cassell, Paul 140
Civil Rights Act 1866 34
civil rights movement 139; backlash to 10, 46, 49; contradictory effects on death

penalty abolitionist efforts 41, 43, 49; and lynching 36
Civil War 10, 33–4; impact on death penalty abolitionist efforts 29, 32
Clinton, President William J. 66
Coker v Georgia 56–7, 119
colonization 14–15, 81, 162–5, 169; abolitionists' rejection of 82, 170–1; comparison with life without parole 171, 176
Colorado 37–8, 48, 200
comparative historical method 7–11
Connecticut 9–10, 121, 123–4, 146, 168, 187
Conservatives Concerned About the Death Penalty (CCATDP) 70, 144–5, 165–6
convict leasing 34–5, 49
costs of capital punishment 2, 6, 69, 83, 101, 137, 144–5, 165–6
critical race theory 27, 63, 91
Critical Resistance 222
Cuomo, Governor Mario 167, 193

Davis v Ayala 120
Davis, Angela 7, 14, 49, 71, 222
Davis, David Brion 24n14, 28–9, 89
"death is different" 41, 118–21, 178
Declaration of Independence 24, 114, 117; providing grounds for radical abolitionism 163; tension between slavery and 92, 111, 113
Delaware 168, 174
Dershowitz, Alan 43–4
dignity 2, 13; and anti-death penalty efforts 6, 83, 87, 93–5, 101, 130, 143–5, 147–55; centrality to radical abolitionism 13, 82–4, 100–01, 138; and colonization 170–1, 176; and the community 95–8; conceptions of 83–8; and the courts 14, 88, 92, 100, 112, 115–18, 120–1, 124–6, 130, 177–80; and the criminal justice system 83; criticisms of 86–7; and the legal institution 98–100; and life without the possibility of parole 163, 171–2, 176–8; and racial degradation 14, 28, 72; and slavery abolitionism 88–91, 148–50; and the US Constitution 83, 88
Douglass, Frederick 148–50; on the death penalty 22; failure to critique post-emancipation convict lease system 49; on slavery 91, 97
Dred Scott v Sandford 8, 63, 92, 108, 114, 210
Du Bois, W.E.B. 13, 32–4, 40–1
Dworkin, Ronald 86, 89, 117

Echols, Damien 148, 208
Eighth Amendment: centrality to anti-death penalty strategy 4; courts' interpretation of 48–9, 65, 115–18, 125–6, 131, 137, 178–80, 209; and the death penalty 4, 92, 108, 115–18, 126, 128–30; and dignity 84–5, 98, 180, 223; and life without the possibility of parole 120, 178–180, 223; and methods of execution 128–9, 196; and secrecy laws 209; and slavery 95; and treatment of prisoners 95
Eighth Amendment Project, The 71, 129
Equal Justice Initiative 36, 71–2
Equal Justice USA 71, 146, 149–50
European Union 180, 194, 197, 200
executions: "botched" executions 202, 206–07; complicity with 194–201; declining rates of 2–3, 5; and dignity 98–101, 117–18, 130, 154; geography of 1, 55; "humane" executions 93–4, 127–8, 195; as "legal lynchings" 42; methods of execution 7, 27, 42, 94, 118, 195, 202; and "positive good" argument 60; and race discrimination 27–8, 205; role in abolitionism 15, 24, 186–7, 201–02, 206–10; of slaves 26, 28; *see also* lethal injections
executioners (former): as abolitionists 138, 152–4; effects of death penalty on 154;
extradition 188–9, 193–4

Fair Punishment Project 208
Florida 59, 142, 152, 223; life without parole 167 176, 178; sentencing scheme 5n31, 174
Foster v Chatman 122, 130–1
Fourteenth Amendment: 107n3, 108, 118; and the death penalty 4, 35, 39, 41, 44, 49, 99, 107; and dignity 88, 108; drafting of 113–14; as product of slavery abolitionism 107, 114, 130, 210–11; and race discrimination 32, 49, 61, 91, 107
freedom suits 10n69, 121
Fugitive Slave Act 1793 188–90
Fugitive Slave Act 1850 187, 191–2, 202, 204–5, 210
fugitive slaves 15, 108, 186–94, 201–02, 204; as abolitionists 147–150, 186
Furman v Georgia 66, 92, 109–10, 118, 125, 128, 168, 178; avoidance of race 46–8; backlash to 48–9; effect on death penalty abolitionism 4

Garland, David 4n22, 11n73, 58, 177, 220
Garrett, Brandon 3, 141n21, 142, 162n3, 223
Garrison, William Lloyd 23, 40, 96–7, 146, 196; and colonization 164, 171, 176; disavowal of US Constitution 82, 98, 110–11; immediatism, and rejection of gradualism 82, 171n50, 222; and non-complicity with slavery 97, 186–7; and radicalism 12, 81–2, 98, 145, 170
Georgia 56n9, 153, 205; and lethal injections 196, 201, 204; racially discriminatory death penalty 27, 59, 62
Givens, Jerry 152–3
Glossip v Gross 108, 118, 202, 207; Justice Breyer's dissenting opinion 129–30, 168
Goldberg, Justice Arthur 43–7
Gorsuch, Justice Neil 3
Gottschalk, Marie: criticisms of anti-death penalty efforts 7, 58, 154, 172; and life without parole 162, 173–5
gradualism 11, 12, 80–2, 147, 171
Graham v Florida 120, 178–80
Grayson, William J 139–40
Gregg v Georgia 10, 46–50, 55–9, 65–7, 110, 119, 126–8; effect on anti-death penalty efforts 4
Guyatt, Nicholas 14, 82n21, 163, 169n42, 221n8

Haines, Herbert 5–6, 44, 58, 64, 67–9, 70, 140
Hall v Florida 5n30, 117, 130
Hands Off Cain 198
Higginbotham Jr, A. Leon 27, 49
Hodgkinson, Peter 7n47, 221–2
human rights 4, 22, 58, 70, 137, 141; and dignity 84, 87; grounds for prohibiting extradition 194; incompatibility of life without parole 172; marginalization from anti-death penalty efforts 145
Hurst v Florida 5, 174

Illinois 6, 45, 69, 142, 168, 174
immediatism 82, 127, 171, 222
Indiana 24, 189, 201
innocence 3, 42, 66, 70, 83, 87, 100, 125, 209, 223; criticisms of innocence in abolitionist discourses 71, 143; prominence in anti-death penalty discourses 68–9, 138, 142, 146, 150–3
international community: role in abolitionist efforts 16, 57–8, 70, 84, 116, 137, 141, 153, 180, 193–4, 197–201, 220n3
international human rights law *see* human rights
Italy 196, 198–9

Jefferson, Thomas 23, 163–5, 170
Johnson, Robert 95–6, 154

Kansas 167
Kant, Immanuel 86–7, 89, 93,95
Kennedy v. Louisiana 100, 117, 120, 130
Kennedy, Justice Anthony 110; invocation of dignity in constitutional interpretation 14, 88, 93, 107, 116–18; use of death penalty jurisprudence in non-capital cases 120, 178–80
Kennedy, Randall 57, 61n48, 64
Kentucky 37, 64
King Jr, Martin Luther 41–2
Kirchmeier, Jeffrey 1n3, 26n26, 38n39, 41, 61n48, 64
Kraditor, Aileen 11–12

La Amistad 112–14
LaChance, Daniel 6, 84, 93
Legal Defense Fund *see* National Association for the Advancement of Colored People Legal Defense Fund
lethal injections 142, 172; adoption of 195; and the appearance of a "humane" execution 94, 118, 127, 130, 195, 207; and the entrenchment of capital punishment 94, 202–04; experimentation 200–01; and involvement of medical personnel 98; legal challenges to 100, 118, 127–8, 196, 201, 207–08; the "medicalization" of the death penalty 27, 195; objections to 195; risk of botched executions 206–07; role in anti-death penalty efforts 5–6, 98, 187, 194–202, 209–210; and secrecy laws 187, 202–04; shortage of drugs 5, 101, 196, 199–200; Stop the Lethal Injection Project 198
Liberator, The 81, 82, 97n91, 97n98, 98n104, 191
life without the possibility of parole (LWOP) 6n39; as an alternative to the death penalty 168–9; comparisons to colonization 83, 176; and dignity 163, 171–2, 176–8; and the Eighth

Amendment 120, 178–180, 223; effect on public support for the death penalty 167–8; effect on the use of the death penalty 168; and the European Court of Human Rights 172; extent of 162; opposition to 71, 143, 171–3, 175; and racial discrimination 175; relationship to costs of capital punishment 144–5; support for by death penalty abolitionists 5, 68, 83, 101, 141, 151, 165–8; and the United States Supreme Court 118, 120, 174, 178–80
Lincoln, President Abraham 9, 114, 164
litigation strategy 44, 56, 64, 71, 137
Louisiana 24, 26, 35, 39, 151–2, 168, 176, 201–2
lynching 1, 13, 35, 41, 50, 55; effect on death penalty 36–8

Marquis, Joshua 140
Marshall, Chief Justice John 112–13
Marshall, Justice Thurgood 47, 61, 98, 110, 124, 126–30
Marshall Hypothesis 47, 141
Maryland 142, 150, 168, 174, 190, 223
Massachusetts 24, 57, 190–2; abolition of slavery 24, 121
McCleskey v Kemp 10, 61–3, 115, 124; effect on anti-death penalty efforts 11, 55, 64–5, 83
Meltsner, Michael 43, 45
Michigan 1, 29, 37
Miller-El v Dretke 122
Mississippi 25, 152, 201
Missouri 200, 201, 203, 208
Murder Victims' Families for Reconciliation (MVFR) 154, 223

National Association for the Advancement of Colored People (NAACP) 40–1, 47; NAACP Legal Defense Fund 41, 45, 57, 62
National Coalition to Abolish the Death Penalty 57, 70, 141
National Conference on Wrongful Convictions and the Death Penalty 6, 69, 141, 147; *see also* innocence
Nebraska 3, 199, 201
Nellis, Ashley 176, 179
New Jersey 121, 123, 168
New York 26–7, 67, 167, 173, 193
North Carolina 23, 27, 64, 175

Ohio 3, 24, 59, 201, 206–7, 209
Oklahoma 66, 193; "botched" executions 206; constitutionalization of capital punishment 3, 202–03, 210; costs of capital punishment 69n120, 144; high rate of executions 142; lethal injections 195, 201–03, 208; use of nitrogen gas 203; and race discrimination 4n27; and secrecy laws 203
Other Death Penalty Project, The 173

"peculiar institution" 34, 220
Pennsylvania 91, and anti-death penalty movement 24; burgeoning death row population 55; costs of capital punishment 69n120, 144; deregulating the death penalty 65; and fugitive slaves 188–91; gradual emancipation of slaves 80, 187; life without parole 176; progressive approach to criminal justice 223; restrictions on death penalty 25, 27, 142
Pennsylvania Abolition Society 11, 80
Personal Liberty Laws 189–91, 201
Phillips, Wendell 12, 23, 40
Prigg v Pennsylvania 109, 190–91, 196, 201
prison abolitionism 222
public opinion: among African Americans towards capital punishment 60; challenge for anti-death penalty movement 27, 65–6; role in Eighth Amendment analysis 4, 49, 66, 115–16, 128; support for death penalty 3, 6, 66–7, 137
Public Safety Officials on the Death Penalty 70–1, 151

Quakers 23

race discrimination: and the American criminal justice system 32–4, 222; centrality to anti-death penalty efforts 40–1, 45; and the courts 39, 41–2, 45–50, 55–7, 61–3, 121–4, 130–1; and the death penalty in antebellum America 1, 22–3, 25–8; and the death penalty in America from 1865–1976 34–6, 39–45, 49–50; and the death penalty in America since 1976 55–7, 59; and discretionary death penalty schemes 39; effect on anti-death penalty strategies and tactics 10–11, 64, 71–2; and juries 35, 39–40, 59–62; and legislatures 64; and life

without the possibility of parole 175; and lynching 36–8; marginalization from anti-death penalty efforts 59, 70–1; and methods of execution 27–8, 205; outside the realm of criminal justice 224; perpetuation by anti-death penalty activists 25–8; perpetuation by moderate slavery abolitionists 14; and Reconstruction 32
Racial Justice Acts 64, 66, 175
Reconstruction 13, 32, 36, 38, 49
religion: as basis for racially-disparate death penalty statutes 26; use of death penalty to repress religious groups 58; and dignity 87; and executions 201; and "imagined communities" 96; and life without the possibility of parole 167, 173; to limit the use of the death penalty 115; and opposition to the death penalty 4, 5, 15, 24, 42, 70, 137; and opposition to slavery 15, 24, 81
Reprieve: blamed for botched executions 207; collaboration with pharmaceutical companies 198–200; and Stop the Lethal Injection Project 198; and the United Kingdom government 197–8
Roper v Simmons 116, 119–20, 174, 179
Rudolph v Alabama 44
Rush, Benjamin 24, 27
Ryan, Governor George 142

Sarat, Austin 70–1, 99, 146, 207
Scalia, Justice Antonin 3, 65, 108, 116, 126, 140
Scottsboro Boys 41–2
Sinha, Manisha 79, 82, 147, 186n4
Slave Codes 26, 90
social movement theory 68
Sotomayor, Justice Sonia 99, 110, 117–18
South Africa 84–5, 220–1
South Carolina 25, 26, 27, 35, 123, 196, 201
Southern Center for Human Rights 72
Stanford v Kentucky 65–6, 114–15, 119, 131
State v Santiago 10, 121,123–4
Steiker, Carol: on life without parole 176; on lynching and effect on capital punishment 37; on the Marshall Hypothesis 141n19; on the US Supreme Court's avoidance of race discrimination in the death penalty 46, 48, 57, 63; on the US Supreme Court's death penalty jurisprudence 1n3, 71, 119, 174
Steiker, Jordan: on life without parole 176; on lynching and effect on capital punishment 37; on the Marshall Hypothesis 141n19; on the US Supreme Court's avoidance of race discrimination in the death penalty 46, 48, 57, 63; on the US Supreme Court's death penalty jurisprudence 1n3, 71, 119, 174
Stevens, Justice John Paul 115–16, 126–9
Stevenson, Bryan 1n3, 13n83
Stewart, Alvan 112, 121
Stewart, Justice Potter 47, 118, 169
Stinney, George 35
Stop the Lethal Injection Project *see* Reprieve
Story, Justice Joseph 113, 190–1
Strauder v West Virginia 39, 61
Swain v Alabama 39

Tennessee 24, 25, 38–40, 173, 196, 203
Texas 40, 59, 122–3, 142, 150–1, 167–8 174, 201, 204
Texas After Violence Project 98
Thirteenth Amendment 10, 211; as a cause of racial discrimination in the contemporary criminal justice system 29, 34; placing limitations on slavery 29
Thompson, John 151–2
Till, Emmett 36
Trump, President Donald 3, 9, 224
Truth, Sojourner 1, 154–5
Tubman, Harriett 171, 186

Underground Railroad 10n70, 171, 186
United Kingdom 100, 196–9
United Nations 193, 194, 198
United States Supreme Court: anti-death penalty opinions 7, 38, 43–8, 124–30; and life without parole 120, 178–80; and methods of execution 42, 195–6; perceived institutional incompetency to abolish slavery or the death penalty 108–09; politicization 3, 110; pro-slavery decisions 8, 15, 107–09, 190; and race discrimination 39–40, 44, 48, 62–3, 121–3; regulation of capital punishment 5, 41–2, 56, 59, 65, 174; and reinstatement of death penalty 2–3, 9–11; shaping anti-death penalty strategy 4, 64–5, 107, 203;

see also Eighteenth Amendment; Fourteenth Amendment
Utah 167, 203

victims' rights 7, 55–6, 58–9 65–6, 154; President's Task Force on Victims and Crime 59; Victim and Witness Protection Act 59; victim impact evidence in capital trials 59, 65
Virginia 23, 25–6, 144, 152, 163, 188–9, 192, 205, 224

Walker, David 82, 170–1 *see also* colonization
West Germany 220
Wiecek, William 107–8, 110–11
Witherspoon v Illinois 45, 60–1
Witness to Innocence (WTI) 70, 148, 150

Yarris, Nick 91–2

Zimring, Franklin 4n22, 11n73, 55n4

www.ingramcontent.com/pod-product-compliance
Ingram Content Group UK Ltd.
Pitfield, Milton Keynes, MK11 3LW, UK
UKHW011004180926
475701UK00004B/558
9780367899035